SECTARIANISM, DE-SECTARIANIZATION AND REGIONAL POLITICS IN THE MIDDLE EAST

SECTARIANISM, DE-SECTARIANIZATION AND REGIONAL POLITICS IN THE MIDDLE EAST

Protest and Proxies across States and Borders

Edited by
Ana Maria Kumarasamy, Elias Ghazal, Eyad Alrefai and
Simon Mabon, Samira Nasirzadeh

I.B. TAURIS
LONDON • NEW YORK • OXFORD • NEW DELHI • SYDNEY

I.B. TAURIS
Bloomsbury Publishing Plc, 50 Bedford Square, London, WC1B 3DP, UK
Bloomsbury Publishing Inc, 1385 Broadway, New York, NY 10018, USA
Bloomsbury Publishing Ireland, 29 Earlsfort Terrace, Dublin 2, D02 AY28, Ireland

BLOOMSBURY, I.B. TAURIS and the I.B. Tauris logo are
trademarks of Bloomsbury Publishing Plc

First published in Great Britain 2024
This paperback edition published 2025

Copyright © Ana Maria Kumarasamy, Elias Ghazal, Eyad Alrefai, Simon Mabon,
Samira Nasirzadeh and Contributors, 2024

Ana Maria Kumarasamy, Elias Ghazal, Eyad Alrefai, Simon Mabon, Samira Nasirzadeh have asserted their rights under the Copyright, Designs and Patents Act, 1988, to be identified as Editors of this work.

For legal purposes the Acknowledgements on p. x constitute an extension of this copyright page.

Series design by Adriana Brioso
Cover image © Elena Odareeva/Adobe Stock

This work is published open access subject to a Creative Commons Attribution-NonCommercial-NoDerivatives 4.0 International licence (CC BY-NC-ND 4.0, https://creativecommons.org/licenses/by-nc-nd/4.0/). You may re-use, distribute, and reproduce this work in any medium for non-commercial purposes, provided you give attribution to the copyright holder and the publisher and provide a link to the Creative Commons licence.

Bloomsbury Publishing Inc does not have any control over, or responsibility for, any third-party websites referred to or in this book. All internet addresses given in this book were correct at the time of going to press. The author and publisher regret any inconvenience caused if addresses have changed or sites have ceased to exist, but can accept no responsibility for any such changes.

A catalogue record for this book is available from the British Library.

Library of Congress Cataloging-in-Publication Data
Names: Nasirzadeh, Samira, editor. | Ghazal, Elias, editor. | Kumarasamy,
Ana Maria, editor. | Alrefai, Eyad, editor. | Mabon, Simon, editor.
Title: Sectarianism, de-sectarianization and regional politics in the Middle East : protest and proxies across states and borders / edited by Samira Nasirzadeh, Elias Ghazal, Ana Maria Kumarasamy, Eyad Alrefai, Simon Mabon.
Description: 1st. | New York: I.B Tauris an imprint of Bloomsbury Publishing, 2023.|
Includes bibliographical references and index. | Contents: Introduction / Simon Mabon and Ana Maria Kumarasamy – Section I: Politics of Sectarianism: 1. The Iraqi Protests: Sliding into the Abyss?/Jinan Al-Habbal – 2. Taif at Thirty: On Revolution, Reform, and the Unforgiven / Madonna Kalousian – 3. Carl Schmitt's ineffectual exceptionalism in the case of Syria / Samuel Peter Mace – Section II: Regional Dynamics and Proxies: 4. The Deal of Discontent: Saudi Arabia, Iran and the Nuclear Deal / Olivia Isabell – 5. Securitization of Shi'a to 'violisation': A Response to the Arab Spring in Bahrain / Samira Nasirzadeh – 6. Bridging Ethno-Religious Divides by Proxy? Non-State Sponsorship and Sectarianism in the Case of the Syrian Democratic Forces/ Michel Wyss – 7. Saudi Arabia's rhetorical construction of the Houthis as an Iranian proxy / Maria-Louise Clausen – 8. Sectarianism and civil wars in the MENA region / Francesco Belcastro – Section III: De-Sectarianization: 9. Iran's Soft Power in the Gulf from the Islamic Revolution to Post Intra Gulf Crisis and Prospects for De-sectarianization in the Gulf / Nesibe Hicret Battaloglu – 10. Political and Discursive De-secterianization: Re-Ordering Saudi Foreign and Domestic Policy-Making / Umer Karim – 11. Institutional Faith-based Diplomacy and De-Sectarianisation in the Middle East: How to Understand the Role of Al-Azhar in the Sunni–Shi'l Rapprochement? / Hossam Ed-Deen Allam – Conclusion / Samira Nasirzadeh, Elias Ghazal and Eyad Alrefai. Identifiers: LCCN 2023020513 (print) | LCCN 2023020514 (ebook) | ISBN 9780755639175 (hardback) | ISBN 9780755639212 (paperback) | ISBN 9780755639182 (pdf) | ISBN 9780755639199 (epub)
Subjects: LCSH: Middle East–Politics and government–21st century. | Islamic sects–Political aspects–Middle East. | Islam and politics. Classification: LCC DS63.123 .S428 2023 (print) |
LCC DS63.123 (ebook) | DDC 320.956–dc23/eng/20230508
LC record available at https://lccn.loc.gov/2023020513
LC ebook record available at https://lccn.loc.gov/2023020514

ISBN: HB: 978-0-7556-3917-5
PB: 978-0-7556-3921-2
ePDF: 978-0-7556-3918-2
eBook: 978-0-7556-3919-9

Typeset by Newgen KnowledgeWorks Pvt. Ltd., Chennai, India

For product safety related questions contact productsafety@bloomsbury.com.

To find out more about our authors and books visit www.bloomsbury.com
and sign up for our newsletters.

CONTENTS

Acknowledgements	x
Contributors	xi
INTRODUCTION	1
Simon Mabon and Ana Maria Kumarasamy	
Part I: The politics of sectarianism	6
Part II: Regional dynamics and proxies	7
Part III: De-sectarianization	8
Bibliography	9

Part I
POLITICS OF SECTARIANISM

Chapter 1
THE IRAQI PROTESTS: SLIDING INTO THE ABYSS?   13
    Jinan S. Al-Habbal

Introduction	13
The establishment of Iraq's consociational political system	14
Iraq's resilience: An overview of the protest movements between 2011 and 2018	17
Thawrat Tishreen: The October 2019 protests	20
Conclusion	25
References	26

Chapter 2
TAIF AT THIRTY: OCTOBER 17 AS *THAWRA ʿALA AL-ʾISTISHRĀQ*   31
    Madonna Kalousian

Igniting the Lebanese revolution	33
Thawra ʿala al-ʾistishrāq	34
From amnesty to amnesia	36
New electoral laws	39
New amnesty laws	41
Notes	43
References	44

Chapter 3
CARL SCHMITT'S INEFFECTUAL EXCEPTIONALISM IN THE CASE OF SYRIA — 49
Samuel Peter Mace

Introduction	49
Carl Schmitt's exceptionalism	50
Homogeneity	51
Sectarianism as a concept	52
The limits of sectarian governance and the Syrian state	53
Conclusion	57
References	58

Part II
REGIONAL DYNAMICS AND PROXIES

Chapter 4
THE DEAL OF DISCONTENT: SAUDI ARABIA, THE ISLAMIC REPUBLIC OF IRAN AND THE NUCLEAR DEAL — 65
Olivia Glombitza

Introduction	65
The nuclear deal: Source of discontent	68
Saudi–Iran relationship	69
Saudi and Iranian foreign policy priorities	70
Frames, narratives and the projection of symbolic power	74
Strategic framing of the self and the other and the formation of narratives	76
Conclusion	81
Notes	82
References	83

Chapter 5
SECURITIZATION OF SHI'A TO 'VIOLIZATION': A RESPONSE TO THE ARAB SPRING IN BAHRAIN — 85
Samira Nasirzadeh

Introduction	85
Securitization theory and the 'sectarianization' thesis	86
Securitization of Iran as seen by domestic and regional audiences since 1979	88
Securitization through 'sectarianization' in Bahrain	89
Securitization through 'sectarianization' at the regional level	91
Successful securitization moving to 'violization' in Bahrain	93
Systematic 'violization': A form of cultural and religious violence	96
Conclusion	97
References	98

Chapter 6
BRIDGING ETHNO-RELIGIOUS DIVIDES BY PROXY? NON-STATE SPONSORSHIP AND SECTARIANISM IN THE CASE OF THE SYRIAN DEMOCRATIC FORCES   103
    Michel Wyss
    Introduction   103
    Studying proxy relationships   104
    Theorizing non-state sponsorship   106
    Sectarianism and proxy relations in the Syrian war   107
    Utilizing non-state sponsorship to address sectarianism: The case of the YPG and the Syrian Democratic Forces (SDF)   109
    The YPG and the SDF – primus inter pares?   111
    Addressing sectarianism by proxy   112
    Conclusion   112
    Notes   113
    References   113

Chapter 7
SAUDI ARABIA'S RHETORICAL CONSTRUCTION OF THE HOUTHIS AS AN IRANIAN PROXY   119
    Maria-Louise Clausen
    Introduction   119
    The post-Arab uprising transition in Yemen and its gradual collapse   120
    Identity, friends and enemies   122
    The contested nature of the proxy concept   123
    Saudi Arabia and the Yemeni state: Saudi Arabia as a friend of Yemen and the Houthis as an enemy   124
    Iran and the Houthis: Iran as an enemy to Saudi Arabia and the Houthis as their proxy   127
    Conclusion   130
    Notes   131
    References   133

Chapter 8
SECTARIANISM AND CIVIL WARS IN THE MENA REGION   135
    Francesco Belcastro
    Introduction   135
    Sectarianism and regional involvement in civil wars: An overview   136
    Aims and limitations   138
    Sectarianism, states and foreign fighters   138
    States and foreign fighters   140
    Sectarianism, civil wars and regions   141
    Sectarianism and civil wars: The case of Syria   143
    The Syrian polity   144
    The civil war   145

Conclusion: Civil wars and the sectarianism debate	148
Notes	150
References	150

Part III
DE-SECTARIANIZATION

Chapter 9
IRAN'S SOFT POWER IN THE GULF FROM THE ISLAMIC REVOLUTION TO POST–INTRA-GULF CRISIS AND PROSPECTS FOR DE-SECTARIANIZATION IN THE GULF

Nesibe Hicret Battaloglu

	155
Introduction	155
Soft power: Its definition, sources and limitations	156
The rationale of studying Iran's soft power in the Gulf	157
Iran's soft power resources, currencies, motivations and application in the Gulf region	159
Measuring soft power: Gulf public opinion towards Iran	163
Assessments on Iran's soft power in the GCC countries: From the Green Movement to the Arab Spring	166
Gulf assertiveness, Gulf crisis and Iran as a lesser evil?	168
Iran's soft power and possibilities for de-sectarianization of the Gulf region	170
Conclusion	173
Notes	174
References	174

Chapter 10
POLITICAL AND DISCURSIVE DE-SECTARIANIZATION: RE-ORDERING SAUDI FOREIGN AND DOMESTIC POLICY-MAKING

Umer Karim

	179
Conceptual framework	180
Structural variables impacting upon the sectarian outlook	182
'From sectarian to sectarianization': A regime strategy or a state's ethos?	183
Islamic revolution in Iran and politicization of Saudi Shi'ite identity	185
Sectarian and regional fault lines within Saudi politics	186
Transformation of state–sect relationship under King Salman	188
Changing discourses on the foreign policy front	192
Rapprochement with Iraq	194
Political capital above sectarian identity	195
Conclusion	197
Notes	198
References	198

Chapter 11
INSTITUTIONAL FAITH-BASED DIPLOMACY AND
DE-SECTARIANIZATION IN THE MIDDLE EAST: HOW TO
UNDERSTAND THE ROLE OF AL-AZHAR IN THE SUNNI–SHIʿI
RAPPROCHEMENT? 205
    Hossam Ed-Deen Allam
    Early Muslim scholars' approach to differences of opinion 206
    Tracing the roots of the Sunni–Shiʿi rapprochement 206
    Mapping out the role of Al-Azhar in the Sunni–Shiʿi rapprochement 207
    The significance of Shaykh Shaltūt's fatwa on Shiʿa Madhāhib in 1959 AD 209
    Shaltūt's scholarly works 210
    Shaltūt's impact on the path of rapprochement 211
    Al-Qaradāwi's declaration of principles regarding Sunni–Shiʿi
        rapprochement 214
    A critical assessment of the role of Al-Azhar in the Sunni–Shiʿi
        rapprochement and de-sectarianization 215
    Conclusion 216
    Notes 217
    References 218

CONCLUSION
    Samira Nasirzadeh, Elias Ghazal and Eyad Alrefai 227
    Sectarianism is complicated but not unpredictable 229
    Regional geopolitics of sectarianism and proxies 230
    Moving from sectarianization to de-sectarianization 232

Index 237

ACKNOWLEDGEMENTS

An endeavour such as this requires the involvement of a great many people, and we would like to thank them here. This volume comes out of the inaugural Sectarianism, Proxies and De-sectarianisation (SEPAD) conference, held in the spring of 2019. This event brought together a range of wonderful scholars from across the world, provoking fascinating discussions and serving as the intellectual springboard for what was to follow. We would like to thank our wonderful contributors who have provided such fantastic and provocative chapters. We would also like to thank all of the people who were involved in this event and all other SEPAD events and initiatives that have helped push the intellectual boundaries of debate on sectarianism. SEPAD receives funding from Carnegie Corporation of New York and we would like to thank Hillary Wiesner and Nehal Amer for their ongoing support. Finally, we would like to thank everyone at I.B. Tauris for their patience and support while we navigated Covid-19 and a truly intercontinental editing process.

NOTES ON CONTRIBUTORS

Jinan S. Al-Habbal is the Principal Investigator of the research project 'Consociationalism and Civil Resistance in Lebanon' in the Middle East Centre at the London School of Economics and Political Science (LSE). She is also a Fellow in the Centre for Syrian Studies at the University of St Andrews and the co-author of *The Politics of Sectarianism in Postwar Lebanon* (2015). Jinan holds a PhD in International Relations from the University of St Andrews.

Eyad Alrefai is a PhD candidate in International Relations at Lancaster University. He is a lecturer of Political Science at King Abdulaziz University. His research looks at the interaction between material and ideational aspects in the Middle East through discussing the intersection between comparative politics and IR theory.

Nesibe Hicret Battaloglu is a Research Assistant in the Gulf Studies Center, Qatar University, Doha, Qatar. Currently, she is also a PhD candidate at the Middle East Technical University (METU) in Ankara, Turkey. Battaloglu obtained an MA in Gulf Studies at Qatar University with a thesis on Turkey and Iran's soft power in Gulf Cooperation Council (GCC) countries. Her research interests are International Relations of the Gulf monarchies, Turkey-GCC relations, and identity and foreign policy nexus in the Gulf.

Francesco Belcastro is a Senior Lecturer in International Relations at the University of Derby and a Fellow at the CSS, University of St Andrews. His areas of research are conflict, sport and politics and politics of the Middle East (particularly Israel/Palestine and Syria). His current research looks at external actors' involvement in civil wars. He is also working on a project that deals with sport and politics in the MENA region. In the past he has worked on foreign policy and alliances. His first monograph, published by Routledge, analysed the foreign policy of Syria during the years 1963–89.

Maria-Louise Clausen holds a PhD in Political Science from Aarhus University, Denmark, and is currently a Senior Researcher at the Danish Institute of International Studies (DIIS) and a fellow in the Sectarianism, Proxies and De-sectarianisation (SEPAD) project. Her work centres on external state building as both administrative practices and a site for competing notions of legitimate governance. More broadly, her research critically reflects on ideas and actors involved in political governance at local, national and international levels. Geographically her work focuses on the Middle East, particularly Yemen and Iraq. She has published on these issues in journals such as *Third World Quarterly, Small*

Wars and Insurgencies, Public Administration and Development, Studies in Conflict and Terrorism as well as International Affairs.

Hossam Ed-Deen Allam is a State Counsellor at Egyptian State Lawsuits Authority. He has an MA in Diplomacy and Religion with Distinction from the Department of Politics, Philosophy and Religion at Lancaster University. In parallel, Hossam serves as a Lecturer of Usul al-Fiqh and Research Methods in English at the Department of Sharia and Law in English at Al-Azhar University in Cairo, where he obtained the LLB of Sharia and Law in English with Honours.

Previously, Hossam worked as a member of Al-Azhar Fatwa Global Centre and as an Academic Researcher at Al-Azhar's Observatory for Countering Extremism. His main research areas are faith-based diplomacy, conflict transformation, de-sectarianization, international humanitarian law and peacebuilding. He has published several academic works on interfaith diplomacy and peacebuilding.

While pursuing his MA in the UK, Hossam worked as a Fellow Researcher at the Richardson Institute for Peace and Conflict Research. Additionally, Hossam is a Fellow of the 'International Dialogue Centre' and is globally known by its abbreviation (KAICIID). He is also a project participant with the United Nations Alliance of Civilizations (UNAOC) focusing on safeguarding places of worship. He is also a Chevening Scholar.

Elias Ghazal is pursuing a PhD in International Relations at Lancaster University. He is interested in the intersection between religion and politics in the Middle East.

Elias's thesis is about de-sectarianization in Lebanon. He is exploring structural factors that reproduce sectarianism in Lebanon and the agency of religious leaders to circumvent those structures.

Olivia Glombitza is an Adjunct Professor of International Relations at the Autonomous University of Barcelona (UAB) and the Open University of Catalonia (UOC), and a fellow for the project 'Reconfiguration of Transnational Actors & Elites in the MENA Region' based at UAB and the project 'Sectarianism, Proxies and De-sectarianization' (SEPAD) based at Lancaster University. She holds a master's degree in Media, Communication and Culture from the Autonomous University of Barcelona, and a master's degree in Intercultural Competence and Conflict Management from the University of Verona. She earned her PhD in International Relations from the Autonomous University of Barcelona with a thesis on the symbolic politics of the Islamic Republic of Iran and the Republic of Turkey at the intersection of domestic politics and foreign policy.

She has led projects on the ongoing transformation of the Republic of Turkey and the role of ideational factors in foreign policy and peacebuilding in the Middle East and the Persian Gulf, both supported by the International Catalan Institute for Peace (ICIP). Her research interests include the history, contemporary politics and international relations of the Middle East and the Persian Gulf; Iran's and Turkey's domestic and foreign policies; symbolic politics; relations of power;

conceptualizations of ideology and identity; media representation; and narrative and discourse analysis.

Her articles have been published by *Third World Quarterly*, *The International Spectator*, *Turkish Studies*, *Global Discourse* and the *British Journal of Middle Eastern Studies*.

Madonna Kalousian is a lecturer in Modern Arabic Literature and Culture at the University of Cambridge. She has a PhD in English Literature, with a focus on the Lebanese Civil War, from the Department of English Literature and Creative Writing at Lancaster University. Her current work focuses on postcolonial animal studies, ecocriticism and the Anthropocene in modern Arabic Literature, politics and the visual arts. She is the author of multiple pieces on related questions and her work appears in a number of outlets, including *Alif: Journal of Comparative Poetics*, *Journal of War and Culture Studies* and *Journal of Middle Eastern Studies*.

Umer Karim is a doctoral researcher in the Department of Political Science and International Studies at the University of Birmingham. His academic research focuses on Saudi foreign policy and broader geopolitics of the Middle East. He is an Associate Fellow at the King Faisal Center for Research and Islamic Studies and a Fellow of the SEPAD Project at Lancaster University's Richardson Institute.

Ana Maria Kumarasamy is a PhD candidate in Politics at Lancaster University. Her research focuses on the politics of waste, sovereign power and inequality in Beirut. She is a PhD fellow at the Sectarianism, Proxies and de-sectarianisation (SEPAD) project, and has previously worked as a project coordinator at the Richardson Institute based at Lancaster University.

Simon Mabon is Chair in International Politics at Lancaster University where he directs the Richardson Institute. He holds a PhD in International Relations from the University of Leeds and is the director of SEPAD, a project funded by Carnegie Corporation and the Henry Luce Foundation, which looks at the position and contestation of sectarian identities within the contemporary Middle East (www.sepad.org.uk).

Mabon is the author of a number of books on the contemporary Middle East including: *The Struggle for Supremacy: Saudi Arabia and Iran* (2023); *Houses Built on Sand: Sectarianism, Revolution and Violence in the Middle East* (Manchester University Press, 2020); and *Saudi Arabia and Iran: Soft Power Rivalry in the Middle East* (2013). He has published in a range of Middle East and International Relations journals including: *Review of International Studies*; *Middle East Journal*; *Middle East Policy*; *British Journal of Middle East Studies*; *Politics, Religion and Ideology*; and *Third World Quarterly*. He is the co-editor of a major Middle Eastern book series with Manchester University Press.

Samuel Peter Mace received his undergraduate and MA degrees from Lancaster University. In addition, he has recently finished his PhD in Political Theory from the University of Leeds. His research interests are the intersection of sovereignty and political authority relating to the management of political orders.

Samira Nasirzadeh holds a PhD in International Relations at Lancaster University in the UK. She was previously working as a University Teaching Assistant and Research Assistant at Lancaster University and Research Fellow in the Sectarianism, Proxies and De-sectarianisation (SEPAD) project. She currently works as a University Lecturer and Research Assistant at IPIS. Her research centers on international relations of the Middle East, particularly Bahrain and Yemen; Foreign Policy and Diplomacy; Arab Springs, Post-Arab Springs; Securitization through Sectarianization and desecuritization in Saudi-Iran relations. Her research has appeared in journals such as *The International Spectator, The Review of Faith & International Affairs, Global Discourse, Politics and Law*.

Michel Wyss is a PhD candidate at Leiden University, a lecturer at the Department of Humanities, Social and Political Sciences at ETH Zurich, and a scientific assistant at the Military Academy at ETH Zurich. His research has appeared in *International Security, International Studies Review*, and *Democracy and Security*, and he is the co-editor of the *Routledge Handbook of Proxy Wars* (2023). He also serves as a Specialist Officer in the Swiss Armed Forces Joint Operations Command.

INTRODUCTION

Simon Mabon and Ana Maria Kumarasamy

During his 2016 State of the Union address, President Barack Obama reflected on the multifarious challenges facing the United States in the coming year. Within his remarks, Obama reflected on developments across the Middle East at a time when actors across the region were embroiled in a series of inter- and intra-state conflict, including a bloody war against Da'ish. In the speech, Obama declared that 'the Middle East is going through a transformation that will play out for a generation, rooted in conflicts that date back millennia'. This remark, while factually inaccurate, orientalist and verging on the xenophobic, is regularly used by people professing awareness of the root causes of the rivalry between Saudi Arabia and Iran, and also of broader sectarian tensions in the Muslim world. This approach reduces tensions (between Saudi Arabia and Iran, or between Sunni and Shi'a) to 'ancient hatreds' within Islam that emerged following the death of the Prophet. The schism that emerged initially was driven by political questions – who should guide the *umma* after the prophet's death – but over time took on religious components. Advocates of the 'ancient hatreds' thesis argue that contemporary tensions within Islam are a direct consequence of the events of 1,400 years ago, reducing tensions to monolithic and monocausal reasons, ignoring political, cultural, economic and ideological developments that play a key role in understanding the behaviour of actors across the Middle East.

Instead, developments across the Middle East – locally and regionally – are forged through the complex interplay of local politics and regional rivalries, where material and ideational resources are deployed by actors seeking to impose particular visions of order on the region. This interplay of actors brings together powerful regional actors such as Saudi Arabia or Iran with local actors, be they political elites, tribal leaders, militias or religious figures, with relationships cultivated in pursuit of shared visions of order. Problematic analysis, such as that proposed by Obama, frames regional politics playing out along the lines of 'ancient hatreds', with Saudi Arabia engaging in a rivalry with Iran which pits Sunni against Shi'a. As a result of this, Sunni actors across the region support – and draw resources from – Saudi Arabia, while Shi'a actors ally with Iran. While there is a grain of truth in the claim that Saudi Arabia draws support from Sunnis and

Iran draws support from Shi'a groups, there is much more nuance at play, notably through the existence of a range of other identity markers. Yet the prominence of Islam within the political fabric of states across the region is reflected in the attention given to sectarian identities by scholars working on the geopolitics of the Middle East.

Although adhering to different strands of Islam – Saudi Arabia is Wahhabi and, by extension, Sunni, while Iran is Twelver Shi'a – sectarian tensions are but one feature of a complex rivalry that predates the formation of the modern Kingdom of Saudi Arabia in 1932 (Keynoush 2016). Instead, relations between Riyadh and Tehran are shaped by the congruence of (myriad) security concerns and claims to Islamic legitimacy, albeit also conditioned by the contours of regional politics and the rhythms of global capitalist politics (Keynoush 2016; Mabon 2013; Rubin 2014).

As the modern Saudi state approaches its centenary, relations with neighbouring Iran have oscillated between periods of overt hostility and burgeoning rapprochement, once again shaped by the peculiarities and contingencies of time and space. After revolution led to the establishment of the Islamic Republic of Iran in 1979, relations took an increasingly belligerent turn (Chubin and Tripp 1996). The immediate aftermath of the revolution led to a spiral of rhetoric between Saudi Arabia and Iran over competing claims to legitimacy and leadership of the Muslim world, along with war between Iran and Iraq (Mabon 2013). Over the years that followed, Saudi-Iranian relations oscillated between periods of hostility and apparent rapprochement, yet as regional dynamics evolved, so too did relations between the Kingdom and the Islamic Republic.

While realists hold that regional tensions typically emerge as a consequence of structural factors such as competing claims over territory (Chubin and Tripp 1996; Furtig 2006), the power of ideology, particularly within contested environments, should not be ignored. Indeed, as a number of scholars have articulated, these tensions between material and ideational factors – and how they operate within and between states – are central to understanding much of what happens in Middle Eastern international relations (Darwich 2019). Put another way, the porous nature of borders means that what happens in one state resonates across the region.

It is generally accepted that debate about the role of religion has a prominent role to play in shaping the fabric of states across the Middle East. From Turkey in the north to Yemen in the south, Iran in the east and Israel in the west, both the social fabric and relationship between rulers and ruled are shaped by the position of religion within the state. Perhaps the most obvious examples of this are found on opposite sides of the Persian Gulf, where Saudi Arabia and Iran have instilled religious values at the heart of their respective political projects (Akbarzadeh and Connor 2005; Commins 2006; Farhi 2008; Farquar 2016; Katouzian and Shahidi 2008; Kostiner 1985, 1997). State-building processes revolved around instilling Islamic values across the state while regulating the power of normative principles.

Middle Eastern states are situated in the midst of a regional security environment shaped by concurrent pressures from other states, supra-state ideologies and sub-state actors (Noble 1984). Those who derive legitimacy through recourse to

Islamic rhetoric also position themselves within a normative environment that is shaped through the interactions of its constituent parts. For those states invested in both, geopolitical and religious environments operate in a dialectic manner, shaping domestic and foreign policy.

The US-led invasion of Iraq in 2003 created conditions which led to a dramatic increase in tensions as Riyadh and Tehran sought to increase their influence in Iraqi politics (Dodge 2008), while the Arab Uprisings of 2011 created additional opportunities for the two to engage in competition over regional order, leading to the outbreak of violence in Syria, Bahrain and Yemen, and the continuation of unrest in Lebanon and Iraq. As Gregory Gause (2014) observes, the fragmentation of political projects has created opportunities for increased regional involvement in local politics. Similarly, as others have observed, the presence of shared normative environments – constructed along sectarian, ethnic, (geo)political or tribal lines – aided the penetration of states by regional powers in pursuit of power and influence.

For instance, as Madawi Al Rasheed noted in 2011, unrest in Syria presented Saudi Arabia with the opportunity to bring the country back to the Arab fold. A similar point is made by Mehran Kamrava (2012) about Saudi Arabia's counter-revolutionary capabilities. In contrast, unrest in Yemen – after developments elsewhere across the region – led a senior Iranian official (AP 2017) to claim that Tehran 'controls four Arab capitals', namely Baghdad, Beirut, Damascus and Sana'a. Of the five arenas of rivalry previously mentioned, only Bahrain's capital Manama was absent from this list, reflecting the strength of the ruling Al Khalifa's response to the protests, albeit strongly supported by the House of Saud.

Within each arena, elites declared particular groups to be operating with the support of nefarious regional powers, discursively framing both the local group and regional actor as a threat to the stability of the state. As we shall see below, the salience of sectarian identities within and across states provided opportunities for rulers to exacerbate divisions in pursuit of security and stability, regardless of the veracity of claims of pernicious external involvement.

While many view the external sponsorship of local groups in conflict zones as 'proxy wars' (Mumford 2013), this appears somewhat problematic, ignoring the complexity of transnational relationships and denying the agency of clients. In understanding local and regional developments – and the interaction of sectarian identities and geopolitical agendas – it is imperative to critically reflect on concepts of sectarianism, de-sectarianization and 'proxies'.

Although there is no consensus on the definition of sectarianism, it has typically been used to explain difference and violence across and within states in the Middle East, especially relating to divisions within Islam and the rivalry between Saudi Arabia and Iran. The concept has been widely contested, and as a result, a vast literature has developed seeking to unpack the complexities at play, including publications such as the *Politics of Sectarianism* (Salloukh et al. 2015), *Sectarianization* (Hashemi and Postel 2017), *The New Sectarianism* (Abdo 2016) and *Houses Built on Sand* (Mabon 2020a). Other literature on this topic has sought to challenge dominant perceptions and theoretical perspectives, including Ussama

Makdisi (2019) and his study 'the ecumenical frame', which explores historical instances of coexistence in the Arab world. Similarly, Fanar Haddad (2020) argues that the term 'sectarianism' should be discarded and suggests that the literature on race relations and critical race theory would allow scholars to better understand sectarian identity.

In the past, the debates on sectarianism have revolved around primordial, instrumental and constructivist positions. Primordialists, rarely a feature of contemporary scholarly debate, argue that sectarianism is one of the defining features of the Middle East that is rooted in history and 'ancient hatreds' coupled with territorial locations. Instrumentalists, in contrast, suggest that sectarianism is a part of the political process and is manipulated by political elites in order to advance political and economic interests. However, much emphasis has been placed on discrediting primordialist and instrumentalist positions with various alternative approaches flourishing. Valbjørn (2019) groups these into three types of 'beyond strategies': 'the new saviour', 'the baby and the bathwater' and 'LEGO theorising'. 'The new saviour' approaches argue that primordialist and instrumentalist approaches are so flawed that they need to be completely abandoned. Within these types of approaches emphasis is moved towards other established fields such as identity politics and nationalism studies, including theoretical approaches like constructivism (Hashemi and Postel 2017), institutionalism (Salloukh and Verheij 2017; Al-Habbal Chapter 1), the Copenhagen School (Drawich and Fakhoury 2016; Mabon 2019) and urban geopolitics (Fregonese 2019). Engagement with theoreticians and their ideas has also been significant, including Pierre Bourdieu (Dodge 2020), Giorgio Agamben (Mabon 2020b; Mabon and Kumarasamy 2019; Kalousian Chapter 2) and Carl Schmitt (Mace Chapter 3).

'The baby and the bathwater' strategy acknowledges that 'pure' versions of primordialism and instrumentalism are flawed but that they include some insights and should be revised rather than simply rejected (Valbjørn 2019: 100). Valbjørn's final 'beyond strategy' is labelled 'the LEGO theorising' strategy that follows a call for eclecticism that builds on a variety of approaches and theories that builds like LEGO bricks. These strategies assume that there is not one but a combination of theories and approaches that can sufficiently describe the complexities around sectarianism. For example, Staci Strobl (2018) applies sectarianism and criminal justice in the case of Bahrain and similarly, Samira Nasirzadeh (Chapter 5) employs securitization theory and the sectarianization concept in order to understand the systematic methods of violence in Bahrain.

Sectarian differences are not limited to domestic politics, however, perhaps best seen in the rivalry between Saudi Arabia and Iran (Keynoush 2016; Mabon 2013; Mason 2014). This rivalry – conditioned by the interplay of geopolitical tensions and competition for Islamic legitimacy – plays out across the region, finding traction in states that are fragmented, or societies divided along sectarian lines. From this, the fragmentation of political projects in Iraq, Syria and Yemen opened up space for Riyadh and Tehran to engage in the domestic machinations of domestic politics, cultivating relationships with local actors which are then viewed through the lens of 'proxies'. In Chapter 7, Clausen analyses how Saudi Arabia has justified military intervention through the construction of Saudi Arabia as a 'friend of Yemen' and the Houthis as Iranian proxy. In Bahrain and Lebanon, two states where political contexts differ dramatically from those previously mentioned, Saudi Arabia and Iran have sought to cultivate relations with political, social and religious actors, albeit conditioned by the peculiarities of time and space. Here we see different types of relationships playing out across regional politics from elite relationships to the sponsoring of political parties and movements.

The existence of transnational relationships between regional powers and local actors has often led to the framing of such relations as proxies, where the patron determines trajectories of the client. Yet this, as Amal Saad (2019) persuasively argues, denies much of the agency of the client actor which is deeply problematic given the actions of many so-called proxies across the Middle East. Reflecting on the actions of Hizballah, the Houthis, the Popular Mobilization Units (PMUs), Iraqi tribes or political parties in Lebanon reveals local actors pushing against the wishes of their patrons. Indeed, these transnational relationships themselves are shaped by complex competitions over power and influence rather than purely being examples of patrons controlling clients. As such, more work is needed to better understand the nature of relations between patron and client and to move beyond the simplistic reading of 'proxy' relationships. In this vein, Wyss (Chapter 6) challenges current scholarships by exploring the agency and ability of non-state actors to employ their own 'proxies'.

Frustration at the presence of regional powers in local politics has provoked widespread anger across a number of states, perhaps best seen in protests in Iraq and Lebanon. The legacy of external involvement has created certain forms of political organization which privilege particular individuals and groups above others, leading to a political environment skewed by elite corruption and sectarian difference, supported and enabled by external allies. Despite the power of such elites, an array of recent protest movements has sought to reimagine the nature of political organization. The Arab Uprisings, Lebanon's YouStink protests of 2015 and the 2019 protests in Lebanon and Iraq have sought to challenge the dominant role of sectarian elites in all facets of life. In doing this, individuals and groups have articulated alternative visions of political life and the role of religion. Such processes fall under the rubric of de-sectarianization (Mabon 2020b).

Emerging in response to the sectarianization thesis presented by Hashemi and Postel in 2017, de-sectarianization is the re-imagining of the role of religion within socio-economic and political life, defined broadly. As such, de-sectarianization not only can include the deconstruction of sectarian enmity – in response to the sectarianization construction of such relations – but also can include the privileging of particular identities in opposition to the salience of sectarian identities. This can take place in a range of different ways, from the de-securitization of sectarian identity to the mobilization of other forms of identity. As Mabon (2020b) observes, there are four key questions to be addressed when reflecting on de-sectarianization: how do we understand de-sectarianization? Where does de-sectarianization occur and how? Who is involved in de-sectarianization? And what are the aims of de-sectarianization? Fundamental to these questions are efforts to move beyond sectarianism as an organizing principle of political life, driven by the actions of a range of individuals, different activities and in different spaces. Broadly speaking, de-sectarianization serves as a way of re-imagining the role of religion in trans-sectarian activity, collective action spanning different communal groups; anti-sectarianism, the explicit rejection of sectarian identities and the erosion of communal difference.

While typically stemming from grassroots protests, such as those seen during the Arab Uprisings, the YouStink protests of 2015 or the Iraqi and Lebanese protests of 2019, de-sectarianization can also take place in a top-down process. For example, in Saudi Arabia and Bahrain, ruling elites have privileged national identities as an alternative to sectarian identities as a means of redrawing boundaries within political projects. In Chapter 10, Karim explores a broader shift in Saudi Arabia towards de-sectarianization and broader focus on regional projects.

In pursuit of this, the book is divided into three main sections which allow scope for critical reflection on the ways in which regional politics intersects with local politics. Part I ('The Politics of Sectarianism') features third-way strategies that have been developed in order to further understand sectarianism and contestation. Part II ('Regional Dynamics and Proxies') considers sectarian rivalries and their impact on politics and civil wars. The final part ('De-sectarianization') explores the re-imagining of the role of religion in political projects and policy developments.

Part I: The politics of sectarianism

Jinan Al-Habbal (Chapter 1) examines the development of the liberal consociational political system in Iraq after the US-led invasion. The political changes and de-Ba'thification by former prime minister Nour al-Maliki increased tensions between Sunni and Shi'a groups in the aftermath of the civil war. The manifestation of ethnosectarian identities concurrent with entrenched political divisions has embedded corruption and clientelism, leading to a series of anti-government protests. This chapter focuses on these protest movements during the Arab Uprisings and during the period leading up to the 2018 protests and ends by exploring the October 2019 protests and its implications for Iraqi politics.

Aspects of sectarianism have been researched in a series of different ways. Madonna Kalousian (Chapter 2) considers the sectarian narratives by Lebanese ruling elite after the Taif Agreement. Despite recent widespread popular protests and economic crisis, the political elite has displayed little willingness to change the broader political system. The response to the protests in October 2019 is viewed as an extension of the newly introduced electoral law in 2017 and the proposed amnesty law in 2019. The government's lack of political will to address popular demands, Kalousian argues, highlights the need to move beyond the post-war climate that shapes Lebanon today.

Sam Peter Mace (Chapter 3) observes the development of sectarianism within the Syrian regime. Sectarianism played an increasing role within state institutions leading up to the 2011 Syrian uprisings and it continued to do so during the civil war through the instrumentalization of sectarian identities as a means to secure the state. Through the utilization of Carl Schmitt's 'friend–enemy' dichotomy, Mace argues that the Syrian regime's sovereignty is undermined when it is practising sectarian politics. Mace concludes that the 2011 uprisings and the following civil war have left the regime 'weak internally' and that large sections of society now view the state as an enemy.

Part II: Regional dynamics and proxies

The geopolitical environment in the Middle East is complex and is fragmented by regional dynamics, proxy wars and a multitude of diverse actors. Olivia Isabell Glombitza (Chapter 4) analyses the departure from the Joint Comprehensive Plan of Action, known as the 2015 nuclear deal, and the changing nature of the competition between Saudi Arabia and Iran. The nuclear deal was historically significant, seeking to further peace and stability. The chapter argues that the competition between the two states is feeding into the sectarian divide through the use of symbolic power and by discursively mobilizing sectarian identities. Glombitza concludes that the abandonment of the nuclear deal has supported Saudi narratives and their perceptions of the Islamic Republic of Iran.

Samira Nasirzadeh (Chapter 5) explores the aftermath of the protests in Pearl Roundabout in 2011, in which counter-revolution strategies by the Al Khalifa fuelled sectarian tensions in Bahrain where the Shi'a majority is 'securitized' and ruled by a Sunni minority. In this vein, Nasirzadeh approaches these tensions through the application of a third-way approach that focuses on the successful manipulation of securitization through sectarianization which contributed to the failure of the revolution and the 'violization' against the Shi'a population. Nasirzadeh concludes that the Bahraini ruling family has utilized a variety of violent methods in order to secure long-term stability in order to prevent any repetition of the Arab uprisings in Bahrain.

Michel Wyss (Chapter 6) observes that a focus on state sponsorship and sectarian divides has missed complex issues surrounding contemporary proxies and non-state actors. By utilizing the case study of the Kurdish People's Protection Units (YPG) and the Syrian Democratic forces (SDF), Wyss argues that certain non-state actors are employing proxies themselves and reducing sectarian tensions (perhaps unintentionally) by bridging ethno-religious divisions. The chapter ends with a call to better understand contemporary proxy relations and non-state sponsorships outside state prerogative.

Maria-Louise Clausen (Chapter 7) analyses how Saudi Arabia has discursively justified military intervention in Yemen. The conflict in Yemen is narrated by the actor through the construction of Saudi Arabia as a friend of Yemen and the Houthis as an Iranian proxy. The chapter considers how Saudi Arabia legitimizes and utilizes international law in order to distinguish itself from Iran. The chapter concludes that there are two key components that constitute the distinction between friend and enemy in Saudi Arabian narratives. Firstly, it has positioned itself as a friend of the internationally recognized president ʿAbd Rabbuh Mansour Hadi, and secondly, Iran is positioned as an enemy of Saudi Arabia that is perceived to disregard norms of non-interference and international laws.

Francesco Belcastro (Chapter 8) explores the relationship between sectarianism and civil wars in the Middle East and North Africa (MENA) region. The chapter seek to further unpack the role of the state in the mobilization and recruitment of foreign fighters, and their broader impact on the process of sectarianization within civil wars. In the Syrian civil war, Belcastro finds that the regime exploited sectarian divides within the country and the broader region, and utilized networks in order to secure and recruit fighters from countries such as Afghanistan and Pakistan. Belcastro concludes that states play a crucial role in exploiting sectarian divides to serve their own objectives and contributing to the sectarianization of civil wars.

Part III: De-sectarianization

The literature on de-sectarianization has expanded considerably over the past years. Nesibe Hicret Battaloglu (Chapter 9) examines Iran's soft power and its impacts in the Gulf region since the Iranian Revolution in 1979. Geopolitical developments have deteriorated and curbed the reach of Iranian soft power in the region. However, recent intra-Gulf disputes between Saudi Arabia and Qatar, and historic peace deals with Israel have altered the political agenda in some of the Gulf states. Battaloglu argues that Iran's soft power policies towards the Gulf Cooperation Council (GCC) states would contribute to a better understanding of de-sectarianization and the normalization of inter-state relations between Gulf monarchies and Iran. Improvements of Iran's image reflect a regional shift and awareness of other regional threats and developments since 2011.

Umer Karim (Chapter 10) explores the political shift in Saudi Arabia from King Salman and the emergence of his son Crown Prince Mohammad Bin Salman. Political and economic changes due to this shift have impacted Saudi foreign policies and regional relationships, leading towards a discursive de-sectarianization of its national identity. Karim argues that contemporary Saudi foreign policy frames Iran through their regional projects as opposed to politicizing the broader Shiʿa community. This is displayed through not only Saudi Arabian engagement with Iraq but also other confrontational engagements with Qatar and Turkey.

Hossam Ed-Deen Allam (Chapter 11) seeks to further understand the role of religious institutions within the broader de-sectarianization processes. Through the case study of the Islamic institution of Al-Azhar, Allam explores its thought on Sunni–Shiʿa rapprochement, and its potential role in de-sectarianization. Sunni–Shiʿa rapprochement came to the forefront of the Al-Azhar Institute through Shaykh Shaltūt's fatwa on Shiʿi Madhāhib in 1959 but has since been on the decline. Allam calls for the Al-Azhar Institute to play a larger role in discussions on de-sectarianization and peacebuilding as an extension of its already significant role on the global arena, in which it has confronted waves of violent extremism and Islamophobia.

Bibliography

Abdo, G. (2016), *New Sectarianism: The Arab Uprisings and the Rebirth of the Shi'a-Sunni Divide*, New York: Oxford University Press.

Akbarzadeh, S., and Connor, K. (2005), 'The Organization of the Islamic Conference: Sharing an Illusion', *Middle East Policy*, 12 (2): 79–92.

Associated Press in Dubai (2017), 'Iran Is Seeking "to Control Islamic World", Says Saudi Arabian Prince', *The Guardian*, 2 May. Available online: https://www.theguardian.com/world/2017/may/02/iran-is-seeking-to-control-islamic-world-says-saudi-arabian-prince (accessed 18 May 2021).

Chubin, S., and Tripp, C. (1996), *Iran–Saudi Arabia Relations and Regional Order*, London: Oxford University Press.

Commins, D. (2006), *The Wahhabi Mission and Saudi Arabia*, London: I.B. Tauris.

Darwich, M., and Fakhoury, T. (2016), 'Casting the Other as an Existential Threat: The Securitisation of Sectarianism in the International Relations of the Syria Crisis', *Global Discourse*, 6 (4): 712–32.

Darwich, M. (2019), *Threats and Alliances in the Middle East: Saudi and Syrian Policies in a Turbulent Region*, Cambridge: Cambridge University Press.

Dodge, T. (2008), 'Iraqi Transitions: From Regime Change to State Collapse', *Third World Quarterly*, 26 (4–5): 705–21.

Dodge, T. (2020), 'The Failure of Peacebuilding in Iraq: The Role of Consociationalism and Political Settlements', *Journal of Intervention and Statebuilding*, 15 (4): 1–17.

Farhi, F. (2008), 'The Dilemma of National Interest in the Islamic Republic of Iran', in H. Katouzian and H. Shahidi (eds), *Iran in the 21st Century: Politics, Economics & Conflict*, Oxon: Routledge, 13–27.

Farquhar, M. (2016), *Circuits of Faith: Migration, Education, and the Wahhabi Mission*, Stanford, CA: Stanford University Press.

Fregonese, S. (2019), *War and the City: Urban Geopolitics in Lebanon*, London: I.B. Tauris.

Furtig, H. (2006), *Iran's Rivalry with Saudi Arabia between the Gulf Wars*, Reading: Ithaca Press.

Gause III, G. F. (2014), 'Beyond Sectarianism: The New Middle East Cold War', *Brookings Doha Center Analysis Paper*.

Haddad, F. (2020), *Understanding 'Sectarianism': Sunni–Shi'a Relations in the Modern Arab World*, New York: Oxford University Press.

Hashemi, N., and Postel, D. (2017), *Sectarianization: Mapping the New Politics of the Middle East*, New York: Oxford University Press.

Kamrava, M. (2012), 'The Arab Spring and the Saudi-Led Counterrevolution', *Orbis*, 56 (1): 96–104.

Katouzian, H., and Shahidi, H. (2008), *Iran in the 21st Century: Politics, Economics & Conflict*, Oxon: Routledge.

Keynoush, B. (2016), *Saudi Arabia and Iran: Friends or Foes?* London: Palgrave Macmillan US.

Kostiner, J. (1985), 'On Instruments and Their Designers: The Ikhwan of Najd and the Emergence of the Saudi State', *Middle East Studies*, 21 (3): 298–323.

Kostiner, J. (1997), 'State, Islam and Opposition in Saudi Arabia, the Post-Desert Storm Phase', *Middle East Review of International Affairs*, 1 (2): 75–89.

Mabon, S. (2013), *Saudi Arabia and Iran: Power and Rivalry in the Middle East*, London: I.B. Tauris.

Mabon, S., and Ardovini, L. (2016), 'People, Sects and States: Interrogating Sectarianism in the Contemporary Middle East', *Global Discourse*, 6 (4): 551–60.

Mabon, S., and Kumarasamy, A. (2019), 'Da'ish, Stasis, and Bare Life in Iraq', in J. Eriksson and A. Khaleel (eds), *Iraq after ISIS: The Challenges of Post-War Recovery*, Cham: Palgrave Macmillan, 9–28.

Mabon, S. (2019), 'The End of the Battle for Bahrain and the Securitization of Bahraini Shi'a', *Middle East Journal*, 73 (1): 29–50.

Mabon, S. (2020a), *Houses Built on Sand: Sovereignty, Violence and Revolution in the Middle East*, Manchester: Manchester University Press.

Mabon, S. (2020b), 'Four Questions about De-sectarianization', *The Review of Faith & International Affairs*, 18 (1): 1–11.

Makdisi, U. S. (2019), *Age of Coexistence: The Ecumenical Frame and the Making of the Modern Arab World*, Oakland: University of California Press.

Mason, R. (2014), *Foreign Policy in Iran and Saudi Arabia: Economics and Diplomacy in the Middle East*, London: I.B. Tauris.

Mumford, A. (2013), 'Proxy Warfare and the Future of Conflict', *RUSI Journal*, 158 (2): 40–6.

Noble, P. C. (1984), 'The Arab System: Pressures, Constraints, and Opportunities', in B. Kahgat and A. E. Hillal (eds), *The Foreign Policies of Arab States*, 2nd edn, New York: Routledge, 67–165.

Al-Rasheed, M. (2011), 'Sectarianism as Counter-Revolution: Saudi Responses to the Arab Spring', *Studies in Ethnicity and Nationalism*, 11 (3): 513–26.

Al-Rasheed, M. (2012), 'The Saudi Response to the "Arab Spring": Containment and Co-option', *Open Democracy*, 10 January. Available online: https://www.opendemocracy.net/en/5050/saudi-response-to-arab-spring-containment-and-co-option/ (accessed 18 May 2021).

Rubin, L. (2014), *Islam in the Balance: Ideational Threats in Arab Politics*, Stanford, CA: Stanford University Press.

Saad, A. (2019), 'Challenging the Sponsor-Proxy Model: The Iran–Hizbullah Relationship', *Global Discourse*, 9 (4): 627–50.

Salloukh, B. F., Barakat, R., Al-Habbal, J. S., Khattab, L. W. and Mikaelian, S. (2015), *The Politics of Sectarianism in Postwar Lebanon*, London: Pluto Press.

Salloukh, B. F., and Verheij, R. A. (2017), 'Transforming Power Sharing: From Corporate to Hybrid Consociation in Postwar Lebanon', *Middle East Law and Governance*, 9 (2): 147–73.

Strobl, S. (2018), *Sectarian Order in Bahrain: The Social and Colonial Origins of Criminal Justice*, Lanham, MD: Lexington Books.

Valbjørn, M. (2019), 'Beyond the Beyond(S): On the (Many) Third Way(s) Beyond Primordialism and Instrumentalism in the Study of Sectarianism', *Nations and Nationalism*, 28: 91–107.

Part I

POLITICS OF SECTARIANISM

Chapter 1

THE IRAQI PROTESTS: SLIDING INTO THE ABYSS?

Jinan S. Al-Habbal

Introduction

Following decades of an authoritarian regime under Saddam Hussein, the US-led invasion of Iraq in 2003 sought to bring democracy to the country, albeit failing to implement a nation-building process that could peacefully transition Iraq into a democratic political system. The imposition of a liberal consociational political system has divided state positions along ethnic and sectarian lines while alienating Sunnis and engendering civil wars. The wave of the Arab Spring popular uprisings that started in Tunisia in December 2010 soon spread to other Arab regimes that were overthrown, implemented reforms or have fallen into civil wars. Iraq, however, has been a rather different case. Although the country was not fully immune to the uprisings in the region, with sporadic protests occurring, its consociational power-sharing political system remained unscathed. But the 2011 protests were not the last attempt at socio-economic reforms and political change.

A series of mass demonstrations have taken place in Iraq since 2003, with protesters demanding the eradication of the political system which has rapidly increased corruption and exacerbated the gap between the political elite and citizens. Protests reached their peak during *Thawrat Tishreen* (the October Revolution) in 2019 when demonstrations erupted in Baghdad and then spread across the country. Sporadic, smaller protests continue as an extension of the uprising despite the repressive force used by security forces and militias affiliated with the ruling class. Although a new government was formed as a result of these protests, no reforms or a feasible top-down process of de-sectarianization have been initiated.

This chapter begins by examining the formation of the liberal consociational political system in Iraq after the US occupation and the removal of Saddam Hussein in 2003. It explains how power sharing has entrenched ethnosectarian identities and embedded corruption and clientelism in Iraq. The chapter touches upon the anti-government protest movements that occurred between the Arab Spring and 2018 during the premierships of Nouri al-Maliki and Haider al-'Abadi. The third part focuses on the October 2019 protest movement, the largest in size and scope, with over a million protesters from all walks of life participating, as well as the October 2021 parliamentary elections. The chapter closes by pointing out the research findings and their implications on Iraqi politics.

The establishment of Iraq's consociational political system

As part of his war on terror following the 9/11 attacks, US President George W. Bush launched Operation Iraqi Freedom to remove Saddam Hussein's authoritarian Ba'thist regime that allegedly had weapons of mass destruction and to impose a new democratic political system. By mid-April 2003, Iraq fell into the hands of the US-led coalition forces and was ruled until June 2004 by the Coalition Provisional Authority (CPA) which was administered by Paul Bremer, setting the foundations for the country's current political system (Dodge 2013: 243). The US occupation was met with widespread Sunni Arab insurgency hoping to drive out the United States and regain the power Sunnis possessed under Saddam. By 2004, Iraq fell into an ethnosectarian civil war between Sunnis and Shi'a, which escalated in 2006 with the proliferation of violence by Shi'a militias seeking to defend their sect and dominance against Sunni insurgents (Fearon 2007). Until today, Iraq's social fabric remains broken, and nationalism remains debated, with most citizens belonging to their sects, ethnicities and tribes before being loyal to their country.

However, it was the CPA's tactics and policies that contributed to the institutional collapse in Iraq. Promoted by the United States and some local actors – such as Iraqi Shi'a Arabs, Kurds and returning exiles – a de-Ba'thification ideology was implemented. The CPA Order No. 1: De-Ba'thification of Iraqi Society of 16 May 2003 disbanded the Ba'th Party, banned its top four members from occupying government positions and prohibited former party members from holding positions in the three most senior management levels of any governmental institution. Between 20,000 and 120,000 people were thus purged from their posts. De-Ba'thification along with over a decade of sanctions, Iraq's three wars within twenty years and the unrestricted looting upon the American invasion erased remnants of the state and its skilled workers (Dodge 2013: 252). The de-Ba'thification policy continued to be adopted by the successive Iraqi governments of former Prime Minister Nouri al-Maliki, increasing tensions between Sunnis and Shi'a in the post-war period. It also disproportionately affected Sunni Arab Ba'thists who were excluded from senior posts in the security forces and government, while Shi'a Ba'thists were given the chance to repent by Shi'a parties in power (International Crisis Group 2006: 10). The CPA also forcibly demilitarized the military and security infrastructure upon implementing CPA Order No. 2: Dissolution of Entities of 23 May 2003, which removed 400,000 Iraqi military personnel (Marr 2012: 397). Even though de-Ba'thification and demilitarization were ostensibly utilized as a means to democratize Iraq, they ultimately hindered democracy and nation-building by alienating Sunni Arabs to the advantage of the Shi'a and Kurds.

Following negotiations between the CPA and a few political parties that were previously exiled, the twenty-five-member Iraqi Governing Council (IGC) was established. Based on ethnic and sectarian quotas, the IGC posts were divided among thirteen Shi'a, five Sunnis, five Kurds, one Turkomen and one Christian. Civil society actors, however, criticized the selection process of the IGC that introduced sectarianism to Iraqi politics and appointed members based on their political affiliations rather than their skills (Dodge 2012: 42). Despite being a policy adopted by Saddam's regime, communalism 'never enjoyed widespread support among the Iraqi people, who are accustomed to Shi'is and Sunnis living peacefully together and even intermarrying' (Jabar 2004: 9). Foreign observers and Iraqi burgeoning elites raised concerns about the prospect of implementing a communal political system that could institutionalize ethnic, sectarian and religious fragmentations; increase political tensions; or strengthen radical Islamism (ibid.). Such fears, however, were dismissed and the IGC paved the way for a liberal consociational democracy. The sectarianization and Shi'a-centric state building of post-2003 Iraq have also created Sunni rejection spanning from ambivalence to anti-state violence and stemming from 'a deep sense of Sunni alienation, a sense of loss, and a sense of victimhood beginning with regime change in 2003' (Haddad 2016).

On 30 January 2005, the first post-Saddam elections were held based on a single electoral district and a closed list proportional representation (PR) system. The CPA wanted the electoral system to be as proportional as possible to guarantee the representation of all ethnic and religious groups in Parliament, but the single electoral district encouraged voting along ethnosectarian lines (Younis 2011: 12). The elections led to the formation of a 275-seat transitional National Assembly tasked with drafting a new Constitution for Iraq, and a Constitutional Drafting Committee of fifty-five members from the Assembly was formed. However, the Committee and the Assembly were both sidelined by the main political parties who controlled the undemocratic Constitutional drafting. The Constitution was ratified in October but was opposed by Sunnis, who were not represented in the process, thus emphasizing the 'exclusive elite bargain around which Iraqi politics were organised' (Dodge 2012: 45–6).

Arend Lijphart (1969: 216) defines consociationalism as a 'government by elite cartel designed to turn a democracy with a fragmented political culture into a stable democracy'. A consociational democracy usually has four features: (1) a grand coalition that includes political leaders representing all the plural society's major segments, (2) mutual veto that protects minority groups politically and allows them to oppose decisions that can harm their vital interests, (3) proportionality that divides political representation, civil service positions and public funds between the different segments with respect to their size in the population and (4) segmental autonomy that allows minorities to rule themselves and manage their internal affairs (Lijphart 1977: 25, 36, 38–9, 41). These features can be identified in the 2005 Iraqi Constitution that has institutionalized a self-determined or liberal consociationalism accommodating the various sects and ethnicities in society rather than allocating specific communities or groups to predetermined political positions like Lebanon's corporate consociationalism. John McGarry and Brendan

O'Leary (2007: 675) argue that liberal consociationalism protects the rights of individuals and groups and 'rewards whatever salient political identities emerge in democratic elections, whether these are based on ethnic or religious groups, or on subgroup or transgroup identities'. But the inclusion of the de-Ba'thification policy in the Constitution has marginalized many Iraqis from the political process, especially Sunnis and secularists, as well as engendering civil turmoil and challenging the legitimacy of the political system (Younis 2011: 9).

Although the Constitution does not stipulate consociationalism or a PR electoral system, Article 49 postulates that all components of the Iraqi people shall be represented in the Council of Representatives (CoR). And Article 9 indicates the principle of proportionality in the Iraqi armed forces and security services – reiterated in the General Secretariat Instruction 07/30797 of 4 September 2008, specifying that a multiethnic board recruits cadets in an 'ethnically fair' manner (Gaub 2011: 9–10). Informal consociational rules have also been applied, with the speaker of the CoR being a Sunni, the president a Kurd and the prime minister a Shi'a. Since 2005, every prime minister has assigned a grand coalition cabinet constituting ethnosectarian political parties that were successful in elections (Dodge 2020: 148). As the adoption of a PR electoral system makes a one-party majority unlikely, power-sharing agreements become necessary in post-election periods. But since the premiership offers a high level of executive power, the political rivalry over the position has increased and prevented the effective transfer of power (Younis 2011: 5). Furthermore, the post-Saddam elections have forced citizens to vote along ethnosectarian lines, making elections predetermined by the population's sectarian and ethnic composition. Hence, the majority Shi'a parties will always govern while Sunnis remain alienated (Ottaway 2013: 1).

The failure of the United States to focus on nation-building during the transitional period and its withdrawal from Iraq in December 2011 left the country battered by ethnosectarian violence. Moreover, consociationalism and de-Ba'thification have failed to create a unified national army that can protect Iraq and its citizens, especially as ethnosectarian identities became the main factor for recruitment rather than merit and skills. The weakness of the military allowed the steady advancement of Da'esh in Iraq in 2013. Mass desertions in the Iraqi Army occurred at the early stages of its fight against Da'esh, leading to its disintegration in June 2014. This was mainly due to sectarian divisions along with the rampant corruption that hindered funds from reaching the army and the politicization of the military by al-Maliki who assigned his loyalists to senior military positions (Parker and Ryan 2014). The collapse of the army and its inability to fight Da'esh encouraged the growing presence of ethnic and sectarian non-state armed groups, mainly operating under the umbrella of the Popular Mobilization Units (PMU) or *al-Hashd al-Sha'bi*, an Iran-backed coalition of predominantly Shi'a paramilitaries, that led to the battle that defeated Da'esh. In addition to being utilized by political elites as a method of sectarianization, the PMU have increased Iran's influence in Iraq and served its geopolitical objectives.

Most importantly, consociationalism has made corruption widespread in Iraq. Not only does sectarian apportionment (*muhasasa ta'ifiyya*) divide ministerial posts among ethnosectarian parties who win in national elections, but its subsidiary the *wikala* – a system for temporary contract appointments – gives these leaders the authority to assign senior civil servants. For instance, the allocation of approximately eight hundred senior civil service jobs in different ministries was part of the government formation negotiations following the 2018 elections (Dodge 2019). Assigned by their parties, these civil servants oversee government contracts in every ministry while siphoning off illegal resources for their parties' budgets. Ministries and foreign firms have also been involved in contract fraud, with around 25 per cent of the ministries' annual budget reportedly being misappropriated through contract fraud (Dodge 2020: 148). Corruption has thus become systematically sanctioned and pervasive, marginalizing a large section of society from the political system and its leaders (ibid.: 150). In May 2021, President Barham Salih announced that around US$150 billion had been smuggled outside Iraq since 2003 by corrupt administrations and individuals ('Iraqi President Introduces Law' 2021). Corruption is also no stranger to sectarian institutions that are protected by the ruling class. In September 2019, the Iraqi government suspended the license of al-Hurra, a TV channel funded by the US government, for three months after it broadcast an investigation on alleged corruption within Iraq's Sunni and Shi'a endowments, and accused the channel of defamation and bias ('Iraq Suspends US-funded Broadcaster' 2019).

According to Transparency International (2023), a non-governmental organization combating corruption, Iraq scored twenty-three out of hundred in terms of the perceived level of public sector corruption, with zero being highly corrupt and hundred being very clean, in 2022. The rampant corruption has deprived citizens of their basic rights, including access to health care, safe drinking water, job opportunities, uninterrupted electricity and adequate infrastructure (Transparency International 2021: 18). The lack of these services has frustrated Iraqi youth who constitute the majority of the population, with over 60 per cent of Iraqis under the age of twenty-four and around 700,000 becoming employable each year (Hasan 2019). But the powerful political parties and their non-state armed groups control the government and are the only ones with access to the national budget. This has engendered a 'deep state' constituting the political and religious leaders that influence political processes without necessarily being part of the government (Salam 2019). In the oil-rich country of Iraq, the ethnosectarian system and political leaders have been the main impediments to the fair distribution of oil rent and citizens' access to services and resources, prompting mass protests that demand systemic change and an overhaul to the post-2003 regime.

Iraq's resilience: An overview of the protest movements between 2011 and 2018

In the wake of the Arab Spring uprisings, sporadic protests in Iraq started as of 3 February 2011, with thousands of protesters decrying shortages of food, water, power and other services in the predominantly Shi'a Diwaniyah province (al-Salhy

2011). Protests reached their peak on the 'Day of Rage' on 25 February, in parallel with protests in other Arab countries, including Egypt, Jordan, Yemen and Bahrain. Protesters in Baghdad and other areas across Iraq – such as Basra, Mosul and Hawijah – demonstrated against the inadequate basic services, unemployment and vast corruption that has increased during al-Maliki's tenure. The prime minister cautioned protesters they would be targeted by pro-Saddam and al-Qa'eda violence, but it was his security forces that killed at least six and injured seventy-five people during clashes (Sherwood and Finn 2011). To downplay the significance of the protests, al-Maliki banned live media coverage and prohibited journalists from reporting. These tactics, however, did not deter Iraqis from demonstrating, and many used social media platforms, like Facebook and YouTube, as alternative means to report the events (al-Rawi 2014: 917).

In response to increasing protests and in an attempt to appease the protesters, al-Maliki sought to blame the provinces rather than his government for the lack of services and called for early elections. He even threatened to dismiss his ministers if they fail to progress in fulfilling their programmes within one hundred days, but there was little progress by the 7 June deadline (Ottaway and Kaysi 2011). The prime minister also urged Iraqis not to participate in the protests, charged his political opponents with leading them and questioned the organizers' intentions. Concomitantly, security forces met the protesters with violence and detained organizers and journalists (Kaysi 2011). The overt and covert use of repression made the protest movement lose momentum and no real reforms were implemented. Iraq's consociational political system, in which ethnosectarian elites share a piece of the pie, has also made it hard to overthrow the regime compared to other Arab countries whose power is restricted to one main leader and were successful in toppling their regimes – such as in Tunisia, Libya and Egypt – during the Arab Spring.

In December 2012, anti-government protests reignited in the predominantly Sunni al-Anbar province, the largest Iraqi province west of Baghdad, following the arrest of ten bodyguards assigned to the Sunni Finance Minister Rafi' al-'Issawi. Iraqi Sunnis interpreted these arrests as politically motivated and a marginalization attempt by the Shi'a-led government ('Iraq protests signal growing tension' 2012). Protests continued into January 2013, with tens of thousands accusing al-Maliki of sectarianism, corruption and brutal suppression. They were also outraged by the regime receiving military aid from the United States and significant political support from Iran whose intervention has increased in post-2003 Iraq. Although the protests were centred in al-Anbar province and dubbed 'Sunni' protests, they spread to other cities across Iraq. Numerous cities sent delegations to protest in Ramadi, the largest city in al-Anbar province, and Kurdish delegations participated in the Mosul protests. Several Shi'a religious leaders also supported these demonstrations (Caputi 2013).

The protests between 2011 and 2013 highlighted the weakness and corruption of state institutions, yet simultaneously their effectiveness in repressing protests. 'It is, indeed, this dichotomy between the Iraqi state's ability to secure order and its inability to deliver services that has aided Maliki's march towards a new authoritarianism' (Dodge 2013: 255). Since the prime minister acts as the commander-in-chief of the armed forces based on the Constitution, albeit without defining the exact powers or enabling legislation, al-Maliki referred to himself as the commander-in-chief by 2010 and assigned his loyalists as military officers. The absence of oversight mechanisms and effective civilian opposition enabled the prime minister to control the security sector, including the armed forces. He also created the Office of the Commander in Chief (OCIC) as an informal chain of command and used it as his personal security agency to target his political rivals. In November 2010, al-Maliki refused to appoint defence and interior ministers in his new government, rather occupying both positions himself and turning the OCIC into 'the de facto executive body for the whole security sector, sidelining the relevant ministries' (Gaub 2016). Through the patronage networks he established, al-Maliki controlled the security services that enabled him to quell popular protests and stay in power despite his inability to provide citizens with basic services.

On 14 August 2014, al-Maliki agreed to step down as prime minister after losing support from his local, regional and international allies and was replaced by Haider al-'Abadi on 8 September. The change of prime minister, however, did not stop the protest movements. In July 2015, tens of thousands protested every Friday, eventually reaching around one million across the country. Educated Iraqi male youth under thirty from the middle and lower middle class – mainly teachers, state employees or educators – initiated the protests, but they were led by the older generation – mostly males who were activists affiliated with political or civil society organizations. Protesters held slogans like *bi-isem al-deen baguna al-haramiya* (in the name of religion we were robbed by looters) in reference to the ethnosectarian leaders whom they saw as the cause of institutionalized corruption, sectarianism, unemployment, the absence of basic services like water and electricity, and the lack of adequate education and health infrastructures. They also rejected the sectarianization and Islamization of political and social life and urged a welfare state that can reallocate the country's wealth to citizens. The Islamist Shi'a movement of cleric Muqtada al-Sadr participated in these protests; some viewed it as a co-optation tactic, whereas others supported a wider working-class base. The protests carried on for over five months, before faltering like previous protest movements (Ali 2019).

Although Basra produces three million barrels of oil per day, its residents lack basic services and face diseases linked to oil pollution. On 8 July 2018, young unemployed males demanded employment outside the offices of foreign oil companies in northern Basra. The death of a protester by repressive security forces mobilized protests that spread to other southern Shi'a cities and were led by ordinary citizens rather than political groups or civil society organizations like in 2015. Within the first two weeks of protests, more than a dozen protesters were killed and over six hundred injured by security forces and militias led by political elites. And over six hundred protesters were detained, with many released after being threatened and brutalized. While al-'Abadi promised to hold the culprits accountable, political leaders accused the demonstrators of being Ba'th affiliates or controlled by foreign agents without any evidence. The government also cut telecommunication and the internet for over ten days. But there were no protests in Iraqi Kurdistan despite its economic crisis and in Sunni provinces that were destroyed in post-2003 battles or by Da'esh and whose residents fear being viewed as members of Da'esh or being affiliated with terrorism (Ali and Khalaf 2018).

Protests in Basra reignited in September 2018 after 30,000 people were hospitalized due to drinking polluted water. Demonstrators rallied for proper public services and set fire to the Iranian consulate, government buildings and the offices of pro-Iranian political parties and militias ('Iraq PM Asked to Resign' 2018). Due to mounting pressure from protesters and leading political parties, al-'Abadi was forced to resign and was replaced by 'Adel 'Abdul Mahdi in October. None of the protest movements in post-2003 Iraq have resulted in any tangible change, but this has not dissuaded Iraqis from taking to the streets spasmodically throughout the years to voice their disillusionment with the consociational political system and its sectarian leaders, most recently in 2019.

Thawrat Tishreen: *The October 2019 protests*

Iraq's political system has enabled political elites to abuse public funds and increase their wealth and that of their supporters, thus looting the country's resources and depriving most Iraqi citizens of any benefits. Around a year after the formation of 'Abdul Mahdi's technocratic government, which promised to resolve corruption and the gap between ordinary citizens and leaders, the prime minister made deals with the ruling class that brought him to power instead of opposing them (Mansour 2019). On 25 September 2019, some university graduates organized a peaceful sit-in outside the prime minister's office to protest the lack of job opportunities. They were, however, met with repressive force by the security apparatus, which was condemned by the public, and a call to protest in Baghdad on 27 September went out ('Lajnat al-Ihtijajat' 2019). Furthermore, 'Abdul Mahdi's demotion of Iraq's well-respected Counter Terrorism Service (CTS) Lieutenant General 'Abdul Wahab al-Sa'edi who led the military campaign against Da'esh sparked outrage, with calls on social media for protests to take place on 1 October against the government's corruption and failure to provide jobs and basic public services ('The Iraq Protests Explained' 2019).

Anti-government protests erupted in Baghdad and then spread across the country, particularly in predominantly Shi'a governorates in central and southern Iraq – such as Karbala, Najaf, Babil, Basra, Muthanah, Dhi Qar, Wasit, Missan, Diyalah and Qadisiyah. Protesters, mainly civil society activists and males between the ages of fifteen and thirty-five, decried the lack of education and health care services, housing issues, unemployment and poverty (UNAMI 2019: 3). They also demanded the overthrow of the political establishment and leaders they deem corrupt. Despite Sunni and Kurdish youth facing similar grievances, they were not involved in the protests. Residents of predominantly Sunni areas were still overcoming the destruction caused by the war against Da'esh and feared arrest, but some youth from Mosul and al-Anbar were reportedly unable to reach Baghdad due to road closures. And activists in Iraqi Kurdistan shared videos online to spread the word during internet outages in other parts of Iraq (Bobseine 2019).

Even though the demonstrations were leaderless and lacked a formal organizational structure, their scale was unprecedented compared to previous protest movements. But like former protests, demonstrators were met with violence and the excessive use of force by security forces encompassing militias and armed groups led by some Iraqi politicians. Over a hundred people were reportedly killed and thousands injured in less than a week after armed forces used machine guns, rubber bullets, tear gas, live ammunition and anti-riot tanks. Moreover, the Iraqi regime imposed a curfew and cut internet access to limit the spread of the protests (Ali and Khalaf 2019). The internet blackout also aimed to stop official abuses and attacks from being recorded and shared, a tactic that enabled militiamen to position snipers targeting the protesters on the roofs of government buildings. The protests eventually paused in order to commemorate the Shi'a holiday of Arba'een (Alhassani 2020).

A second wave of protests resumed on 25 October as demonstrators' demands had not been met. The government's promises to provide new jobs and additional funds for housing, establish a special court to clamp down on corruption, and prosecute police and military commanders involved in the use of force did not convince aggrieved Iraqis who lacked trust in the government and its ability to implement reforms. 'Abdul Mahdi's post-midnight televised speech addressing protesters' grievances also failed to deter the renewal of the protest movement in Baghdad and other cities. In this second wave of protests, over a million protesters came from all walks of life, including students and even former members of the PMU who had been injured and unable to work (Rubin 2019). Thousands of Iraqi women also practised their inalienable right to protest and spearheaded rallies – similar to Lebanese women who became symbols for the protest movement during Lebanon's October 2019 uprising – to express their dissent against the political system and leaders while risking their lives amid the use of violence. They even defied patriarchal norms and rejected al-Sadr's calls for gender segregation in protests in February 2020 (Barbarani 2020). Despite the majority of Shi'a protesters and the participation of al-Sadr's supporters, the movement was anti-sectarian and not initiated by any organization or party. Rather, demonstrators explicitly rejected the manipulation of sectarian identities in political life and its damaging consequences, while reimagining a secular national Iraq, a process of de-sectarianization.

While the 2019 uprising reiterated the demands of previous protests, there was a categorical criticism of Iranian intervention that has steadily increased since 2003. Protesters accused Iran of being part of Iraqi corruption and failed governance due to its links to Shi'a political elites and the PMU. They also blamed pro-Iranian militias and parties for the repressive force used and set ablaze the Iranian consulates in Karbala and Najaf, to protest Iranian intervention in Iraq's internal affairs (al-Nashmi 2020). As the demonstrations progressed, protesters demanded the resignation of key government officials, electoral reforms and early elections, constitutional change and the dissolution of Parliament and provincial councils

(Alshamary and al-Amin 2019). In early November 2019, they issued a ten-point manifesto of demands, which was published in their own newspaper Tuktuk and promoted through banners in Baghdad's Tahrir Square. These demands created an alternative secular national ideology urging equal rights and citizenship for all Iraqis regardless of their ethnosectarian affiliations, as well as underscoring Iraqis' cynicism of the consociational political system and its rampant corruption (Dodge and Mansour 2020: 65–6).

Although there were numerous events of burning and mobbing buildings of different militias and parties during the early weeks of the uprising, protesters mostly relied on non-violent strategies. However, they faced extreme and disproportionate repression by the state security forces and the non-state repressive agents that political elites deployed during violent clampdowns. The uprising has delineated that the protests in Iraq, which ostensibly has a democratic government, can be as intense and violent as those occurring in authoritarian countries, partly because the ethnosectarian regime can utilize militias and thugs linked to certain governmental factions to perform the most violent acts of repression. But as the regime crackdown on protests increased, new rounds of mobilization by outraged protesters erupted (Berman, Clarke and Majed 2020: 21). In the face of the excessive use of force, the three-wheeled tuk-tuk vehicle emerged as a symbol of the Iraqi protests, with drivers using them as ambulances to transport the wounded from Tahrir Square to areas where they can receive medical aid. Medical students and volunteers also ran makeshift medical stations in Tahrir Square to treat injured protesters for free (Alkhudary 2019).

In addition to the direct use of physical violence which killed hundreds and injured thousands, some protesters were arrested and charged according to the Iraqi penal code, others were detained and tortured by security forces and tens of people were kidnapped or disappeared. To further silence the protest movement and crack down on dissent, well-known protest organizers, activists and journalists were targeted, threatened, kidnapped, arrested, killed and assassinated (EASO 2020: 27–32). Ibrahim Halawi (2020: 130) contends that the regime's violence is part of a 'longer process of counter-revolutionary strategy'. Indeed, consociationalism excludes those outside the ethnosectarian cartel from any significant participation in the political and economic spheres and impedes inclusionary cross- and anti-sectarian mobilization through tactics of co-optation, coercion, repression and containment (ibid.: 132). Protesters are thus disadvantaged as ethnosectarian elites have had time and history to entrench their interest groups, establish political alliances and economic networks regionally and internationally, and amass resources to defend their counterrevolution (ibid.: 133).

Following the deadliest day of protests on 28 November, with over forty protesters reported killed, Iraq's top Shi'a Muslim cleric Grand Ayatollah 'Ali al-Sistani denounced the use of violence against demonstrators and called for a new government, prompting 'Abdul Mahdi to submit his resignation to Parliament ('Iraq Unrest' 2019). The killing of the Iranian General Qassem Soleimani, the head of Quds Force, Iran's Islamic Revolutionary Guard Corps (IRGC), and Abu Mahdi al-Muhandis, the deputy leader of the PMU, by a US airstrike in Baghdad on 3 January 2020 temporarily halted the anti-government protests for several weeks. It also led al-Sadr to urge his followers to stop participating in the protests and instead march against the US 'occupation' (Coles 2020).

Anti-government demonstrations, however, resumed, albeit with fewer numbers. Protesters also relied on online activism through social media platforms to protest virtually and attract the attention of international media and organizations and foreign governments, including the UK and the United States, which denounced the violence in Iraq. When Mohammed Tawfiq 'Allawi was named prime minister-designate, protesters used the hashtag 'March 1, Voice of the Martyrs' to mobilize demonstrators and reject 'Allawi whom they viewed as affiliated with the established political parties (al-Rubaie 2020). 'Allawi resigned from the position after failing to form a cabinet, but the protests ended abruptly on 21 March due to the Covid-19 pandemic. Protesters vowed to resume their activism when the coronavirus threat subsided if the ruling class failed to meet their demands (al-Nashmi 2020).

In May 2020, Mustafa al-Kadhimi, seen as a political independent, became the new prime minister of Iraq. At a time when protests resumed against the new government, al-Kadhimi promoted al-Sa'edi to lead counterterrorism operations, released detained protesters, promised justice to the relatives of those killed and urged Parliament to adopt a new electoral law in order to hold early elections ('New Iraq PM Releases Protesters' 2020). But only in October 2020 did al-Kadhimi form an official committee to investigate the crimes committed during the protests. Activists thus raised doubts about his ability to achieve justice, implement reforms or put an end to the kidnappings and assassinations of civil society activists during his term in office, such as the murder of security researcher Hisham al-Hashimi. Additionally, al-Kadhimi sought to restrict paramilitaries and maintain state control over arms, but to no avail. He instructed the CTS to arrest Kata'eb Hezbollah militiamen in relation to rocket attacks against the International Zone and requested it confront armed tribes in Nasiriyah to search for a kidnapped civil activist. Nonetheless, on these two occasions, he later rescinded his orders and apologized to the armed groups, weakening the CTS and its reputation (Alshamary 2020). Al-Kadhimi also scheduled parliamentary elections on 6 June 2021, in an attempt to meet protesters' demands of holding early elections, before postponing them to 10 October, a decision that angered demonstrators (Menmy 2021).

Sporadic protests, with significantly fewer demonstrators, continued to take place across Iraq and were seen as an extension of *Thawrat Tishreen*. Political leaders downplayed the significance of the protests by claiming they were a result of a few disorganized movements without clear political objectives and contending that the decrease in the number of protesters stresses that the majority of Iraqis are discontent with the protests' tactics and demands. But a survey commissioned by Chatham House between July and August 2020 indicates that the majority of over 1,200 Iraqi respondents supported the protests and had the same grievances against the regime irrespective of their gender, age, employment status or income (Cooke and Mansour 2020).

The killing of civil activist Ihab Jawad al-Wazni in Karbala on 9 May 2021 sparked another round of mobilization. On 25 May, one protester was killed and dozens were injured in Baghdad during a rally by thousands demanding an end to impunity and seeking accountability for the assassinations of eminent protesters and activists. The continuous attacks on and murders of journalists and activists raised appeals to boycott the October parliamentary elections, as many protesters were outraged by a system that does not protect them (Barbarani 2021). Political parties also co-opted some protest organizers and activists running for elections under existing or new party names, while others founded new independent parties to represent those discontented with the existing regime. These activists represented less than 15 per cent of the protest movement but saw no option for achieving reforms outside the system. Other protesters, however, denounced co-optation by an establishment that cannot reform and called for an electoral boycott despite the ratification of a new electoral law in November 2020 (Jiyad 2021: 13).

On 10 October 2021, Iraqis went to the polls, but voter turnout was the lowest in the post-2003 era at 43.54 per cent. The newly adopted electoral law based on the single non-transferable vote (SNTV) allowed al-Sadr's movement to win the most seats in the 329-member CoR, with 73 seats compared to 54 in 2018. The defeated pro-Iranian Shi'a political parties, however, established the Coordination Framework political bloc, which includes al-Maliki's political alliance, to challenge al-Sadr. Some groups belonging to the PMU also protested outside Baghdad's Green Zone before clashing with security forces. The leader of *Asa'ib Ahl al-Haq* faction blamed al-Kadhimi for the death of two protesters, and an unclaimed drone attack struck al-Kadhimi's residence the next day, resulting only in structural damage. The attack was viewed as a signal that al-Kadhimi should not be the prime minister of the new government (Higel 2021).

Nevertheless, various emerging political movements and independent candidates from the *Tishreen* movement unexpectedly garnered a substantial number of seats. The greatest victory was by *Imtidad* party that secured nine seats in its home base in Nasiriyah and in Najaf and Babel. Their victory emphasized that alternatives could reach Parliament and that there is a 'public appetite for new faces in Iraqi politics' (ibid.). But this success was short-lived as protest parties have been unable to unite and have started disintegrating due to accusations of corruption, infighting and mass resignations, namely the resignation of five *Imtidad* MPs from the party (Alkhudary 2022).

Amid months of deadlock over the appointment of a new prime minister, al-Sadr's parliamentarians resigned in June 2022, and his supporters camped outside Parliament, storming it in July and August. On 29 August, al-Sadr announced his retirement from political life, prompting deadly clashes between his followers and rival Shi'a parties ('Buildings Stormed' 2022). Days after the clashes, thousands of Iraqis affiliated with *Thawrat Tishreen* took to the streets to renew their demand of a complete overhaul of the regime and its political elites ('Thousands in Iraq' 2022). And on 1 October, protesters marked the third anniversary of the 2019 protest movement in Baghdad and southern provinces, clashing with security forces who used teargas, stun grenades, and rubber bullets that wounded several protesters ('Scores of Iraqis' 2022).

Ranj Alaaldin (2020) argues that the Iraqi environment is not favourable to a regime overhaul, nor do the major internal and foreign actors want the post-2003 political system completely changed. The lack of viable institutions, the abundance of armed groups and the presence of non-state actors that replace the state play a role in hindering any kind of change. Therefore, the regime will remain intact, and its ruling class will stay in power even if protests increase due to a 'whole host of formal and informal, state and para-state actors that dominate, shape, and manage the structures of governance and power'. But only time will tell if protests and secular emerging political movements can become effective and efficient in changing the political system and whether protesters will lose hope in demanding this change.

Conclusion

This chapter traces the establishment of the liberal consociational political system in Iraq after the US-led invasion in 2003 and the removal of Saddam Hussein's Ba'thist regime. This system, however, has institutionalized ethnosectarian identities, while marginalizing Sunnis, and engendered sectarian violence rather than ameliorating fragmentations, as Lijphart argues. It has also increased competition between the political elite over government positions, thus drastically aggravating corruption and neopatrimonial networks. Moreover, the lack of good governance and accountability has worsened the socio-economic status of millions of Iraqis who are deprived of basic services and employment. It has also enabled the prevalence of militias that are led by or affiliated with the ruling class, hence paralysing the national army and leading to its disintegration in 2014 while the sectarian PMU fought Da'esh. The power-sharing model has failed to achieve authentic democracy in Iraq, proving that a democratic system cannot be externally imposed or prevail overnight. Iraqi citizens have voiced their disillusionment of the post-2003 establishment over the years through mass protests across the country.

In the wake of the Arab Spring uprisings that swept the region, the Iraqi regime remained unscathed. Over the next few years, protests kept on reigniting, with thousands of protesters, mainly young unemployed males, demanding an end to corruption and regime change. The protests reached their peak, in terms of scope and scale, during *Thawrat Tishreen* in 2019. Over a million Iraqis from different backgrounds, including women and children, took to the streets calling for a systemic overhaul of the political system and its corrupt leaders. The peaceful protests that started in Baghdad soon spread to other cities and towns, mainly the Shi'a south. The movement was met with overt and covert use of repression and violence by security forces and militias. But as the use of force increased, the mobilization of protests increased and continued even after a new government was formed. Nonetheless, the spread of the Covid-19 pandemic and lockdown restrictions abruptly ended the protests, and protesters shifted to online platforms to share their grievances. In October 2021, al-Sadr's party garnered the majority of seats in parliamentary elections, engendering an impasse and deadly clashes between different Shi'a factions. Political movements and independents emerging from the protests surprisingly won seats, paving the way for new faces in Iraqi politics, but have failed to unite. Sporadic protests that are an extension of the 2019 protest movement continue to take place in Iraq, but their size has immensely shrunk.

Since the existing political system serves the interests of the ruling elites, meaningful reforms or top-down processes of de-sectarianization will be hard to achieve. As the demands of the protest movement are yet to be met and with the worsening socio-economic situation of many Iraqis, protests are likely to resume. However, will a new round of grassroots protests be able to force change through bottom-up de-sectarianization, or will they be to no avail like previous movements due to the resilience of the consociational regime and its oppressive methods? This chapter opens up the debate on examining means that can effectively bring about a bottom-up change beyond protest movements. Adopting new methods and strategies of non-violent resistance might provide the people of Iraq with their inalienable human rights and bring about the country they aspire for.

References

Alaaldin, R. (2020), 'The Irresistible Resiliency of Iraq's Protesters', *Brookings*, 31 January. Available online: https://www.brookings.edu/blog/order-from-chaos/2020/01/31/the-irresistible-resiliency-of-iraqs-protesters/ (accessed 1 February 2021).

Alhassani, M. (2020), 'The Evolution of Iraq's Protests: Excessive Force Pushes Protesters to Adapt', *Washington Institute*, 4 February. Available online: https://www.washingtoninstitute.org/policy-analysis/evolution-iraqs-protests-excessive-force-pushes-protesters-adapt (accessed 2 February 2021).

Ali, Z. (2019), 'Protest Movements in Iraq in the Age of a "New Civil Society"', *LSE CRP Blog*, 3 October. Available online: https://blogs.lse.ac.uk/crp/2019/10/03/protest-movements-in-iraq-in-the-age-of-new-civil-society/ (accessed 24 October 2019).

Ali, Z., and Khalaf, S. (2018), 'Iraq's Protest Movement Reveals the Failure of the Post-2003 Regime', *openDemocracy*, 8 August. Available online: https://www.opendemocracy.net/en/north-africa-west-asia/iraq-s-protest-movement-reveals-failure-of-post-2003-r/ (accessed 1 February 2021).

Ali, Z., and Khalaf, S. (2019), 'In Iraq, Demonstrators Demand Change – and the Government Fights Back', *Washington Post*, 9 October. Available online: https://www.washingtonpost.com/politics/2019/10/10/iraq-protestors-demand-change-government-is-fighting-back/ (accessed 1 February 2021).

Alkhudary, T. (2019), 'Tuk-tuks of Tahrir: The Unlikely Symbol of a Revolution in Iraq', *New Arab*, 4 November. Available online: https://english.alaraby.co.uk/opinion/tuk-tuk-unlikely-symbol-revolution-iraq (accessed 10 December 2020).

Alkhudary, T. (2022), 'The Fragmentation of Iraq's "Protest Parties" Attests to the Muhasasa System's Resilience', *LSE Middle East Centre*, 7 June. Available online: https://

blogs.lse.ac.uk/mec/2022/06/07/the-fragmentation-of-iraqs-protest-parties-atte sts-to-the-muhasasa-systems-resilience/ (accessed 1 July 2022).

Alshamary, M. (2020), 'Six Months into His Premiership, What Has Mustafa al-Kadhimi Done for Iraq?', *Brookings*, 13 November. Available online: https://www.brookings.edu/ blog/order-from-chaos/2020/11/13/six-months-into-his-premiership-what-has-must afa-al-kadhimi-done-for-iraq/ (accessed 10 January 2021).

Alshamary, M., and al-Amin, S. (2019), 'Iraqi protestors Demand Constitutional Change. Can They Make It Happen?', *Washington Post*, 7 November. Available online: https:// www.washingtonpost.com/politics/2019/11/07/iraqi-protesters-demand-constitutio nal-change-can-they-make-it-happen/ (accessed 10 January 2021).

Barbarani, S. (2020), 'Hundreds of Iraqi Women Challenge al-Sadr's Call for Segregation', *Al-Jazeera*, 14 February. Available online: https://www.aljazeera.com/news/2020/2/14/ hundreds-of-iraqi-women-challenge-al-sadrs-call-for-segregation (accessed 1 February 2021).

Barbarani, S. (2021), ' "Country Has No Future": Iraqi Protester Killed at Baghdad Rally', *Al-Jazeera*, 25 May. Available online: https://www.aljazeera.com/news/2021/5/25/one-killed-as-iraqs-anti-government-protests-resume (accessed 26 May 2021).

Berman, C., Clarke, K. and Majed, R. (2020), 'Patterns of Mobilization and Repression in Iraq's Tishreen Uprising', *MENA's Frozen Conflicts*, POMEPS Studies 42, 21–8, Washington, DC: George Washington University. Available online: https://pomeps.org/ pomeps-studies-42-menas-frozen-conflicts (accessed 1 December 2020).

Bobseine, H. (2019), 'Iraqi Youth Protesters: Who They Are, What They Want, and What's Next', *Middle East Institute*, 14 October. Available online: https://www.mei.edu/ publications/iraqi-youth-protesters-who-they-are-what-they-want-and-whats-next (accessed 1 February 2021).

'Buildings stormed after Moqtada al-Sadr, Iraqi political leader, retires' (2022), *BBC News*, 29 August. Available online: https://www.bbc.co.uk/news/world-middle-east-62713026 (accessed 30 August 2022).

Caputi, R. (2013), 'Iraqi Protests Defy the Maliki Regime and Inspire Hope', *Guardian*, 17 January. Available online: https://www.theguardian.com/commentisfree/2013/jan/17/ iraq-protest-defy-maliki-regime (accessed 23 January 2013).

Coles, I. (2020), 'Iraqi Security Forces Push to Regain Control of Cities from Protestors', *Wall Street Journal*, 25 January. Available online: https://www.wsj.com/articles/ iraqi-security-forces-push-to-regain-control-of-cities-from-protesters-11579974901 (accessed 1 February 2021).

Cooke, G., and Mansour, R. (2020), 'Iraqi Views on Protesters One Year after the Uprising', *Chatham House*, 29 October. Available online: https://www.chath amhouse.org/2020/10/iraqi-views-protesters-one-year-after-uprising (accessed 1 February 2021).

Dodge, T. (2012), *Iraq: From War to a New Authoritarianism*, Abingdon: Routledge.

Dodge, T. (2013), 'State and Society in Iraq Ten Years after Regime Change: The Rise of a New Authoritarianism', *International Affairs*, 89 (2): 241–57.

Dodge, T. (2019), 'Corruption Continues to Destabilize Iraq', *Chatham House*, 1 October. Available online: https://www.chathamhouse.org/2019/10/corruption-continues-dest abilize-iraq (accessed 2 February 2021).

Dodge, T. (2020), 'Iraq's Informal Consociationalism and Its Problems', *Studies in Ethnicity and Nationalism*, 20 (2): 145–52.

Dodge, T., and Mansour, R. (2020), 'Sectarianization and De-sectarianization in the Struggle for Iraq's Political Field', *Review of Faith & International Affairs*, 18 (1): 58–69.

EASO (European Asylum Support Office) (2020), *Iraq: The Protest Movement and Treatment of Protesters and Activists*, Luxembourg: EASO. Available online: https://euaa.europa.eu/publications/coi-report-iraq-protest-movement-and-treatment-protesters-and-activists (accessed 12 January 2021).

Fearon, J. (2007), 'Iraq's Civil War: No Graceful Exit', *Foreign Affairs*, March/April. Available online: http://www.foreignaffairs.com/articles/62443/james-d-fearon/iraqs-civil-war (accessed 7 June 2007).

Gaub, F. (2011), *Rebuilding Armed Forces: Learning from Iraq and Lebanon*, Carlisle: Strategic Studies Institute.

Gaub, F. (2016), 'An Unhappy Marriage: Civil-Military Relations in Post-Saddam Iraq', *Carnegie Endowment for International Peace*, 13 January. Available online: https://carnegieendowment.org/2016/01/13/unhappy-marriage-civil-military-relations-in-post-saddam-iraq-pub-61955 (accessed 1 February 2016).

Haddad, F. (2016), 'Shia-Centric State Building and Sunni Rejection in Post-2003 Iraq', *Carnegie Endowment for International Peace*, 7 January. Available online: http://carnegieendowment.org/2016/01/07/shia-centric-state-building-and-sunni-rejection-in-post-2003-iraq-pub-62408 (accessed 10 January 2016).

Halawi, I. (2020), 'Consociational Power-Sharing in the Arab World as Counter-Revolution', *Studies in Ethnicity and Nationalism*, 20 (2): 128–36.

Hasan, H. (2019), 'Iraq Is Currently Being Shaken by Violent Protests', *Carnegie Middle East Center*, 4 October. Available online: https://carnegie-mec.org/diwan/79993 (accessed 1 February 2021).

Higel, L. (2021), 'Iraq's Surprise Election Results', *International Crisis Group*, 16 November. Available online: https://www.crisisgroup.org/middle-east-north-africa/gulf-and-arabian-peninsula/iraq/iraqs-surprise-election-results (accessed 20 September 2022).

International Crisis Group (2006), *The Next Iraqi War? Sectarianism and Civil Conflict*, Middle East Report N°52, 27 February, Amman/Baghdad/Brussels: International Crisis Group. Available online: https://www.crisisgroup.org/middle-east-north-africa/gulf-and-arabian-peninsula/iraq/next-iraqi-war-sectarianism-and-civil-conflict (accessed 1 March 2006).

'Iraq PM Asked to Resign Amid Basra Unrest' (2018), *Al-Jazeera*, 8 September. Available online: https://www.aljazeera.com/news/2018/9/8/iraq-pm-asked-to-resign-amid-basra-unrest (accessed 24 January 2021).

'The Iraq Protests Explained in 100 and 500 words' (2019), *BBC News*, 2 December. Available online: https://www.bbc.co.uk/news/world-middle-east-50595212 (accessed 24 January 2021).

'Iraq Protests Signal Growing Tension between Sunni and Shia Communities' (2012), *Guardian*, 26 December. Available online: https://www.theguardian.com/world/2012/dec/26/iraq-protests-tension-sunni-shia (accessed 5 January 2013).

'Iraq Suspends US-funded Broadcaster Al Hurra over Graft Investigation' (2019), *Reuters*, 2 September. Available online: https://www.reuters.com/article/us-iraq-censorship/iraq-suspends-us-funded-broadcaster-al-hurra-over-graft-investigation-idUSKCN1VN1GT (accessed 20 February 2021).

'Iraq Unrest: PM Abdul Mahdi to Resign after Bloodiest Day in Protests' (2019), *BBC News*, 29 November. Available online: https://www.bbc.co.uk/news/world-middle-east-50600495 (accessed 6 December 2020).

'Iraqi President Introduces Law to Fight Corruption' (2021), *Asharq al-Awsat*, 24 May. Available online: https://english.aawsat.com/home/article/2989251/iraqi-president-introduces-law-fight-corruption (accessed 24 May 2021).

Jabar, F. A. (2004), *Postconflict Iraq: A Race for Stability, Reconstruction, and Legitimacy*, Special Report 120, Washington, DC: United States Institute of Peace. Available online: https://www.usip.org/publications/2004/05/post-conflict-iraq-race-stability-reconstruction-and-legitimacy (accessed 12 November 2017).

Jiyad, S. (2021), *Protest Vote: Why Iraq's Next Elections Are Unlikely to Be Game-Changers*, LSE Middle East Centre Paper Series 48, London: LSE Middle East Centre. Available online: http://eprints.lse.ac.uk/110201/ (accessed 24 April 2021).

Kaysi, D. A. (2011), 'Iraq's Protests Test Maliki's Leadership', *Foreign Policy*, 3 March. Available online: https://foreignpolicy.com/2011/03/03/iraqs-protests-test-malikis-leadership/ (accessed 4 November 2011).

'Lajnat al-Ihtijajat al-Sha'biyah Tad'ou li-Tantheem Waqfa fi Baghdad lil-Tandeed bi-Hadethat Fadd I'tisam Hamalat al-Shahadat al-'Olya' (2019), *Baghdad Today*, 26 September. Available online: https://baghdadtoday.news/news/97225/ -لجنة-الاحتجاجات-الشعبية- (accessed 15 December 2020).

Lijphart, A. (1969), 'Consociational Democracy', *World Politics*, 21 (2): 207–25.

Lijphart, A. (1977), *Democracy in Plural Societies: A Comparative Exploration*, New Haven, CT: Yale University Press.

Mansour, R. (2019), 'Iraq Protests: What's Behind the Anger?', *BBC News*, 7 October. Available online: https://www.bbc.co.uk/news/world-middle-east-49960677 (accessed 1 February 2021).

Marr, P. (2012), *The Modern History of Iraq*, Boulder, CO: Westview Press.

McGarry, J., and O'Leary, B. (2007), 'Iraq's Constitution of 2005: Liberal Consociation as Political Prescription', *International Journal of Constitutional Law*, 5 (4): 670–98.

Menmy, D. T. (2021), 'Iraqi Anger Grows after Election Postponement', *Al-Jazeera*, 30 January. Available online: https://www.aljazeera.com/news/2021/1/30/iraqi-anger-grows-after-election-postponement (accessed 1 February 2021).

al-Nashmi, F. (2020), 'Coronavirus Brings Abrupt End to Iraq Protest Movement', *Asharq al-Awsat*, 22 March. Available online: https://english.aawsat.com//home/article/2193021/coronavirus-brings-abrupt-end-iraq-protest-movement (accessed 1 February 2021).

'New Iraq PM Releases Protesters; Promotes Respected General' (2020), *Al-Jazeera*, 10 May. Available online: https://www.aljazeera.com/news/2020/5/10/new-iraq-pm-releases-protesters-promotes-respected-general (accessed 8 January 2021).

Ottaway, M. (2013), *Sectarianism and Political Participation in Iraq*, Political Participation, Pluralism, and Citizenship Project Occasional Paper, Center on Democracy, Development and the Rule of Law, Stanford, CA: Stanford University. Available online: http://cddrl.fsi.stanford.edu/arabreform/publications/sectarianism_and_political_participation_in_iraq (accessed 23 August 2013).

Ottaway, M., and Kaysi, D. A. (2011), 'Iraq: Coalition Under Stress', *Carnegie Endowment for International Peace*, 8 June. Available online: https://carnegieendowment.org/2011/06/08/iraq-coalition-under-stress-pub-44441 (accessed 21 October 2011).

Parker, N., and Ryan, M. (2014), 'Iraqi Military Breakdown Fueled by Corruption, Politics', *Reuters*, 14 June. Available online: https://www.reuters.com/article/us-iraq-security-military-analysis-idUSKBN0EO2FK20140614 (accessed 15 June 2014).

al-Rawi, A. K. (2014), 'The Arab Spring and Online Protests in Iraq', *International Journal of Communication*, 8: 916–42.

al-Rubaie, A. (2020), 'Despite Political Turmoil and Coronavirus, Iraq's Protest Movement Continues', *Washington Institute*, 23 March. Available online: https://www.washingt

oninstitute.org/policy-analysis/despite-political-turmoil-and-coronavirus-iraqs-protest-movement-continues (accessed 24 January 2021).

Rubin, A. J. (2019), '"All of Them Are Thieves": Iraqis Defy Security Forces to Protest Corruption', *New York Times*, 25 October. Available online: https://www.nytimes.com/2019/10/25/world/middleeast/iraq-protests.html (accessed 24 January 2021).

Salam, D. (2019), 'Will Protests Herald a New Era in Iraqi Politics?', *Atlantic Council*, 31 October. Available online: https://www.atlanticcouncil.org/blogs/menasource/%ef%bb%bfwill-protests-herald-a-new-era-in-iraqi-politics/ (accessed 6 January 2021).

al-Salhy, S. (2011), 'Iraqis Protest Power and Food Shortages; 3 Shot', *Reuters*, 3 February. Available online: https://www.reuters.com/article/iraq-electricity-protest/iraqis-protest-power-and-food-shortages-3-shot-idINALS33563120110203 (accessed 24 November 2011).

'Scores of Iraqis Injured in Anti-government Protests in Baghdad' (2022), *Guardian*, 1 October. Available online: https://www.theguardian.com/world/2022/oct/01/scores-of-iraqis-injured-in-anti-government-protests-in-baghdad (accessed 2 October 2022).

Sherwood, H., and Finn, T. (2011), 'Thousands Join "Day of Rage" across the Middle East', *Guardian*, 25 February. Available online: https://www.theguardian.com/world/2011/feb/25/thousands-join-day-of-rage-across-middle-east (accessed 20 October 2011).

'Thousands in Iraq Demand Regime Change after Shia Factions Clash' (2022), *Al-Jazeera*, 2 September. Available online: https://www.aljazeera.com/news/2022/9/2/thousands-in-iraq-demand-regime-change-after-shia-factions-clash (accessed 3 September 2022).

Transparency International (2021), *Corruption Perceptions Index 2020*, Berlin: Transparency International. Available online: https://www.transparency.org/en/cpi/2020/index/nzl (accessed 1 February 2021).

Transparency International (2023), 'Corruption Perceptions Index', *Transparency International*. Available online: https://www.transparency.org/en/cpi/2022/index/irq (accessed 17 July 2023).

UNAMI (United Nations Assistance Mission for Iraq) (2019), *Demonstrations in Iraq: 1-9 October 2019*, Baghdad: Human Rights Office UNAMI. Available online: https://reliefweb.int/report/iraq/human-rights-special-report-demonstrations-iraq-1-9-october-2019-enar (accessed 18 January 2021).

Younis, N. (2011), 'Set Up to Fail: Consociational Political Structures in Post-War Iraq, 2003-2010', *Contemporary Arab Affairs*, 4 (1): 1–18.

Chapter 2

TAIF AT THIRTY: OCTOBER 17 AS *THAWRA 'ALA AL-'ISTISHRĀQ*

Madonna Kalousian

Since the ratification of the Taif Agreement on 22 October 1989, attempts at sustaining a functioning framework of power sharing within the post-war Lebanese political establishment through the distribution of key ministerial, executive and legislative posts to ethno-sectarian party-aligned groups have coincided with the conceiving of political power by the entrenched ruling elites in terms of mutually exclusive objectives. Gradually redefining the way 'the state' exercises its power and working, in tandem with other variables, to foster strong patronage networks within sects, Taif has re-envisioned a multifaceted power-sharing system premised on an allocated, mutually recognized *ḥiṣa*.[1] Respective political parties, therefore, do not necessarily cooperate or *share* power, but rather, in the case of Lebanon, compete for, partition and *divide* power into *ḥiṣaṣ* within what Reinoud Leenders calls a 'distributive state' (Leenders 2012: 233). The *muḥaṣaṣa* system of governance brought about by Taif proposes to execute a degree of 'stateness' amidst conflicting visions of governance offered by various actors exercising their own degree of non-state 'stateness'.

Within the context of Lebanon, the stateness of the state and non-state stateness overlap, compete and blur into each other, resulting in what Giorgio Agamben terms a 'state of willed exception' (Agamben 1998: 139). These resulting exceptions work to segregate and organize citizens along sectarian lines,[2] to ensure that the sect and its affiliated political party continue to serve as the vessel through which the state–citizen relation is mediated, to regulate access to 'the state' itself, and, more importantly, to formalize and promote the idea of power being divided among a number of unanimously excluded 'others'. More importantly, these exceptions propagate, under the veneer of a false equation between the persistence of Taif and that of 'sectarianism' in the country, the idea that the removal of a sect-based power sharing arrangement would inevitably lead to a return to civil war hostilities.

In reality, however, Taif ceased to be a framework through which Lebanon effected a transition into peace. Instead, Taif has become a means for the elite to perform a flawed semblance of post-war unity, sovereignty and stateness. It is within this context – and against the ruling class which nurtured and benefited from this false equation – that the October revolution erupted. It was exactly thirty years from Taif, on 22 October 2019, when the set of plans announced by the minister of telecommunications to impose a monthly $6 tax on internet voice calls were scheduled to be brought into effect. This announcement, however, was only the trigger of what was later dubbed the 'WhatsApp revolution'. The evening of 17 October 2019 marks the beginning of the largest anti-establishment inherently decentralized protests in Lebanon's modern history. Unlike the perhaps equally momentous protests of the Cedar Revolution of 2005, protesters took to the streets to celebrate, in unity and without any specific party flags in sight, a national identity as Lebanese. Envisioning what the symbolically charged thirtieth anniversary of Taif would bring to the Lebanese political scene, John Nagle and Mary-Alice Clancy argue that, 'rather than a unifying moment, the anniversary of Taif will feature the major political actors generating polarizing memories and antagonistic interpretative frames' of the Lebanese Civil War and its ongoing formally unacknowledged repercussions (Nagle and Clancy 2019: 1).[3] However, the course of events on the thirtieth anniversary of Taif took a different, yet unsurprising, turn.

This chapter argues that the ruling elite's narrative of 'sectarianism' is losing some of its relevance within the context of current and post-Taif political activism in Lebanon. This growing irrelevance does not imply a complete abolishing of sectarianism, but rather brings to the fore the fact that political stalemate in Lebanon coincides with the consolidation of a compromised power-sharing system which the elite are unwilling to reform. To this end, they legitimize and instrumentalize a narrative of sectarianism, one according to which the abolishing of the political system of governance from which they have endlessly benefited will inevitably lead to a return to sectarian violence. With this in mind, I first examine the course of events surrounding and leading up to the eruption of the October protests. I then investigate the extent to which the newly proposed amnesty law pledging to pardon allegations of what the government originally framed as an economic mismanagement of the crisis is a manifestation of the continuation of the very politics which allowed the 1990 amnesty law to slowly and gradually define the country's current political climate. Drawing on my analysis of Taif and the ensuing amnesty law of 1991, I situate my reading of the October protests in the context of an analogy I present with the newly introduced electoral law of 2017 and the government's proposed amnesty law of 2019. As the political climate following the protests is constantly evolving, this chapter is not an attempt to capture what has taken place in Lebanon since October 2019, but rather an examination of the protests within the context of and in relation to these two events specifically. The fact that these new laws have even been considered, albeit not entirely implemented eventually, not only exposes, as I conclude this chapter, the government's lack of political will to address any of the popular demands of the protesters but also highlights its disregard of the urgency to depart from the sedimented post-war political history that continues to define the political landscape in Lebanon today.

Igniting the Lebanese revolution

On 13 October 2019, unprecedented wildfires broke out in and quickly spread across vast forest areas throughout the country. The lack of funds, resources and appropriate equipment required to respond to such events not only exacerbated the situation but also exemplified, at least for the protesters, yet another incident in which 'the state' was completely unable and unprepared to respond to a natural disaster, or to any other emergency, of this scale. In an unsuccessful attempt to divert the dissatisfied public's attention from this failure, Member of Parliament Mario Aoun's comment on the fires is a manifestation of the scapegoating of a violently defined 'sectarian other'. Aoun alluded, during a television interview with him, to the possibility that the fires were motivated by sectarianism and that they affected Christian areas only. In a similar vein, Environment Minister Fadi Jreisati claimed that the fires might have been set in these areas intentionally, thus, like Aoun, ignoring the fact that the fires broke out in other areas throughout the country (Helal and Geha 2019). Catastrophic fires were raging in Syria as well at the same time, and, in fact, fires broke out in a Syrian refugee camp in Deir Al-Ahmar earlier that year. However, those who blamed Syrian refugees for the October fires could not afford but to overlook these other fires (Vohra 2019).

On 17 October, when the government was still grappling with the public outrage over its response to the wildfires, the state approved a bill that would impose new taxes on all phone calls made using internet-based services, including WhatsApp, in its 2020 budget. Being fully aware of the public condemnation this proposal would receive, yet unaware of the scale of outrage into which this was going to spiral, the government presented the new taxes as part of a comprehensively studied reform plan, the implementation of which would result in the release of eleven billion dollars' worth of aid promised to the Lebanese economy and infrastructure at the CEDRE conference in Paris in April 2018.[4] Triggered by the government's plan to impose these new taxes as part of so-called austerity measures, embodying an overwhelming spirit of unity and transcending the sectarian differences that the established political order has systematically instrumentalized since the end of the war, hundreds of thousands of people spontaneously took to the streets to demand the immediate resignation of the entire ruling class. This has been expressed in the popular rallying cry *killun ya'ni killun*, or 'all of them means all of them', in reference to all politicians and their networks across the political spectrum. Protesters also called for a political alternative and a complete overhaul of the unstable post-war political system which has helped engender numerous crises during the post-war era. These include widespread corruption, a near, if not imminent, collapse of an already crippled economy and the Lebanese Lira, a rapidly deteriorating public infrastructure, a lack of a waste management plan, an inadequate administration of social security, as well as an unresolved power and water shortage.

Following the announcement of the WhatsApp tax, an implosion of this large scale was not entirely foreseeable, but was undoubtedly inevitable. These subsequent protests are not an isolated incident. Rather, they draw on numerous recent campaigns of public dissent in Lebanon, including, for example, the 2013 campaign for the rights of domestic foreign workers, the 2015 'You Stink' campaign to protest the country's waste mismanagement, as well as the political alliance of Beirut Madinati. The October protests, therefore, draw on and are inspired by a long and complex history of contested state–citizen relations. The government quickly withdrew the proposal, but it was too little too late. The official response from the state has so far took the form of no more than few televised speeches in which a number of Lebanese politicians addressed the nation. These included a statement issued by Saad Hariri, before he resigned as prime minster, in which he promised to perform a set of necessary and urgent political and economic reforms. This was met with increasing public disappointment and had only little, if indeed any, impact on the possibility of reaching a political settlement (Molana-Allen 2019).

Thawra ʿala al-ʾistishrāq

Despite the controversial and contentious politics inherent in its reconfiguration of a post-war Lebanese state and the consequences it has brought onto a wide range of societal, political and national dynamics (Makdisi, Kiwan and Marktanner 2011: 115–41; Salloukh 2019: 43–60), the ratification of the Taif Agreement did provide a political, albeit narrowly envisioned, framework to bring the cycle of violence that ravaged the country since the early 1970s to an end. Taif, however, only formally ended the Lebanese Civil War. This is because, instead of facilitating a genuine political unity across ethnic, sectarian and confessional groupings, Taif obscured and failed to address the 'unfinished nature of the end of the civil war' (Haugbolle 2005: 192), thus maintaining only a post-conflict veneer of unity which, in reality, disguised many of the grievances and injustices of the war which remain unsettled and unresolved at a national level. The framework of governance outlined by Taif has legitimized, institutionalized and exacerbated sectarianism and communal divisions under the guise of democratic governance and representation. 'On a popular level', this, according to Sune Haughbolle, has fed 'into simplified antagonistic discourses of "the other"', exacerbating the division between the Lebanese along sectarian lines' (ibid.: 192). Political parties in Lebanon today do not represent different political ideologies or ideas to rebuild the state. They do not reflect a diversity of political thought, but rather the ethnic and/or sectarian defined communities they are appointed to represent.

Prolonging a period of inevitable polarization, the fact that Taif gradually transformed itself from a temporary re-envisioning of political life in post-war Lebanon to one more permanent framework of governance in the country which has survived for over thirty years following the end of the hostilities has indeed contributed to the conceptualization of sectarian and confessional identification as central to political life in post-conflict Lebanon. However, this political ordering depends on and has resulted in the envisioning and misrepresentation of a culture of 'sectarianism' as inherent to the sociopolitical life in Lebanon, rather than in a critical engagement with 'the overlapping social and religious layers and the limits inherent in modern sectarian identity' (U. Makdisi 2000: 98). Taif was necessary to end the war, but, by not being a transitory framework of governance and outliving its initial status of a peace agreement (Nucho 2016: 30–50), it deliberately and systematically cemented, rather than settled, the divisions that contributed to the war in the first place. It intensified a fear of a return to hostilities if this formula of political sectarianism is overhauled 'too soon'. Under this regime of peacekeeping, an end to political sectarianism is repeatedly equated with the exacerbation of the 'sectarian sensitivity [which] has precluded a census since 1932' (Harris 2012: 95). The resilience of the system through which Taif upholds the appointment of political office as well as its persistence, permeance and relevance in present-day Lebanon as the main avenue through which political contestation occurs has been 'often taken as evidence of the persistence of "sectarianism"' itself (Haddad 2019; Saouli 2019: 67–87).

Two fundamental paradoxes lie at the heart of the peacekeeping logic of Taif. The very politicians who owe their parliamentary seats to a system of political sectarianism are tasked with the responsibility of de-sectarianization, the suspension of the sociopolitical exclusions that promote the practice *not* of sectarian identification per se but of sectarianism. The second factor is succinctly summarized by Maya Mikdashi as follows:

> This temporality of the temporary is grounded in colonial and mandate logics – that a group of people must be ruled until they are 'ready' for freedom and equality, expressed as citizenship in an independent nation-state, and citizenship in a direct liberal democracy. Mandate rule in the Middle East and its medium – the colonial nation-state – was thus framed as a civilising mission. The independent nation-state has inherited the architecture and ideology of the civilising mission through the temporality of the temporary. (Mikdashi 2019)

It is within this context of the often orientalized sectarianism through the frequent representation of Taif as a mandate to keep the menace of sectarianism 'under control' that on 27 October, one of the protesters sprayed *thawra ʿala al-ʾistishrāq*, Arabic for 'a revolution against orientalism', on the side of the Ring Bridge, a notoriously strategic site of political division during the Lebanese Civil War now repurposed into one unifying site of protest in central Beirut (Sinno 2017: 79). This orientalization of sectarianism manifests itself through repeated statements issued by a number of Lebanese politicians inciting fear of a return to civil war hostilities should the protests continue. For example, on 14 November, Defence Minister Elias Bou Saab commented on recent incidents in Jal Al-Dīb and Nahr Al-Kalb,[5] including the killing of Alaa Abou Fakhr, telling reporters that 'we have been reminded of the civil war and of what happened in 1975, which is a very dangerous situation'.[6]

The political project of Taif, significantly undermined by a range of regional and international powers who have 'become perennially embroiled in domestic political processes and outcomes' (Samir Makdisi and R. Sadaka 2005: 79), has so far failed to provide a cohesive formula for a long-term political solution. While Makdisi and Sadaka argue that 'the Taif settlement notwithstanding, there is no guarantee that, as in the past, sectarianism will not be a destabilizing influence' (ibid., 80). I believe that there is no guarantee that sectarianism *will* be – and, in fact, 'every history of sectarianism is also a history of coexistence' (U. Makdisi 2019: 1). Taif might be said to have entrenched sectarian divisions in Lebanon, but it has not solely given rise to 'sectarianism'. Nor is 'sectarianism' the sole predicament of political life in Lebanon today (Kiwan 2004: 51–74; Salloukh and Verheij 2017: 147–73).[7] In what follows, I argue that what has been most detrimental to the current political climate in Lebanon emanates tremendously, but not exclusively, from the fact that the post-war model of relative political stabilization and conflict alleviation has enabled the same self-serving political elites – those whose participation in decision-making is imbricated in decades of corruption and intrastate grievances over governance – to remain in power and continues today to empower them over the masses. Examining what they term a 'collegiate governance in the post-Taif period' (Samir Makdisi and R. Sadaka 2005: 79), Samir Makdisi and Richard Sadaka raise 'a fundamental question concerning the long-term workability of the Taif Accord. ... Does it constitute the ultimate political framework that will ensure stability in the long run' (ibid.: 80)? The following section begins to answer this question by examining the extent to which what remains at stake here is not Taif itself but rather the 1991 general amnesty law whose stipulations it continues to drive.

From amnesty to amnesia

Almost thirty years after the end of hostilities in Lebanon, there is a noticeable absence of an official documentation of the war. There has been no governmental initiative to establish a unifying account of the atrocities committed. In fact, 'when the war ended in Lebanon, it was like it never happened' (Haugbolle 2010: 1). This instrumentalized absence of memorialization has not only resulted in the enabling of the same ruling warlords to remain in power but was itself the result of the Lebanese government's 1991 general amnesty law which, 'on the basis of a "no victor, no vanquished" formula', legitimized the forgiving – *and forgetting* – of all war crimes committed by all involved parties prior to that date (El-Khazen 2000: 239). This deliberate political act of forgetting the past became a tactic to obliterate collective memory and replace it with a state-sponsored homogenized political consciousness that ensures that those who committed war crimes are never punished and, therefore, retain their position within a post-war government. Recognizing amnesty as a tactic discreetly undertaken by those whose authority is challenged by acts of remembering, Paul Ricoeur argues that 'the proximity, which is more than phonetic, or even semantic, between amnesty and amnesia signals the existence of a secret pact with the denial of memory, which ... distances it from forgiving, after suggesting a close simulation' (Ricoeur 2006: 453).

Therefore, the answer to the question Samir Makdisi and Richard Sadaka raise above is that even more detrimental to political life in Lebanon than the implementation of Taif is the issuing of this equally controversial parliamentary amnesty law which pardoned all war crimes committed before 1990.[8] The ensuing consolidation of a state-sponsored amnesia under what Ussama Makdisi and Paul Silverstein conceive of as 'the rubric of letting bygones be bygones' legitimized the political dominance many of those who committed war crimes continue to exercise over Lebanon's fragile political landscape (U. Makdisi and Silversteign 2006: 15).

Corresponding to this fragile political landscape is a fragile memorialization of pre-Taif Beirut. The political amnesia brought about in 1991 enables and resonates with 'urban amnesia' of Solidere's politics (Elias 2018: 23). It is for this reason that the protests seeking to *un*imagine and *re*imagine Beirut's 'downtown', an area rebuilt by Solidere, are highly symbolic. The implementation of Solidere's plans for a new space undermined the potential of urban architecture to enable a more nuanced understanding of post-war Lebanese identity through the physical repurposing of Beirut's pre-war history.

Against the backdrop of the failure of former Prime Minister Rachid Al-Solh's newly elected government of 1990 to de-confessionalize post-war Lebanon, to address the sense of injustice felt by the Lebanese public and to produce a reconciled Lebanese identity, Solidere was tasked with the fabrication of a commissioned spectacle of legitimacy around and on behalf of the complicit government itself. Solidere's intended spectacle did not revolve around formulating an informative understanding of the war through architecture, but was, instead, dependent on bulldozing through Beirut's historical ruins, conveniently erasing the memory of the war that the Lebanese government, at the time, could not afford to acknowledge or include in a public narrative of what had happened between 1975 and 1990. Through its links to a number of investors from the private sector as well as to elite Lebanese politicians, including former Prime Minister Rafik Hariri, who partly owned and financially benefited from the project, Solidere operated an architectural erasure of the aftermath of the war and, therefore, contributed to the suppression of the political, social and sectarian divisions which underpin Lebanon's recent history.

With that in mind, one can argue that when the war had ended, it was not only as if it had never happened, to use Haugbolle's words, but also as if a new historical and cultural past had to be refashioned onto what remains of Beirut's architecture, as though the city had been devoid of any authentic past. Within Haugbolle's understanding of this culturally emptied space, the newly restored central district of Solidere's Beirut exhibits very little, if any, resemblance to and continuity with its pre-war past. It is as if this district has been stripped off its historical context.

Examples of central Beirut buildings restored by Solidere include the iconic Hamidiyyeh Clock Tower and Le Grand Serail, a historic Ottoman-era building on Rue des Capuchins now used as the prime minister's office. Beirut's Roman Baths, which are located just across the road from Le Grand Serail, remain almost intact. However, nowhere is Solidere's obliterating of Beirut's architectural memory more visible than in the appropriation of the city's Old Souks and the surrounding area. Solidere demolished the entire historic Old Souks district, built a parking space underground and constructed the new Souks above to house hundreds of shops, restaurants and cafes which certainly planned to cater more for its regional and international investors than for the local Lebanese consumer to whom Solidere did not consider it was accountable. Critiquing the positioning of Solidere's new Souks vis-à-vis Lebanese pre-war memory, Saree Makdisi fears that Solidere's remanufacturing of Beirut's post-war architectural reality will turn the city into:

> a space that has been disemboweled literally and cleansed of its past. It will be marketed as a recreation of what was there before, rather than as something that is entirely novel, something that has no historical depth. It is, rather, part of a much broader process that has from the beginning stripped away the past and laid bare the surface of the city as sheer surface – spectacle – and nothing more. (Saree Makdisi 1997: 204)

In his article 'Reconstructing History in Central Beirut' Makdisi argues that once the generation who personally experienced the war and had a first-hand knowledge of pre-war Beirut dies, there will no longer be a living memory of the space that once existed prior to the materialization of the image cultivated by Solidere. At that point, Solidere's new space and the way people experience and interact with it will have entirely overshadowed the demolished history and consumed it in favour of maintaining a mere spectacle, a reconstructed surface which does not resemble itself, and a permanent 'hiatus of history'. An indefinite discontinuity has now come to occupy the centre of modern Lebanese politics, while an indeterminate emptiness continues to articulate a gap between Beirut's historical past and present.

In a critique of Solidere's obliterating politics, Aseel Sawalha argues that:

> While the reconstruction company destroyed what remined of the city centre, dynamiting the buildings and bulldozing the streets, Beirut residents (both powerful and powerless) expressed sorrow at seeing the downtown area disappearing and many of the city's landmarks being demolished. This massive destruction provoked many Beirutis to document their personal prewar and wartime experiences and to express their pain about the damage caused by the bulldozers. (Sawalha 2010: 29)[9]

Solidere's visualization of post-war Beirut has thus broken the memory of the war into indiscernible gestures (Agamben 2000: 49), and then re-incorporated these gestures into a homogenized state-sponsored amnesiac memory that, today, continues to be alienated from the sphere of everyday experience and to alienate human experience of the war as a reconstructed exterior devoid of its historical depth (Hayek 2015; Sawalha 2010; Hanssen 2015; Khalaf 2013; Young 2010; Bou Akar 2018; Naeff 2018; Fregonese 2019), a 'sheer surface – [a] spectacle – and nothing more' (Saree Makdisi 1997: 8) and 'a ghost town, or a setting for a war movie in a city anywhere in the world' (Khoury 2015: 305). Mobilizing the attachment of many Lebanese to pre-war Beirut, Solidere has portrayed itself as a newly launched nationalist unifying project whose plans are part of a larger endeavour for the city to reclaim its pre-war financial and regional role. In reality, however, Solidere's plans were designed as though the old centre of Beirut and its five thousand years of history, colonialism and architecture had never existed.

Through its reformulated, yet still confessional, power-sharing arrangement, Taif, propelled by both the general amnesty law and Solidere's amnesiac architectural reformulation of physical space around central Beirut, ended up incorporating wartime factional dynamics into the post-war political and national fabric of Lebanon and failed, therefore, to mediate a sustainable post-war public reconciliation. In this way, Taif, as Norman Saadi Nikro and Sonja Hegasy argue, ensured that any 'memory of violence and trauma would not only have no role on political accountability and legal redress, but also have no consequence for national identity' (Nikro and Hegasy 2017: 18). Under Taif, the memory of pre-war and wartime Beirut has been diffracted into inauthentic, conflicting and irreconcilable narratives of nationalism, national subjectivity and self-definition as a nation that continues to be emblematic of and detrimental to contemporary Lebanese politics.

When the Lebanese Civil War was brought to an end, the country began, by the summer of 1992, to nurture a degree of normality. The political settlement brought about by Taif was, and still is, precarious. Fighting continued, accompanied by a series of politically motivated assassinations targeting a number of prominent political figures, activists and journalists, such as Samir Kasir, former Lebanese Communist Party leader George Hawi, journalist Gebran Tueni, MP Pierre Amine Gemayel, terrorism investigator Wissam Eid and General Wissam al-Hassan. Today, questions surrounding the electoral laws brought about by Taif and the politics of amnesia which accompanied Taif's progression from a transitory peace agreement into what appears to be a compromised and permanent power-sharing arrangement re-emerge. The new electoral and amnesty laws introduced in June 2014 and October 2019, respectively, have not only provoked increasing public outrage but have also – and more importantly – been conceived of, by the protesters of 17 October, as an articulation of the fact that the politics they propose to bring about remain irremediably indistinct from the politics that followed the end of the hostilities – the very politics against which the protesters have been campaigning.

New electoral laws

Lebanon's new electoral law, which was approved by the Lebanese government on 14 June 2017, continues to justify and enable the operating of exclusive sectarianism by inviting voters in parliamentary elections to choose their representatives on the basis of sect. This new law divides Lebanon into fifteen, instead of twenty-six, electoral constituencies, each of which is allocated a number of seats in Parliament. This law maintains the fifty–fifty Christian–Muslim division of seats which was introduced by Taif in 1991 and introduces, for the first time since 1920, a proportional system of representation. Under the old system, voters were able to vote for each seat individually, regardless of the political party to which their chosen candidate belonged. Under the new system, voters are able to vote exclusively for the candidates presented to them on an already published list, in an attempt to regulate what candidates run for what sectarian-based constituency. While this new system promises to replace the old system which, arguably, did not recognize the changing social and sectarian demographics of Lebanon, the way it reconfigures the country's constituencies nevertheless implicitly strives to maintain the same political balance between the various governing parties. For example, the predominantly Christian constituency of Jbeil has been allocated eight Members of Parliament, seven of whom are to be Maronite Christian and one Shi'a Muslim. The predominantly Sunni Muslim northern constituency of Al-Dnayya has been allocated eleven Members of Parliament, eight of which are to be Sunni Muslim. Just as the new power-sharing system ensures that the Jbeil remains under Maronite Christian control, it, likewise, ensures that Al-Dnayya remains under Sunni Muslim control.

This law has received the same criticism the old law did. This is at least because a democratic system of representation in Lebanon is tied to factors that go beyond what a census-based electoral law can offer. Lucia Volk argues that the distribution of power 'was not derived from a census, and hence the numbers [of the fifty-fifty division] are not linked to Lebanon's current demographic realities' (Fahrenthold 2019: 137–59; Maktabi 1999: 219–41; Volk 2010: 8). Volk explains that this is due to the fact that

> This [new 50:50] formula [as opposed to the old 6:5] was not derived from a census, and hence the numbers are not linked to Lebanon's current demographic realities. Because of proportionally higher Maronite, Christian Orthodox, and Druze emigration from Lebanon and proportionally higher birth rates among Shiite and Sunni Lebanese, it is generally assumed that Shiites and Sunnis now significantly outnumber all Christian communities combined. This means that relative to their actual numbers, Sunnis and Shiites are underrepresented in parliament. (Volk 2010: 8)

Volk goes on to explain that during a recent visit to Lebanon, she 'heard both Sunnis and Shiites claim, but in the absence of a census they could not prove, that *their* community now constitutes the *absolute* majority of Lebanon's population' (ibid., 8). In a similar vein, Joshua Gleis and Benedetta Berti argue that the Taif Agreement 'better appropriated the ratio of seats allocated to Muslim and Christian representatives' (Gleis and Berti 2012: 15), as it abolished the old 6:5 formula and introduced the current fifty–fifty one. However, contra the arguments presented by Volk, Gleis and Barti, I argue that there is no evidence that links census-based recognition of demographic realities to effective democratic representation. Nor is it clear why an updated census is able to better distribute representational powers. The question, in fact, is not whether the link Volk theorizes does exist, but whether it *should* do. Within the critique I present of Lebanon's uncomfortable relationship with its past, I argue that this link between democracy and a census to assess the demographic reality of constituencies would be detrimental to Lebanese politics should it be allowed to inform post-war Lebanese politics. However, the fact that Lebanon's ruling class is still unwilling to let go of a political system which has so far kept it in power explains why this proposed electoral law is still 'confessional'. Arguably, this new law will further establish what is referred to in Arabic as *al-manaṭiqiyya*, or the geo-demographic division of Lebanon into the newly introduced fifteen districts, each of which is given a voting list of candidates predominantly belonging to its confessional majority. The rising exclusive *manaṭiqiyya* socially, culturally and politically alienates the districts from each other, thus further enabling a representation of them as competing sectarian others.

The very proposal that democratic political representation is synonymous with and dependent on majority/minority population census figures not only undermines the possibility of arriving at an inclusive paradigm of a post-war nation state but also revives and legitimizes the religious and confessional basis of power sharing that fuelled the civil war in the first place. In Lebanon, a permanently compromised religious structure of power redistribution, as opposed to a system based on political competence and expertise (Khalaf 2013: 328), has, so far, produced a failing state apparatus that continues to violently build and exclude others from 'the political'.

New amnesty laws

State representatives have so far struggled to formulate a comprehensible response which would meet the demands of the protesters. Evoking a similar sense of incapability and incompetence with which the October wildfires have been met, the state has so far grappled with how to navigate an escalating nationwide crisis they have never anticipated. The fact that the early protests have been co-opted and demonized by those in power symptomizes the dilemma in which the state has found itself. For example, in a speech he gave on October 19, Hassan Nasrallah accused the protesters of being funded by foreign embassies, leading protesters to respond in the viral *ana mumawil al-thawara*, or 'I am funding the revolution'.[10]

On October 20, the parliamentary bloc of the Lebanese Forces resigned in response to increasing public pressure calling for the dissolution of the government. They have, since then, attempted, albeit unsuccessfully, to use their resignation to score political goals against their rivals, thus also essentially exporting the historical rivalry between the Lebanese Forces and the Free Patriotic Movement into the contemporary political landscape of Lebanon (Arsan 2018: 27–59; Corstange 2016: 50–89). However, the first major victory of the revolution was that, on October 29, following just under two weeks of unprecedented protests, Prime Minister Saad Al-Hariri announced the resignation of the government. As of the end of the first month of the protests, the caretaker government was yet to appoint new ministers.

Instead of using this as an opportunity to undertake necessary, real and realistic reform measures to mitigate the public outrage, the parliament announced that it was planning to chair a session in order to debate and propose yet *another* general amnesty law under which crimes related to matters such as the governance of state resource and the management, or, in fact, the mismanagement, of the escalating economic crisis would be forgiven, thus illegally allowing the establishment of a legal loophole through which politicians could escape accountability, potential scrutiny and prosecution. The proposal further deepened the mounting national frustrations in two different ways. On the one hand, it became more evident to the protesters, especially to those demanding the issuing of an amnesty law for their family members arrested during the protests, that the government is yet to take the uprising and its demands seriously. On the other hand, the fact that the government even planned to debate this law demonstrates that they are still unwilling to recognize and act upon the divisions that the 1991 amnesty law brought about. In a bid to prevent the planned session from taking place, protesters gathered to block every road the members of parliament could take. The session was eventually cancelled and rescheduled, for the second time since 12 November, to take place on a yet to be announced date.

The dysfunctional political, governmental and consociational apparatus of power, meanwhile, has, since then, remained unyielding. While protesters are determined to challenge the legitimacy of the rule of the political establishment, a pan-sectarian counterrevolution is seeking to nurture exclusionary politics, to generate antagonistic group mobilization through the prism of sectarian difference, to advocate for the crafting of a general amnesty law in order to establish a mandate of unaccountability and to engage in disinformation campaigns by reiterating allegations that the protests are funded and infiltrated by proxies of foreign powers. At the time of writing this chapter, answers to questions surrounding how to advocate an effective management of a looming financial collapse, to nurture a more democratic system of governance and to hold the responsible leaders accountable cannot be anticipated. This is not to imply an absence of a way forward, but to emphasize the precarity of the emerging alternatives being articulated as the situation constantly evolves.

As Lebanon approaches the first anniversary of the protests, it is expected that former prime minister Saad Hariri is to return to form a new government. One year on, Lebanon comes full circle: it was the government under Hariri which the protesters brought down, and the country is still in need of an urgent financial bailout. The Beirut port explosion of 4 August 2020 was historically powerful. It is estimated that 2,750 tonnes of the highly explosive ammonium nitrate were stored irresponsibly and neglected at the port. Hundreds of people lost their lives in the blast; thousands were injured; 300,000 became homeless as the blast completely destroyed more than one-third of the city. For the outraged public, this is always going to be one of the most devastating and most scarring examples of the state's negligence, incompetence and disregard of the lives of its own citizens. Within this political climate, even if the outcome of the uprising turns out to be only short term, the reconsolidated unity that the Lebanese people have shown to and against the ruling political apparatus and that a reimagination of an inclusive trans-sectarian nation-building project is indeed possible remain the long-term outcome that nothing is going to be able to undo.

Notes

1 Throughout this chapter, I follow the *International Journal of Middle East Studies* (IJMES) transliteration system for Arabic, but leave people and place names in the familiar English form.
2 For an analysis of the way in which the relinquishing of differentiated personal status jurisdictions to religious courts evokes this segregation, see Mikdashi 2014; Salloukh and Clark 2013.
3 This is not to suggest that the protests taking place today were intended to mark the anniversary of Taif, but they certainly are set against the background of the divided politics that Taif has cemented.
4 For the full final statement of the CEDRE conference, see Ministry for Europe and Foreign Affairs 2018.
5 This is in reference to clashes between a number of protesters and local residents, followed by scuffles with soldiers of the Lebanese Army deployed to the area. Video footage of an armed man shooting at protesters have been widely circulated. See ahāli jal al-dīb yaḍbuṭūn bil video rajulan musalaḥan yuṭleq annār bi'itijāh al-mutaẓahirīn 2019.
6 The full statement of Elias Bou Saab is available to watch on Aljadeed; 'Bu ṣab ba'd liqā' Berri: mā jara fi jal el-dīb wa nahr al-kalb dhakaranā bil ḥarb al-ahliyya 2019.
7 I must note here that the words 'Maronite', 'Sunni' and 'Shia' do not appear in either the Taif Agreement or the Lebanese Constitution. Despite this fact, many assume that the current power-sharing arrangement, whereby the president must be a Maronite Christian, the prime minister a Sunni Muslim and the speaker of parliament a Shia Muslim, is a constitutional stipulation. It is noteworthy here that the Lebanese constitution mentions the words 'Muslim' or 'Christian' only four times, two of which are found in the current text of Article 24, and the other two in Article 95, which is an amendment introduced by Taif.
8 Of all the participants in the fighting, only Samir Geagea was tried and prosecuted. The most notorious case to exemplify the impunity brought about by the parliamentary amnesty is, I believe, that of Elie Hobeika. Hobeika was found guilty of overseeing and perpetrating the Sabra and Shatila massacres with Ariel Sharon, but was assassinated, along with a number of his bodyguards, in 2002 before he was tried. Despite the fact that he was widely suspected of plotting for these massacres, Hobeika held a number of important positions in the Lebanese government. He was appointed Minister of Electricity, Minister of the Displaced, with heavy irony, and a Member of Parliament to represent the governorate of the East of Beirut, thus benefitting from the ratification of the Taif Agreement, the close ties he had established with Damascus and the parliamentary immunity that the Lebanese government grants to its members so they cannot be investigated for any offences committed during their tenure. Even the report of the Kahan Commission, also known as the Commission of Inquiry

into the Events at the Refugee Camps in Beirut, that Israel sanctioned at the end of September 1982 to investigate Israeli involvement in the events finds that Sharon was responsible, but also mentions that Hobeika is a key perpetrator. See Hegasy 2018; S. Posner 1987: 262–3 and Silverstein and U. Makdisi 2005; Va'adat ha-ḥakirah la-ḥakirat ha-eru'im be-maḥanot ha-peliṭim be-Berut 1983: 20.

9 Specific examples of Solidere's deconstruction and appropriation of Beirut's architectural memory can be found in examples of Solidere's activities can be found in M. Cooke 2002: pp. 393–424; Saree Makdisi 1997: 660–705. Photographic evidence of Solidere's development can be found in E. Charlesworth 2006.

10 There has also been an online effort to counter fake news spread by supporters of the government. Examples of these platforms include Daleel Thawra, TeleThawa, Fawra Media, Sawt Alniswa and Megaphone News. Participating in the co-option of the revolution, writer and director Charbel Khalil claims, during a pro-state rally on October 10, that, underlying the anti-sectarian demands of the revolution is an implicit call to bring about new laws relating to homosexuality in Lebanon, a statement which is problematic in several ways. For an analysis of the political instrumentalization of homosexuality by 'the state' in times of revolution in the Middle East, see J. Massad 2007: 160–90; Merabet 2014: 112–56.

References

Agamben, G. (1998), *Homo Sacer: Sovereign Power and Bare Life*, trans. Daniel Heller-Roazen, Stanford, CA: Stanford University Press.

Agamben, G. (2000), *Means without End: Notes on Politics*, trans. Vincenzo Binetti and Cesare Casarino, Minnesota: University of Minnesota Press.

'Ahāli jal al-dīb yaḍbuṭūn bil video rajulan musalaḥan yuṭliq annār bi'itijāh al-muṭaẓahirīn' (2019), *Aljadeed*, 13 November. Available online: https://www.aljadeed.tv/arabic/news/local/1411201991 (accessed 14 November 2019).

Arsan, A. (2018), *A Country in Fragments*, London: Hurst.

Bou Akar, H. (2018), *For the War Yet to Come: Planning Beirut's Frontiers*, Stanford, CA: Stanford University Press.

'Bu ṣab ba'd liqā' Berri: mā jara fi jal el-dīb wa nahr al-kalb dhakaranā bil ḥarb al-ahliyya' (2019), *Aljadeed*, 13 November. Available online: https://www.aljadeed.tv/arabic/news/local/1411201991 (accessed 14 November 2019).

Charlesworth, E. (2006), *Architects without Frontiers: War, Reconstruction, and Design Responsibility*, Oxford: Elsevier.

Cooke, M. (2002), 'Beirut Reborn: The Political Aesthetics of Auto-Destruction', *Yale Journal of Criticism*, 15 (2): 393–424.

Corstange, D. (2016), *The Price of a Vote in the Middle East: Clientelism and Communal Politics in Lebanon and Yemen*, New York: Cambridge University Press.

El-Khazen, F. (2000), *The Breakdown of the State in Lebanon 1967–1976*, London: I.B. Tauris.

Elias, C. (2018), *Posthumous Images: Contemporary Art and Memory in Post-Civil War Lebanon*, Durham, NC: Duke University Press.

Fahrenthold, S. (2019), *Between the Ottomans and the Entente: The First World War in the Syrian and Lebanese Diaspora, 1908–1925*, Oxford: Oxford University Press.

Fregonese, S. (2019), *War and the City: Urban Geopolitics in Lebanon*, London: I.B. Tauris.

Gleis, J., and Berti, B. (2012), *Hezbollah and Hamas: A Comparative Study*, Baltimore, MD: Johns Hopkins University Press.

Haddad, F. (2019), 'The Waning Relevance of the Sunni–Shia Divide', *The Century Foundation*, 10 April. Available online: https://tcf.org/content/report/waning-relevance-sunni-shia-divide (accessed 10 May 2019).

Hanssen, J. (2005), *Fin de Siècle Beirut: The Making of an Ottoman Provincial Capital*, Oxford: Oxford University Press.

Harris, W. (2012), *Lebanon: A History 600–2011*, Oxford: Oxford University Press.

Haugbolle, S. (2005), 'Public and Private Memory of the Lebanese Civil War', *Comparative Studies of South Asia, Africa, and The Middle East*, 25 (1): 191–203.

Haugbolle, S. (2010), *War and Memory in Lebanon*, New York: Cambridge University Press.

Hayek, G. (2015), *Beirut, Imagining the City: Space and Place in Lebanese Literature*, London: I.B. Tauris.

Hegasy, S. (2018), 'Letter to Oneself: Acknowledging Guilt in Post-War Lebanon', in K. Deslandes, F. Mourlon and B. Tribout (eds), *Civil War and Narrative: Testimony, Historiography, and Memory*, Aberdeen: University of Aberdeen, 39–58.

Helal, N., and Geha, C. (2019), 'Wildfires Engulf Lebanon amid Rise in Temperature', *Annahar*, 15 October. Available online: https://en.annahar.com/article/1049637-sudden-rise-in-temperature-sets-lebanons-forests-on-fire (accessed 17 October 2019).

Joseph, S. (2000), *Gender and Citizenship in the Middle East*, New York: Syracuse University Press.

Khalaf, S. (2013), *Heart of Beirut: Reclaiming the Bourj*, London: Saqi Books.

Khoury, E. (2015), *The Broken Mirrors: Sinalcol*, London: MacLehose Press.

Kiwan, F. (2004), 'Decentralization: Choosing a Model', in N. Salam (ed.), *Options for Lebanon*, London: I.B. Tauris, 51–74.

Leenders, R. (2012), *Spoils of Truce, Corruption and State-Building in Postwar Lebanon*, New York: Cornell University.

Lucia, V. (2010), *Memorials and Martyrs in Modern Lebanon*, Indiana: Indiana University Press.

Makdisi, S., and Sadaka, R. (2005), 'The Lebanese Civil War, 1975–90', in P. Collier and N. Sambanis (eds), *Understanding Civil War: Europe, Central Asia, and Other Regions*, Washington: World Bank, 59–86.

Makdisi, S., Kiwan, F. and Marktanner, M. (2011), 'Lebanon: The Constrained Democracy and Its National Impact', in I. Elbadawi and S. Makdisi (eds), *Democracy in the Arab World: Explaining the Deficit*, Oxon: Routledge, 115–41.

Makdisi, S. (1997a), 'Laying Claim to Beirut: Urban Narrative and Spatial Identity in the Age of Solidere', *Critical Inquiry*, 23 (3): 660–705.

Makdisi, S. (1997b), 'Reconstructing History in Central Beirut', *Middle East Report*, 203: 59–89.

Makdisi, U. (2000), *The Culture of Sectarianism: Community, History, and Violence in Nineteenth-Century Ottoman Lebanon*, California: University of California Press.

Makdisi, U. (2019), *Age of Coexistence: The Ecumenical Frame and the Making of the Modern Arab World*, California: University of California Press.

Makdisi, U., and Silverstein, P. (2006) 'Introduction', in U. Makdisi and P. Silverstein (eds), *Memory and Violence in the Middle East and Africa*, Bloomington: Indiana University Press, 1–24.

Maktabi, R. (1999), 'The Lebanese Census of 1932 Revisited: Who Are the Lebanese?', *British Journal of Middle Eastern Studies*, 26 (2): 219–41.
Massad, J. (2007), *Desiring Arabs*, Chicago: University of Chicago Press.
Merabet, S. (2014), *Queer Beirut*, Austin: University of Texas Press.
Mikdashi, M. (2014), 'Sex and Sectarianism: The Legal Architecture of Lebanese Citizenship', *Comparative Studies of South Asia, Africa, and the Middle East*, 34 (2): 279–93.
Mikdashi, M. (2019), 'The Magic of Mutual Coexistence in Lebanon: The Taif Accord at Thirty', *Jadaliyya*, 23 October. Available online: https://www.jadaliyya.com/Deta ils/40134/The-Magic-of-Mutual-Coexistence-in-Lebanon-The-Taif-Accord-at-Thirty (accessed 23 October 2019).
Ministry for Europe and Foreign Affairs (2018), 'Lebanon: CEDRE Conference', *France Diplomacy*, 6 April. Available online: https://www.diplomatie.gouv.fr/en/coun try-files/lebanon/news/article/lebanon-cedre-conference-06-04-18 (accessed 9 September 2018).
Molana-Allen, L. (2019), 'Lebanon's Hariri Announces Economic Reforms in Response to Days of Protests', *France 24*, 21 October. Available online: https://www.france24.com/en/20191021-lebanon-s-hariri-announces-economic-reforms-in-response-to-days-of-protests-2 (accessed 21 October 2019).
Naeff, J. (2018), *Precarious Imaginaries of Beirut: A City's Suspended Now*, Cham: Springer Nature.
Nagle, J., and Clancy, M. (2019), 'Power-Sharing after Civil War: Thirty Years since Lebanon's Taif Agreement', *Nationalism and Ethnic Politics*, 25 (1): 1–8.
Nucho, R. (2016), *Everyday Sectarianism in Urban Lebanon: Infrastructures, Public Services, and Power*, Princeton, NJ: Princeton University Press.
Posner, S. (1987), *Israel Undercover: Secret Warfare and Hidden Diplomacy in the Middle East*, New York: Syracuse University Press.
Ricoeur, P. (2006), *Memory, History, Forgetting*, Chicago: University of Chicago Press.
Saadi Nikro, N., and Hegasy, S. (2017), 'Memory Between Lieu and Milieu, in N. Saadi Nikro and S. Hegasy (eds), *The Social Life of Memory: Violence, Trauma, and Testimony in Lebanon and Morocco*, 1–24, Cham: Springer Nature.
Salloukh, B. (2019a), 'Taif and the Lebanese State: The Political Economy of a Very Sectarian Public Sector', *Nationalism and Ethnic Politics*, 25 (1): 43–60.
Salloukh, B. (2019b), 'War Memory, Confessional Imaginaries, and Political Contestation in Postwar Lebanon', *Middle East Critique*, 28 (3): 341–59.
Salloukh, B., and Clark, J. (2013), 'Elite Strategies, Civil Society, and Sectarian Identities in Post War Lebanon', *International Journal of Middle East Studies*, 45 (4): 731–49.
Salloukh, B., and Verheij, R. (2017), 'Transforming Power-Sharing: From Corporate to Hybrid Consociation in Postwar Lebanon', *Middle East Law and Governance*, 9 (2) (2017): 147–73.
Saouli, A. (2019), 'Sectarianism and Political Order in Iraq and Lebanon', *Studies in Ethnicity and Nationalism*, 19 (1): 67–87.
Sawalha, A. (2010), *Reconstructing Beirut: Memory and Space in a Postwar Arab City*, Austin: University of Texas Press.
Sinno, N. (2017), 'A War of Colors: Beirut Street Art and the Reclamation of Public Space', *ASAP Journal*, 2 (1): 71–107.
Va'adat ha-ḥakirah la-ḥakirat ha-eru'im be-maḥanot ha-peliṭim be-Berut (1983), *The Beirut Massacre: The Complete Kahan Commission Report*, Michigan, Karz-Cohl.

Vohra, A. (2019), 'Lebanon's Deir al-Ahmar: How an Incident Displaced 600 Refugees', *Aljazeera*, 9 June. Available online: https://www.aljazeera.com/news/2019/06/lebanon-deir-al-ahma-incident-displaced-600-refugees 190609095940222.html (accessed 20 October 2019).

Young, M. (2010), *The Ghosts of Martyrs Square: An Eyewitness Account of Lebanon's Life Struggle*, New York: Simon and Schuster.

Chapter 3

CARL SCHMITT'S INEFFECTUAL EXCEPTIONALISM IN THE CASE OF SYRIA

Samuel Peter Mace

Introduction

The Syrian state relies on the state of exception to govern as a matter of routine; thus this chapter focuses on the state of exception and the resulting tools of governance emerging from it. Exceptional governance in Schmittian terms requires an explanation of the underlying framework underpinning the claim *'Sovereign is he who decides upon the exception'*. Specifically, the underlying framework that is explored in this chapter consists of analysing the *'friend–enemy'* dichotomy and attempts to construct a homogeneity manifest in the state. The *'friend–enemy'* dichotomy for Schmitt represents the basis of politics that cannot be ameliorated acting as the basis for the construction of homogeneity inside the state and among the citizens. The state supposedly representing and invoking the *'friend'* as opposed to the *'enemy'* can thus make decisions on behalf of the citizenry but with their support as a united whole. Ideally, this provides the state with sufficient political support to guarantee decisionism's sovereignty.

However, the Syrian illustration highlights the folly of this idea. Rather than producing homogeneity and sovereignty as claimed by Schmitt, this chapter examines the limitations of this mode of politics. Rather than representing homogeneity, the Syrian state functions as a deeply heterogeneous state. The *'friend–enemy'* dichotomy can be seen as turned inwardly against citizens, specifically in relation to the politics of sectarianism producing a dysfunctional political system devoid of genuine representation for those treated as internal *'enemies'*.

The result has been a regime suffering from domestic political strain under both Hafez and Bashar Al-Assad. While the context may be different for both, the strain is directly related to the forms of politics that were practised by the Assad regime. Focusing on the recent Arab Spring uprising that descended into a civil war from 2011 onwards allows for a fruitful examination of its causes, the regime's reaction and the limitations of the current political condition of the Syrian state. Rather than a strong historical examination of the Assad regime, the chapter maintains it focus on recent events affecting the function, or rather dysfunction, of the Syrian state.

The Syrian state has faced severe challenges to its claim of sovereignty since 2011. Both domestic forces have revolted against the regime and international actors have undermined the state's capacity to control its recognized territories. Rather than seeing this as part of an unavoidable, unpredictable series of events, this chapter claims that the political framework adopted by the regime was unsustainable, inevitably leading to this conclusion. In this chapter, this claim is primarily analysed via the lens of the *'friend–enemy'* dichotomy focusing on sect relations. Tactics such as promoting concrete differences between sect groups via both rhetoric and action have been used by the regime attempting to remain in power. The result has not been a homogeneous, united populace, but a disunited, heterogeneous citizenry, the majority of which have made the regime the *enemy* turning Schmitt's formulation for sovereignty on its head.

Carl Schmitt's exceptionalism

Exceptionalism as discussed above cannot be viewed without sufficient grounding in the political framework that makes it up. Decisionism if exercised without a stable political basis unravels itself, leaving it reliant upon pure naked power to enforce its will. Inevitably, this does not lead to stability and sovereignty but fragility and challenges. This claim differs from that of other scholars who work off the basis that the exception itself is the ultimate form of sovereignty.

Despite Schmitt's controversial politics (Wolin 1990; Turner 2002; Kennedy 2004) his thinking on exceptionalism as a form of governance can tell us something new about the case of Syria. Rather than focusing on biopower as the mechanism of control, Schmitt instead forms a framework of supposed legitimation underpinning decisionism via the *friend–enemy* dichotomy, homogeneity and the sovereign god (Schmitt 2005). This framework allows for the diagnoses of new problems within the exercise of decisionism that can be explicitly seen in the Syrian case contrasting power with sovereignty. Linking political capacity in relation to perceived authority is central to the case study.

Indeed, a combination of economic stagnation, political inertia and a state of emergency which had been maintained for over fifty years had wilted the state's authority and provided the perfect storm for the mobilization of citizens against the regime (Abboud 2018). Exceptionalism itself was unable to hold back the tide of anger that confronted the regime as has been seen in Chapters 1 and 2. While the state of emergency was in effect since 1963 (Hadad 2009) accompanied by a further seven laws consolidating executive power via a combination of suspending civil liberties, press freedom and the power of arbitrary arrest and detention (Ghadry 2005; Kawakibi 2010), this did not produce sovereignty. Rather, it created a mask of sovereignty underpinned by fear and distrust, hiding the hope of political reform. Akin to the second chapter, the Syrian regime appeared to hope that people would forget hopes for reform once Bashar ascended the leadership that promised real change culminating in the Damascus Spring but was quickly suppressed (Wieland 2012).

Homogeneity

Schmitt's decisionist thought has a strong basis in claims of homogeneity (Mouffe 1998; Schmitt 2005, 2008; Hoelzl 2016). Political homogeneity for Schmitt is found in the unity of a people raising the state above distinct political groupings giving the sovereign authority to rule (Bredekamp et al. 1999; Mouffe 2000; Suganami 2007; Shapiro 2008; Falk 2014). Schmitt's critique of Hobbes's apparent disconnect between sovereign will and private thought highlights his belief in the necessity of ideological unity to maintain the state machine functioning via the decision (Schmitt 2008; Fischer 2010; Tralau 2010). By basing the state off unity this removes the need in Schmitt's mind for distinct political categories allowing the state to uniquely occupy the space of 'the political' as opposed to partisan political groupings (Schmitt 2008; Ifergan 2010).

The political homogeneity that Schmitt envisions is predicated via the *friend–enemy* dichotomy (Schmitt 2008). The *friend–enemy* dichotomy is not normative but descriptive, politics for Schmitt revolves around concrete groups of *friends* and *enemies* founded upon a deep enmity threatening one's safety (Hohendahl 2008; Dean 2013; Pankakoski 2013). Therefore, the *friend–enemy* distinction is not one of a personal dislike of the other. Rather, it is a political opposition to a group deemed to represent a threat, thus representing an otherness that exists both outside and within the state existing politically not just legally (Norris 1998; Arditi 2008; Beckstein 2011).

However, Schmitt's homogeneity hypothesis is problematic for two reasons. First, in a heterogeneous population attempting to create a homogeneous state system is difficult. It relies upon tools of power and coercion to eradicate heterogeneity creating a false homogeneity. Rather than fostering a unity to unite against political enemies this merely creates division in the state and various minorities competing against one another.

Second, baked into this claim is the assumption that the citizens have consented to the state in some form. Different groups often disagree on political first principles, ensuring that homogeneity is simply not possible without significant coercion undermining the state's legitimacy (Mearsheimer 2018). As the chapter goes on to show, attempting to force homogeneity when attempted to be applied is a brutal exercise which only harms both the state and the citizens. A state resorting to violence to coerce the population is not a sign of its strength but rather a signal of its weakness (Arendt 1970). In the context of the case study of Syria and sectarianism this is an especially important point which undermines the ability of the state to rule by exception.

We can therefore find inherent problems in Schmitt's framework regarding the state's maintenance of legitimacy. The Syrian case study demonstrates these limitations in Schmitt's framework. The Syrian state has attempted to practice 'on paper' homogeneity constituting secular 'Arabism' in the constitution as a unifying cause of the Syrian people and constituting the Ba'ath party as the party of society in article 8 of the constitution (Kienle 1995; Ossorio 2012; Saleh 2017). The Syrian state has also made illegal alternative political associations; examples include law No. 49 in 1980 making membership of the Muslim Brotherhood punishable by death and the clampdown on political associations during the Damascus Spring (Pierret 2014).

Accompanying 'on paper' attempts to foster political unity via authoritarian methodologies has been manipulation of communal relations fostering internal *friends* and *enemies*. Using traditional Alawite insecurity as a process of securing minority loyalty the regime has engaged in two generations of cronyism providing a narrow but deep base to the regime (Robinson 1998; Goldsmith 2011; Jasser 2014; Balanche 2018). It is this manipulation of communal relations which the chapter is focusing on, explaining the theoretical relationship with the practical.

Sectarianism as a concept

It has been argued sectarianism as a term suffers from so many different interpretations that it should be tossed aside (Haddad 2017). However, sectarianism can still be a useful term to frame political relations. In this chapter, sect is used to understand the limitations of exceptional governance imagined by Schmitt. Politics utilizing sect, not as an ancient hatred but as a distinct relationship between the state and its citizens, undermines the necessary claim of homogeneity that underpins Schmitt's decisionism (Migdal 2011; Hinnebusch 2016; Hashemi and Postel 2017).

This is not to suggest that relations between Shi'a and Sunni define and solely explain the politics of the region (Hashemi 2016). Rather than seeing sect as an intractable identity and central to people's identities as primordialists do (Lewis 2002; Al-Qarawee 2004), this chapter takes the approach that sectarian identities are oftentimes instrumentalized by elites creating 'in' and 'out' group dynamics (Hashemi 2016; Haddad 2017). Thus, 'sectarian' political relationships can be construed as mirroring other forms of identity splits rather than being specifically religious in nature (Valbjorn and Hinnebusch 2019). As a result, sectarianism should not be analysed simply via religious disputes but as akin to other identities such as ethnicity and tribe melding together the religious and the secular politically (Little 2011; Hashemi 2016).

The notion of instrumentalization regarding sectarian relations can be analysed via Schmitt's notion of homogeneity. By creating 'in' and 'out' groups this undermines the idea of homogeneity underpinning decisionism. Rather than creating whole united groups defined via the same '*friend–enemy*' dichotomy sectarianized relations crack the necessary unity for sovereign decisionism. This process undermines the ability of the sovereign to make decisions representing a homogeneous whole but instead fosters an empty decisionism that cannot be sustained.

Sectarian relations and their instrumentalization are not simple but consist of multiple, overlapping identities at both national and sub-national levels that are fluid rather than fixed (Hadaya 2020). Sectarianism fundamentally describes feelings to a sect within a social context, but this context is ever changing and shifting that can include other forms of identity (Saouli 2019; Alsarghali 2020). The malleable nature of identity helps create a contestation between different political forms of identities that sect threatens to subsume. One example used by Mabon (2017) is that of Lebanon where sect identities have infiltrated political and economic differences. This is also relevant in relation to the Syrian case study, as Jasser (2014) has argued: 'Like the regime, some of the more extremist groups utilize sectarian rhetoric and iconography to perpetuate fear' (64), highlighting the utilization of sect in relation to conflict.

Sectarian conflict when analysed this way can be understood via Carl Schmitt's claim of the sovereign god. Schmitt scrutinized the links between theological and political structures, including a link for Schmitt between the divine and secular sovereignty with both resting upon a decision to enforce an established order guaranteeing their status as sovereign (Pankakoski 2013). Sectarianism affects Schmitt's claim of the 'sovereign god' and not just homogeneity. The godly sovereign is directly linked to homogeneity, if heterogeneous political groupings disagree and can effectively challenge the sovereign that renders the sovereign akin to a mortal. Therefore, when a sovereign presides over sectarian division it undermines the ability of the sovereign to take decisions and rule.

The limits of sectarian governance and the Syrian state

The San Remo treaty defined the boundaries of Syria, not the Sykes Picot treaty as has been widely stated; despite this fact the Sykes Picot treaty set the scene for the treaty of San Remo which eventually defined the borders of Syria, ensuring the modern borders of Syria are a form of 'colonial enterprise' (Phillips 2015). But it was not just the borders that were affected by colonialism. Under French colonial rule, Syria was layered with different governing units defined by their sect and ethnic make-up stressing differences in identities in a bid to cool down for Arab nationalism, leading to a policy of 'divide and rule' (Fildis 2011, 2012). Rather than these processes remaining historical, traditional social discrimination faced by Alawites combined with divide-and-rule policies enabled the political opposition during the Arab Spring to be labelled the work of sectarian *enemies* (Hof and Simon 2013; Hokayem 2013; Gelvin 2015; Phillips 2015).

While Syria is a land of minorities, with 10–12 per cent Alawite, 10 per cent Christian, 10 per cent Kurdish, with Ismailis and Druze making up small portions of the population, there is a Sunni Arab majority consisting of around 65 per cent of the population (Hokayem 2017). Sect demographics on their own do not indicate anything, but when they exist alongside historical divisions exacerbated by outside and native actors, they can acquire a meaning eroding civil consensus in times of political upheaval (Rustow 1970). Not only has historical imperialism helped create an environment of 'divide and rule', the Assad regime has helped activate such tensions; thus, blaming Western imperialism for such tensions is short-sighted and ignores the current regime's role in activating and maintaining sectarian divisions.

Syrians are not blind to sectarian divisions when they exist but oftentimes remain silent on the matter due to the regime's insistence not to discuss or push 'sectarian politics' (Van Dam 2011). But is the Syrian regime really sect neutral? The Assad regime to maintain stability has utilized coup proofing from the very beginning which is not uncommon among authoritarian regimes. Bashar Al-Assad inherited a regime that was functional but perpetuated divisions across the country (Phillips 2012). However, rather than ameliorating these divisions, more recently Bashar Al-Assad increasingly installed familial relations as well as sect and tribal allies in key positions (Quinlivan 1999; Pilster and Bohmelt 2012; Phillips 2012; Pierret 2014; Selvik 2014). In addition, institutions have been increasingly sectarianized such as the ranks of the SAA (Syrian Arab Army) where Alawites were more likely to be promoted, better equipped and more likely to receive benefits even before the uprisings occurred (Van Dam 2011; Dukhan 2014; Nassif 2015). Coup proofing both at the elite and lower levels can thus be one way we can see the regime using sect as a dividing line in relation of who to trust and who not to (Afzaal 2016).

Thus, sectarianism and its thinking do not have to blister into open conflict for it to be present but can act as a broader governance strategy in a bid to maintain 'stability'. When analysed from a Schmittian perspective this strategy appears to make sense for the authoritarian. Fostering a homogeneous group guided by the state creating 'in' and 'out' groups directed by the *'friend–enemy'* dichotomy eliminates heterogeneity supposedly creating a stable basis from which to govern via the decision. However, as seen in the Syrian case, this is not true. Even without explosive conflicts, governing upon a narrow base is inherently problematic for any non-democratic regime seeking to assert its authority, sowing the seeds for future challenges to emerge.

Despite the longing for certainty and stability among the population the Assad regime has had continual challenges to its power resulting in uprisings in 1973, 1980, 1982, 2005 and 2011, with a civil war in 2011 almost completely fracturing the state (Al Shami and Kassab 2016). The opposition that arose in 2011 was not defined by sect initially, instead it crossed sect lines with a message defined by justice, freedom and dignity (Van Dam 2011; Littell 2015; Saleh 2017). Thus, despite historic manipulation and sectioning off, sect relations on the ground at the beginning of the uprising were good, pouring cold water on the idea that sect is necessarily a feature of conflict from below. Instead, sect relations and their deterioration were cultivated institutionally by the regime that can be analysed via increasing intensity of relations opening the door to the *'friend–enemy'* dichotomy.

This was achieved in several ways. First, rhetoric from Bashar Al-Assad himself claiming an international conspiracy was responsible for the uprising denied the domestic reasons for the uprising such as economic difficulties and an almost unique degree of authoritarian rule (Fielding Smith 2015; Kassab 2015).

Not only have the regime presented the uprising as the result of international intrigue sabotaging the Ba'ath party, they have also equated the opposition that emerged in 2011 to terrorists. Presenting a picture of a terroristic, sectarianized mob opposition demanding their ethnographic majoritarian rights led to many in the Alawite block seeing the civil war as a 'life or death' situation (Doran and Shaikh 2011, Falk 2013). The Assad regime did not stop at mere rhetoric to cultivate fear of the 'other'. They also infected the opposition with terrorists who they released from prisons across the country to further sectarianize and polarize the emerging conflict, hoping to create a reality to match their rhetoric (Kassab 2015; Abboud 2018).

In some ways this approach could be deemed as 'successful'. Through a combination of arrests, extrajudicial murder, international intervention and releasing terrorists, the uprisings of 2011 transformed from a non-violent, democratic outpouring for dignity and human rights into one ladled with increasing sectarian strife as citizens acquired fear of the 'other' (Diehl 2012; Wimmen 2014). It can be argued that this strategy of rhetoric and action, analysed via the *'friend–enemy'* dichotomy, painting the opposition (largely albeit not exclusively made up from the Sunni Muslim majority) bound many members of minority groups to the state in fear of the consequences of the result. It is rhetoric and action seen not just in Syria but more widely in countries in the region such as Bahrain that have faced similar troubles (Lynch 2013). The result was that 'In April 2013, Syria's battle map largely aligns with the map of its sectarian distribution' (Balanche 2018: 3), highlighting the renewed importance of sect and ethnic identity.

However, this approach came at a large cost both to the citizens of Syria as well as ultimately to the regime. The insular nature of the regime turned a domestic uprising demanding greater dignity and democratic rights into an international free-for-all where Syrian sovereignty was not just questioned but obliterated. While the map of Syria in 2013 reflected sectarian divisions across the country, this could hardly be good news for the regime given they were a regime of minorities. Sam Dagher's inside look at the Assad regime in *Assad or We Burn the Country* highlights the limitations of attracting a minoritarian approach to governance which centred a violent response and sectarianization over reconciliation, and de-sectarianizing (Phillips 2012; Dagher 2019).

As discussed previously in this chapter it was not simply Bashar Al-Assad and the elite who were sectarianizing the conflict, their influence spread throughout institutions. Institutions such as the national armed forces fostered the *'friend–enemy'* dichotomy. This dichotomy was fostered in a distinct way related both to sect and the relationship of the armed forces to violence. The coup-proofed nature of the regime along communal lines ensured a lack of defections from the upper echelons of the SAA, except for a small cadre of those who felt increasingly isolated by the regime and disagreed with Assad's violent approach. However, the distinct difference between the sect relationship of officers in the SAA and the rest of society and the use of such violence against citizens helped engender an antagonistic, fractious, war-like relationship between the officer class of the SAA and the citizenry (Khaddour 2015; Dagher 2019). Rather than creating the conditions for peace and sovereignty, it cemented continual contestation and war, eliminating sovereign control rather than strengthening it.

The Assad regime has not only institutionalized sectarianism inside regime structures but has actively used sectarian 'armed forces' outside of the framework of supposedly national institutions such as the SAA. The most prominent case of this is the use of the Shabiha as a way of utilizing sectarianism to build upon a ground base of support among the minority communities of Syria (Sullivan 2014; Phillips and Valbjorn 2018). The term 'Shabiha' was used in a narrow sense until the revolution where it referred to males, specifically males in strong Alawite families who were close to the regime, involved in smuggling and were brutal in their approach to those who defied them (Saleh 2012). But they remain defined by a couple of essential characteristics. First is the bond of blood and sect which links them to the ruling Assad family. Second is the hostility towards wider society which has led to a predisposition of practising violence against civilians (Saleh 2017). The Shabiha have been implicated in massacres across Syria with a sectarian element being at the core to mobilize young Alawites to the defence of the regime (Chapman 2014). In addition, there was also a mobilization of clans forming committees for pro-regime mobilization acting as a dual connector promoting regime support while sectarian violence was being meted out and the regime paying for members to pretend to commit sectarian acts to stir up communal tensions (Jasser 2014; Leenders and Giustozzi 2019).

The result of this was the intensification of the conflict and uprising. However, the result was not the production of a homogeneous united state clearly identifying the '*enemy*' that represents the apotheosis of sovereignty. Instead, the result was a disunited, fractured state that could not contain the violence it had unleashed on the citizenry. Rather than the state remaining a united homogeneous whole, it had lost control of large swathes of the country where armed gangs were responsible for much of the violence during the uprising. By increasing the sectarian overtones of the conflict by using the Shabiha championing repression but simultaneously de-centralizing violence via these non-state actors, this highlights the weakness of the state, a victim of their own attempts to control the conflict (Van Dam 2011).

These processes can be analysed via the '*friend–enemy*' distinction, homogeneity and the supposed sovereign god. Those who opposed the state were deemed internal '*enemies*', with the rhetoric and actions of the regime functioning as the bedrock of this designation. The homogeneous structure of the regime in its total loyalty to the Assad family meant that its support base necessarily narrowed. Assad hoping the coalition of minorities which has held the state together since the Assad family rose to power could continue to band together in order to defeat the largely Sunni armed rebellion who were considered '*enemies*' of the state necessarily created the conflict that continually defines the state today. The result is not a 'sovereign god' who can intervene at will over a homogeneous entity but a defanged sovereign, weak, desperate to retain office over a fractured broken state.

The relationship of sectarianism to politics highlights the problematic nature of building a decisionist state off the back of a minoritarian regime. The Assad regime has created a sectarian model of governance unable to satisfy a populace and contain disapproval of the regime. Sectarianism provided the framework for ruling via the *friend–enemy* distinction within the regime, leading to a breakdown of order in the state. This highlights the problematic nature of attempting to build a decisionist state which requires homogeneity when you represent a small subsection of the populace. Thus, rather than creating sovereignty and stability, the minority coalition standing by President Assad have declared *enemies* on the majority of the population, with the majority turning the *friend–enemy* dichotomy back on the state.

As Jasser (2014) has noted: 'Once the civil war started in 2011, Assad began pitting groups against each other and amplified long quiet ethno-sectarian divisions (59), highlighting the need to discuss 'quiet sectarianism' as opposed to simply 'loud sectarianism'. The ruling elite and security forces may have kept in check an outright rebellion until 2011, but this did not mean consensus or stability was provided politically. Political conditions such as chronic unemployment among the Arab Sunni majority, privatization and gobbling up of companies by the regime, and the disproportionate Alawite representation in positions going back to the 1920s allowed the Sunni vs Alawite schism to remain socially intact Hof and Simon 2013). Thus, the uprising created the opportunity for actors to release sectarian feelings and grievances, highlighting sectarianism not as a primary cause or feature of conflict on its own terms but something that can be used to mask other grievances (Haddad 2020; Wahab 2021). Thus, de-sectarianization can only take place once structural grievances and quiet sectarianism have been addressed in full, otherwise sectarianism can remain and be used to mask other forms of conflict.

Conclusion

To conclude, this chapter highlights exceptionalism is not necessarily a tool which enhances power and thus sovereignty but instead ultimately undermines both. The exception is not simply about the power to decide, after all we can all make exceptions to the rules, rather it is concerned with attaining the requisite authority to exercise the decision. The requisite authority within the decisionist state can be understood as the creation and maintenance of the homogeneous state. Exceptionalism is reliant upon the creation of a homogeneous state as a way of grounding decisionism, yet this necessary homogeneity is difficult to accomplish due to the ever-changing nature of politics and this is especially so in a heterogeneous state. The case study of Syria has demonstrated the inability to create a homogeneous form of state when practising sectarian politics as the Syrian state does.

Despite Schmitt advocating a state that rises above partisan political groupings, the state itself is politicized and needs to be for the *friend–enemy* dichotomy to exist. This creates a paradox inside the model that Schmitt advocates for where the *friend–enemy* dichotomy is supposed to bind together, but as the case study of Syria highlights it merely draws the state into defining the *friend–enemy* dichotomy. The chapter identifies the *friend–enemy* dichotomy being drawn in the form of sectarianism within the Syrian state.

The role that sectarianism has played in the Syrian state can directly be seen in the weakening of Assad's rule. Sectarianism as this chapter examines has become an increasing issue as the backdrop of the Assadist authoritarian structure. The Assadist state has always suffered from some amount of sectarianism – with the minority coalition maintaining a disproportionate amount of powerful positions among the hierarchy of the regime and armed forces. Alongside this, the Syrian state has maintained a state of emergency since 1963 and has consistently acted unilaterally and brutally to maintain the veneer of a 'homogeneous' state on paper with the adoption of Arab Nationalism.

However, since the death of Hafez Al-Assad and the rise of Bashar Al-Assad the state has become increasingly sectarianized, reaching a tipping point following the protests in 2011. Instead of responding to the protestors' concerns the sectarianized institutions of the state followed a similar trajectory to the response to the Hama uprising in 1982, that is, attempting to militarily crush the uprising. This approach was combined with a sectarian framing of the uprising by instrumentalizing sectarian identities to forge division during the civil war. By sectarianizing the institutions of the state and increasingly relying upon the sectarian Shabiha militias this has entrenched the friend–enemy dichotomy that prevails within the dynamics of the state and society. Indeed, Assad consistently claimed that the uprisings were the result of terrorists and appealed to Syria's minorities that a cleansing would be conducted if he were to lose control of the state. Assad attempted to make this a reality by releasing extremists from his own prisons to infect and radicalize the opposition.

The case study of Syria identifies the chronic weakness that in the face of an increasingly sectarianized state the authority of the sovereign has been corroded and the exercise of power through decisionism is insufficient to change this. Indeed, a decisionist state combined with sectarianism formulated by minority rule actively disrupts the sovereignty of the state rather than enforcing it. The results of the 2011 uprising and resulting civil war are not a renewed state but one which is internally weak and reliant upon outside actors. Ultimately, this has led to the majority of society seeing the regime itself as the *enemy*. This chapter highlights the overall weakness to the claim that exceptionalism is an exemplification of sovereignty, but can undermine sovereignty by using the Syrian case study to show this through the existence of sectarianism which undermines the political framework of the model of sovereign decisionism.

References

Abboud, S. N. (2018), *Syria: Hot Spots in Global Politics*, Cambridge: John Wiley.
Afzaal, M. O. *The Syrian Crisis: Sectarianism – a Foreign Agenda?* Centre for Strategic and Contemporary Research Islamabad, http://cscr.pk/pdf/rb/The%20Syrian%20Crisis.pdf

Al-Qarawee, H. H. (2004), 'Heightened Sectarianism in the Middle East: Causes, Dynamics and Consequences', *Theory and Society*, 33 (1): 31–64.

Al-Shami, L. and Yassin-Kassab, R. (2016), *Burning Country: Syrians in Revolution and War*, London: Pluto Press.

Alsarghali, S. (2020), 'Sectarianism and Constitutional Identity', *The Review of Faith & International Affairs*, 18 (1): 97–108.

Alvarez-Ossorio, I. (2012), 'Syria's Struggling Civil Society', *Middle East Quarterly*, 19 (2): 23–32.

Arditi, B. (2008), 'On the Political: Schmitt contra Schmitt', *Telos*, 2008 (142): 7–28.

Arendt, H. (1970), *On Violence*, Houghton Mifflin Harcourt.

Balanche, F. (2018), *Sectarianism in Syria's Civil War*, The Washington Institute for Near East Policy.

Beckstein, M. (2011), 'The Dissociative and Polemical Political: Chantal Mouffe and the Intellectual Heritage of Carl Schmitt', *The Dissociative and Polemical Political*, 16 (1): 33–51.

Bredekamp, H., Hause, M. T. and Bond, J. (1999), 'From Walter Benjamin to Carl Schmitt, via Thomas Hobbes', *Critical Inquiry*, 25 (2): 247–66.

Chapman, A. (2014), 'Defining and Dangerous? An Examination of the Assad Regime's Use of the Shabiha Militia in the Syrian Conflict'. Center for International Studies and Diplomacy Yearbook of Global Studies', School of Oriental and Asian Studies, *University of London*, 1 (1): 98.

Dagher, S. (2019), *Assad or We Burn the Country: How One Family's Lust for Power Destroyed Syria*, Hachette, UK: Little Brown and Company.

David Little (2011), 'Religion, Nationalism and Intolerance', in Tim Sisk (ed.), *Between Terror and Tolerance: Religious Leaders in Deeply Divided Societies*, Washington, DC: Georgetown University Press, 2011, 9–28.

Dean, M. (2013), *The Signature of Power: Sovereignty, Governmentality and Biopolitics*, London: Sage.

Diehl, J. (2012), 'Lines in the Sand: Assad Plays the Sectarian Card', *World Affairs*, 7: 7–15.

Doran, M. S. and Shaikh, S. (2011), *Syria: The Ghosts of Hama. The Arab Awakening, America and the Transformation of the Middle East, Part IV: States in Crisis*, The Brookings Institution, Washington, DC, 230–43.

Dukhan, H. (2014), 'Tribes and Tribalism in the Syrian Uprising', *Syria Studies*, 6 (2): 1–28.

Falk, H. (2013), 'What Should Be Done About the Syrian Tragedy? Citizen Pilgrimage', in *The Syria Dilemma*, edited by Nader Hashemi and Danny Postel, Cambridge, MA; London: The MIT Press, 61.

Falk, H. (2014), 'The "Theological Nihilism" of Friedrich Gogarten: On a Context in Karl Löwith's Critique of Carl Schmitt', *European Review*, 22 (2): 217–30.

Fielding-Smith, A. (2015), ASSAD'S 'AS IF', *The New Authoritarians: Ruling through Disinformation*, 25.

Fildis, A. T. (2011), 'The Troubles in Syria: Spawned by French Divide and Rule', *Middle East Policy*, 18 (4): 129–39.

Fildis, A. T. (2012), 'Roots of Alawite-Sunni Rivalry in Syria', *Middle East Policy*, 19 (2): 148–56.

Fischer, K. (2010), 'Hobbes, Schmitt, and the Paradox of Religious Liberality', *Critical Review of International Social and Political Philosophy: Thomas Hobbes and Carl Schmitt. The Politics of Order and Myth*, 13 (2–3): 399–416. https://doi.org/10.1080/13698231003787828.

Gelvin, J. L. (2015), *The Arab Uprisings: What Everyone Needs to Know. What Everyone Needs to Know*, New York: Oxford University Press.

Ghadry, F. N. (2005), 'Syrian Reform: What Lies Beneath', *Middle East Quarterly*, 12 (1): 61–70.

Goldsmith, L. (2011), 'Syria's Alawites and the Politics of Sectarian Insecurity: A Khaldunian Perspective', *Ortadoğu Etütleri*, 3 (1): 33–60.

Hadad, D. (2009), 'Human Rights in Syria: The Never-Ending Emergency', *International Journal of Middle East Studies*, 41 (4): 545–47.

Hadaya, S. (2020), 'Sectarianisation in Syria: The Disintegration of a Popular Struggle', *Conflict, Security & Development*, 20 (5): 607–29.

Haddad, F. (2017), '"Sectarianism" and Its Discontents in the Study of the Middle East', *The Middle East Journal*, 71 (3): 363–82.

Haddad, F. (2020), *Understanding 'Sectarianism': Sunni–Shi'a Relations in the Modern Arab World*, Oxford: Oxford University Press.

Hadaya, S. (2020), 'Sectarianisation in Syria: The Disintegration of a Popular Struggle', *Conflict, Security & Development*, 20 (5): 607–29.

Hashemi, N. and Postel, D. (2017), 'Sectarianization: Mapping the New Politics of the Middle East', *The Review of Faith & International Affairs*, 15 (3): 1–13.

Hashemi, N. (2016), 'Toward a Political Theory of Sectarianism in the Middle East: The Salience of Authoritarianism over Theology', *Journal of Islamic and Muslim Studies*, 1 (1): 65–76.

Hashemi, N. and Postel, D. (2017), 'Sectarianization: Mapping the New Politics of the Middle East', *The Review of Faith & International Affairs*, 15 (3): 1–13.

Hinnebusch, R. (2016), *The Sectarian Revolution in the Middle East*, Revolutions: global trends and regional issues.

Hoelzl, M. (2016), 'Ethics of Decisionism: Carl Schmitt's Theological Blind Spot', *Journal for Cultural Research*, 20 (3): 235–46.

Hof, F. C. and Simon, A. (2013), *Sectarian Violence in Syria's Civil War: Causes, Consequences, and Recommendations for Mitigation*. Paper commissioned by the Center for the Prevention of Genocide, United States Holocaust Museum.

Hohendahl, P. U. (2008), *Political Theology Revisited: Carl Schmitt's Postwar Reassessment*.

Hokayem, E. (2013), *The Regional Struggle over Syria. Syria's Uprising and the Fracturing of the Levant*.

Hokayem, E. (2017), *Syria's Uprising and the Fracturing of the Levant*, London: Routledge.

Ifergan, P. (2010), 'Cutting to the Chase: Carl Schmitt and Hans Blumenberg on Political Theology and Secularization', *New German Critique*, 37 (3 (111)): 149–71.

Jasser, M. Z. (2014), 'Sectarian Conflict in Syria', *Prism*, 4: 58–67.

Kassab, S. (2015), *The Resiliency of Authoritarianism: The Assad Regime of Syria*. NCUR.

Kawakibi, S. (2010), *The Private Media in Syria. The Knowledge Programme: Civil Society in West Asia*.

Kennedy, E. (2004), *Constitutional Failure: Carl Schmitt in Weimar*, Durham, NC: Duke University Press.

Khaddour, K. (2015), Assad's officer ghetto: Why the Syrian army remains loyal. The Carnegie Middle East Center. http://carnegie-mec. org/2015/11/04/assad-s-officer-ghetto-why-syrian-army-remains-loyal-pub-61449.

Kienle, E. (1995), 'Arab Unity Schemes Revisited: Interest, Identity, and Policy in Syria and Egypt', *International Journal of Middle East Studies*, 27 (1): 53–71.

Leenders, R. and Giustozzi, A. (2019), 'Outsourcing State Violence: The National Defence Force, 'Stateness' and Regime Resilience in the Syrian War', *Mediterranean Politics*, 24 (2): 157–80.

Lewis, B. (2002), *What Went Wrong? Western Impact and Middle Eastern Response*, Oxford: Oxford University Press.

Littell, J. (2015), *Syrian Notebooks: Inside the Homs Uprising*, London: Verso Books.

Lynch, M. (2013), 'The Entrepreneurs of Cynical Sectarianism', *Foreign Policy*, 13.

Mabon, S. (2017), 'Sovereignty, Bare Life and the Arab Uprisings', *Third World Quarterly*, 38 (8): 1782–99.

Mearsheimer, J. J. (2018), *Great Delusion: Liberal Dreams and International Realities*, New Haven, CT: Yale University Press.

Migdal, J. S. (2011), *State in Society: Studying How States and Societies Transform and Constitute One Another*, Cambridge: Cambridge University Press.

Mouffe, C. ed. (1998), *The Challenge of Carl Schmitt*, London: Verso.

Mouffe, C. (2000), *The Democratic Paradox*, London: Verso.

Nassif, H. B. (2015), 'Generals and Autocrats: How Coup-Proofing Predetermined the Military Elite's Behavior in the Arab Spring', *Political Science Quarterly*, 130 (2): 245–75.

Norris, A. (1998), 'Carl Schmitt on Friends, Enemies and the Political', Telos-St Louis Mo Then New York-, 68–88.

Pankakoski, T. (2013), 'Carl Schmitt Versus the "Intermediate State": International and Domestic Variants', *History of European Ideas*, 39 (2): 241–66.

Phillips, C. and Valbjørn, M. (2018), '"What Is in a Name?": The Role of (Different) Identities in the Multiple Proxy Wars in Syria', *Small Wars & Insurgencies*, 29 (3): 414–33.

Phillips, C. (2012), *After the Arab Spring: Power Shift in the Middle East?: Syria's Bloody Arab Spring*.

Phillips, C. (2015), 'Sectarianism and Conflict in Syria', *Third World Quarterly*, 36 (2): 357–76.

Pierret, T. (2014), 'The Syrian Baath Party and Sunni Islam: Conflicts and Connivance', *Middle East Brief*, 77 (2014): 1–8.

Quinlivan, J. T. (1999), 'Coup-proofing: Its Practice and Consequences in the Middle East', *International Security*, 24 (2): 131–65.

Robinson, G. E. (1998), 'Elite Cohesion, Regime Succession and Political Instability in Syria', *Middle East Policy*, 5 (4): 159–79.

Rustow, D. A. (1970), 'Transitions to Democracy: Toward a Dynamic Model', *Comparative Politics*, 2 (3): 337–63.

Saleh, Y. A. H. (2012), *The Syrian Shabiha and Their State*. Heinrich-Böll-Stiftung-Middle East Office.

Saleh, Y. A. H. (2017), *The Impossible Revolution: Making Sense of the Syrian Tragedy*. Oxford: Oxford University Press.

Saouli, A. (2019), 'Sectarianism and Political Order in Iraq and Lebanon', *Studies in Ethnicity and Nationalism*, 19 (1): 67–87.

Schmitt, C. (2005), *Political Theology: Four Chapters on the Concept of Sovereignty*. Chicago: University of Chicago Press.

Schmitt, C. (2008), *The Leviathan in the State Theory of Thomas Hobbes: Meaning and Failure of a Political Symbol*. Chicago: University of Chicago Press.

Selvik, K. (2014), *Roots of Fragmentation: The Army and Regime Survival in Syria*. CMI Insight.

Shapiro, K. (2008), *Carl Schmitt and the Intensification of Politics*, Rowman & Littlefield.
Suganami, H. (2007), 'Understanding Sovereignty through Kelsen/Schmitt', *Review of International Studies*.
Sullivan, M. (2014), *Hezbollah in Syria*. Institute for the Study of War.
Tralau, J. (2010), 'Order, the Ocean, and Satan: Schmitt's Hobbes, National Socialism, and the Enigmatic Ambiguity of Friend and Foe', *Critical Review of International Social and Political Philosophy*, 13 (2–3): 435–52.
Turner, B. S. (2002), 'Sovereignty and Emergency: Political Theology, Islam and American Conservatism', *Theory, Culture & Society*, 19 (4): 103–19.
Valbjørn, M. and Hinnebusch, R. (2019), 'Exploring the Nexus between Sectarianism and Regime Formation in a New Middle East: Theoretical Points of departure', *Studies in Ethnicity and Nationalism*, 19 (1): 2–22.
Van Dam, N. (2011), 'Syria: The Dangerous Trap of Sectarianism', *Syria Comment*, 14.
Wahab, H. (2021), 'Syria's Sect-coded Conflict: From Hezbollah's Top-down Instrumentalization of Sectarian Identity to Its Candid Geopolitical Confrontation', *Contemporary Review of the Middle East*, 8 (2): 149–67.
Wieland, C. (2012), 'Syria: A Decade of Lost Chances', *opendemocracy. net*, 29 (8): 2012.
Wimmen, H. (2014), *Divisive Rule: Sectarianism and Power Maintenance in the Arab Spring: Bahrain, Iraq, Lebanon and Syria*.
Wolin, R. (1990), 'Carl Schmitt, Political Existentialism, and the Total State', *Theory and Society*, 19 (4): 389–416.

Part II

REGIONAL DYNAMICS AND PROXIES

Chapter 4

THE DEAL OF DISCONTENT: SAUDI ARABIA, THE ISLAMIC REPUBLIC OF IRAN AND THE NUCLEAR DEAL

Olivia Glombitza

Introduction

The Iran nuclear deal, also known as the Joint Comprehensive Plan of Action or JCPOA, was preceded by more than ten years of intense negotiations until the final agreement was eventually signed in 2015 by the Islamic Republic of Iran and the five permanent members of the UN Security Council, that is, the United States, the UK, France, Russia, China as well as Germany. The deal prompted high expectations and was hailed as an historical deal that would further peace, stability and security by restraining the Islamic Republic's nuclear programme. However, with alliances seemingly shifting in favour of the Islamic Republic, tipping the balance of power in the region, the deal became a source of discontent for Saudi Arabia. Departing from the two countries' contrasting positions, with Saudi Arabia being critical of the nuclear deal and with the Islamic Republic being in favour of it, the chapter argues that the competition between the two countries has a symbolic dimension, where both parties aim at shaping the image of the Islamic Republic in accordance with their positions towards the nuclear deal. To this end, they are exercising symbolic power, which includes among others, the discursive employment of sectarian identities that have the potential to tap and feed into existing sectarian narratives. It further contends that both countries' foreign policy discourses are interdependent and are shaped by the symbolic discursive exchange on the international stage. The chapter examines how the political elite of Saudi Arabia and the Islamic Republic purposefully construct and strategically frame the other and the self, respectively, and how their discursive interaction and deployment of symbolic power in foreign policy discourse is on the one hand conducive to obstructing and on the other hand conducive to facilitating a process of de-sectarianization as well as endeavours of peace, security and stability. The timeframe examined ranges from the signing of the deal in 2015 until the United States' unilateral abandonment of it in 2018. Interrogating the creation of meaning for political ends, the chapter seeks to contribute to the literature on the rivalry between the Islamic Republic and Saudi Arabia, the instrumental mobilization of sectarian identities and to further add to the understanding of the complicated relationship between the two countries.

Since the establishment of the Kingdom of Saudi Arabia in 1932, Saudi-Iranian relations had been fluctuating regularly between moments of careful rapprochement and moments of ardent contestation. The Islamic Republic of Iran and Saudi Arabia are ambitious. And while both are continuously reiterating that they are interested in peace, stability and security in the region, however, at the same time, both of them also wish to emerge as leading regional actor. In this vein, each of them seeks to influence the regional order in their respective favour and both try to exert substantial influence on their neighbours in the region. Saudi Arabia sees itself as being at 'the core of the Arab and Islamic worlds' representing 'the heart of Islam' (Kingdom of Saudi Arabia 2017) and contends that 'geographic, cultural, social, demographic and economic advantages' and riches had enabled it 'to take a leading position in the world' (Kingdom of Saudi Arabia 2017). The Islamic Republic similarly understands itself as a 'solid regional power' with 'significant potential for a prominent regional and global role' (Zarif 2014: 52). Potential conflicts of interest seem inevitable. However, Saudi Arabia and the Islamic Republic depart from very different vantage points. The Islamic Revolution of 1979 signified a fundamental and abrupt turning point for Iran and its regional and international relations. It meant the rupture of old alliances and brought about a drastic reorientation and reordering of relations in line with the leaders' ideological vision of the country as an Islamic Republic on the one hand and the perception of the Islamic Republic's ambitions on the other hand. One of the casualties of that time was the Islamic Republic's alliance with the United States. No more was the country a regional anchor of American foreign policy or an 'island of stability'.[1] In consequence, Saudi Arabia was able to improve its position and traded places with the Islamic Republic to solely occupy the role as the United States' preferred partner in the region, whereas the Islamic Republic, now fallen from grace, was increasingly isolated and subsequently placed under long-lasting and intense sanctions. Not least due to its reignited and heavily scrutinized nuclear programme. With the advent of the nuclear deal, however, seemingly contributing to the normalization of relations with the Islamic Republic, the status quo of regional arrangements seemed to have reached a turning point. The Islamic Republic now seemed to have the chance to substantially better its position and international standing and to be able to emerge from the sanctions regime and to re-enter the international community and economic system. For some, the nuclear agreement was significant, because it meant increased security and stability by restraining the Islamic Republic's nuclear programme; for others, it meant the opposite, or so it is represented, a threat to security and stability and therefore to peace. In any case, a change in the balance of power was looming on the horizon, leading to increased discontent on part of Saudi Arabia, which was increasingly and strongly verbalized.

Nevertheless, the nuclear deal is certainly not the only issue or event that impacted or impacts on Saudi-Iranian relations. There is a whole host of other factors and issues, such as the wars in Yemen and Syria, for example, and for years their relationship has been oscillating between more and less favourable times. Sometimes relations were better, sometimes worse, but generally they were restrained and not really amicable. However, it remains to point out that their differences are not a result of – as often mediatized – a centuries-old conflict between religious denominations, that is, a conflict based on sect-based difference between a Saudi Arabia whose population mostly adheres to Sunni Islam and an Islamic Republic whose population mostly adheres to Shia Islam. While religion does play an important role in the political and social life of both countries, 'sectarianism is not an inherent historical quality' (Al-Rasheed 2017: 158), in neither Saudi Arabia nor the Islamic Republic. Among others, religious or sectarian identities are however, as this chapter will show, employed in political discourse in order to mobilize support both regionally and internationally (Mabon 2019: 26), by discursively legitimizing oneself and one's actions or by delegitimizing other actors and their actions. Sectarianism is therefore rather 'a modern political phenomenon that is nourished by persistent actors whose rule depends on invoking religious identities that become lethally politicized' (Al-Rasheed 2017: 158). The discursive act of positive self and negative other representation and, for this purpose, the discursive mobilization of salient identities occur within a frame that the political elite is on the one hand able to influence, but which, on the other hand, equally constrains them. As Warnaar (2013: 5) has pointed out, foreign policy discourse is a historical, ever-evolving and changing construct, which makes reference to other, previous discourses. While conditioned by a certain discursive frame, political elites take part in renegotiating, reshaping and reorienting this discursive frame over time (Warnaar 2013: 5). In the context of this chapter, this may be a conscious process, where the political elite refers to frames and narratives that are meaningful to their audience in order to mobilize support for political ideas and actions. As there is a deep connection between the domestic realm and the international, pronouncements on the international stage are never unidirectional, but reciprocally addressed to a domestic as well as an international audience. Topics that resonate with the domestic audience, such as shared beliefs or concerns, are therefore popular themes of symbolic value, and this includes shared religious beliefs (see Barnett 1998).

The chapter focuses on the discourses surrounding the JCPOA as well as the discourses of those members of the Saudi and Iranian political elite who are the most important representatives of their country on the international stage and in foreign policy-related issues. In what follows, the chapter will first provide useful context on the nuclear deal before drawing a brief sketch of the Saudi-Iranian relationship and their foreign policy priorities. The chapter then explores the theoretical background in order to understand how the Saudi and Iranian political elites use frames and narratives, that is, the deployment of symbolic power in their discourses, to influence the perception of the Islamic Republic.

The nuclear deal: Source of discontent

Hassan Rouhani's election as president of the Islamic Republic of Iran on 15 June 2013 marked a significant change after eight years of the neo-conservative government of his predecessor Mahmoud Ahmadinejad (see Ehteshami and Zweiri 2007). Since the beginning of its mandate, Rouhani's government had placed great importance on the pursuance of negotiations for a nuclear agreement, and it had also been one of Rouhani's most important campaign promises leading up to the elections. Under Ahmadinejad, the Islamic Republic had spiralled far away from potentially coming to an arrangement regarding Iran's nuclear activities. With Rouhani, however, such agreement had come again within close reach. Midway through Rouhani's first term (2013–2017), negotiations had made significant advances and eventually culminated in the JCPOA, signed on 14 July 2015 in Vienna. The deal had taken more than ten years to be negotiated and finalized. The signing of the deal led to the Islamic Republic experiencing a brief upsurge in its position in the international community and its relations with the world seemed to take a positive turn and improve after many years of negative press and containment. The Islamic Republic, just like its image, now seemed to rise like a phoenix from the ashes. Media coverage on the country also took a positive turn, and for a while, the Islamic Republic was represented in much more favourable terms than before the agreement. Apart from positive news coverage, a series of favourable reports and documentaries emerged, increasingly advertising the Islamic Republic as an appealing tourist destination, highlighting its ancient history and cultural sites and assets. But not only the Islamic Republic's image benefitted from the outcome of negotiations, also the outlook regarding economics and finances took an optimistic turn. With the signing of the JCPOA, the Islamic Republic's economy started to draw a long-denied breath and the growth rate increased significantly, while the inflation rate decreased to single digits. With a considerably large and young population, Iran constitutes a very attractive market for foreign investors. While Rouhani himself ventured out on a 'shopping trip', among others, to acquire much needed new aircraft for the country's ageing fleets, other countries were quick to send diplomatic and economic delegations to the Islamic Republic to be at the forefront of unearthing new business and investment possibilities. Future prospects were promising and initially, the signatories seemed satisfied with the deal. A year later, the enthusiasm that had gripped the Islamic Republic's government could be felt in President Rouhani's speech at the UN General Assembly on 22 September 2016. Full of optimism, Rouhani affirms that the nuclear deal 'confirmed the peaceful nature of Iran's nuclear program through devising confidence-building mechanisms, closing the so-called "possible military dimension" file and reinstating Iran's right to develop a peaceful nuclear program. This deal also put an end to unfounded concerns and led to the removal of the brutal sanctions against Iran' (Rouhani 2016). Nevertheless, a possible pull-out on part of the United States had already been looming on the horizon at that time. In 2017, the term of office of Democrat Barack Obama was followed by that of Republican Donald Trump. With the election of a new president, the United States had soon changed its stance on the nuclear deal and started to voice dissatisfaction with the overall framework. Before long, the euphoria initially surrounding the signing of the deal and the beginning normalization of the Islamic Republic's foreign relations, the positive aspirations quickly turned sour. Less than three years after its inception, the United States unilaterally withdrew from the JCPOA, reinstated sanctions and subsequently began a campaign of maximum pressure on the Islamic Republic. Both moves have been supported by Saudi Arabia (Al-Jubeir 2019), who considered the JCPOA to be a weak deal.[2] Until the US' withdrawal, however, Saudi Arabia had started to grow increasingly uneasy in regard to the possibilities opening up for the Islamic Republic and therefore the potential consequences that were arising from the JCPOA for the regional balance of power and consequently itself. As a result, Saudi-Iranian relations reached a new low point.

Saudi–Iran relationship

Describing the Saudi-Iranian relationship, while remaining tacitly optimistic about future developments, Al-Badhi has remarked that 'geography has made the two countries neighbors, but history has not made them friends, economics has not made them partners, and necessity has not made them allies' (Al-Badi 2017: 189). Saudi Arabia and the Islamic Republic aspire to occupy equally powerful and dominant positions in the region and positions of influence in the international system, leading to regular disputes and conflicts. While the relation between Saudi Arabia and the Islamic Republic is marked by periodical changes in amicability, ranging from tacit rapprochement to the hostile breakdown of diplomatic relations, both states' interaction with one another is overall conditioned by a drive for regional influence and competition over the oil market. In this sense, the nature of their relation is therefore marked by geopolitics rather than religion and their at times complicated relationship is consequently a product of conflicting interests rather than sect-based difference (Matthiesen 2013: 20). With foreign policy serving to balance domestic politics, the struggle of Saudi Arabia and the Islamic Republic at foreign policy level also reveals the battles that both countries fight at the domestic level to secure the continuity of existing structures of power (Mabon 2018: xiii).

The Iranian Revolution represents a major turning point in Iran's contemporary history. From the perspective of the Islamic Republic, in the words of its foreign minister Mohammad Javad Zarif (2014: 51), 'the repercussions were drastic, and the revolution deeply affected the country's foreign relations, not only in its immediate neighborhood but also throughout the greater Middle East and the rest of the world'. A major consequence for the revolutionary Islamic Republic was its increasing isolation by regional and international actors. Since the revolution, the Saudis were the sole occupants of a position that the Islamic Republic could not challenge anymore from its place in isolation. Before the revolution, both countries had been allied with the United States, which subsequently turned its back on the

Islamic Republic after the rupture of relations and elevated Saudi Arabia as its main anchor and energy provider in the region. A mutually beneficial relationship, where in exchange the United States acted as Saudi Arabia's security provider. Ongoing tensions and developments during the timeframe of analysis have given rise to much speculation about the possibility of a direct military confrontation between Saudi Arabia and the Islamic Republic. While to date, they are not engaging in a direct war with one another, they do, however, assume militarily active or passive supporting roles for opposing sides in a number of regional conflicts, such as the wars in Yemen and Syria (see Phillips 2016) or in other hotly contested arenas such as Lebanon, Iraq, the Gulf states or even Afghanistan.

In addition, there are a number of other issues of contention, leading repeatedly to disputes. One of them is the *Hajj*, the annual pilgrimage to Mecca, which represents an important and indispensable pillar in the exercise of the Islamic faith.[3] Though following different currents of Islam, the annual *Hajj* and the holy cities of Mecca and Medina are equally important to Muslims of both countries. Although there are numerous other popular holy cities open to pilgrimages, and particularly the sites in Kerbala and Najaf in Iraq have increasingly been promoted by the Islamic Republic and, hence, gained in importance, they are no substitute to Mecca. Consequently, every year, Saudi Arabia is the recipient of a large flow of pilgrims and will therefore always occupy a special role when it comes to the annual ritual of pilgrimage. Nonetheless, not every year is peaceful and various incidents during the *Hajj* itself have further contributed to the souring of relations on a regular basis (Graham-Harrison, Kamali Dehgan and Mohammed Salih 2015). The *Hajj* has been highly politicized for decades and depending on the state of relations between Saudi Arabia and the Islamic Republic, Saudi Arabia might decide not to open its doors, while the Islamic Republic might ask its citizens to refrain from travelling there (Bozorgmehr and Kerr 2016; Reuters 2016). The last time the Islamic Republic 'boycotted' the *Hajj* was after the breakdown of diplomatic relations in 2016, following an attack on the Saudi embassy in Tehran in January of the same year that succeeded in the execution of Shia cleric Sheikh Nimr al-Nimr in Riyadh.

Saudi and Iranian foreign policy priorities

Saudi Arabia

Foreign policy is an important means of engagement for Saudi Arabia and the Islamic Republic on a regional and international scale. However, it is also an important tool when it comes to supporting domestic politics and accomplishing domestic priorities and safeguarding their national interests. They share these objectives as well as a desire for peace, security and stability in the region. In consequence, both name the region as their foremost foreign policy priority.

It is the kingdom's vision to lead 'Saudi diplomacy to achieve and safeguard national interests, and promote the Kingdom's contribution to security, stability

4. The Deal of Discontent

and prosperity in the region and in the world' (Kingdom of Saudi Arabia Ministry of Foreign Affairs 2016). On the domestic front, Saudi Arabia seeks to modernize the country, to foster a large number of changes and to explore new avenues of income in preparation for the post-oil era. With its Vision 2030, Saudi Arabia sets forth an ambitious national project, driven by the Saudi leadership in order to effect changes that will lead to the diversification of its economy and the development and strengthening not only of a number of different public service sectors such as health, education, infrastructure, recreation and tourism, but also of sectors such as mining, minerals as well as innovation and technology. By opening up new areas of investment, Saudi Arabia seeks to attract not only domestic but also new foreign investors (Al-Jubeir 2019). While becoming less oil dependent in the coming years, the overall aim is to sustain and develop other parts of its economy. At the same time, Saudi Arabia faces a growing, young population that demands change, but not less comfort and security than previous generations. It becomes a balancing act to sustain the traditional Saudi social contract amidst a shifting regional power structure and to satisfy the aspirations of a growing, majorly young population. The empowerment of Saudi Arabia's youth is therefore one of its main domestic policy priorities, along with the empowerment of women, the opening up of public spaces and the encouragement of a culture of innovation and technology (Al-Jubeir 2019). Promoted and projected in positive terms both at home as well as abroad, these changes are not only important Saudi domestic policy priorities but in fact essential pillars for the realization of Crown Prince Mohammad Bin Salman's Vision 2030. And furthermore, providing people with opportunity, with hope and with jobs, according to Al-Jubeir (2019), is ultimately also a way to secure domestic stability and peace.

What is it that Saudi Arabia is looking for in the region? With domestic politics being its utmost priority and in order to be able to pursue overriding domestic goals such as the preservation of domestic stability and domestic relations of power, Saudi Arabia is looking for a stable region to be able to concentrate on its internal affairs (Al-Jubeir 2019). In that spirit, Saudi Arabia's foreign policy priorities focus on the neighbours that surround it, across the Persian Gulf and the Red Sea. In line with their aims, this includes particular focal points and sources of tension with the Islamic Republic such as Syria, Yemen, but also Iraq, Lebanon, the Gulf States – particularly Bahrain and Qatar – and Afghanistan.

In Syria, a conflict where the Islamic Republic and Saudi Arabia have taken up opposing positions, with the Islamic Republic supporting the regime of Bashar Al-Assad and Saudi Arabia supporting several opposition groups, Saudi Arabia – though militarily involved – is looking for a political settlement. However, this settlement shall result, according to the Saudi view, in 'a stable, unified Syria with no Iranian influence' (Al-Jubeir 2019). Similarly, in Yemen, a strategically important country for Saudi Arabia, Saudi Arabia and the Islamic Republic find themselves on opposing sides. The Islamic Republic, however, is much less militarily involved than often portrayed. And here too, Saudi Arabia is looking for a political process that will lead to 'a unified Yemen, and the objective is a Yemen in which Iran has no role'.[4] In Iraq, Saudi Arabia would like to foster trade relations and investment in an overall stable Iraq, which from the Saudi perspective would equally necessitate a retreat on the part of the Islamic Republic. Lebanon represents another arena where both actors seek to exert influence. Saudi Arabia's endeavours became apparent in 2017, when Lebanese Prime Minister Saad Hariri resigned publicly on live television and failed to return to Lebanon as planned, when on official invitation in Saudi Arabia. However, shortly after arriving back in Lebanon, he resumed his post. Lebanon is also home to Hezbollah, a politically and militarily active, Shia Islamist movement, often portrayed as a 'puppet of Iran' or 'Iranian proxy' because of its alliance of interdependence with its religio-political patron, the Islamic Republic of Iran (Saouli 2019). In the eyes of the Saudis, Hezbollah is simply a 'terrorist group'.[5] Saudi Arabia is also the main instigator of an ongoing diplomatic crisis and blockade of the neighbouring state of Qatar, which started in 2017, according to Al-Jubeir 'because Qatar continues to fund extremists and terrorists and continues to involve itself in our internal affairs'.[6] The blockade hasn't been lifted since. In Afghanistan, Saudi Arabia seeks to exert influence on the balance of power by mediating between the government and the Taliban (Al-Jubeir 2019). Across the Red Sea, Saudi Arabia actively engages with countries such as Ethiopia, Eritrea and Djibouti, which have endured a long-lasting severance of relations with one another.

Nonetheless, Saudi Arabia's greatest concern remains its most important competitor for regional influence, the Islamic Republic of Iran. The Islamic Republic is perceived as a threat and an obstacle to Saudi Arabia achieving the goals it has set for itself. The leadership is therefore interested in supplanting the Islamic Republic by diminishing 'Iranian influence' (Al-Jubeir 2019) across the region.

The Islamic Republic

Similar to Saudi Arabia, the Islamic Republic's foreign policy priorities are closely connected to its domestic priorities. As mentioned earlier, the Islamic Republic's economy had been badly affected by the years of sanctions and isolation prior to the nuclear deal. As a consequence, the Islamic Republic experienced growing economic hardship, including difficulty to trade oil, its most important asset and primary source of foreign currency. Also tensions with countries within and outside of the region had risen perceptibly. As a result, the new government is under heavy pressure and therefore, improving the economic situation and stabilizing the internal state of affairs was a primary objective for Rouhani and his government. The path to this went through the improvement of international relations in order to emerge from the ongoing and decades-long isolation, to re-enter the international financial system and regain legitimacy on the international stage. Rouhani and his government build on a more pragmatic approach on the international stage and reengage in dialogue in order to seek relief from the sanctions and to enable the Islamic Republic to re-enter the international community (Glombitza and Zaccara, 2021). The nuclear deal forms part of a series of efforts by subsequent Iranian governments to normalize relations on a regional and international level.

The nuclear deal was an opportunity to gain trust, better its foreign relations and, therefore, its economic and financial situation.

In line with the constitution, but in contrast to the preceding government of Ahmadinejad, Rouhani placed his fortunes on fostering the normalization of relations with countries in the region and beyond with an approach of constructive engagement (Glombitza and Zaccara, 2021). In commitment to its identity as an Islamic Republic, among the obligations of the government set forth in the Iranian Constitution,[7] the government is supposed to 'develop foreign policy based on Islamic standards, brotherly obligations vis-à-vis all Muslims and unqualified support for all the oppressed nations of the world'.[8] In an article published in 2014 in *Foreign Affairs*, the Foreign Minister Mohammad Javad Zarif laid out further principles of post-revolutionary Iranian foreign policy, which include

> the preservation of Iran's independence, territorial integrity, and national security and the achievement of long-term, sustainable national development. Beyond its borders, Iran seeks to enhance its regional and global stature; to promote its ideals, including Islamic democracy; to expand its bilateral and multilateral relations, particularly with neighboring Muslim-majority countries and nonaligned states; to reduce tensions and manage disagreements with other states; to foster peace and security at both the regional and the international levels through positive engagement; and to promote international understanding through dialogue and cultural interaction. (Zarif 2014: 49)

In addition, the constitution underlines that while supporting 'the rightful struggle of the oppressed people against their oppressors anywhere in the world', the Islamic Republic would completely refrain 'from any interference in the internal matters of other nations'.[9] Interference in the internal affairs of others is in fact a major point of criticism towards the Islamic Republic from the Saudi side, which will be discussed later in the chapter.

Similar to Saudi Arabia's foreign policy priorities, apart from a focus on domestic politics, its region and its neighbours are the Islamic Republic's main concern (Zarif 2013) and a peaceful, stable and secure region is cited as desirable aim (Araghchi 2018). Not unlike Saudi Arabia, the Islamic Republic advocates for political settlements for ongoing conflicts rather than military solutions (Araghchi 2018). These include the previously mentioned wars in Syria and Yemen in the preceding section on Saudi Arabia's foreign policy priorities. Regional focal points overlap with those of Saudi Arabia and those are, apart from Syria and Yemen, Iraq, Lebanon, the Gulf States and Afghanistan. Promoting dialogue, the Islamic Republic is looking to first improve its relations in the Persian Gulf region through initiating a regional dialogue forum, with the potential to extend it to the neighbouring area (Araghchi 2018).

Therefore, regionally, the Islamic Republic's first priority is its neighbours in the Persian Gulf, and this is because the Islamic Republic believes that its own domestic security and stability is intertwined with the stability and security of other countries in the region (Zarif 2013). Consequently, while pursuing its aims regarding the normalization of relations with Western countries, the normalization of relations with regional states, that is, particularly the states comprising the Gulf Cooperation Council (GCC), such as Saudi Arabia, the United Arab Emirates, Bahrain, Kuwait, Oman and Qatar, is equally important to the Islamic Republic. In the foreign minister's own words, 'in our interconnected world, the fate of one nation is tied to the destinies of its neighbors' (Zarif 2013). The Rouhani government has therefore endeavoured to engage with the region in general and the GCC countries in particular through the launch of a set of discursive and practical measures including initiatives such as the 'World Against Violence and Extremism' (WAVE), the 'Hormuz Peace Endeavor' (HOPE) as well as strategies of discursive persuasion that were supposed to build confidence, enhance the Islamic Republic's image and to overall improve the country's foreign relations (Glombitza and Zaccara, 2021). All in the spirit of dialogue, exercising what the foreign minister calls 'constructive interaction', he directs attention to common interests, common threats and common challenges, but also common opportunities and a common destiny that Saudi Arabia and the Islamic Republic share with the rest of their neighbouring countries (Zarif 2013). Zarif (2013) cites a number of so-called imperatives for common security and development. Among those are the prevention of tension in the region, curbing extremism and terrorism, the promotion of harmony between various Islamic sects, the preservation of the Islamic Republic's territorial integrity, the assurance of the Islamic Republic's political independence, ensuring the free flow of oil and the protection of a shared environment.

Frames, narratives and the projection of symbolic power

In their interactions with one another as well as with third parties Saudi Arabia and the Islamic Republic are engaging regularly and repeatedly in strategic framing and the creation of narratives about themselves, current and past affairs and, importantly, about others. As the chapter argues, the competition that Saudi Arabia and the Islamic Republic engage in has a symbolic dimension and both of them equally endeavour to shape the image of the Islamic Republic in accordance with their convictions. In so doing, they are capitalizing, among others, on the symbolic power of discursive phenomena such as narratives and frames to legitimize or delegitimize themselves or the other and their actions respectively. The discourses are interdependent, and each narrative produces a reply or counter-narrative. To understand Saudi Arabia's and the Islamic Republic's purposeful representation of the other and the self respectively through narratives and frames, the following section discusses what narratives and frames actually are and the potentials ascribed to them.

Narratives are a powerful means to interpret and make sense of the world around us and through narratives it is possible to connect with and to transmit political views to an audience in a more direct way than through the mere use of rational arguments. Because of their more immediate quality, prospective recipients more easily internalize messages that are conveyed through narratives (De Fina 2018: 239). When narratives are employed purposefully to reach certain goals, they become strategic: the goal being here to direct one's audience to act or think in a way they otherwise might not have done (Miskimmon, O'Loughlin and Roselle 2013: 34). Concretely, 'strategic narratives are representations of a sequence of events and identities, a communicative tool through which political actors, usually elites – attempt to give determined meaning to past, present, and future in order to achieve political objectives. Critically, strategic narratives integrate interests and goals – they articulate end states and suggest how to get there' (Miskimmon, O'Loughlin and Roselle 2013: 7). In this sense, actors' strategic goals include, among others, the legitimation and delegitimation through positive and negative self- and other representation and 'may be designed with short-term and/or long-term goals in mind' (Miskimmon, O'Loughlin and Roselle 2013: 11). By constructing a shared meaning of the past, present and future of political circumstances through strategic narratives, political actors are able to shape the behaviour of other actors domestically and internationally (Miskimmon, O'Loughlin and Roselle 2013: 3). In consequence, strategic narratives become 'a tool for political actors to extend their influence, manage expectations, and change the discursive environment in which they operate' (Miskimmon, O'Loughlin and Roselle 2013: 3). In this sense, the one who is able to dominate or influence certain narratives, and the ways in which they are told, consequently occupies a powerful position (Bottici 2010: 919). And especially when narratives are widely shared and circulated through the media and especially social media, narratives are capable of shaping 'public perception about politically relevant events, relations and people' (De Fina 2018: 236). Furthermore, they filter into people's minds and become part of their habitus through a process of 'accrual' (De Fina 2018: 237). In this context, Ali Ansari (2006: 5) has observed, 'an opinion repeated often enough becomes fact. Consensus becomes common sense, and common sense structures our thoughts.'

However, it is important to point out that while political actors engage in the strategic use of narratives, their ability to construct them is not limitless. Strategic narratives are malleable and dynamic and subject to a continuous process of negotiation and re-negotiation. And they are also shaped by political actors' interactions with their societies, their own and their societies' belief system and by the 'domestic and international political contexts, the communication environment, and the goals of the political leadership' (Miskimmon, O'Loughlin and Roselle 2013: 6–7). In other words, the 'parameters of a state's strategic narratives are bounded by prevailing domestic and international understandings and expectations of that state, readings of its history, and evaluations of its reputation' (Miskimmon, O'Loughlin and Roselle 2013: 11). In this sense, narratives are understood here as both, as structuring the thoughts and actions of actors as well as tools of persuasion (Miskimmon, O'Loughlin and Roselle 2013: 20). In order to work, the narrative needs to be embedded in the political or social imaginary and resonate in a certain context with a certain audience, at home and abroad. In other words, while actors have a certain amount of agency, they are also constrained by existing structures.

Frames make narratives more tangible, by adding an evaluative, categorizable interpretation. Frames make an event politically meaningful and intelligible by situating it 'within a particular story line in order to locate that event, organize the experience, and guide the action' (Barnett 1998: 40–1). Frames are 'specific metaphors, symbolic representations, and cognitive cues used to render or cast behavior and events in an evaluative mode' (Zald 1996: 262) and therefore take part in shaping our interpretation of the world. They are established and preconceived ideas that are activated in people's minds through the use of certain language, that is, certain terms. In order to make reference to an existent frame and hence to conjure up certain ideas, terms that connect to that frame will be used. Once a frame is created and established through repetition, it can be called upon any time. Frames, as mental structures, are invisible, but nonetheless are defining our approach to our environment, how we perceive it and how we interpret it. In other words, framing consists of the filtering of certain elements of reality and the reassembly into a comprehensive narrative. Frames therefore do influence how we act, think, feel, form an opinion and take decisions. Consequently, through a dedicated and focused process of reframing public discourse, by using different language repeatedly, it is possible to change how the public sees the world. Therefore, careful and strategic framing constitutes a means for actors to advance their interests and thus, they compete over the representation of certain events, other actors or also themselves in order to shape people's view of them. Put differently, in Lisa Wedeen's (2015) words, 'politics is not merely about material interests but also about contests over the symbolic world, over the management and appropriation of meanings'. Frames shape actors' self- and other representation and serve to legitimize and delegitimize the actions of the other and the self and to enhance or diminish the image of the self and the other, that is, influence how the world interprets actors, their actions and behaviour and, in consequence, to galvanize regional and international support for their positions. This power of influence is referred to here as symbolic power. Studying the deployment of symbolic power tells us a lot about how the two actors themselves *would like* to be perceived and how the other *should* be perceived. Through strategic framing and the construction of strategic narratives, actors define and enable certain postures, actions, what can or cannot be said about oneself and others. In this sense, the purposeful employment of sectarian identities is not necessarily the expression of the feeling of a threat, but rather deployed for strategic aims because of a fear of losing power or influence, at home and abroad.

Strategic framing of the self and the other and the formation of narratives

The advent of the nuclear deal tapped into Saudi Arabia's fears of a change in the regional balance of power and that the Islamic Republic would be empowered to significantly expand its influence and cross-border relations, with Saudi Arabia falling far behind. This is reflected in the way Saudi Arabia represents the Islamic Republic discursively, where it can be observed that Saudi Arabia is generally portraying the Islamic Republic as a threat and, in order to do so, frames the Islamic Republic in explicitly negative terms, which is supposed to evoke suspicion, insecurity, distrust and fear. With this, Saudi Arabia is offering an interpretation of the character, behaviour and actions of the Islamic Republic, aimed at delegitimizing the Islamic Republic and therefore affect change in the way other states view and deal with the Islamic Republic. For every narrative Saudi Arabia produces about the Islamic Republic, the Islamic Republic delivers a counter-narrative about itself. Consequently, while engaging in the construction of narrative and counter-narrative, Saud Arabia and the Islamic Republic mutually shape their discourses through this exchange. While their discourses are pronounced on the international stage, in what can be considered foreign policy discourse, they are never unidirectional. They are reciprocally directed at an international as well as a domestic audience. Saudi Arabia and the Islamic Republic equally try to appeal to the international and regional community, their relations and allies, their contenders, as well as their own population and the population of the other.

In principle, Saudi Arabia is continuously and repeatedly resorting to the same narratives and frames and they permeate Saudi's official communication on the Islamic Republic. Narratives formed by Saudi representatives that are especially prominent include: 'Iran talks pretty, but its actions show otherwise'; 'Iran intends to export the revolution'; 'Iran commits and supports acts of terrorism'; 'Iran interferes in other countries' affairs'. An opinion piece published in the *New York Times* in early January 2016, written by then Saudi foreign minister Adel Bin Ahmed Al-Jubeir (2016) where he asks, 'Can Iran Change?', serves to exemplarily exhibit some of these narratives:

> The world is watching Iran for signs of change, hoping it will evolve from a **rogue** revolutionary state into a respectable member of the international community. But Iran, rather than confronting the isolation it has created for itself, opts to **obscure** its **dangerous sectarian** and **expansionist** policies ... The Iranian government's behavior has been consistent since the 1979 revolution. The constitution that Iran adopted states the objective of **exporting** the revolution. As a consequence, Iran has supported **violent extremist groups**, including Hezbollah in Lebanon, the Houthis in Yemen and **sectarian militias** in Iraq. (author's emphases)

Al-Jubeir uses negatively connoted, classificatory adjectives to frame the Islamic Republic, its actions and relations. The inference that the recipients of this discourse are supposed to make is that while the Islamic Republic *should* be a respectable member of the international community, in fact, it *is* a rogue revolutionary state that acts in obscure, dangerous, sectarian and expansionist ways and all the while supports violent extremist groups and sectarian militias. The excerpt bears the implicit question, 'knowing all of this, how can you trust the Islamic Republic?' The reference to expansionary policies and the export of the revolution along with references to its activities in Lebanon and Yemen are supposed to display the

Islamic Republic's interference in other countries' affairs and its disregard for their sovereignty. In this context, an intention of restoring the Persian Empire and to take over the region is alluded to alongside the supposed call for the destruction of Saudi Arabia in accordance with Khomeini's will.[10] The use of qualitatively negative nouns and adjectives to construct frames of crime, violence and terror plays on feelings of fear and insecurity and brings the Islamic Republic in close association with illegality, dishonesty and illegitimacy. Sectarianism here has a clear negative connotation and is used to underline divisionary practices on the part of the Islamic Republic. While conceding that relations with the Islamic Republic have not always been poor, and there is hope for a betterment of current relations in the future, nevertheless,

> after the revolution of 1979, Iran embarked on a policy of **sectarianism**. Iran began a policy of expanding its revolution, of interfering with the affairs of its neighbors, a policy of assassinating diplomats and of attacking embassies. Iran is responsible for a number of terrorist attacks in the Kingdom, it is responsible for smuggling explosives and drugs into Saudi Arabia. And Iran is responsible for setting up **sectarian** militias in Iraq, Pakistan, Afghanistan and Yemen, whose objective is to destabilize those countries. (author's emphases)[11]

The Islamic Republic is largely portrayed as responsible for acts of crime and terror in Saudi Arabia and the immediate and further region. The negative framing contributes to shaping the perception of the Islamic Republic and therefore to delegitimize the Islamic Republic and its actions and to offset the Islamic Republic's narratives about itself. The terms 'assassination, attack, terror, smuggle, drugs and militias' equate the Islamic Republic to a criminal and illegitimate actor instead of a legitimate self-interested acting state in the region. In response, and in connection to the sectarian allegations, the Islamic Republic puts forward the following during the UN General Assembly in 2016, where President Rouhani declares:

> Iran opposes any kind of sectarianism and any attempt to promote religious gaps. The Muslim people, be they Shi'as or Sunnis have and continue to live together for centuries in harmony and mutual respect. Attempts to turn religious dissimilarities into tense confrontations is rooted in vested interests of certain countries, which try to hide their quest for power covered in religious slogans. (Rouhani 2016)

President Rouhani portrays the Islamic Republic as actively rejecting the mobilization of sectarian identities for political ends, while at the same time promoting the unity of Muslims. In line with this statement, the Islamic Republic overall tries to strike a rather conciliatory tone regarding its foreign relations, and particularly when it comes to its neighbours. The Islamic Republic seeks to portray itself as benevolent, cooperative and trustworthy, possessing a good portion of 'team spirit'. To this end, emphasis is generally placed on togetherness, common goals and guiding principles such as mutual respect and non-interference that should inform relations in order to achieve a better outcome for all countries of the region (Zarif 2013: 2). At the inception of his assignment, the Islamic Republic's foreign minister Mohammad Javad Zarif stresses therefore, for example, common bonds of religion, history and culture and assures the neighbours of the Islamic Republic that they had a reliable partner in the Islamic Republic that extended its hand in friendship and Islamic solidarity to them (Zarif 2013: 2). Thus, as outlined previously, the Islamic Republic's primary foreign policy priority is its region and its neighbours (Zarif 2013: 1). And, in fact, in the opinion of the foreign minister, good neighbourly relations in the immediate and further neighbourhood and the mutual consideration of interests are pivotal for the Islamic Republic's own national security. Zarif has written in this context that 'prosperity cannot be pursued at the expense of others' poverty, and security cannot be achieved at the expense of the security of others. We will either win together or lose together. We are capable of working together, trusting one another, combining our potential, and building a more secure and prosperous region' (Zarif 2013: 1). In this continuous competition to influence and shape the perception of itself, the counter-narratives that the Islamic Republic produces in response to the Saudi narratives include, 'our nuclear program is for peaceful purposes only'; 'nuclear energy is our right'; 'we do not interfere in the affairs of others, we respect the sovereignty of other countries'; 'our neighbors are our priority, and we extend our hand in friendship'.

Furthermore, apart from recounting the present, Saudi Arabia regularly and frequently resorts to narrating a number of specific past events to show that the Islamic Republic's behaviour has a recurring pattern and that it is not a phenomenon exclusive to the present. Reaching into the past, Al-Jubeir, therefore, seeks to evoke a projection and extrapolation of the Islamic Republic's expected future conduct. The revolution of 1979 is used to mark a decisive moment and turning point in Iran's behaviour. According to Saudi Arabia, 'the Iranians are on a rampage and have been on a rampage since 1979' (Al-Jubeir 2019) and 'since the Iranian revolution forty years ago, all we've seen from Iran is death and destruction'.[12] The 'nefarious' actions that the Islamic Republic is supposed to have committed since the revolution, as claimed by Saudi Arabia, include attacks on embassies in Beirut and Tehran, the kidnapping and assassination of Saudi diplomats as well as diplomats of other nationalities, an attack on the Hajj, the blow-up of Khobar Towers in Saudi Arabia and a synagogue in Argentina (Al-Jubeir 2019). The stated past events and actions, showing 'a consistent record of evil',[13] that Saudi Arabia finds condemnable, are brought up time and again. They are cited with regular frequency and purposefully connect the Islamic Republic to frames of crime, terror and unlawfulness. The intended message that is supposed to be understood by the audience is that even if the Islamic Republic talks pretty today, it cannot be trusted, as since 1979, there has not been a positive change in its 'murderous' and 'aggressive' behaviour and all they have engaged in were criminal activities.[14] The continuous repetition of these negative statements about the Islamic Republic is supposed to permanently influence the image of the Islamic Republic in a derogatory way and to gradually turn into facts.

The nuclear deal is placed in this context of a criminally acting Islamic Republic, that would receive now even more money to further its previously described and negatively portrayed activities in the region: 'The Iranians took money from the nuclear deal, and they used it to double down in Syria, and Yemen, and Iraq, and they increased the budgets for the Revolutionary Guards and the Quds Forces.'[15] In addition, while using 'the income from the JCPOA in order to fund its mischievous activities', the Islamic Republic 'didn't use that income to improve the living standard of its people' (Al-Jubeir 2019). Al-Jubeir lends himself as witness to underline the argument by giving it the strength of a personal testimony: 'I personally have not read about any infrastructure project that Iran did since the nuclear deal. I haven't heard of them building a university or hospital.'[16] In this sense, the Islamic Republic is said to not only carry out reprehensible activities but also to do so to the disadvantage of its people. The Saudi foreign minister is building on the presupposition that if actions are carried out to the detriment of one's own people, they cannot be justified by any means. Because of the Islamic Republic's incorrigible nature, Saudi Arabia 'would like to see actions rather than words' (Al-Jubeir 2019) and this means 'no nukes for Iran under any scenario whatsoever, no missiles, and no terrorism and interference in the affairs of other countries'.[17]

The Islamic Republic counters the allegations by referring to a fatwa by Khamenei that it had 'never had the intention of producing a nuclear weapon' (Rouhani 2015) and that its programme was for peaceful purposes only.[18] Contrary to Saudi Arabia's perspective, the Islamic Republic does of course not portray itself as prime instigator of regional discord, instability and insecurity, but rather as a catalyst for peace, security and stability:

> Any objective analysis of Iran's unique attributes within the larger context of its tumultuous region would reveal the country's significant potential for a prominent regional and global role. The Islamic Republic can actively contribute to the restoration of regional peace, security, and stability and play a catalytic role during this current transitional state in international relations. (Zarif 2014: 52)

By implication, anyone rationally assessing the Islamic Republic should be inclined to agree with Iran's foreign minister. However, this, by further implication excludes Saudi Arabia. Still, the Islamic Republic promotes regional engagement and cooperation with all actors and the nuclear deal is portrayed as enabling these activities that will bring the region together in reciprocally beneficial ways:

> After the JCPOA, Iran will stand ready to show that the practical path to security and stability is through the development that comes with economic engagement. … Iran is also eager to show that we can all choose a lasting peace based on development and shared interests that will lead to a sustainable security rather than a volatile peace based on threats. We hope to engage with our neighbors in a wide range of social and economic cooperation, which will enable the achievement of political understanding and even foster structural security

cooperation. In the international system today, mutual economic ties are deemed the foremost factors in facilitating political cooperation and reducing security-related challenges. (Rouhani 2015)

With the intention to build trust and regional legitimacy and to enhance the image and perception of the Islamic Republic, Iranian officials are bringing the Islamic Republic in close association with positively connoted terms such as contribution, development, shared interests, engagement, cooperation as well as achievement and links itself with regional desirabilities such as peace, security and stability. Just as Saudi officials repeat its narratives about the Islamic Republic, Iranian officials are repeating their own positively framed narratives about the country throughout official communication channels attempting to dominate public perception, and therefore the ways in which the Islamic Republic and its actions are interpreted and dealt with. For Saudi Arabia, the way forward, however, before any cooperation can happen is summed up in a statement by Al-Jubeir:

> So change your policy. Become a good neighbor. Stop this nonsense of terrorism, implanting terrorist cells, assassinations, providing ballistic missiles to militias. Stop that, respect the sovereignty of nations, ..., and international law, and we'd love to be your best friend.[19]

Conclusion

The quest for international, regional, but also domestic legitimacy permeates the discourses of both countries' officials and their symbolic exchange on the international stage is simultaneously directed at an international and a domestic audience. The nuclear deal signified a major incision in the regional balance of power, going beyond but also amplifying the effects of any other current issue or conflict on the regional status quo. The chapter has examined how Saudi Arabia and the Islamic Republic are engaging in the purposeful and strategic construction of frames and narratives to evaluate, qualify and categorize the character and actions of the Islamic Republic in accordance with their respective positions towards the implementation of the JCPOA. Saudi Arabia had grown ever more uneasy about the upheaval in the regional equilibrium and started to increasingly proliferate the portrayal of the Islamic Republic as a threat to the region and beyond.

Through their discursive interaction, conditioned by the signing of the nuclear deal, both actors aim therefore at dominating the public perception of the Islamic Republic. Saudi Arabia does so by employing frames and narratives that contribute to delegitimizing and negatively representing the Islamic Republic, its actions and relations, while the Islamic Republic aims at positive self-representation and the legitimation of itself and its actions. To this end, their deployment of symbolic power in foreign policy discourse includes the mobilization or demobilization, for that matter, of sectarian identities. The chapter has demonstrated that the upsurge in sectarian language in foreign policy discourse is directly related to political tensions and alterations or potential alterations in the balance of power and regional order. The use of sectarian language makes these alterations or potential alterations palpable and intelligible. The competition of words over representation and perception will continue until both states settle comfortably in their positions and will feel their priorities and interests fulfilled. Until then, and because words matter, their discursive struggle over influence and legitimacy to ultimately secure their own regimes' survival will continue to make its mark on possibilities for regional peace, stability and security.

However, with the United States unilaterally abandoning the nuclear deal in 2018, the Saudi narrative seemed to have gained vindication at the time and therefore the upper hand in the contest over shaping the perception of the Islamic Republic. However, the United States remains a critical factor in Saudi-Iran relationship, a factor that conditions also what is discursively possible. The US presidential elections of November 2019 resulted in Democrat Joe Biden becoming president. While the United States continues to maintain its relations with Saudi Arabia, they have significantly cooled down and President Biden has continued to voice criticism of the country's leadership, resulting in the capping of Saudi Arabia's discursive boldness. Under President Biden, the United States also started to resume talks with the Islamic Republic and the remaining signatories of the 2015 nuclear deal to renegotiate it. While negotiations remain inconclusive to date, a potential agreement might yet again alter the situation by influencing the Islamic Republic's position in the international system and the balance of power anew.

Notes

1 During a brief stopover in Iran on New Year's Eve 1977, Jimmy Carter had called Iran an 'island of stability', only a little more than a year before the Shah left Iran and the Islamic Revolution. See Gil Guerrero 2016: 57.
2 A Conversation with Minister Adel Al-Jubeir of Saudi Arabia.
3 Essentially, there are two different types of pilgrimage. The *Hajj*, carried out once a year during certain specified periods, and the *Umrah*, which is shorter than the *Hajj* and subject to less stringent requirements and can be carried out any time during the year.
4 A Conversation with Minister Adel Al-Jubeir of Saudi Arabia.
5 A Conversation with Minister Adel Al-Jubeir of Saudi Arabia.
6 A Conversation with Minister Adel Al-Jubeir of Saudi Arabia.
7 See the Iranian Constitution and particularly articles 3, 152–5.
8 Iranian Constitution, p. 11.
9 Iranian Constitution, article 154.
10 A Conversation with Minister Adel Al-Jubeir of Saudi Arabia 2019.
11 Interview with Al-Jubeir in Der Spiegel, 2016.
12 A Conversation with Minister Adel Al-Jubeir of Saudi Arabia 2019.
13 A Conversation with Minister Adel Al-Jubeir of Saudi Arabia.
14 A Conversation with Minister Adel Al-Jubeir of Saudi Arabia.

15 A Conversation with Minister Adel Al-Jubeir of Saudi Arabia.
16 A Conversation with Minister Adel Al-Jubeir of Saudi Arabia.
17 A Conversation with Minister Adel Al-Jubeir of Saudi Arabia 2019.
18 Opening Debate between Mohammad Javad Zarif and David Ignatius. https://securityconference.org/en/medialibrary/collection/munich-security-conference-2015/.
19 A Conversation with Minister Adel Al-Jubeir of Saudi Arabia.

References

Al-Jubeir, A. (2016), 'Can Iran Change?' *New York Times*. 19 January 2016. Available online: https://www.nytimes.com/2016/01/19/opinion/saudi-arabia-can-iran-change.html (accessed 30 July 2020).

Al-Jubeir, A. (2019), *Saudi Arabia's Foreign Policy Priorities*. Royal Institute of International Affairs. 21 October 2019. Available online: https://chathamhouse.soutron.net/Portal/DownloadImageFile.ashx?objectId=3483 (accessed 30 July 2020).

Ansari, A. (2006), *Confronting Iran*, London: Hurst.

Al-Rasheed, M. (2017). "Sectarianism as Counter-revolution: Saudi Responses to the Arab Spring." In *Sectarianization: Mapping the New Politics of the Middle East*, edited by N. Hashemi, and D. Postel. London: Hurst, 143–58.

Al-Rasheed, M. (2010), *A History of Saudi Arabia*, Cambridge: Cambridge University Press.

Araghchi, Abbas H. E. (2018), *Iran's Foreign Policy Priorities*. Royal Institute of International Affairs. 22 February 2018. Available online: https://chathamhouse.soutron.net/Portal/DownloadImageFile.ashx?objectId=1304 (accessed 30 July 2020).

Barnett, M. (1998), *Dialogues in Arab Politics*, New York: Columbia University Press.

Basic Law of Governance of the Kingdom of Saudi Arabia, 1992. Available online: https://www.saudiembassy.net/basic-law-governance (accessed 30 July 2020).

Bottici, C. (2010), 'Narrative', in Mark Bevir (ed.), *Encyclopedia of Political Theory*, Thousand Oaks, CA: Sage, 919–20.

Bozorgmehr, N., and Kerr, S. (2016), 'Iran Boycotts Hajj as Anger with Saudi Arabia Grows'. *Financial Times*. 30 May 2016. Available online: https://www.ft.com/content/0ac4c056-2666-11e6-8b18-91555f2f4fde (accessed 30 July 2020).

Council on Foreign Relations (2019), *A Conversation with Minister Adel al-Jubeir of Saudi Arabia*. Tuesday, 24 September 2019. Available online: https://www.cfr.org/event/conversation-minister-adel-al-jubeir-saudi-arabia-0.

De Fina, A. (2018), 'Narrative Analysis', in Ruth Wodak and Bernhard Forchtner (eds), *The Routledge Handbook of Language and Politics*, Abingdon: Routledge, 233–46.

Ehteshami, A., and Zweiri, M. (2007), *Iran and the Rise of Its Neoconservatives*, London: I.B. Tauris.

Gil Guerrero, J. (2016), *The Carter Administration & the Fall of Iran's Pahlavi Dynasty*, New York: Palgrave Macmillan.

Graham-Harrison, E., Kamali Dehgan, S. and Mohammed Salih, Z. (2015), 'Hajj Pilgrimage: More Than 700 Dead in Crush Near Mecca'. *The Guardian*, 24 September 2015. Available online: https://www.theguardian.com/world/2015/sep/24/mecca-crush-during-hajj-kills-at-least-100-saudi-state-tv (accessed 30 July 2020).

Glombitza, O. and Zaccara, L. (2021), 'The Islamic Republic's Foreign Policy through the Iranian Lens: Initiatives of Engagement with the GCC', *The International Spectator*, 56 (4): 15–32.

Islamic Republic of Iran (1989), 'The Constitution of the Islamic Republic of Iran'. *Islamic Consultative Assembly*. Available online: http://en.parliran.ir/UploadedData/previmages/iran-parliament_English_SHR01.pdf (accessed 30 July 2020).

Kingdom of Saudi Arabia (2017), 'Vision 2030'. Available online: https://vision2030.gov.sa/sites/default/files/report/Saudi_Vision2030_EN_2017.pdf (accessed 30 July 2020).

Kingdom of Saudi Arabia Ministry of Foreign Affairs (2016), '*Ministry's Vision*'. Available online: https://www.mofa.gov.sa/sites/mofaen/aboutMinistry/vision/Pages/default.aspx (accessed 30 July 2020).

Mabon, S. (2018), *Saudi Arabia and Iran: Power and Rivalry in the Middle East*, London: I.B. Tauris.

Mabon, S. (2019), 'Desectarianization: Looking beyond the Sectarianization of Middle Eastern Politics', *Review of Faith and International Relations*, 17 (4): 25–35.

Matthiesen, T. (2013), *Sectarian Gulf*, Stanford, CA: Stanford University Press.

Miskimmon, A., O'Loughlin, B. and Roselle, L. (2013), *Strategic Narratives: Communication Power and the New World Order*, Abingdon: Routledge.

Phillips, C. (2016), *The Battle for Syria*, London: Yale University Press.

Reuters (2016), 'Iranian Pilgrims Won't Attend Hajj Amid Row with Saudi Arabia'. *The Guardian*, 29 May 2016. Available online: https://www.theguardian.com/world/2016/may/29/iran-pilgrims-will-not-attend-hajj-amid-row-with-saudi-arabia (accessed 30 July 2020).

Saouli, A. (2019), *Hezbollah: Socialisation and Its Tragic Ironies*, Edinburgh: Edinburgh University Press.

Shafy, S., and Zand, B. (2016), *Der Spiegel*, interview with Saudi Foreign Minister Adel Al-Jubeir, 2016. 'I Don't Think World War III Is Going to Happen in Syria'. Available online: https://www.spiegel.de/international/world/interview-with-saudi-foreign-minister-adel-al-jubeir-on-syrian-war-a-1078337.html (accessed 30 July 2020).

United Nations. Statement by H.E. Dr. Hassan Rouhani, President of the Islamic Republic of Iran at the General Debate of the General Assembly of the United Nations. New York, 28 September 2015.

Warnaar, M. (2013), *Iranian Foreign Policy during Ahmadinejad: Ideology and Actions*, New York: Palgrave Macmillan.

Wedeen, L. (2015), *Ambiguities of Domination*, Chicago: University of Chicago Press.

Zald, M. N. (1996), 'Culture, Ideology, and Strategic Framing', in D. McAdam, J. McCarthy and M. Zald (eds), *Comparative Perspective on Social Movements: Political Opportunities, Mobilizing*, New York: Cambridge University Press, 261–71.

Zarif, M. J. (2014), 'What Iran Really Wants: Iranian Foreign Policy in the Rouhani Era', *Foreign Affairs*, 93 (3): 49–59.

Zarif, M. J. (2013), 'Our Neighbors Are Our Priority', *Iran Times*, 29 November 2013.

Chapter 5

SECURITIZATION OF SHI'A TO 'VIOLIZATION': A RESPONSE TO THE ARAB SPRING IN BAHRAIN

Samira Nasirzadeh

Introduction

On the first day of protests at the Pearl Roundabout in 2011, security forces of the Al Khalifa regime arrested a Sunni citizen for criticizing the government's policies of granting citizenship to foreigners (Interviewee 6, Code 6: 29 January 2020), which changed the demographic structure of the country. However, the Al Khalifa regime labelled the massive demonstrations in 2011 a 'Shi'a-led' uprising against the Sunni minority regime; the presence of Sunni protestors revealed the nature of the cross-sectarian national movement of uprisings in Bahrain. The largest non-sectarian protests in the history of Bahrain, demanding social, political and economic reforms as a result of long-standing grievances of Bahrainis, shook the power of the Al Khalifa ruling family during the Arab Spring of 2011.

The failure of counter-revolutionary policies of the Al Khalifa ruling family to control the massive protests at home led to locating demonstrations in a geopolitical regional struggle to give domestic issues a regional character by calling its Shi'a citizens 'agents' (Gengler 2015: 148) for Iran in order to receive military aid from its allies. These divisive policies, manipulated by the regime to counter the revolution, not only fuelled sectarian tensions within Bahraini society but also intensified the regional security environment of the Middle East. Through the successful manipulation of securitization via sectarianization both domestically and regionally, the Al Khalifa family gave the green light to Saudi Arabia for intervention in Bahrain and a crackdown on Bahrainis, which led to using force against Bahraini citizens. In the following section, this chapter will explore the theoretical and conceptual frameworks of 'securitization' and 'sectarianization', which led to a form of 'violization' in Bahraini society, and its transformation into a regional geopolitical struggle.

Securitization theory and the 'sectarianization' thesis

Since March 2011, many Shi'a Bahrainis have been forced to leave their homeland due to violent counter-revolutionary measures instigated by the Al Khalifa regime. In contrast to a number of successful demonstrations during the Arab Spring to overthrow authoritarian regimes in the Arab world, the failure of the Bahraini revolution led to the Al Khalifa family remaining in power. However, the failed revolution in Bahrain can be scrutinized at three levels: national, regional and international; this chapter explores the national and regional levels of the securitization process, which led to systematic violence against Shi'a citizens. To do this, the chapter applies the securitization framework from the Copenhagen School, focusing on the securitization of Shi'a as short-term strategy of the Al Khalifa regime to retain power post-2011. After securitization, the regime, to preserve its long-term stability, manipulated systematic 'violization' against its Shi'a citizens. The contribution of this chapter is to consider the extent to which securitization of the Shi'a population through 'sectarianization' shifted to systematic methods of religious and cultural 'violization', thus changing the demographic structure of Bahrain for long-term stability. To facilitate this analysis, I will develop the argument through insights from interviewees who experienced securitization through 'sectarianization' and 'violization' within Bahrain.

The so-called Copenhagen School introduced a 'new' security agenda driven by political, economic, societal and environmental aspects to international relations (Buzan et al. 1998). As Buzan, Wæver and De Wilde contend, 'security is about survival, it is when an issue is presented as posing an existential threat to a designated referent object … the special nature of security threats justifies the use of extraordinary measures to handle them' (Buzan et al. 1998: 21). Furthermore, it raises the question of 'what makes something a security problem'. Wæver explains that securitization is about the 'construction of issues as security problems' (Wæver 2000: 252). Hence, '(de)securitisation combines the politics of threat design with that of threat management' (Wæver 2011: 472). In other words, securitization studies seek to understand 'who pursues security, on what issues (threats), for whom (referent objects), why, with what results, and not least, under what conditions' (Buzan et al. 1998: 32). The final stage in the securitization process is the use of force to fend the 'threat' off.

Considering the prominent feature of securitization theory, which is the use of extraordinary measures, it justifies the suspension of 'normal' politics. However, some scholars have criticized the Western-liberal features of the theory, as normal politics differs in 'non-Western' contexts (Bilgin 2011; Huysmans 1998: 483; Wilkinson 2007: 5, 2010: 96). With regard to the Middle East, normal politics itself is nonetheless 'problematic', but all states have rules to govern the society and the suspension of normal politics means the suspension of particular rules within the country (Mabon 2019a: 44). Thus, the suspension of particular rules and laws can be seen as the suspension of 'normal' politics to apply securitization theory in Middle Eastern case studies.

The central role of securitization theory is to explain the 'effects' of securitization in case studies (Wæver 2003: 18). Within the Middle Eastern context, it is possible to 'anticipate' whether a condition or case is more or less likely to be securitized; some cases, due to 'mutual fear' perceptions among the actors, are more likely to be securitized (Wæver 2000: 252). In the Middle East, where religion and politics are intertwined, 'religion serves as a mechanism for regimes to secure their legitimacy and survival' (Mabon 2019a: 45). With this in mind, Arab rulers perceived a 'threat' from minority groups, leading to framing the 'other' as a security 'threat' to their survival within and outside their borders. Since the Arab Spring, top-down 'sectarianism' has been manipulated by some authoritarian regimes to ensure their survival (Gause 2020: 38; Mabon 2018; Matthiesen 2013; Valbjørn 2018: 46). The 'top-down' process of religious securitization during the Arab Spring led to a divide between rulers and ruled and within plural societies. In Bahrain, the Al Khalifa regime succeeded in framing Shi'a groups as a security 'threat' to the stability of the regime and the country, it targeted Sunni audiences through security speech acts against the Shi'a, which intensified the sectarian rift between Sunni and Shi'a – locally and regionally – in order to legitimize the use of force against Shi'a Bahrainis via the Saudi-led intervention of Bahrain.

The successful process of securitization of Shi'a in Bahrain ensured the failure of the Bahraini revolution. However, the regime's manipulation of 'sectarianization' provided fertile ground for such a successful process. Meanwhile, the Bahraini uprising in 2011 has been considered a political 'project' manipulated by an authoritarian regime to divide the society into sectarian blocs. As defined by Hashemi and Postel (2017: 4), 'sectarianization is a process shaped by political actors operating within specific contexts, pursuing political goals that involve popular mobilization around particular religious identity markers. Class dynamics, fragile states and geopolitical rivalries also shape the sectarianization process.' Within Bahrain, where the regime feels threatened by the majority Shi'a population, the use of 'sectarianization' to block cross-sectarian movements and divide society into Sunni–Shi'a kin can be considered as an effective tool for the regime. Via the successful manipulation of securitization through 'sectarianization' in Bahrain, the Al Khalifa regime could ensure its short-term survival in 2011.

To understand the failure of the Bahraini revolution in 2011, it is necessary to explore the successful use of securitization through the 'sectarianization' framework of the regime in the divided society of Bahrain. To do this, I have argued elsewhere in a co-authored article how the 'sectarianization' thesis fills a gap in securitization theory. First, we add 'religion' as an independent security sector, which has basically been considered under the societal sector in securitization theory, and the prescient role that religious identity can play. Second, I address the Western understanding of securitization theory, whereas the 'sectarianization' thesis sheds light on specific contexts in the Middle East as far as securitizing practices are understood and articulated (Nasirzadeh and Wastnidge 2020: 25). Regarding the contribution of this chapter to bridge the gap between the two frameworks in order to analyse the Bahraini case, the models show how 'sectarianization' as a tool can be used in specific 'contexts', such as Bahrain, to fill a gap in securitization theory. However, while securitization theory has been used to analyse Middle Eastern cases, more specifically, 'sectarianization' helps to understand the particularity of contexts like Bahrain. To be more specific, 'sectarianization' is an instrument manipulated by the Al Khalifa regime in the plural society of Bahrain through the mobilization of a Shi'a identity to ensure the short-term survival of the regime. Viewing Bahrain as a 'specific' case, which is located at the heart of the regional geopolitical competition between Saudi Arabia and Iran, the manipulation of 'sectarianization', which results in the securitization of Shi'a, is more likely to happen.

Securitization of Iran as seen by domestic and regional audiences since 1979

In the case of Bahrain, wherein the 'threat' perception of the Sunni Al Khalifa regime from the Shi'a population is fabricated within political discourse, the securitization of Iran is more likely to happen. A number of scholars have explored it in the context of regional 'rivalry' between Sunni Arab monarchies with Iran, which has dominated the security calculations of Arab regimes, particularly Saudi Arabia (Chubin and Tripp 1996; Fürtig 2007; Keynoush 2016; Mabon 2012, 2013; Mason 2014; Matthiesen 2013). With this in mind, the emergence of a Shi'a state in 1979 within a Sunni-dominant region altered the security environment of the region. While Middle Eastern rulers have long relied on the West – particularly the United States – as a 'security guarantor' (Mason 2014), the Islamic Republic rejected dependence on the West for its security and autonomy.

Since the emergence of the Islamic Republic of Iran, the foreign policy agenda of Iran has been challenging the claim of leadership of Saudi Arabia over Muslim countries. In the meantime, the fundamental principles of the foreign policy of Iran have led to the rise of a 'threat' perception among Arab regimes from Iran. The fundamental foreign policy agenda of the Islamic Republic includes: '1) rejection of all forms of external domination, 2) preservation of Iran's independence and territorial integrity, 3) defence of the rights of all Muslims without allying with hegemonic powers, 4) the maintenance of peaceful relations with all non-belligerent states' (Ehteshami and Zweiri 2008: xiii). For the House of Saud, the emergence of a Shi'a state, which challenges its Wahhabi interpretation of Islam and rejects an absolute monarchical system, is perceived as a primary 'threat' to its foreign policy. Within this context, the Shi'a population of Sunni countries has often been linked to Iran by Sunni rulers, labelling them 'agents' of Iran (Gengler 2015: 148), and undeniably playing a key role in the current turmoil in the Middle East.

Historically, the Shi'a population within Sunni Arab countries has been viewed as the primary source of 'threat' to the survival of Middle Eastern regimes. Thus, any rise of Shi'a groups within and outside the borders of Sunni regimes has been considered a 'threat' to the survival of their rulers. In the meantime, the security environment of the Middle East has been exacerbated by the US invasion of Iraq in

2003, which led to the emergence of an Iraqi Shi'a government in the post-Saddam era. As Wehrey (2014: 8) articulates, the invasion of Iraq provided fertile ground for the 'activation' of a Shi'a identity once again post-1979 in the region. The shift of power from a Ba'athist regime to a Shi'a government in Iraq has been perceived as a double 'threat' to the Arab monarchies, in which the balance of power has shifted in favour of Iran (Fürtig 2007; Mason 2014; Terrill 2011; Wehrey 2009, 2014). The events in Iraq, which led to the activation of Shi'a groups, exacerbated the 'threat' perception of Sunni Arab regimes vis-à-vis Iran and Shi'a power.

Since 2003, the 'anti-Shi'a' and 'anti-Iran' rhetoric has become entrenched in the political discourse of frightened Sunni regimes and alarms internal, regional and international audiences of Iranian influence in the region. Accordingly, the King of Jordan, Abdullah II, in 2004 coined the term 'Shi'a Crescent' (*al-Hilal ash-Shi'i*), explicitly warning Sunni rulers about Iranian power in the Middle East (Wright and Baker 2004: A01). In this respect, Jones argues for a sense of 'victimhood' by Sunni Arab rulers to justify their prejudice and discrimination against the Shi'a population both domestically and regionally, while ignoring the colonizing of the Middle East by the US invasion (Jones 2020: 94). More specifically, Saudi Arabia has attempted to spread its 'anti-Shi'a position of official Wahhabism throughout the Muslim world' (Gause III: 12; Mabon 2019a; Matthiesen 2013: 21). Consequently, Sunni rulers have embraced such speech acts by iterating them to a domestic audience, particularly within plural societies with both Sunni and Shi'a populations. Sunni rulers have by default linked the Shi'a of Arab countries to Iran, perceiving them as a security 'threat' to their regimes' survival.

Considering the 'threat' perception of Arab rulers from Shi'a citizens, and by default Iran, the Al Saud and Al Khalifa ruling families, by linking the Shi'a population to Iran, have often justified their discriminatory policies towards Shi'a citizens prior to and post-2011. More specifically, in Bahrain, where a Sunni minority regime rules over a Shi'a majority population, regional geopolitical conflicts feed into the security rhetoric against Shi'a, and by default Iran. As Jones contends, there is 'overemphasis' of the Islamic Revolution in Iran as a motivation for the 'anti-Shi'a' and 'anti-Baharna' discourse in Bahraini politics, while exaggeration of the effect of the Iranian Revolution on Bahraini politics has diverted attention from exploring the discriminatory political system of Bahrain to securitizing the Shi'a since independence (Jones 2018). Such a system of discrimination against the Shi'a population has intensified since the Arab Spring in Bahrain 2011.

Securitization through 'sectarianization' in Bahrain

Regarding the population of Bahrain, estimated to be 60–70 per cent Shi'a and 30–40 per cent Sunni, demographics in Bahrain have often been an issue in the country (Bassiouni 2011: 13). However, sectarian, tribal and ethnic variety in Bahrain has often been viewed by the regime as a 'threat' to its survival. In this respect, Matthiesen argues that if these groups share some linguistic or ethnic affiliation with a powerful neighbour, then securitization is even more 'effective'

(Matthiesen 2017: 201). To counter this 'threat', since 2011, the Al Khalifa regime has attempted to alter the demographic structure of Bahrain, so that now half of the population of Bahrain consists of non-citizens (Hafidh and Fibiger 2019: 114). Within this context, Bahraini society is more likely to become involved in geopolitical regional tension regarding its Sunni–Shi'a religious identities, Arabs and ethnic Persian groups.

Moving from the regional sphere to the domestic level, the 'threat' perception of the Shi'a majority population by the regime has led to constant friction between rulers and ruled within Bahrain. With this in mind, the speech act of the 'Shi'a Crescent' has been embraced by the regime of Al Khalifa, with regard to its majority Shi'a population. The Al Khalifa regime, by polarizing Bahraini society into Sunni and Shi'a citizens, has ensured its survival for decades. Thus, the divisive policy of the regime led to long-term discrimination against the Shi'a population within the islands, leading to long-standing grievances among the population.

Bahrainis have long been suffering from political, social and economic discrimination targeting the majority population. Historically, since the 1920s, every ten years Bahrain has witnessed demonstrations demanding civil rights and political and social reform. For instance, in the 1990s, the protests lasted for four years and led to the death of dozens of people, the exile of many families and human rights violations (Al-Khawaja 2014: 190). The 1990s uprisings marked the highest level of conflict between rulers and ruled prior to the Arab Spring in 2011. In the meantime, the death of Emir Isa, the Bahraini ruler, on 6 March 1999, led to a pause in the uprisings. As a result, Sheikh Hamad bin Isa Al Khalifa, son of the former ruler, became the new ruler of Bahrain (Joyce 2012: 111). The new emir, Sheikh Hamad, graduated from the British military academy at Sandhurst as an experienced military commander and assumed power in Bahrain (Jehl 1999).

To end the intifada, the so-called 'reformist' (Gengler 2013: 54) king promised to return the 'suspended' constitution of 1973, the people believed him and the 1999 uprisings ended (Al-Khawaja 2014: 190). Accordingly, in February 2001, the 'National Action Charter' was presented to the people in a referendum that promised a parliament with full legislative power. But in 2002, the king – calling himself king not emir – 'reneged' on his promises and announced a new 'constitution', through which power was concentrated in the king of Bahrain. The parliament, in contrast to the referendum promise, has no legislative powers (Zill 2012). As a result, the promised political reforms have not been accomplished, leading to continuity in the grievances of the Bahraini people regarding the Al Khalifa regime in subsequent years.

However, the 1990s uprisings having been ended by fake promises, and the long-standing grievances of Bahraini citizens led to the largest protests in the country's history in 2011. The long-term social, political and economic grievances brought demonstrators into the streets in line with the Arab Spring across the region in 2011. In response to the Arab Spring, the regime launched a massive crackdown on the population and took counter-revolutionary steps to tackle the protests within Bahrain. Long-standing grievances led to massive protests within the context of the Arab Spring. As Lynch (2012: 109–10) articulates, like in Yemen,

Bahrain's revolution emerged in the context of long-lasting political unrest seeking democratization. In light of the Arab Springs, Bahrainis went into the streets to air long-standing grievances on 14 February 2011.

Inspired by the Tunisian revolution, the Bahraini people aired long-standing grievances, such as unfulfilled promises and the return of political trials, torture and arrests by the regime (Al-Khawaja 2014: 190–1). However, the Arab Spring in Bahrain can be seen as the apex of multilayered grievances that surfaced on the 'day of rage' (Hafidh and Fibiger 2019); the regime labelled the national, non-sectarian demonstrations in Bahrain 'Shi'a-led Uprisings', 'Shi'a protests' and actions of the 'Shi'a majority' (Gengler 2015: 143). This sectarian speech act, manipulated by the regime, sought to divide protestors into Sunni and Shi'a to prevent the spread of revolution.

The Bahraini regime, by the manipulation of securitization through sectarianization during the Arab Spring, ensured its short-term survival. The ultimate goal of the Al Khalifa regime was to preserve its survival at any cost. Thus, securitization of the Shi'a through sectarianization was the only way for the regime to remain in power. Unlike in Tunisia and Egypt, Libya and Yemen, where dictators were overthrown (Bayat 2017: 156; Matthiesen 2013), the revolution in Bahrain failed to topple the authoritarian regime of Al Khalifa. The failure of the revolution in Bahrain can be discussed in terms of the sectarian counter-revolutionary policy of the regime. In the following discussion, I will explore how cross-sectarian Bahrainis' movements were crushed by the regime through 'sectarianization', leading to the securitization of Shi'a at the national and regional levels.

Securitization through 'sectarianization' at the regional level

Bahraini society with its Shi'a majority population remains fertile ground for securitization through 'sectarianization' at the regional level. Within this context, for Saudi Arabia, Bahrain remains a 'red line' (Mabon 2012). Hence, it was unlikely that the House of Saud would leave its strategic ally alone during the Arab Spring. The importance of Bahrain for Riyadh shifted the security stance of Saudi Arabia from indirect involvement to direct intervention in Bahrain in 2011. The process of securitization through sectarianization, manipulated by the Al Khalifa regime to divert attention from internal turmoil to borders, has intensified the regional security environment. By locating Bahrain at the heart of the geopolitical struggle between Saudi Arabia and Iran, the Al Khalifa regime achieved support from its ally Saudi Arabia to ensure its survival.

More specifically, the Al Khalifa regime's failure to control the protests within its borders played a crucial role in changing the unrest into a regional geopolitical conflict. As Mabon argues, the Al Khalifa ruling family sought to 'locate the struggle within broader geopolitical events, thus ensuring that regional allies remain committed to the regime' (Mabon 2019b: 42). On the other hand, by framing the Shi'a as a 'fifth column', both the Al Saud and Al Khalifa regimes convinced 'intended' and 'unintended' audiences that Iran was behind the unrest in Bahrain (Mabon 2019a: 42). To increase the fear of Sunni audiences of their fellow Shi'a citizens and Shi'a in neighbouring countries, both the Al Khalifa and Al Saud ruling families framed the demonstrators as 'agents' of Iran to put an end to the cross-sectarian movement in order to control the unrest at any cost.

In fact, the Al Khalifa regime's policy served two purposes in 2011: first it delegitimized any Shi'a-led opposition activity demanding reform by calling them 'agents' of Iran. Second, by portraying the protests as a 'foreign meddling' plot, the Al Khalifa regime played a 'divide-and-rule' card to stop any unification of cross-sectarian movements (Ulrichsen 2013: 9). It can be said that the intelligence strategy of securitization through 'sectarianization', manipulated by both Al Khalifa and Al Saud, legitimized the use of force against the Shi'a population internally and externally. To legitimize its intervention in Bahrain, Riyadh and Manama played an intelligence card in the form of regional 'sectarianization' of Shi'a and Iran to convince audiences of the need for military action against Shi'a Bahrainis.

Securitization through 'sectarianization' at the regional level was guaranteed via massive political, military and economic patronage of GCC states amounting to around US$10bn paid to the Al Khalifa regime to crack down on its people (Shehabi and Jones 2015: 21). King Hamad bin Isa Al Khalifa, on 21 March 2011, praised the Saudi-led intervention, while blaming Iran for the protests within Bahrain. The king declared: 'I do hereby announce the failure of the subversive plot fomented against security and stability' (Independent 2011, 21 March). As Jones argues, the Al Khalifa regime has always been able to play off the regional geopolitical struggle between Saudi Arabia and Iran for its own 'benefit' (Jones 2020: 333). The attempt of the Al Khalifa regime to locate the domestic unrest in a geopolitical regional struggle with Iran to distract from its internal issues led to a reaction from Iran to the claim. In response, the Supreme Leader of Iran, Ayatollah Sayyed Ali Khamenei, criticized the Saudi-led intervention in Bahrain, declaring 'what Shi'ite-Sunni dispute? It's the protest of a nation against oppression' (Independent 2011, 21 March). The speech acts reveal the rise of regional tensions, which were exacerbated after the 2011 Arab Spring in Bahrain.

Through shifting domestic issues into a regional geopolitical struggle, the Al Khalifa regime ensured its survival, in comparison with other Arab dictators during the Arab Spring in 2011. Both Al Saud's and Al Khalifa's allegations of an Iranian role in the Arab Spring in Bahrain were a scheme to legitimize the Saudi-led intervention in Bahrain through framing the Shi'a as an Iranian 'fifth column' (Bayat 2017: 147; Mabon 2019a: 42). As interviewees 2 and 3 emphasize, 'there is no Iranian role in Bahrain, Iran does not fund us or grant us citizenship, it is a geopolitical game in which Shi'a Bahrainis have often paid the cost as victims in a sectarian game' (Interviewee 2, Code 2, 21 December 2019; Interviewee 3, Code 3, 23 December 2019). In this respect, Lynch (2012: 61) argues that the growth of Sunni–Shi'a 'sectarianism' serves the agenda of Saudi Arabia and Bahrain, which hopes to isolate Iran in order to 'browbeat' their own Shi'a populations into silence. Therefore, 'sectarianism', rather than being a primordial factor in Bahraini society, has been a political 'project' relying on 'sectarianization' to suspend democratic movements and legitimize a crackdown on Bahraini citizens in the name of a regional geopolitical struggle.

For the Al Khalifa and Al Saud ruling families, the securitization of Shi'a groups within and outside their borders has long been a policy to deceive Sunni citizens in order to maintain their power through 'sectarianization'. As Wehrey articulates, the main regional actor in Bahrain is Saudi Arabia, as Riyadh does not want a democratic state with a Shi'a majority in the neighbourhood (Wehrey 2012). However, the Shi'a in Bahrain are nationalists rather than being proxies for Iran, but securitization of the Shi'a is an excuse to suspend the democratization process in Bahrain and neighbouring countries. Despite a range of propaganda portraying the Shi'a of Bahrain as 'agents' for Iran, a report by a *Bahraini Independent Commission of Inquiry* rejected Al Khalifa's claim of Iranian involvement in Bahrain. The report by Mahmoud Cherif Bassiouni rejects the claims of Al Khalifa made through speech acts against the Shi'a population, calling them 'agents' of Iran (BICI 2011: 3–4). In this respect, Strobl argues that there has often been a 'nexus' between Al Khalifa and Sunni 'survival', and violence against the Shi'a in Bahrain (Strobl 2019). The Al Khalifa regime has manipulated securitization through 'sectarianization' domestically and regionally to ensure its survival during and post the uprisings in 2011.

However, King Hamad bin Isa Al Khalifa claims foreign 'influences' fuelled the protests in Bahrain and praised the Saudi-led forces that came to his aid (*The Guardian* 2011). Many Bahrainis, mostly Shi'a, believe that Bahrain has been under massive Saudi occupation since the Arab Spring (Matthiesen 2013: 51). It is worth noting that the securitization of Shi'a, and by default Iran, has intensified regional conflicts, not only at the domestic level but also at the regional level. However, the Saudi-led intervention in Bahrain kept the Al Khalifa ruling family in power but exacerbated the internal and regional security environment through sectarianization.

Successful securitization moving to 'violization' in Bahrain

In recent years, studies on securitization have advanced our understanding of the contemporary turmoil in the Middle East, particularly in Bahrain, seeing it as fertile ground for geopolitical tensions in the region. However, securitization of the Shi'a population during the Arab Spring ensured the short-term survival of the Al Khalifa regime, leading to an increase in concerns for long-term stability through the continuity of grievances and the massive crackdown on citizens. To do this, the regime applied a variety of violent methods in order to prevent future uprisings and guarantee long-term stability in Bahrain. Building on Neumann's argument, there are two processes after securitization in security problems: it can move to conflict and 'violization' or 'de-securitization'. The Al Khalifa regime has opted to shift from the securitization of Shi'a citizens to a systematic violent method to counter potential unrest within its borders.

Regarding the successful securitization process of Shi'a groups post-Arab Spring in the islands, the Al Khalifa ruling family moved to a violent form to cope with its Shi'a majority population. However, the regime achieved its goal to stop the revolution and ensure its short-term survival in 2011, and the desire of the ruling family to pursue long-term stability triggered its use of violent measures to control the country. Moving from securitization to 'violization' of Shi'a groups could ensure long-term stability. As Neumann (2012: 8–10) notes, the use of violence on a substantial scale highlights the transformation from securitization to 'violization'. It is the nexus of 'identity' and 'war', it starts with politicization, leading to securitization and 'violization'. To be more specific, when an issue is politicized, then it is moved to a securitization process by political actors, and so, it is more likely to be transformed into a 'violized' form instead of de-securitization. The model below demonstrates the process of 'violization' of an issue:

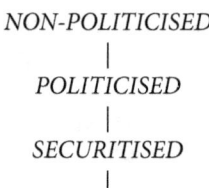

In the case of Bahrain, to counter the revolution, the Al Khalifa regime manipulated securitization through 'sectarianization' by dividing protestors into Sunni, Shi'a sectarian kin and calling the Shi'a 'agents' (Gengler 2015: 148) for Iran. The regime's depiction of non-sectarian demonstrations as 'Shi'a-led Uprisings', 'Shi'a protests' and 'Shi'a majority' (Gengler 2015: 143) intensified 'sectarianism' at the domestic and regional levels. Since the Arab Spring in 2011, the acceptance by domestic and regional audiences of such speech acts legitimized the use of systematic violence against Shi'a citizens to ensure the regime's long-term stability. The following section provides further evidence to that effect. It examines how the Al Khalifa regime has manipulated 'violization' after the successful securitization of the Shi'a population to change the demographic structure of Bahrain as the only way to prevent future unrest and solve the 'threat' from its majority population.

The transformation from securitization to systematic 'violization' against Shi'a Bahrainis can be viewed as an ongoing war against its citizens. The successful process of securitization of the Shi'a population, manipulated by the regime, led to the failure of the Bahraini revolution and to systematic violence against Shi'a citizens. The violent crackdown on the Shi'a population by Al Khalifa's security forces and the silence of Sunni citizens regarding the use of force against local citizens in Bahrain provided a vacuum for the regime to shift the demographic structure of the country for long-term stability. As Gengler (2013: 54) asserts, the Al Khalifa regime's policies towards Shi'a citizens have often been viewed as a 'security' problem rather than in 'political' terms. With this in mind, to sustain the

Al Khalifa regime's stability, it met large-scale challenges, such as the protests in 2011, with violent 'repression' (Jones 2020: 336).

Considering the variety of 'violized' methods used against Shi'a Bahrainis, Holmes articulates that between March and May 2011, 4,500 employees were fired from their jobs, 2,500 from the private sector and 2,000 from the public sector, albeit not all of them for taking part in the strikes, but for continuing to work and providing medical treatment to those who were wounded as a result of regime violence against its own citizens (Holmes 2016: 113; Shehabi 2015: 8). In this respect, Matthiesen refers to these measures as a form of 'economic punishment' in line with physical repression, targeting some Sunnis, but particularly Shi'a professionals (Matthiesen 2017: 212–13). As mentioned by interviewee 8, for fear of arrest, civilians wounded during the Arab Spring refused to go to hospital for treatment and preferred to be treated at home (Interviewee 8, 27 February 2020). The regime's strategy of punishing Shi'a citizens led to dismissing people from their jobs and educational institutions.

According to a 503-page report by the *Bahrain Independent Commission of Inquiry*, post-2011, Shi'a citizens have been targeted with systematic violence and arrests, and subsequently deaths, detention, torture, sexual abuse, rapes, unfair trials, deprivation or destruction of private property, demolition of religious buildings, restrictions on free speech, suspension from public and employment sectors, suspension of students, media harassment and travel bans (BICI 2011: 3–4). The wide range of violence inflicted in Bahrain shows that the Al Khalifa regime is well equipped to tackle internal challenges during its dynasty. As Jones asserts, the massive aggressive tactics utilized by the regime's security forces reveal the deep-rooted 'institutionalization' of such methods in Bahrain (Jones 2020: 166).

Al Khalifa's use of different violent methods has not been limited to physical methods; it went further with change to the demographic balance of the country. As Valbjørn and Hinnebusch (2018) articulate, the regime has launched demographic 'engineering', including revoking the citizenship of five hundred Shi'a Bahrainis. The regime's policies have affected 'social dynamics' by cultivating 'fear' among its citizens. As Matthiesen articulates, he was shocked to find that many Bahraini citizens whom he met during the Arab Spring are 'now either dead, in jail, or in exile'. According to personal interviews with Bahrainis, most of them have been arrested by the regime (Interviewee 2, Code 2, 21 December 2019; Interviewee 3, Code 3, 23 December 2019; Interviewee 5, Code 5, 6 February 2020; Interviewee 6, Code 6, 29 January 2020; Interviewee 7, Code 7, 28 February 2020); some are in exile (Interviewee 4, Code 4, 28 January 2020; interviewee 2, interviewee 5; interviewee 6) and some subjected to citizenship revocation and so stateless (Interviewee 1, Code 1, 19 December 2019; interviewee 3). This can be viewed as ethno-religious cleansing of the Shi'a population of Bahrain. As articulated by my interviewees (interviewee 1; interviewee 2; interviewee 3; interviewee 4; interviewee 5; interviewee 6; interviewee 7; interviewee 8; interviewee 9), the Shi'a are however still a majority in Bahrain, though the regime's policies seek to make Shi'a citizens a minority in the near future. With this in mind, it is not surprising that the demographic structure of Bahrain is shifting from local Bahrainis to non-Bahraini citizens.

Referring to *World Bank Data* in 2018, the population of Bahrain was reportedly 1,569,43. This number is made up of 689,714 Bahrainis and 813,377 non-Bahrainis, or 45 per cent of the population are local citizens and 55 per cent are foreigners (Fanack.com). But in 2001 the population of Bahrain comprised 409,619 Bahrainis and 251,698 non-Bahrainis (Information & eGovernment Authority 2020). As the data indicate, the number of foreigners is increasing in Bahraini society. As interviewees (interviewee 1; interviewee 3; interviewee 4; interviewee 5; interviewee 6; interviewee 7; interviewee 8) articulate, 'the large-scale citizenship revocations of local Bahrainis, alongside the systematic demographic shift in Bahrain, increased after the Arab Spring and this rapid shift is a political goal of the regime to change the demography of Bahrain'.

According to a report by *SALAM* for *Human rights and Democracy*, 'since 2011, 985 Bahrainis have been stripped of their citizenship by the regime. The human rights issue in Bahrain took a massive violent form, with a number of Bahrainis executed, while by 2018, 26 death sentences were issued' (SALAM Media 2020, 19 February). The deprivation of citizenship, a violation of human rights and a form of 'violization', has increased, denying Shi'a Bahrainis of their basic rights. Since 2011, 550 Shi'a have had their citizenship revoked, and this rate is increasing; as Al Wadaei asserts, Bahrain has stripped 990 people of their nationality and made them stateless (Amnesty International, TRT World). For the long-term stability of the regime, the revocation of Shi'a citizenship while granting citizenship to Sunni foreigners meets the end goal of the Al Khalifa regime, no matter what the cost or damage to Bahraini society.

Systematic 'violization': A form of cultural and religious violence

The Al Khalifa regime's violence has targeted not only the Shi'a population, but also cultural and religious Shi'a buildings post-2011. For instance, the national symbol of Bahrain, Pearl Roundabout, was targeted for destruction as it was a reminder of the history of revolution against the Al Khalifa ruling family. The regime decreed the destruction of Pearl Roundabout with its symbolic monument of Bahrain, because the people renamed it 'Martyrs' Square', after the death of two protestors at the hands of riot police in Bahrain (Bayat 2017: 131; Gengler 2015: 4). In response, the regime not only demolished Pearl Roundabout but also went further, erasing all images of Pearl Roundabout from shops and government websites, taking the 500 Fils coin with its Roundabout feature out of circulation, to erase this reminder of pro-democracy national movements (Dibell 2017). The Al Khalifa regime changed Pearl Roundabout's name to *Plaza Faruq Junction* in honour of Caliph Umar ibn al-Khattab, who is revered by Sunnis as a great military leader. A national symbol was turned into a Sunni symbol and considered by a majority of people to be a provocative name fuelling sectarianism in Bahrain (Matthiesen 2013: 71).

The violent measures implemented by the regime against the Shi'a led to international allies breaking their silence. For instance, Obama criticized the destruction of Shi'a mosques in his 19 May speech on the Arab Spring, saying the 'Shi'a must never have their mosques destroyed in Bahrain' (The Wichita eagle 2011). Though the Al Khalifa regime has been blamed for its ant-Shi'a crackdown methods, the violent actions have continued with the demolition of at least 35 Shi'a mosques and mourning halls (*Hossayniyya*). As interviewee 2 articulated (21 December 2019),

> The Al Khalifa regime along with Saudi troops demolished the historical mosque of Shi'a which dates back to 400 years ago. The regime expected the Shi'a to react against the destruction of their mosques, but the Shi'a were aware of the regime's policy to promote 'sectarianism' through retaliation. The Shi'a wisely avoided responding to the regime's violence against Shi'a sites.'

While these historical mosques have been registered by the government for decades, the hostility against Shi'a historical and cultural sites has continued, including bulldozing the historical mosque of Shi'a Al Barbaghi dating back four hundred years (Jafariya News).

Following the regime's hostility towards the Shi'a Bahrainis, the level of violence implemented by the regime can be viewed as the result of acceptance by domestic, regional and international audiences, which have legitimized violent actions against Shi'a citizens in the country. Al Khalifa's manipulation of securitization through 'sectarianization' resulted in 'violization' against Shi'a Bahrainis, which has transformed from local to regional level, exacerbating the security environment of the Middle East.

Conclusion

This chapter has discussed how in contrast to Arab dictators who were toppled during the Arab Spring in 2011, the Al Khalifa ruling family maintained its power through the securitization of Shi'a Bahrainis. The process of securitization through 'sectarianization', implemented by the regime, was successful and kept in power during the revolution in 2011. The chapter has built a bridge between securitization theory and the 'sectarianization' concept to explore the end goal of the Al Khalifa regime, which uses systematic methods of violence to target its people and maintain long-term stability in Bahrain. To do this, the regime, by framing Shi'a citizens as a security 'threat' to survival of the state and nation, has achieved short-term survival. To guarantee its long-term stability, the Al Khalifa regime moved from a successful securitization process to 'violization' by manipulating a wide variety of violent methods. In the first phase of securitization through 'sectarianization', the regime, by labelling Shi'a citizens as 'agents' for Iran, was able to convince domestic and regional audiences that Iran was behind the unrest in Bahrain and shifted internal unrest into a regional struggle between Saudi Arabia and Iran.

By locating national demonstrations within a regional geopolitical conflict, the Saudi-led intervention alongside Al Khalifa security forces legitimized the crackdown on citizens, which led to the failure of the Bahraini revolution in 2011. However, while the successful securitization process of the Shi'a could maintain the power of the Al Khalifa regime during the Arab Spring, the regime has required intelligent strategies to ensure long-term stability in the country. To do this, as Neumann articulates, the regime moved from a securitization process to 'violization', which includes an outbreak of 'war' and the use of force, which highlights acceptance of security speech acts by various audiences (Neumann 2012: 8–10).

The suspension of normal politics and using force against the Shi'a population shifted the security environment of Bahrain and, broadly, the region. According to the 503-page report by the Bahrain Independent Commission of Inquiry, a range of measures involving deaths, arrests, detentions, torture, sexual abuse, rapes, unfair trials, deprivation or destruction of private property, demolition of religious building, restrictions on free speech, suspension from public and employment sectors, suspension of students, media harassment and travel bans, as systematic violence, have targeted Shi'a citizens post-2011. More specifically, the Shi'a citizens of Bahrain are victims of these policies that have been long implemented by the Al Khalifa ruling family. The transformation from securitization to violent methods has been used by the regime to secure its long-term stability and prevent any repetition of the Arab Spring in the country no matter what the cost in human lives or damage to the social and cultural bases of Bahraini society.

References

Al-Khawaja, M. (2014), 'Crackdown: The Harsh Realities of Nonviolent Protests in the Bahraini Civil Conflict', *Journal of International Affairs*, 68 (1): 189–200.

Amnesty International, Bahrain: Government Expels Citizens after Having Revoked Their Nationality, Available online : https://www.amnesty.org/en/latest/news/2018/01/bahrain-government-expels-citizens-after-having-revoked-their-nationality/ (accessed 20 May 2020).

Bassiouni, M. C. (November 2011), final revision December 2011. *Report of the Bahrain Independent Commission of Inquiry*. Available online: http://www.bici.org.bh/BICIreportEN.pdf (accessed 12 November 2019).

Bayat, A. (2017), *Revolution without Revolutionaries: Making Sense of the Arab Spring*, Stanford, CA: Stanford University Press.

Bilgin, P. (2011), 'The Politics of Studying Securitization? The Copenhagen School in Turkey, *Security Dialogue*, 42 (4–5): 399–412.

Buzan, B., Wæver, O., Wæver, O. and De Wilde, J. (1998). *Security: A New Framework for Analysis*. Lynne Rienner Publishers.

Chubin, S., and Tripp, C. (1996), *Iran-Saudi Arabia Relations and Regional Order*. London. Adelphi Paper No: 304.

Dibell, A. (2017), *Bahrain Reopens Pearl Monument but Obscures Its Legacy. Americans for Democracy & Human Rights in Bahrain*. Available online: https://www.adhrb.org/2017/06/12883/ (accessed 20 December 2019).

Ehteshami, A., and Zweiri, M. (2008), *Iran's Foreign Policy: From Khatami to Ahmadinejad*, Garnet.
Fanack.com, *Population of Bahrain*. Available online: https://fanack.com/bahrain/population/ (accessed 19 May 2020).
Fürtig, H. (2007), Conflict and Cooperation in the Persian Gulf: The Interregional Order and US Policy *Middle East Journal*, 61 (4): 627–40.
Gause III, G. (2020), *Saudi Arabia and Sectarianism in Middle East International Relations*. Sectarianism and International Relations, *POMEPS Studies*, 38.
Gengler, J. J. (2013), 'Royal Factionalism, the Khawalid, and the Securitization of "the Shi'a Problem"', Bahrain*Journal of Arabian Studies*, 3 (1): 53–79.
Gengler, J. J. (2015), *Group Conflict and Political Mobilization in Bahrain and the Arab Gulf: Rethinking the Rentier State*, Bloomington: Indiana University Press.
Hafidh, H., and Fibiger, T. (2019), Civic Space and Sectarianism in the Gulf States: The Dynamics of Informal Civil Society in Kuwait and Bahrain beyond State Institutions *Studies in Ethnicity and Nationalism*, 19 (1): 109–26.
Holmes, A. A. (2016), Working on the Revolution in Bahrain: From the Mass Strike to Everyday Forms of Medical Provision *Social Movement Studies*, 15 (1): 105–14.
Huysmans, J. (1998), Revisiting Copenhagen: Or, on the Creative Development of a Security Studies Agenda in Europe *European Journal of International Relations*, 4 (4): 479–505.
Independent. (2011, 21 March *Bahrain's King Makes Veiled Charge against Iran*. Available online: https://www.independent.co.uk/news/world/middle-east/bahrains-king-makes-veiled-charge-against-iran-2248634.html (accessed 23 November 2019.
Information & eGovernment Authority, Bahrain Open Data Portal. Available online: https://www.data.gov.bh/en/ResourceCenter (accessed 19 May 2020).
Interviewee 1, Personal Interview with Code 1, 19 December 2019.
Interviewee 2, Personal Interview with Code 2, 21 December 2019.
Interviewee 3, Personal Interview with Code 3, 23 December 2019.
Interviewee 4, Personal Interview with Code 4, 28 January 2020.
Interviewee 5, Personal Interview with Code 5, 6 February 2020.
Interviewee 6, Personal Interview with Code 6, 29 January 2020.
Interviewee 7, Personal Interview with Code 7, 28 February 2020.
Interviewee 8, Personal Interview with Code 8, 27 February 2020.
Interviewee 9, Personal Interview with Code 9, 1 March 2020.
Jehl, D. (1999) Bahrain Emir Dies in Palace after Meeting on U.S. Arms. *New York Times*. Available online: https://www.nytimes.com/1999/03/07/world/bahrain-emir-dies-in-palace-after-meeting-on-us-arms.html (accessed 15 March 2020).
Jones, M. O. (2020), *Political Repression in Bahrain*, Cambridge: Cambridge University Press.
Joyce, M. (2012), *Bahrain from the Twentieth Century to the Arab Spring*. New York: Palgrave Macmillan.
Keynoush, B. (2016), *Saudi Arabia and Iran: Friends or Foes?* New York: Palgrave Macmillan.
Lynch, M. (2012), *The Arab Uprising: The Unfinished Revolutions of the Middle East*, New York: Public Affairs.
Mabon, S. (2012), 'The Battle for Bahrain: Iranian-Saudi Rivalry', *Middle East Policy*, 19 (2): 84.

Mabon, S. (2015), *Saudi Arabia and Iran: Soft Power Rivalry in the Middle East*. London: I.B. Tauris.

Mabon, S. (2019a), 'Existential Threats and Regulating Life: Securitization in the Contemporary Middle East, in Mabon, Simon, Kapur, Saloni', *Securitization in the Non-West*, London: Routledge, 40–52.

Mabon, S. (2019b), 'The End of the Battle for Bahrain and the Securitization of Bahraini Shi'a', *Middle East Journal*, 73 (1) 29–50. Project MUSE muse.jhu.edu/article/721755.

Mabon, S. (2018) 'Existential Threats and Regulating Life: Securitization in the Contemporary Middle East', *Global Discourse*, 8 (1): 42–58.

Matthiesen, T. (2013). *Sectarian gulf: Bahrain, Saudi Arabia, and the Arab Spring That Wasn't* Stanford, CA: Stanford University Press.

Matthiesen, T. (2017). 'Sectarianization as Securitization: Identity Politics and Counter-Revolution', in Bahrain, in N Hashemi and D. Postel (eds), *Sectarianization: Mapping the New Politics of the Middle East*, United Kingdom: Glasgow, Hurst, 201–23.

Mason, R. (2014), *Foreign Policy in Iran and Saudi Arabia: Economics and Diplomacy in the Middle East*, London: I.B. Tauris.

Mason, R. (2014), 'Back to Realism for an Enduring US-Saudi Relationship', *Middle East Policy*, 21 (4): 32–44.

Nasirzadeh, S. and Wastnidge, E. (2020), 'De-securitizing through Diplomacy: De-sectarianization and the View from the Islamic Republic', *Review of Faith & International Affairs*, 18: 123–33.

Neumann, I. B. (2012), 'After Securitisation: Diplomats as De-securitisers', *Baltic Journal of Political Science*, 1 (1): 7–21.

SALAM Media (2020, 19 February), *Briefing on the Human Rights Situation in Bahrain in 2019*. Available online: https://salam-dhr.org/?p=3934 (accessed 23 February 2020).

Shehabi, A. and Jones, M. O. (2015), *Bahrain's Uprising: Resistance and Repression in the Gulf*, London: Zed Books.

Strobl, S. (2019), 'A Curious of Justice in Modern Bahraini History: Being Hard on Shi'a and Soft on Sunnis', in S. Mabon, T. Dodge, B. Salloukh and S. Strobl (eds), Ghazal, Elias; Kumarasamy, Ana; Nasirzadeh, Samira. (Editorial Assistant). 2019. *Sectarianism in the Longue Durée*. Lancaster, SEPAD: Sectarianism, Proxies & De-sectarianisation.

Terrill, W. A. (2011), *The Saudi-Iranian Rivalry and the Future of Middle East Security*, Department of the Army. Strategic Studies Institute. Available: US Army War College Press, https://press.armywarcollege.edu/monographs/562.

The Guardian (2011), *Bahrain Hints at Iranian Role over Country's Shia Uprising*, Associate Press in Manama. Available online: https://www.theguardian.com/world/2011/mar/21/bahrain-iran-role-uprising-shia (accessed 26 November 2019).

The WichitaEagle (2011), *Obama Slams Bahrain's Crackdown*, Roy Gutman President Obama Criticized the Destruction in His May 19 Speech on the Arab Spring. Shia Must Never Have Their Mosques Destroyed in Bahrain', Obama Said. Available online: https://www.kansas.com/latest-news/article1064363.html (accessed 12 January 2020).

The World Bank (2018), *Population, Total-Bahrain*. Available online: https://data.worldbank.org/indicator/SP.POP.TOTL?locations=BH (accessed 19 May 2020).

TRT World (n.d.), *Why Is Bahrain Revoking Nationality of Its Citizens?* Availableonline: https://www.trtworld.com/middle-east/why-is-bahrain-revoking-nationality-of-its-citizens-25949 (accessed 20 May 2020).

Ulrichsen, K. C. (2013), 'Bahrain's Uprising: Regional Dimensions and International Consequences', *Stability: International Journal of Security and Development*, 2 (1): 1–12.

Valbjørn, M. (2018, June), Studying sectarianism while beating dead horses and searching for third ways. In *workshop 'The Comparative Politics of Sub-State Identity in the Middle East', LSE Middle East Centre.*

Valbjørn, M., and Hinnebusch, R. (2018), 'Playing "the Sectarian Card in a Sectarianized New Middle East', *Babylon Nordisk tidsskrift for Midtøstenstudier,* 2018: 242–55. https://doi.org/10.5617/ba.6727.

Wæver, O. (2011), 'Politics, Security, Theory', *Security Dialogue,* 42 (4–5): 465–80.

Wæver, O. (2003), *Securitisation: Taking Stock of a Research Programme in Security Studies; Appraising Theories and Research Programmes – or Continuing the Paradigm Wars?* Paper started as a *presentation at a 1999 BISA roundtable organized by Theo Farrell,* where the Copenhagen School was the most mainstream approach to be superseded by first cultural-constructivist security studies, then critical security studies and finally radical security studies. Available online: https://docplayer.net/62037981-Securitisation-taking-stock-of-a-research-programme-in-security-studies.html (accessed 16 February 2019).

Wæver, O. (2000), 'The EU as a Security Actor: Reflections from a Pessimistic Constructivist on Post-Sovereign Security Orders', *International Relations Theory and the Politics of European Integration,* 250–94.

Wehrey, F. (2009), 'Smith Richardson Foundation, & Rand Corporation. National Security Research Division', in *Saudi-Iranian Relations since the Fall of Saddam [Electronic Resource]: Rivalry, Cooperation, and Implications for U.S. Policy.* (Monograph / Rand Corporation) Santa Monica, CA: Rand.

Wehrey, F. M. (2014), *Sectarian Politics in the Gulf: From the Iraq War to the Arab Uprisings,* Columbia University Press. Available online: https://doi.org/10.7312/wehr16512

Wehrey, F. (2012), *Bahrain's Lost Uprising.* Carnegie Endowment for International Peace, Available online https://carnegieendowment.org/2012/06/12/bahrain-s-lost-uprising-pub-48475#proxy (accessed 26 November 2019).

Wilkinson, C. (2007), The Copenhagen School on Tour in Kyrgyzstan: Is Securitization Theory Useable Outside Europe?' *Security Dialogue,* 38 (1): 5–25.

Wilkinson, C. (2010), 'The Limits of Spoken Words: From Meta-Narratives to Experiences of Security', *Securitization Theory: How Security Problems Emerge and Dissolve,* 108–29. Routledge.

Wright, R. and Baker, P. (2004, 8 December), *Iraq, Jordan See Threat to Election from Iran: Leaders Warn against Forming Religious State.* Washington Post. Available online: http://www.washingtonpost.com/wp-dyn/articles/A43980-2004Dec7.html (accessed 25 July 2018).

Zill, Z. (2012), Bahrain and The Arab Spring. Available online: https://socialistworker.org/2012/02/01/bahrain-and-the-arab-spring.

Chapter 6

BRIDGING ETHNO-RELIGIOUS DIVIDES BY PROXY?
NON-STATE SPONSORSHIP AND SECTARIANISM IN
THE CASE OF THE SYRIAN DEMOCRATIC FORCES

Michel Wyss

Introduction

In April 2016, Hezbollah, the Lebanese-Shi'i 'Party of God', announced the 'martyrdom' of Muhammad al-Kabash, a nineteen-year-old Sunni Muslim from Sidon, alongside six of its fighters in Syria. al-Kabash's father proudly confirmed that his son had fought as a regular member of the Lebanese Shi'a organization, claiming that the group had sent him to Syria three years earlier (Chbaro 2016). Other reports, however, suggested that al-Kabash had not been a member of Hezbollah, but rather of the so-called Lebanese Resistance Brigades – a militia composed of members of a variety of Lebanon's religious sects that Hezbollah had founded in the late 1990s (Bis-souwar 2016; Groisman 2016). In either case, the fact that al-Kabash had been fighting side by side with Hezbollah against Syrian rebels sharing his faith seems at odds with the often expressed notion (Hanau Santini 2017; Rabi and Muller 2018) that the war in Syria is primarily a sectarian conflict and the manifestation of a broader, region-wide competition between Sunni and Shi'a constituencies. Furthermore, it calls into question a number of common assumptions about proxy conflicts in general and their occurrence in the Middle East specifically. Conventional wisdom defines proxy warfare as a form of indirect intervention or 'war delegation' (Salehyan 2010: 496, 503) in which external state sponsors back insurgent groups in an ongoing conflict (Hughes 2012: 5; Hughes 2014: 523–4). With regard to the Middle East, scholars have primarily focused on proxy rivalries between Iran and Saudi Arabia in different conflict theatres such as Syria (Berti and Guzansky 2014: 26–30) and Yemen (Terrill 2014). In the case of Syria, a number of studies (Rondeaux and Sterman 2019b: 6; Seely 2017: 54) have additionally identified major powers such as the United States and Russia as sponsors of several proxies on opposing sides of the ongoing conflict.

While these actors and their increased employment of surrogate forces undeniably play a crucial role in the current conflicts in the Middle East and beyond, a narrow focus on them obscures a more dynamic and nuanced picture. To that effect, this chapter makes two interrelated arguments:

> *First*, recent armed conflicts have created conditions for large swathes of territory to be – at least temporarily – controlled by non-state armed groups. Some of these groups, most prominently the so-called 'Islamic State' (IS), have relied on extreme violence, repression and coercion (Jones et al. 2017: 3). Others have instead opted to employ other smaller non-state actors as proxies to advance their goals, thus emulating the strategic behaviour of external state sponsors. There is an important distinction, however. Rather than as military surrogates, non-state sponsors use their proxies as political tools in order to gain, maintain or enhance legitimacy and support from local audiences as well as external backers (Moghadam and Wyss 2020).
>
> *Second*, these non-state sponsors often rely on their proxies to try and bridge ethno-religious tensions and divisions between themselves and local populations under their control. Contrary to assertions about Middle Eastern proxy wars occurring along sectarian lines and further stoking ostensibly 'ancient hatreds' (Burleigh 2014; Dahan 2018), therefore, the proxy strategies of some non-state actors may well be geared towards easing such tensions and reducing common mistrust; or those actors may at least pretend to do so.

The remainder of this chapter is structured as follows. First, I offer a critical appraisal of the current scholarship on proxy relations while also highlighting certain blind spots, particularly regarding the role of non-state sponsors. Next, I discuss the role of proxy relations and sectarianism in the war in Syria, which is often regarded as the epitome of an Iranian-Saudi proxy struggle and of broader Sunni–Shia sectarian tensions. Utilizing the case study of the Kurdish People's Protection Units (YPG), I argue that by myopically focusing on state sponsorship and sectarian divides, previous studies have missed a more complex dynamic: certain non-state actors increasingly employ proxies themselves and by doing so, they may help – perhaps inadvertently – to reduce sectarian tensions. I conclude by summarizing the findings of the chapter and discussing the need for further research.

Studying proxy relationships

The use of proxies (Mumford 2013: 11–12, 26–9), or surrogate forces (Krieg and Rickli 2019: 5), has been described repeatedly as a perennial feature in the history of armed conflict (Hughes 2016; Marshall 2016). Becoming particularly salient as a means of limited war during the great power confrontation following the Second World War, it has remained a fixture of intra-state conflicts in the post-Cold War period (Mumford 2013: 3–4). A 2019 study by New America (Rondeaux and Sterman 2019a) identified more than a dozen proxy relationships in the three conflict theatres of Syria, Iraq and Yemen alone. At the same time – and a burgeoning academic interest over the past two decades notwithstanding – the relationship between proxies and their sponsors has remained somewhat opaque and the study of these relations leaves much to be desired. According to Rondeaux and Sterman (2019b: 10), 'the current state of proxy warfare analysis is reminiscent of the state of post-9/11 counterinsurgency research in the early stages of the Afghanistan and Iraq conflicts'. As noted by Rauta (2018: 450), 'no overarching theory [of proxy wars] has emerged, and the existing models complement, rather than integrate each other'.

One primary obstacle towards the emergence of a coherent theory of proxy relationships has been the lack of terminological clarity. Studies have in various ways referred to 'proxy intervention', 'proxy war', 'proxy warfare' or 'proxy conflicts' – some of them interchangeably – even though these terms arguably carry different meanings and implications.[1] As Rauta (2018: 453) points out, there is even greater variance with regard to terminology describing the principal actors in proxy relationships. At the same time, scholars seem to be in agreement on the nature of these relations: one party agrees to act at the behest of another party in an armed conflict, in exchange for aid provided by the latter (Hughes 2012: 11; Mumford 2013: 11; Rauta 2018: 457; Salehyan 2010: 503). Put differently, a sponsor uses its proxy to reach its strategic goals in exchange for providing it with tangible assistance (Moghadam and Wyss 2020: 124–5). It is this author's conviction that the interaction between sponsors and proxies is at the centre of this phenomenon and that their relation may extend beyond any spatially or temporally limited 'proxy conflict'. Thus, this chapter will henceforth solely refer to *proxy relationships*, unless it is directly quoting other works employing different terminology.

In general, previous research on proxy relationships has adhered to two common assumptions. First, most studies rely on a state-centric paradigm. This is particularly true with regard to research throughout the Cold War period, which only considered states as principal actors and typically defined a so-called 'war by proxy' as 'war between regional states that may be regarded as a substitute for direct confrontation between the superpowers' (Bar-Siman-Tov 1984: 263).[2] Meanwhile, newer scholarship typically ascribes the role of the proxy to armed non-state actors but continues to exclusively consider states as sponsors. Hughes (2014: 523), for example, defines a proxy war as 'one in which states aid and abet non-state proxies involved in a conflict against a common adversary, or a target', whereas Brown (2016: 247) views proxy wars as cases in which '*governments* [emphasis added] … subcontract proxies to fight the country's wars'. Similar definitions can be found in the works of Salehyan (2010), Byman and Kreps (2010), Bapat (2011) and Popovic (2017). Second, based on this first assumption, there is also broad agreement regarding the rationale for states to sponsor proxies. The proxy relations scholarship typically emphasizes three potential benefits (Ahram 2011: 14; Berkowitz 2018: 715; Byman and Kreps 2010: 3–6; Carey, Colaresi and Mitchell 2015: 852–3; Hughes 2012: 22–5; Mumford 2013: 41–2; Salehyan 2010: 504;

Salehyan, Skrede Gleditsch and Cunningham 2011: 713–14). First, proxies offer military value based on their superior knowledge of terrain and population as well as their specific capabilities; second, the use of proxies is perceived as a cheaper option compared to the cost of direct military action; and finally, employing proxies allows sponsors to attain plausible deniability and dissociate themselves from the actions of their surrogates. Scholars also typically agree on the potential risks and costs of sponsorship, which include proxies pursuing divergent interests and preferences; diverting resources; engaging in uncooperative behaviour ranging from devoting suboptimal effort up to switching sides and turning against their own benefactors (Ahram 2011: 14–15; Bapat 2011: 4; Berkowitz 2018: 717–21; Byman and Kreps 2010: 6–9; Hughes 2012: 49–51; Popovic 2017: 924–5; Salehyan 2010: 504–5; Salehyan, Skrede Gleditsch and Cunningham 2011: 714–15).

Theorizing non-state sponsorship

In recent years, several studies on proxy relationships have yielded a wealth of insights and considerably advanced our understanding of the phenomenon. Compared to Cold War-era notions, which considered proxies as 'little more than third-party tools of statecraft without any agency, intent, or indeed interest visibly separable from those of a well-resourced state sponsor' (Innes 2012: xiii), the field has made considerable strides.

However, while recent studies on proxy relationships rightly point out the agency of non-state proxies, they still underutilize this theoretical insight. For them, the fact that non-state proxies have agency is significant because it suggests that these actors have their own preferences and interests, and hence make choices that are independent of – and may even contradict – the designs of their sponsors. Missing from this analysis, however, is another important consequence of the growing agency of non-state actors: agency affects not only preferences and interests but also the nature of the agent proper. Agency-structure theorists have noted that the choices that agents make are transformative in the sense that they can effect change not only in the agent's environment but also in the agent himself (Wight 2006: 212). As some non-state armed groups amass greater powers, they may also adjust their strategies to achieve their objectives. For some of those who may have previously served as proxies for other parties, such strategic adjustments can take the form of adopting new roles as sponsors themselves.

Thus, by failing to appreciate the full scope of the transformative capacity that agency has on the nature of non-state actors, a substantial part of the current research on proxy relationships misses an opportunity to recognize the capacity of non-state armed groups to serve as sponsors.

Indeed, only a few studies have paid attention to this phenomenon and those that did have typically done so in passing only (Byman et al. 2001: 71; Phillips and Valbjørn 2018). Even the aforementioned New America report, which explicitly argues that non-state sponsors 'should not be excluded from an effort to address the dangers of proxy warfare strategies by dint of their not being states' (Rondeaux and Sterman 2019b: 27), does not provide any empirical examples or theoretical insights.

So far, only Moghadam and Wyss (2020: 128–9) have put forth a theory of non-state sponsorship, arguing that unlike state sponsors, non-state sponsors use their proxies for their perceived political value rather than their military capabilities. According to their study, non-state sponsors select proxies that are representative of certain sections of the population to gain or improve access to these specific communities (ibid.: 133). While these proxies at times may be involved in military operations on the frontlines, they are more likely to carry out rear guard duty such as providing security and logistics as their military contributions are of secondary importance. Instead, they serve as political tools to enhance the legitimacy of their sponsors by means of negotiation, mediation or providing governance on the latter's behalf (ibid.: 135). As Moghadam and Wyss (2020: 133–5) also note, non-state sponsors do not seek to attain plausible deniability; rather, they are open about the ties to their proxies and often make an effort to portray these relations as egalitarian partnerships.

To be clear, armed non-state actors already relied on surrogate forces decades ago. Palestinian militants in the 1960s and 1970s, for example, provided training, funding and weapons to European and other left-wing organizations, with the latter carrying out occasional attacks for their sponsors. The 1972 Lod Airport massacre, perpetrated by members of the Japanese Red Army on behalf of the Popular Front for the Liberation of Palestine, is a case in point (Steinhoff 1976: 837–9). Similarly, according to a former member of the German far-left terror organization Revolutionäre Zellen (Revolutionary Cells), he and his comrades were fully aware that their Palestinian sponsors expected attacks on Jewish and Israeli targets in return for material aid (Klein 1977: 33–4). In these instances, however, the geographical distance between the groups meant that these non-state sponsors had little operational control over their proxies and the latter's utility was generally limited to carrying out selective terror attacks. Conversely, recent civil wars, insurgencies and areas with weak governance have created opportunities for non-state armed groups to capture, hold and administer territory, often while relying on local proxies (Horton 2017; International Crisis Group 2017b).

Sectarianism and proxy relations in the Syrian war

One conflict that has provided many opportunities for non-state armed groups to – at least temporarily – capture and control territory is the ongoing war in Syria, which emerged from a multifaceted protest movement in early 2011 following the successful overthrow of the Ben Ali and Mubarak regimes in Tunisia and Egypt respectively. The Syrian uprising, on the other hand, was quickly met with a violent crackdown by Bashar al-Assad's security forces and subsequently turned into an armed insurgency (Hinnebusch 2012: 108–10; Lister 2015: 12–17; 61–2).

As a number of observers have pointed out, the Syrian opposition initially made considerable efforts to emphasize its non-sectarian and secular character

(Hinnebusch 2012: 109; Lister 2015: 61).³ Despite these efforts, however, certain ethno-sectarian overtones accompanied the conflict from the outset and informed the agendas and calculations of its principal actors to at least some extent (Phillips 2015: 359–60). Some deliberate actions soon exacerbated sectarian tensions, chiefly among them Assad's decision to release imprisoned Jihadist militants in order to both radicalize the opposition and sow the fear of a Sunni Islamist insurgency while simultaneously presenting himself as the only protector of Syrian minorities (Lister 2015: 53; Phillips 2015: 369). This, in turn, led to further fragmentation of the – never truly unified – opposition and provided ample opportunity for regional powers such as Saudi Arabia, Qatar and Turkey to back increasingly radical Islamist militias (Landis 2012: 74–7; Phillips 2015: 370). Considering that these groups were better equipped and funded, the ranks of the so-called Free Syrian Army (FSA) experienced an increasing number of defections to Islamist outfits (Dettmer 2013; Mahmood and Black 2013).

Yet Turkey and the Gulf States were hardly the only external actors to meddle in Syria. Fearing to lose its most important ally, Iran propped up the Assad regime through the deployment of the Islamic Revolutionary Guard Corps Qods Force (IRGC-QF) as well as the Lebanese Hezbollah and several proxy militias from Iraq, Afghanistan and Pakistan (Hokayem 2014: 74; Smyth 2015). In addition, as Hokayem (2014: 73) notes, Iran played a crucial role in the creation of the Syrian National Defence Forces (NDF). Still, despite Iran's vigorous efforts, it is far from clear if Assad would still be in power had it not been for the large-scale Russian intervention in September 2015 (Charap, Treyger and Geist 2019). Conversely, the United States and several European countries had initially provided limited non-lethal aid (and later small arms) to previously vetted rebel groups starting in 2013 (Mohammed and Yacoub Oweis 2013). Following the lightning advance of the Islamic State (IS) in Iraq and Syria, US President Obama authorized a train-and-equip programme that sought to compel Syrian rebels to fight IS instead of the Assad regime but proved an abject failure (McKelvey 2015). Instead, the United States came to rely increasingly on the Kurdish People's Protection Units (YPG), which proved exceptionally capable in halting and later rolling back IS but also caused unprecedented tensions between Washington and Ankara (Ustun 2016) – and which will be examined in more detail in the following section.

Given the preceding discussion, it is unsurprising that scholars, pundits and policy makers have frequently framed the conflict in Syria as 'sectarian war' (Recknagel 2012), 'proxy conflict' (Hughes 2014) or 'Iranian-Saudi proxy struggle' (Fisher 2016: 8). At the same time, several observers have cautioned that, while certainly among the drivers of the war in Syria, a focus on sectarian divides and external proxy interference risks missing a more complex picture (Hokayem 2014: 60–1; Phillips 2015). The following section provides further evidence to that effect by examining how the Kurdish YPG militia has relied on smaller non-state armed groups in its fight against IS. It demonstrates that the sponsorship of local proxies is not limited to external state backers and that non-state sponsors may employ their proxies not to further aggravate sectarian divides but in an effort to mitigate them.

6. Bridging Ethno-religious Divides by Proxy?

Utilizing non-state sponsorship to address sectarianism: The case of the YPG and the Syrian Democratic Forces (SDF)

The history of the Kurds in Syria and their relations to the central authority in Damascus have always been intricate. A comparatively small minority within Syria (particularly compared to the numbers of Kurds in Turkey and Iraq), Kurdish aspirations for autonomy, chiefly in the Jazira region in Northern Syria, can be traced back to the time of the French mandate lasting from 1924 to 1946 (Savelsberg 2014: 86–90). These efforts, however, came to no fruition and Syrian Kurds were forced to accept Syrian citizenship after the French withdrawal (Halhalli 2018: 30). Subsequent years in Syria were characterized by a swift succession of military coups and dictators, and the latter's unrelenting efforts to create a homogeneous Arab–Muslim state. Inevitably,

> Kurds, Assyrians and Armenians soon felt the alienating effects of a string of decrees requiring for example that hotels, cafes and cinemas be given purely Arab names, that only Arabic might be spoken at any public meetings, festivals or celebrations, and that Muslims must sit in equal numbers with non-Muslims on all committees of minority organisations. (McDowall 2004: 471)

Anti-Kurdish measures became even more comprehensive as Kurdish-language music records and publications were seized and destroyed and their owners imprisoned (ibid.). In 1962, 120,000 Kurds had their citizenship revoked and their properties confiscated (Halhalli 2018: 31–2; McDowall 2004: 474). During the 1970s, the Syrian Ba'ath party, after seizing power in 1963, established a *cordon sanitaire* along the border to Turkey and Iraq and constructed forty-one new villages for Arab inhabitants in this so-called 'Arab belt' (Halhalli 2018: 32; McDowall 2004: 475). While efforts to weaken Kurdish cultural and political identities in Syria continued unabatedly, the government of Hafez al-Assad was happy to offer a safe haven to the Kurdish Worker Party (PKK) in 1980, looking to use it as leverage against Turkey over territorial disputes (Phillips 2012). Initially, the PKK found support among Syrian Kurds and thousands of them joined its ranks. Starting from the 1990s, however, Kurds in Syria expressed increasing resentment for the preferential treatment the PKK received from the Syrian government and the fact that the party chose to ignore Kurdish aspirations for autonomy within Syria (McDowall 2004: 479) and demanded that Syrian Kurds 'put up with discrimination and oppression by the central government there' (Buchen 2012). In 1998, however, the PKK lost its Syrian patronage when Turkey threatened to invade Syria unless it expelled the foreign insurgents. The PKK was forced to relocate to the Qandil Mountains in Northern Iraq where a group of Syrian Kurds in its ranks founded the Kurdish Democratic Union Party (PYD) in 2003 ('The Kurds' Precarious Balancing Act' 2017: v).

Following the outbreak of protests in 2011, the Kurdish position vis-à-vis the Syrian opposition was ambivalent. One the one hand, Syrian Kurds had little sympathy for Bashar al-Assad's government. One the other hand, memories of the

2004 Qamishli riots and the subsequent crackdown by the government's security forces against Kurdish protesters (resulting in the death of at least thirty Kurds and the arrest of more than two thousand) as well as of non-Kurdish Syrians' indifference at the time have remained vivid (International Crisis Group 2013: 7; Savelsberg 2014: 93). After Qamishli, the Syrian Kurds had achieved an informal accommodation with Assad, and there was additional concern about the more radical elements within the Syrian opposition (International Crisis Group 2013: 37; Savelsberg 2014: 93). The PYD and its YPG militia, which quickly emerged as the most powerful faction among the Syrian Kurds, embody this ambivalence. In July 2012, the YPG forced Syrian government forces to withdraw and took control of the Kurdish regions in Northern Syria (International Crisis Group 2013: 15–16). Initially, the YPG reached a modus vivendi with rebel forces and tried to keep the Kurdish territories out of the conflict. However, the ascent of the Jihadist Al-Nusra Front led to increased tensions, with clashes between the YPG, Al-Nusra and the latter's allies becoming more frequent (ibid.: 36). At the same time, the YPG still sought to keep at least some relations with the Syrian opposition (Allsopp and van Wilgenburg 2019: 126), including by means of Jabhat al-Akrad (the Kurdish Front), apparently a PYD proxy founded in January 2013, which operated within the framework of the FSA and was created with the intention 'to gain access to mixed Arab-Kurdish areas and to make logistics between the three Kurdish enclaves easier' (van Wilgenburg 2013: 7). In addition, Jabhat al-Akrad may have been a means to keep anti-PYD Kurdish factions within the FSA in check as its emergence appeared to coincide with the decline of some of them (Evran 2016; International Crisis Group 2013: 36). Furthermore, PYD and YPG began cooperating with a number of Arab tribes such as the Shammar, which had been the only local Arab tribe to refuse fighting the Kurdish protesters on behalf of the government during the 2004 Qamishli riots (Allsopp and van Wilgenburg 2019: 126). Ironically, it was the rise of yet another Jihadist group, IS, and its relentless targeting of other opposition groups that paved the way for cooperation between the YPG and several FSA factions, including the joint YPG–FSA operations room Euphrates Volcano (Allsopp and van Wilgenburg 2019: 127; Lister 2015: 185).

IS's assault and subsequent siege of the Kurdish town of Kobane starting in September 2014 proved as a decisive moment for the YPG (Lister 2015: 189). Had it not been for the air strikes and material support by the US-led military intervention against IS, the town would not have withstood the Jihadist offensive (Letsch 2014; Morris 2015). Instead, the YPG became the anti-IS coalition's preferred partner force on the ground and – given its ability to call-in air strikes and the lethal and non-lethal material aid it received – one of the most powerful actors in the conflict (Stephens and Stein 2015). These attributes made the YPG a potentially attractive benefactor to many smaller rebel groups fighting to survive the onslaught of both the Syrian regime and IS (ibid.). In a bid to appease Turkey and to obscure ties to the PKK, which it designated a foreign terrorist organization in 1997, the United States eventually encouraged the establishment of the so-called Syrian Democratic Forces, nominally a coalition of Kurdish, Sunni Arab,

Turkmen and Syriac Christian militias (International Crisis Group 2017c: 12–13; Lund 2016).

The YPG and the SDF – primus inter pares?

Officially, the Syrian Democratic Forces (SDF) likes to portray its various groups as equals striving together for 'a decentralized state, where there are local civilian councils, local governments that guarantee the rights of the different Syrian groups, freedom of religion, freedom of expression, gender equality' (Seligman 2019). In some instances, it has also used anti-regime messaging and revolutionary imagery, seeking to lower the threshold for (former) FSA groups to join its ranks (Mullah Darwish 2016).

As several observers have noted, however, the real command authority within SDF belongs to the YPG, which surpasses the other factions not only in strength(according to US officials, it makes up at least three-quarters of the SDF's total number of fighters) but also in combat discipline and access to supplies (Gutman 2015; Sly 2017; Wilkofsky and Fatah 2017). While the SDF used local Arab dignitaries as figureheads after liberating cities such as Manbij, the YPG remained in control (International Crisis Group 2017a: 4). Some YPG officials publicly acknowledged as much, admitting that they are in 'overall command of the joint Kurdish-Arab force' (Gutman 2015). Given this power differential, it is obvious that the SDF is not an alliance between partners and with shared responsibility. Rather, it provides a convenient framework for the YPG to use the smaller militias as proxies. There is also an understanding that the YPG's strategic goals and vision take precedence and recruits from other minorities are required to undergo ideological training (Gutman 2015; Sly 2017). The smaller groups accept the YPG's supreme role for several reasons. They have mutual interests (i.e. the defeat of IS) and they hope that aligning with the Kurds will bring them material gains or political influence, increase their survivability thanks to the aerial support by the anti-IS coalition or even enhance their credibility at the international level with respect to an eventual post-conflict settlement (Wilkofsky and Fatah 2017). In short, their cost–benefit calculus matches the reasoning of non-state armed groups that accept the support of state sponsors (Byman 2018).

As can be expected, the relationship between the YPG and other SDF groups has not been without tensions. In April 2017, for example, the Syriac Military Council (SMC) publicly complained about being treated unequally and pleaded with the United States to be provided with the 'same military supplies as Arab and Kurdish forces are receiving' ('Assyrian Militia in Syria' 2017). The unequal distribution was also cited by several groups as the reason why they were defecting from the SDF, along with human rights abuses, forced conscription of Arab youths and, most importantly, the YPG's unwillingness to hand over control or at least share power in ethnically mixed or even majority-Arab areas after liberating them from the IS (Wilkofsky and Fatah 2017). Meanwhile, the YPG has made sure to keep its SDF proxies from getting too powerful by fragmenting them, spreading discord among different factions and arresting key leaders (Hassan 2017).

Addressing sectarianism by proxy

These internal conflicts notwithstanding, the SDF has at least to some degree played a role in addressing and even reducing some of the sectarian tensions in the Syrian civil war. At the most basic level, it proves that ethno-religious differences do not preclude cooperation across such divides, particularly in the face of shared interests and mutual enemies. The United States, which had been instrumental in the SDF's establishment, had sought, with varying degree of success, to both 'assuage Turkish concerns and avert tensions between Arabs and Kurds' (Sly 2017). More specifically, given the Kurd's minority status within Syria, the YPG had little choice but to work with militias and groups from other ethnicities if it hoped to gain local or even international legitimacy. While most of the other SDF groups have little impact on the battlefield, they are a means for the YPG to reach out to, influence and even recruit among other ethno-religious communities that are traditionally wary of Kurdish aspirations (Hisham 2017; Tabler 2017). Put differently, without the political cover provided by its non-Kurdish proxies, the YPG would have found it far more difficult to push further south and administer territories beyond the majority-Kurdish settlements in Northern Syria. According to the International Crisis Group, the external military aid, which facilitated the territorial expansion in the first place, has created a somewhat paradoxical situation. While it helped the YPG consolidate its regional control and governance, it also forced it 'to relax its internal rules and ideological purity in order to attract new fighters' (International Crisis Group 2017c: 13). To summarize, while reducing sectarian tension has never been the YPG's top priority in creating the SDF, it has certainly proven a side benefit.

Conclusion

As this chapter has shown, and contrary to conventional wisdom, neither do proxy relationships occur exclusively between state sponsors and non-state armed groups, nor do they necessarily further aggravate sectarian tensions. Indeed, as the YPG case study highlights, non-state actors can use proxies to try and bridge ethno-religious divides. There is no reason to assume that the case of the YPG is an outlier. There are several ongoing civil wars and insurgencies in the Middle East and beyond, and most of these conflicts feature multiple armed movements with varying and often fluctuating ties to each other.[4] It stands to reason that some of these belligerents seek to employ other non-state actors as proxies. At the same time, and as the US pullback and the subsequent Turkish invasion in October 2019 demonstrate, even relatively powerful non-state sponsors remain susceptible to external interference, which can considerably affect the relation to their surrogates (Holland-McCowan 2019). Finally, whereas a few studies have acknowledged the existence of non-state sponsorship, the phenomenon remains understood. To better understand the complex dynamics of contemporary proxy relations, scholars will need to pay closer attention to variation in actors, actor pairings and context.

Notes

1. 'Proxy intervention', for example, focuses on the act of an external interference in a local conflict, whereas 'proxy warfare' describes a certain way of waging war, that is, a strategy involving the use of proxies. Meanwhile, 'proxy war' (or 'proxy conflict') denotes an armed conflict in which at least one of the warring parties is surrogate forces. See also Rauta (2018).
2. An interesting exception, and possibly the first study to consider non-state actors as proxies, is Weinberger (1986).
3. A comprehensive discussion of the concept of sectarianism is beyond the scope of this chapter, instead it follows Phillips (2015) defining it as 'discrimination, hate or tension based on differences between sects'. See also Haddad (2011) and Valbjørn (2020).
4. For two additional examples, see Moghadam and Wyss (2020).

References

Ahram, A. (2011), *Proxy Warriors: The Rise and Fall of State-Sponsored Militias*, Stanford, CA: Stanford University Press.

Allsopp, H., and van Wilgenburg, V. (2019), *The Kurds of Northern Syria: Governance, Diversity and Conflicts*, London: Bloomsbury.

'Assyrian Militia in Syria Asks for Full Support from U.S.' (2017), *Assyrian International News Agency*, 4 April. Available online: http://www.aina.org/news/20170404121950.htm (accessed 30 September 2020).

Bapat, N. A. (2011), 'Understanding State Sponsorship of Militant Groups', *British Journal of Political Science*, 42 (1): 1–29.

Bar-Siman-Tov, Y. (1984), 'The Strategy of War by Proxy', *Cooperation and Conflict*, 19 (4): 263–73.

Berkowitz, J. M. (2018), 'Delegating Terror: Principal–Agent Based Decision Making in State Sponsorship of Terrorism', *International Interactions*, 44 (4): 709–48.

Berti, B., and Guzansky, Y. (2014), 'Saudi Arabia's Foreign Policy on Iran and the Proxy War in Syria: Toward a New Chapter', *Israel Journal of Foreign Affairs*, 8 (3): 25–34.

'Bis-souwar: bis-sabab ibnihi al-azi qada ma'a Hizb'allah al-shaykh Khadir al-Kabash yata'arradu lid-darb' (2016), *Janoubia*, 3 September. Available online: http://janoubia.com/2016/09/03/بالصور-بسبب-ابنه-الذي-قضى-مع-حزب-الله/ (accessed 30 September 2020).

Brown, S. (2016), 'Purposes and Pitfalls of War by Proxy', *Small Wars & Insurgencies*, 27 (2): 243–57.

Buchen, S. (2012), 'Alliance between the PKK and the Assad Regime: A Political Sect on the Wrong Track', *Qantara*, 2 August. Available online: https://en.qantara.de/content/alliance-between-the-pkk-and-the-assad-regime-a-political-sect-on-the-wrong-track (accessed 30 September 2020).

Burleigh, M. (2014), 'The Ancient Muslim Hatreds Tearing Apart the Middle East', *Daily Mail*, 13 June. Available online: https://www.dailymail.co.uk/news/article-2656734/Ancient-hatreds-tearing-apart-Middle-East-How-1-400-year-old-feud-Shia-Sunni-Muslims-flared-life-fall-dictators-like-Gaddafi-Saddam-threatens-swallow-Iraq.html (accessed 30 September 2020).

Byman, D. (2018), 'Why Be a Pawn to a State? Proxy Wars from a Proxy's Perspective', *Lawfare*, 22 May. Available online: https://www.lawfareblog.com/why-be-pawn-state-proxy-wars-proxys-perspective (accessed 30 September 2020).

Byman, D., Chalk, P., Hoffman, B., Rosenau, W. and Brannan, D. (2001), *Trends in Outside Support for Insurgent Movements*, Santa Monica: RAND.

Byman, D., and Kreps, S. E. (2010), 'Agents of Destruction? Applying Principal-Agent Analysis to State-Sponsored Terrorism', *International Studies Perspectives*, 11 (1): 1–18.

Carey, S. C., Colaresi, M. P. and Mitchell, N. J. (2015), 'Governments, Informal Links to Militias, and Accountability', *Journal of Conflict Resolution*, 59 (5): 850–76.

Charap, S., Treyger, E. and Geist, E. (2019), 'Understanding Russia's Intervention in Syria'. Research Report No. 318, Santa Monica: RAND. Available online: https://www.rand.org/content/dam/rand/pubs/research_reports/RR3100/RR3180/RAND_RR3180.pdf (accessed 30 September 2020).

Chbaro, A. (2016), 'Muhammad al-Kabash min qisas shabaab as-sounna ladina qadaw kilal al-qital ma'a "Hizb'allah" fi Souriya', *An-Nahar*, 5 April. Available online: https://www.annahar.com/article/347611-محمد-الكبشمن-قصص-الشباب-السنة-الذين-قضوا-خلال-الق تال-مع-حزب-الله-في-سوريا (accessed 30 September 2020).

Dahan, N. (2018), 'Sunni vs Shia: The New Statesman's Latest Cover Draws Ire', *Middle East Eye*, 6 March. Available online: https://www.middleeasteye.net/news/sunni-vs-shia-new-statesmans-latest-cover-draws-ire (accessed September 2020).

Dettmer, J. (2013), 'Al Qaeda-Linked Jihadists Are Hunting and Killing Moderate Syrian Rebels', *The Daily Beast*, 18 December. Available online: https://www.thedailybeast.com/al-qaeda-linked-jihadists-are-hunting-and-killing-moderate-syrian-rebels?ref=scroll (accessed 30 September 2020).

Evran, S. (2016), 'Erdoğan's Kurdish Gangs', *ANF News*, 26 December. Available online: https://anfenglish.com/features/erdogan-s-kurdish-gangs-17742 (accessed 30 September 2020).

Fisher, M. (2016), 'How the Iranian-Saudi Proxy Struggle Tore the Mideast Apart', *New York Times*, 20 November: 8.

Groisman, M. (2016), 'The Iran-Backed Sunni Group That Aids Hezbollah in the Syrian Battlefield', *Jerusalem Post*, 3 April. Available online: https://www.jpost.com/Middle-East/The-Iran-backed-Sunni-group-that-aids-Hezbollah-in-the-Syrian-battlefield-450094 (accessed 30 September 2020).

Gutman, R. (2015), 'New Allies in Northern Syria Don't Seem to Share U.S. Goals', *McClatchy*, 27 October. Available online: https://www.mcclatchydc.com/news/nation-world/world/article41559747.html (accessed 30 September 2020).

Haddad, F. (2011), *Sectarianism in Iraq: Antagonistic Visions of Unity*, New York: Oxford University Press.

Halhalli, B. (2018), 'Kurdish Political Parties in Syria: Past Struggles and Future Expectations', in E. E. Tugar and S. Al (eds), *Comparative Kurdish Politics in the Middle East: Actors, Ideas, and Interest*, Cham: Springer International, 27–53.

Hanau Santini, R. (2017), 'A New Regional Cold War in the Middle East and North Africa: Regional Security Complex Theory Revisited', *International Spectator*, 54 (4): 93–111.

Hassan, M. (2017), 'Kurdish and Syrian Regime Forces Take Very Different Routes to Control in Deir Ez-Zor', Chatham House. Available online: https://syria.chathamho use.org/research/kurdish-and-syrian-regime-forces-take-very-different-routes-to-cont rol-in-deir-ez-zor (accessed 30 September 2020).

Hinnebusch, R. (2012), 'Syria: From "Authoritarian Upgrading" to Revolution?', *International Affairs*, 88 (1): 95–113.

Hisham, M. (2017), 'I Fled the Islamic State's "Caliphate" in Raqqa – But Fear Its Liberators', *Foreign Policy*, 23 June. Available online: https://foreignpolicy. com/2017/06/23/i-fled-the-islamic-states-caliphate-in-raqqa-but-fear-its-liberators/ (accessed 30 September 2020).

Hokayem, E. (2014), 'Iran, the Gulf States and the Syrian Civil War', *Survival: Global Politics and Strategy*, 56 (6): 59–86.

Holland-McCowan, J. (2019), 'Will "We Won" Become "Mission Accomplished"? A US Withdrawal and the Scramble for Northeastern Syria', London: International Centre for the Study of Radicalisation. Available online: https://icsr.info/wp-content/uplo ads/2019/12/ICSR-Report-Will-'We-Won'-Become-'Mission-Accomplished'-A-US-Wit hdrawal-and-The-Scramble-for-Northeastern-Syria.pdf (accessed 30 September 2020).

Horton, M. (2017), 'Fighting the Long War: The Evolution of al-Qaʿida in the Arabian Peninsula', *CTC Sentinel*, 10 (1): 17–22.

Hughes, G. (2012), *My Enemy's Enemy: Proxy Warfare in International Politics*, Eastbourne: Sussex Academic Press.

Hughes, G. (2014), 'Syria and the Perils of Proxy Warfare', *Small Wars & Insurgencies*, 25 (3): 522–38.

Hughes, G. (2016), 'Militias in Internal Warfare: From the Colonial Era to the Contemporary Middle East', *Small Wars & Insurgencies*, 27 (2): 196–225.

Innes, M. A. (2012), 'Preface', in M. A. Innes (ed.), *Making Sense of Proxy Wars: States, Surrogates & the Use of Force*, Washington, DC: Potomac Books, xiii–xvi.

Innes, M. A. (ed.) (2012), *Making Sense of Proxy Wars: States, Surrogates & the Use of Force*, Washington, DC: Potomac Books.

International Crisis Group (2013), 'Syria's Kurds: A Struggle within a Struggle', Middle East Report N°136, Brussels: International Crisis Group. Available online: https://d20 71andvip0wj.cloudfront.net/syrias-kurds-a-struggle-within-a-struggle.pdf (accessed 30 September 2020).

International Crisis Group (2017a), 'Fighting ISIS: The Road to and beyond Raqqa', Middle East Briefing N°53, Brussels: International Crisis Group. Available online: https://d2071andvip0wj.cloudfront.net/b053-fighting-isis-the-road-to-and-bey ond-raqqa.pdf (accessed 30 September 2020).

International Crisis Group (2017b), 'How the Islamic State Rose, Fell and Could Rise Again in the Maghreb', Middle East and North Africa Report N°178, Brussels: International Crisis Group. Available online: https://d2071andvip0wj.cloudfr ont.net/178-how-the-islamic-state-rose_0.pdf (accessed 30 September 2020).

International Crisis Group (2017c). 'The PKK's Fateful Choice in Northern Syria', Middle East Report N°176, Brussels: International Crisis Group. Available online: https:// d2071andvip0wj.cloudfront.net/176-the-pkks-fateful-choice-in-northern-syria.pdf (accessed 30 September 2020).

Jones, S. G., Dobbins, J., Byman, D., Chivvis, C. S., Connable, B., Martini, J., Robinson, E. and Chandler, N. (2017), *Rolling Back the Islamic State*, Santa Monica: RAND.

Klein, H.-J. (1977), 'Ich habe genug angestellt', *Der Spiegel*, (20): 33–4.

Krieg, A., and Rickli, J.-M. (2019), *Surrogate Warfare: The Transformation of War in the Twenty-First Century*, Washington, DC: Georgetown University Press.

Landis, J. (2012), 'The Syrian Uprising of 2011: Why the Asad Regime Is Likely to Survive to 2013', *Middle East Policy*, 18 (1): 72–84.

Letsch, C. (2014), 'US Drops Weapons and Ammunition to Help Kurdish Fighters in Kobani', *The Guardian*, 20 October. Available online: https://www.theguardian.com/world/2014/oct/20/turkey-iraqi-kurds-kobani-isis-fighters-us-air-drops-arms (accessed 30 September 2020).

Lister, C. R. (2015), *The Syrian Jihad: Al-Qaeda, the Islamic State, and the Evolution of an Insurgency*, New York: Oxford University Press.

Lund, A. (2016), 'Origins of the Syrian Democratic Forces: A Primer', *Syria Deeply*, 22 January. Available online: https://www.newsdeeply.com/syria/articles/2016/01/22/origins-of-the-syrian-democratic-forces-a-primer (accessed 30 September 2020).

Mahmood, M., and Black, I. (2013), 'Free Syrian Army Rebels Defect to Islamist Group Jabhat al-Nusra', *The Guardian*, 8 May. Available online: https://www.theguardian.com/world/2013/may/08/free-syrian-army-rebels-defect-islamist-group (accessed 30 September 2020).

Marshall, A. (2016) 'From Civil War to Proxy War: Past History and Current Dilemmas', *Small Wars & Insurgencies*, 27 (2): 183–95.

McDowall, D. (2004), *A Modern History of the Kurds*, 3rd edn, New York: I.B. Tauris.

McKelvey, T. (2015), 'Arming Syrian Rebels: Where the US Went Wrong', *BBC News*, 10 October. Available online: https://www.bbc.com/news/magazine-33997408 (accessed 30 September 2020).

Moghadam, A., and Wyss, M. (2020), 'The Political Power of Proxies: Why Nonstate Actors Use Local Surrogates', *International Security*, 44 (4): 119–57.

Mohammed, A., and Yacoub Oweis, K. (2013), 'West to Send Syrian Rebels Aid, Not Arms', *Reuters*, 28 February. Available online: https://www.reuters.com/article/us-syria-crisis-us/west-to-send-syrian-rebels-aid-not-arms-idUSBRE91R0KM20130228 (accessed 30 September 2020).

Morris, H. (2015), 'ISIS Still Strong Despite Major Defeat in Kobani', *TIME*, 27 January. Available online: https://time.com/3683806/isis-kobani-defeat-kurds/ (accessed 30 September 2020).

Mullah Darwish, S. (2016), 'Raqqa Brigade Continues to Raise Flag of Syrian Revolution', *Al-Monitor*, 18 March. Available online: https://www.al-monitor.com/pulse/originals/2016/03/syria-raqqa-revolutionaries-brigade-liberation-isis.html (accessed 30 September 2020).

Mumford, A. (2013), *Proxy Warfare*, Cambridge: Polity Press.

Phillips, C. (2012), 'Into the Quagmire: Turkey's Frustrated Syria Policy', MENAP BP 2012/04, London: Chatham House. Available online: https://www.chathamhouse.org/sites/default/files/public/Research/Middle%20East/1212bp_phillips.pdf (accessed 30 September 2020).

Phillips, C. (2015), 'Sectarianism and Conflict in Syria', *Third World Quarterly*, 36 (2): 357–76.

Phillips, C., and Valbjørn, M. (2018), '"What Is in a Name?": The Role of (Different) Identities in the Multiple Proxy Wars in Syria', *Small Wars & Insurgencies*, 29 (3): 414–33.

Popovic, M. (2017), 'Fragile Proxies: Explaining Rebel Defection against Their State Sponsors', *Terrorism and Political Violence*, 29 (5): 922–42.

Rabi, U., and Muller, C. (2018), 'The Geopolitics of Sectarianism in the Persian Gulf', *Asian Journal of Islamic and Middle Eastern Studies*, 12 (1): 46–65.

Rauta, V. (2018), 'A Structural-Relational Analysis of Party Dynamics in Proxy Wars', *International Relations*, 32 (4): 449–67.

Recknagel, C. (2012), 'Is Syria Seeing Start of Sectarian War?', *Radio Free Europe/Radio Liberty*, 15 June. Available online: https://www.rferl.org/a/syria-backgrounder-sectarian-war/24615642.html (accessed 30 September 2020).

Rondeaux, C., and Sterman, D. (2019a), 'Proxy Warfare in the Greater Middle East and its Periphery: An Atlas'. New America, 19 February. Available online: https://www.newamerica.org/international-security/reports/twenty-first-century-proxy-warfare-confronting-strategic-innovation-multipolar-world/proxy-warfare-in-the-greater-middle-east-and-its-periphery-an-atlas (accessed 30 September 2020).

Rondeaux, C., and Sterman, D. (2019b), 'Twenty-First Century Proxy Warfare: Confronting Strategic Innovation in a Multipolar World', Washington, DC: New America. Available online: https://d1y8sb8igg2f8e.cloudfront.net/documents/Twenty-First_Century_Proxy_Warfare_Final.pdf (accessed 30 September 2020).

Salehyan, I. (2010), 'The Delegation of War to Rebel Organizations', *Journal of Conflict Resolution*, 54 (3): 493–515.

Salehyan, I., Gleditsch, K. S. and Cunningham, D. E. (2011), 'Explaining External Support for Insurgent Groups', *International Organization*, 65 (4): 709–44.

Savelsberg, E. (2014), 'The Syrian-Kurdish Movements: Obstacles Rather Than Driving Forces for Democratization', in D. Romano and M. Gurses (eds), *Conflict, Democratization, and the Kurds in the Middle East: Turkey, Iran, Iraq, and Syria*, New York: Palgrave Macmillan, 85–107.

Seely, R. (2017), 'Defining Contemporary Russian Warfare', *RUSI Journal*, 162 (1): 50–9.

Seligman, L. (2019), 'Trump Wants U.S. Troops to Guard Syria's Oil. The Kurds May Not Welcome Them', *Foreign Policy*, 24 October. Available online: https://foreignpolicy.com/2019/10/24/ilham-ahmed-trump-syria-kurds-turkey-oil/ (accessed 30 September 2020).

Sly, L. (2017), 'U.S. Military Aid Is Fueling Big Ambitions for Syria's Leftist Kurdish Militia', *Washington Post*, 7 January. Available online: https://www.washingtonpost.com/world/middle_east/us-military-aid-is-fueling-big-ambitions-for-syrias-leftist-kurdish-militia/2017/01/07/6e457866-c79f-11e6-acda-59924caa2450_story.html (accessed 30 September 2020).

Smyth, P. (2015), 'The Shiite Jihad in Syria and Its Regional Effects', *Policy Focus* 138, Washington, DC: The Washington Institute for Near East Policy. Available online: http://www.washingtoninstitute.org/policy-analysis/pdf/the-shiite-jihad-in-syria-and-its-regional-effects (accessed 30 September 2020).

Steinhoff, P. G. (1976), 'Portrait of a Terrorist: An Interview with Kozo Okamoto', *Asian Studies*, 16 (9): 830–45.

Stephens, M., and Stein, A. (2015), 'The YPG: America's New Best Friend', *Al Jazeera*, 28 June. Available online: https://www.aljazeera.com/indepth/opinion/2015/06/ypg-america-friend-isil-kurds-syria-150627073034776.html (accessed 30 September 2020).

Tabler, A. J. (2017), 'Eyeing Raqqa: A Tale of Four Tribes', *Policy Note* 39, Washington, DC: The Washington Institute for Near East Policy. Available online: https://www.washingtoninstitute.org/uploads/Documents/pubs/PolicyNote39-Raqqa.pdf (accessed 30 September 2020).

Terrill, W. A. (2014), 'Iranian Involvement in Yemen', *Orbis*, 58 (3): 429–40.

'The Kurds' Precarious Balancing Act in Syria' (2017), *Strategic Comment*, 23 (4): v–vi.

Ustun, K. (2016), 'US Alliance with Syrian PYD Alienates Turkey', *Al-Jazeera*, 2 June. Available online: https://www.aljazeera.com/indepth/opinion/2016/06/alliance-syrian-pyd-alienates-turkey-160601095726203.html (accessed 30 September 2020).

Valbjørn, M. (2020), 'Beyond the Beyond(S): On the (Many) Third Way(s) beyond Primordialism and Instrumentalism in the Study of Sectarianism', *Nations and Nationalism*, 26 (1): 91–107.

Van Wilgenburg, W. (2013), 'Kurdish Strategy towards Ethnically-Mixed Areas in the Syrian Conflict', *Jamestown Foundation Terrorism Monitor*, 11 (23): 7–9.

Weinberger, N. J. (1986), *Syrian Intervention in Lebanon*, New York: Oxford University Press.

Wight, C. (2006), *Agents, Structures and International Relations: Politics as Ontology*, New York: Cambridge University Press.

Wilkofsky, D., and Fatah, K. (2017), 'Northern Syria's Anti-Islamic State Coalition Has an Arab Problem', *War on the Rocks*, 18 September. Available online: https://warontherocks.com/2017/09/northern-syrias-anti-islamic-state-coalition-has-an-arab-problem/ (accessed 30 September 2020).

Chapter 7

SAUDI ARABIA'S RHETORICAL CONSTRUCTION OF THE HOUTHIS AS AN IRANIAN PROXY

Maria-Louise Clausen

Introduction

In the Middle East today regional dynamics are less defined by formal alliances and increasingly by more informal relations including external support to (armed) non-state actors. This is also reflected in suggestions that the regional politics of the Middle East can be defined as a 'new' cold war in which Iran and Saudi Arabia play the leading roles (Gause 2014). The geopolitical rivalry between Iran and Saudi Arabia has contributed to a politization of sectarianism. This is not only part of the overall competition between a Saudi-led Sunni bloc against an Iran-led Shia bloc but also in growing intra-Sunni and intra-Shia cleavages. Consequently, the regional security environment has become increasingly fragmented. This process is particularly visible and complex as armed non-state actors have grown in the weak and conflict-affected states of the Middle East such as Yemen. The conflict in Yemen began as a civil war following the transition after the popular uprising in 2011 but is increasingly seen as a sectarianized proxy conflict between Iran and Saudi Arabia.

In March 2015, a Saudi-led coalition began a military intervention into Yemen at the request of the then-internationally recognized president 'Abd Rabbuh Mansour Hadi. This intervention has, at the time of writing, been ongoing for more than seven years and resulted in what is referred to as one of the world's current largest humanitarian crises. Saudi Arabia linked the Houthis to Iran from the onset of the military intervention and continued to frame the Houthis as controlled by Iran as a way of justifying the intervention. This has been possible because the Houthis are Zaydi, a form of Shiism. Furthermore, the Houthis have received military and organizational support from Iran, and as such become part of Iran's regional axis of resistance (Clausen, 2022).

This chapter explores how Saudi Arabia, the leader of the coalition who intervened in Yemen in March 2015, has discursively justified the intervention. The chapter shows how the Saudi justification of the intervention reflects a construction of Saudi Arabia as a friend of Yemen and the Houthis as a proxy of

Iran, linked together by belonging to the Shia camp. The chapter does not evaluate the accuracies of these claims but seeks to lay out the elements in the narrative that have been used to justify the military intervention into Yemen. By linking the Houthis to Iran and its network of proxies in the region, Saudi Arabia sought to elevate the perceived Yemeni threat from being a domestic Yemeni concern, to a question with regional or even international implications. This has exacerbated the conflict by regionalizing and sectarianizing it. While these processes are not necessarily linked, understanding how they interacted in the Yemeni case can help facilitate or impede regional processes of desectarianization.

The chapter draws on official statements from key Saudi officials in documents from the United Nations Security Council (UNSC), press releases and other statements and interviews related to the intervention in Yemen to explore the official Saudi discourse on the Houthis. These have been located in three ways: first, through the United Nations Official Document System (ODS) that can be accessed online through the UN website. In the database, it is possible to carry out themed searches in documents and debates from the UN Security Council.[1] Second, through the home page of the Saudi Press Agency (SPA) and finally, through a general search of statements and speeches made by Adel bin Ahmed Al-Jubeir, who has played a key role in framing the Saudi Arabian representation of the intervention into Yemen to an English-speaking audience as first Saudi ambassador to the United States, then foreign minister and latest minister of state for foreign affairs. These sources are then discussed and contextualized by referring to the secondary sources.

The post-Arab uprising transition in Yemen and its gradual collapse

Yemen was one of the first countries that followed the lead from Tunisia and Egypt in 2011 and saw a popular uprising against the regime of long-time president 'Ali Abdullah Saleh. The situation in Yemen had been deteriorating for decades and protests pointing at the lack of economic development and growing insecurity had been occurring for years leading up to 2011. During the months of largely peaceful protests that were met with increasingly violent methods from the regime of President 'Ali Abdullah Saleh, Saleh became under increasing pressure. In November 2011, he was forced to sign the Gulf Cooperation Council (GCC) Initiative, which outlined a two-year transition process. The first step was a negotiated transfer of power from Saleh to his long-time vice-president 'Abd Rabbuh Mansour Hadi. Hadi was charged with overseeing the envisioned two-year transition process that was to result in a new constitution and elections. At the time, the GCC deal was celebrated for preventing the outbreak of a looming civil war, but its focus on maintaining stability and securing buy-in from the elites that had been part of Saleh's regime at least partly explains why the transition eventually collapsed. Saleh was allowed to remain in Yemen with immunity and to continue his position as head of the ruling party, the General People's Congress (GPC).

In February 2012, 'Abd Rabbuh Mansour Hadi was formally elected as the transitional president in an election where he was the only candidate. A key element of the transitional phase was the National Dialogue Conference (NDC) where 565 delegates envisioned to represent a broad spectrum of the Yemeni society including political parties as well as representatives from all regions of Yemen and social categories met to deliberate the future of Yemen. The deliberations of the NDC, divided into nine working groups, were to form the foundation of a new constitution that was to be approved through a referendum at the end of the transition process. However, while the Houthis were engaged in deliberations inside the NDC, they were simultaneously engaged in armed struggle north of Sana'a. The backdrop to this power struggle was the Sa'ada wars between the Houthis and the Saleh regime between 2004 and 2010 (Brandt 2017). The fight against the Houthis had been led by General 'Ali Mohsin al-Ahmar, a key commander of the north-western military district and the First Armoured Division, who had long been one of Saleh's closest allies. He had broken the alliance with Saleh and sided with the protestors in 2011. The power vacuum that followed these intra-elite splits were exploited by the Houthis to expand their control of the northern parts of Yemen, moving northwards from Sa'ada to the governorates of Hajja, 'Amran and al-Jawf and in the process defeating army segments and tribes, many of them associated with Islah (the Yemeni Congregation for Reform, generally known as Islah). Islah had emerged strengthened following the deposing of Saleh but was unable to militarily defeat the Houthis. The transitional president, Hadi, was unwilling (or unable) to deploy the Yemeni military to stop the Houthis' onward march towards the Yemeni capital, Sana'a. The NDC, which is still generally perceived to be an impressive feat, was concluded in January 2014. However, although the level of debate was impressive, no agreement was reached on the future structure of the Yemeni state and the fact that the NDC resulted in over 1800 recommendations underscores how key political decisions and priorities were to be made after the conclusion of the NDC.[2] A key decision that was postponed was the structure of the future Yemeni state (Clausen 2018). Yemen was to be a federal state but after the closure of the NDC, the decision on the number of regions as well as their organization was delegated to smaller working groups. This fed a growing feeling of discontent as some actors, including the Houthis, felt that they were being sidelined from real power. The Houthis continued towards Sana'a and in September 2014, they, with the aid of the former president Saleh who remained in control of large parts of the Yemeni military, took over control of the Yemeni capital. After the Houthis takeover of Sana'a in September 2014, attempts were made to reach a political compromise which resulted in the Peace and National Partnership Agreement (PNPA) with the help of United Nations special advisor on Yemen, Jamal Benomar. The PNPA had positive elements and seemed to usher in a more truly inclusive political reality in line with the uprising in 2011. However, the situation continued to deteriorate, in part because the Houthis did not honour the agreement but continued to exert power over state institutions. When the first draft of the new constitution was presented by the Constitution Drafting Committee (CDC), the Houthis kidnapped Ahmed 'Awadh bin Mubarak, the director of President Hadi's office, and subsequently placed the government and Hadi under house arrest. In February Hadi escaped from house arrest and fled to Aden, which he announced as his interim capital. The Houthis, supported by forces loyal to Saleh, moved towards Aden and Hadi was forced to flee to Riyadh. On 25 March 2015 the Saudi-led coalition intervened.

Identity, friends and enemies

The approach of the chapter is inspired by constructivist approaches to International Relations (IR) as it focuses on the construction of identity and how the articulation of identity constitutes foreign policy. That is, an articulation of identity creates reality through language (Campbell 1998). Whereas constructivist IR has mainly focused on how the Global North (the West) has constructed the Global South (the 'Rest'), fewer works have studied how identity constructions take place between non-Western states (Doty 1996). This chapter shows how a non-Western state, Saudi Arabia, has constructed the identity of another non-Western actor, the Houthis, a Yemeni non-state actor, as a proxy of Iran. Second, the chapter shows how this construction has helped Saudi Arabia build and sustain its relationship to the United States by feeding into established frames about Iran which has been used to place the Houthis in the terrorist camp. In order to do this, the chapter approaches the proxy concept as an essentially contested concept (Gallie 1956). The analytical framework of essentially contested concepts underscores how conceptual confusion is built into some concepts, making their core meaning a matter of contestation. W. B. Gallie claims that concepts are essentially contested in virtue of their norm-invoking functions, thus giving them either a positive or a negative valuation (Collier, Hidalgo and Maciuceanu 2006). Consequently, an essentially contested concept is defined by internal complexity that makes it plausible that different users may describe its meaning in different ways. In the context of this chapter, it is argued that the proxy concept is essentially contested but is given a specific meaning by Saudi Arabia when it constructs the Houthis *as an Iranian-backed terrorist militia*. This construction builds on two key components that refer to a basic distinction between friend and enemy in politics. *First*, the relationship between Saudi Arabia and the Yemeni state. This is structured around two interlinked narratives: (1) that the Houthis are an illegitimate militia threatening the legitimate government of Yemen and hence the Yemeni state and (2) that Saudi Arabia is a friend of Yemen, working to save the Yemeni state. The *second* component is the relationship between the Houthis and Iran which also has two elements: (1) Iran as an enemy to Saudi Arabia and a threat to international security as exemplified by its support to terrorists and expansionist ideals, and (2) that the Houthis are Iran's proxy through references to overlapping policies and sectarian identity. The construction of the Houthis as an Iranian-backed terrorist militia is an ongoing and dynamic process but based on a certain level of historical learning to secure some coherence.

The narrative of the Houthis as an Iranian proxy is built on perceptions of friendship and hostility in politics. The idea of identity as relational is formulated by William E. Connolly as 'Identity requires difference in order to be, and it converts difference into otherness in order to secure its own self-certainty' (Connolly 2002: 64). Consequently, it is in the process of establishing difference to the Other that the Self is constructed. The emphasis has typically been on the role of the threatening Other, the enemy, in the form of analysis of how perceptions of danger and difference work to establish state identity (Campbell 1998). Self and the (negative) otherness are co-constructed. The link between identity and conflict is seen in the act of locating 'the evil' in the actions of the Other, the enemy, who is positioned in relation to the 'good' character of the Self (Strömbom 2012: 175). However, as underlined by Felix Berenskoetter the role of positive otherness in constructing state identity is largely overlooked (Berenskoetter 2007). Yet, references to friendship between states are common. The idea of friendship between states is differentiated to more paternalistic and uneven relations between states and their former colonies or assumptions about linkages based on shared cultural parameters (ibid.: 661). According to Berenskoetter, friendship is 'a process of building a "common world" to which states become emotionally attached' (Berenskoetter 2007: 670). His example of friendship between two states is the relationship between France and Germany through the project of European integration.

However, the distinction between 'good' Others (friends) and 'bad' Others (enemies) is a limited one (Zhukova 2017). Lene Hansen has accounted for differences within enemies by reference to degrees of badness (Hansen 2006), whereas Morozov and Rumelili point to how Self/Other relations are constituted along multiple dimensions and that positive and negative representations of the Other can coexist and be projected upon different aspects of the Other's identity (Morozov and Rumelili 2012: 31). This chapter investigates these elements in the Saudi construction of the Houthis as an Iranian proxy. This adds a glimpse into how a non-Western state (Saudi Arabia) constructs an image of an armed non-state actor by activating and playing on the relationship of this group to an established enemy state, Iran. Although the focus of this chapter is on Saudi Arabia, it is recognized that both the Houthis and Iran have agency in this process. Neither are passive recipients of a given identity. Importantly, the focus on the Saudi narrative should not be read as implicit support for that narrative.

The contested nature of the proxy concept

The issue of proxy warfare has been gaining attention in the last years, and in the Middle East this is not least driven by the perception that Iran uses proxies to further its foreign policy aims. Proxy war can be defined as 'conflicts in which a third party intervenes indirectly in order to influence the strategic outcome in favour of its preferred faction' (Mumford 2013). It is often assumed that third parties intervene to win wars but objectives might include delegating limited resources to a relatively low-importance conflict to impact indirectly another conflict or feeding chaos when the patron has little interest in the conflict per se but sees it as an opportunity to deny another state the ability to attain its interests (Groh 2019: 36–7). This chapter does not discuss whether the conflict in Yemen is in fact best understood as a proxy war, but takes the contested nature of the concept as a starting point (Rauta 2021). The terminological ambiguity helps us understand how it remains essentially contested what constitutes a proxy *actor* and thus a point of continued contention whether the Houthis are in fact an Iranian proxy.

Generally, it is agreed that in a proxy relationship there must be some sort of principal–agent relationship, where an outside actor, usually a state but not necessarily, seeks to influence another state's internal affairs through support to an actor that is willing to act, to some degree, on the intervening state's behalf. But this is not very precise in terms of how much or which kind of support it takes to make a proxy relationship. Geraint Hughes has suggested a focus on non-state actors (Hughes 2012: 11). This is the case here where the focus is on the Houthis, a non-state actor. Tyrone L. Groh has argued that groups that have agency and interests beyond those of the patron should not be excluded while, at the same time, recognizing that proxies should be distinguished from actors that have no separate interest in the conflict such as, for example, mercenaries (Groh 2019: 27). Depending on the context, the proxy will to some degree be dependent on the support of the patron and more or less able to and interested in pursuing its own objectives that may or may not be separate from those of the patron. The dependency comes from the patron's willingness and ability to back the proxy with hardware, intelligence or other key operational forms of support that augment the proxy's forces. Since there is no clear threshold for when a group is a proxy group, there is often a normative element in when and how the concept is used. Moreover, in many proxy relationships one or both of the parties might have an interest in concealing the involvement of the third party in the conflict which further accentuates how contested it can be to define an actor as a proxy.

Saudi Arabia and the Yemeni state: Saudi Arabia as a friend of Yemen and the Houthis as an enemy

The Saudi-led coalition 'Operation Decisive Storm' began in March 2015 (renamed to Operation Restoring Hope in April 2015) following a call for help issued to both the United National and the Arab League from 'Abd Rabbuh Mansour Hadi, the transitional president of Yemen (Clausen 2019a). Hadi became president in 2012 as part of a negotiated transfer of power from his predecessor, 'Ali Abdullah Saleh, who grudgingly signed over the presidential office. The position of Hadi was, as already mentioned, confirmed in a general election where he was the only candidate, but a voter turnout of nearly 65 per cent was widely accepted as a sign of popular support for the transitional process. President Hadi was initially elected for two years which ended in February 2014, but Hadi's term was prolonged by a year as the transition process was delayed. As Hadi was forced to flee Yemen as the Houthis entered Sana'a and launched an attack on southern Yemen, Hadi remained president until April 2022, where Hadi transferred his powers to an eight-member Presidential Leadership Council (Ardemagni 2022).

This step had been underway some time but was made more difficult by the key UN Security Council resolution 2216 that was adopted on 14 April 2015. In the resolution, it is stated that the UN reaffirms its support for the legitimacy of the president of Yemen, 'Abd Rabbuh Mansour Hadi, and it calls for all parties and member states to refrain from actions that undermine the sovereignty, unity and territorial integrity of Yemen, and the legitimacy of the president of Yemen. The resolution goes on to demand that the Houthis unconditionally withdraw their forces from all seized areas, relinquish arms seized from the Yemeni military and security forces, cease all actions that are exclusively within the authority of the legitimate Government of Yemen and refrain from provocation or threats to neighbouring states.[3]

The need for the full and unconditional implementation of resolution 2216 has been continuously accentuated by Saudi Arabian officials and the internationally recognized government since the onset of the Saudi-led military campaign. Resolution 2216 positions President Hadi as the legitimate ruler of Yemen and the Houthis as an illegitimate actor who must relinquish control of materials and territory as a precondition for negotiations. Unsurprisingly, the Houthis have objected, whereas the Hadi government uses resolution 2216 as sanctioning its claim to absolute power. Resolution 2216 was early on linked to key documents from the transition in Yemen in 2012–14, namely the GCC Initiative, its Implementation Mechanism and the outcomes of the NDC. The GCC Initiative and the Implementation Mechanism are two relatively short documents that outline the key elements of the transition process including the transfer of power from Saleh to Hadi, the formation of a unity government split between members of the General People's Congress (GPC) – Saleh's party – and the main opposition collation, the Joint Meeting Parties (JMP) and the formation of the NDC. The transitional period would end with general elections in accordance with the new constitution, written by a Constitutional Commission and based on the outcomes from the NDC, and the inauguration of the new president of the Republic.[4] These documents, the outcomes from the NDC, the GCC deal and resolution 2216, are referred to as the three references for peace.

When the Saudis announced the intervention in March 2015, the then-Saudi Ambassador to Yemen, Adel al-Jubeir, stated that the 'objective is to defend the legitimate government of President Hadi from the takeover attempts by the Houthi militia in Yemen'.[5] The importance of rhetorically linking Hadi and legitimacy was constantly pushed by the Saudis, for example, by referring to the coalition as the 'Coalition to support legitimacy' and the aim of the intervention as being 'to restore legitimacy in Yemen'. Generally, the official Saudi approach was to rhetorically underline that President Hadi was the legitimate president by using the word 'legitimate' as a prefix whenever Hadi and his government is mentioned. The positioning of the Yemeni government as the legitimate representative of Yemen is contrasted to the illegitimacy of the Houthi movement. The Houthi militia, as it is referred to, deposed of the legitimate government through a coup and did so with actions that are 'flagrant violations of international law'.[6] I will return to the presentation of the Houthis in the next section in more detail.

The establishment of Hadi as the legitimate president of Yemen provided the legal cover for the intervention as well as helped Saudi Arabia justify the intervention. Saudi Arabia argues that the intervention is sanctioned by international law. President Hadi requested the GCC and the Arab League for support by all available means including military intervention with reference to the UN Charter article 51 and the right to self-defence, as well as the Charter of the Arab League and the Treaty on Joint Defence, in March 2015 just before the commencement of the Saudi-led military intervention.[7] Whereas the validity of the legal claim of self-defence, as well as the relevance of the intervention by invitation doctrine, has been critically examined by a few authors, it has generally been accepted that Hadi, as the internationally recognized president, could issue a call for intervention to which the Saudi-led coalition could legally respond with a military intervention (Ruys and Ferro 2016). Additionally, Saudi Arabia has sought to frame its activities as being in accordance with international humanitarian law.[8] This claim is undermined by reoccurring reports of breaches of humanitarian law by the Saudi-led campaign, as well as instances of non-cooperation by the coalition forces with independent actors seeking to investigate violations by parties to the conflict.[9] However, the Saudi Arabian narrative maintains that Saudi Arabia acts within international and humanitarian law, and that, when mistakes are made, they are rectified, which is very different from that of the Houthis. While international critique of the humanitarian consequences has been growing, Saudi Arabia has met with limited consequences for its actions in Yemen.

Saudi Arabia aims to present itself as a friend of Yemen that has intervened to 'serve the interests of the Yemeni people'.[10] It is presented as almost a moral obligation for Saudi Arabia to help its 'Yemeni brothers'. It is underscored that Saudi Arabia has no independent agenda in Yemen but acts out of brotherly love and will remain unwavering in its diplomatic, financial and military support to the people of Yemen, and their internationally recognized government. Within this narrative, the humanitarian assistance provided by Saudi Arabia to Yemen is framed as evidence or as a demonstration of the Saudi commitment to the welfare of the Yemeni people. The Saudi role in creating the humanitarian disaster in the first place is overlooked as the Houthis, the Iranian-backed militia, are pointed to as carrying the responsibility for the humanitarian disaster. In relation to the signing of the Riyadh Agreement on 5 November 2019, an agreement that focused on solving strife within the anti-Houthi coalition, it was, for example, argued that Saudi Arabia is not only doing all it can to help Yemen politically but is also supporting Yemen with humanitarian assistance.

On the home page of the King Salman humanitarian Aid & Relief Center (KSrelief) it is accentuated that Yemen is by far the largest receiver of aid from KSrelief, amounting to USD 2,414,279,576 distributed on 381 projects.[11] According to the Financial Tracking Service (FTS) that is managed by the UN Office for the Coordination of Humanitarian Affairs (OCHA), Saudi Arabia has distributed USD3.2 billion to Yemen since 2015.[12] Saudi Arabia has also made a number of direct transfers to the Central Bank of Yemen after president Hadi moved it to Aden in September 2016 (Rageh, Nasser and al-Muslimi 2016). Although the precise numbers are difficult to verify, there is no doubt that Saudi Arabia is a main donor to Yemen. This is used to argue that the Houthis are those creating the humanitarian disaster, whereas Saudi Arabia is trying to ameliorate the suffering of the Yemeni people.[13]

The Saudi framing of its relationship to Yemen has similarities to the paternalistic-type formulations found in descriptions of former colonies. Certainly, if friendship is a relationship among equals, that immediately disqualifies the relationship between Saudi Arabia and Yemen (Berenskoetter 2007: 670). The Yemeni president Hadi resided in Saudi Arabia and his government had a limited on-ground presence in Yemen. The limited legitimacy and support to Hadi within Yemen was part of the reason why Hadi transferred his powers to the Presidential Leadership Council in 2022. The Presidential Council consists of eight members with ground legitimacy and support by armed groups. Several of these received funding from Saudi Arabia and United Arab Emirates. Consequently, despite changes that reflect dynamics on the ground, the side in the Yemeni conflict representing the Yemeni state depends on the support of regional and international actors. Hadi hardly set foot in Yemen from 2015 until 2022, and therefore depended on Saudi Arabia to keep him relevant. In response, Hadi would continuously express his gratitude of the Saudi support as he called for continued and increased involvement. This was done through Hadi's official social media accounts and through official Saudi channels such as the SPA. These statements from official Yemeni and Saudi sources appear to mirror each other, where Saudi Arabia uses the legitimacy enshrined in the presidential office to justify their intervention into Yemen as one of saving the Yemeni people from the Houthi militia, while Yemeni representatives from the internationally recognized government uses the Saudi support to retain or build relevance in Yemen.

Iran and the Houthis: Iran as an enemy to Saudi Arabia and the Houthis as their proxy

The framing of Saudi Arabia as a friend of the legitimate government and the people of Yemen is juxtaposed to the framing of Iran as the enemy. Iran is presented as undermining international peace and security which is used to construct an image of Iran as the main destabilizer in Yemen. A key element is the oft-repeated claim that the Iranian constitution mandates the export of the Iranian revolution. Adel al-Jubeir, who has played a key role in framing the Saudi Arabian presentation of the intervention into Yemen to an English-speaking audience as first ambassador to the United States, then foreign minister and latest minister of state for foreign affairs, has repeatedly reiterated that Saudi Arabia believes there is an 'Iran Problem' that includes Iranian support of terrorist groups, its ballistic missile programme and its destabilizing effect in the region.[14] The argument is that whereas Saudi Arabia will do its part, the world has a responsibility to check the 'aggressive behaviour' of Iran.[15] It is argued that Iran needs to act like a 'normal country' which means moving away from the idea of exporting the revolution and refrain from interference in member states' internal affairs. The claim that Iran is aggressively seeking to export its revolution is generally stated without further explication, but it is used to argue that Iran must abide by international law if it wants to be treated like a normal country. This includes respecting 'fundamental principles of good-neighbourliness, respect for the sovereignty of states, non-interference in internal affairs and the non-use of force or threat of force'.[16] In the specific context of the intervention in Yemen, the official Saudi narrative speaks of an 'Iranian expansion project in Yemen'.[17] While it is often implicit that the rivalry between Iran and Saudi Arabia has a sectarian component, there are references to how the 'Iranian project' include 'distortion of the Islamic faith' through a 'sectarian strategy'.[18] These types of statements juxtapose Iran and Saudi Arabia, as Saudi Arabia, as discussed in the previous section, presents itself as upholding international and humanitarian law and as respecting the sovereignty of other states.

This way, the presentation of Iran as an enemy of the Yemeni people builds on an image of Iran as an irresponsible international actor that is the anti-thesis to the Saudi state. The positioning of both Iran and Saudi Arabia is framed within the language of international and humanitarian law that has a clear normative element (Morozov and Rumelili 2012: 32).

The Houthis are presented as wanting to establish a pro-Iranian regime in Yemen. They are referred to as an 'Iranian-backed Houthi militia' that will undermine international peace and security.[19] It is generally presented as a fact that the Houthis are linked to Iran, which is rhetorically evident in how Saudi Arabian officials continuously refer to the Houthis as 'the Houthi terrorist militia' or the 'Iranian-backed Houthi militias' or a combination such as 'the Iranian-backed Houthi terrorist militias'. The Yemeni government has rhetorically sought to portray the Houthis as being controlled by Iran. Yemen's information minister has for example argued that 'the Iranian regime controls Houthis' political and military decisions and manages the militia to carry out its agenda'.[20] The idea that the Houthis are controlled from Tehran has limited support among Yemen researchers, but the relationship between the Houthis and Iran has been growing (Perkins 2019; Vantanka 2020).[21]. This includes growing evidence that the Houthis receive Iranian military support as they are using and displaying weaponry that was not in the Yemen prewar stockpile.[22] This adds to the Houthis' military capability which also includes the estimated 68 per cent of the Yemeni pre-war military stockpile that the Houthis gained control over through their partnership with the former president Saleh.[23] The UN panel of experts for example documented a decline in price on the black market for small arms ammunition which they linked to the illicit proliferation of the government stockpile.[24] Hence, whereas the level of Iranian support to the Houthis is debated, it is generally agreed that the Houthis receive support from Iran. This is also evidenced by the Houthis' growing ability to carry out increasingly sophisticated attacks on Saudi Arabia using drones and missiles. Moreover, there has been rhetorical support to the Houthis from the Iranian regime and occasional boasting of Iran's influence in Yemen (Kendall 2017; Salisbury 2015). Iran has on multiple occasions refused that it provides or smuggles missiles to the Houthis.[25] It would be in direct violation of UN resolution 2216 (2015) if Iran supplies or does not take all measures to prevent supply of arms and related materiel of all types to the Houthis in Yemen. Saudi Arabia has on multiple occasions raised the question in the UN Security Council and called on the UN to hold the Iranian regime accountable for perceived violations.[26]

The narrative that the Houthis act on behalf of Iran as a proxy is often emphasized or taken as a natural starting point that the Houthis are Shia and therefore aligned with Iran in the wider Middle Eastern conflict (Albloshi 2016). In the Saudi narrative, the policies of Iran are not just expansionist but also sectarian and, consequently, so are the Houthis.[27] The Yemeni defence minister has referred to the Houthis takeover of Sana'a in Yemen as the 'Persian project'. But whereas it is true that technically the Houthis are Shia, they are Zaydi, sometimes referred to as 'Fiver' Shiism. This is a version of Shiism that is different from the more prevalent 'Twelver' Shiism practised in Iran and one that is considered relatively close to the form of Sunni Islam practised in Yemen. Approximately 35 per cent of Yemen's population is Zaydi but importantly not all Houthis are Zaydi, nor are all Zaydis Houthis. The introduction of sectarianism to Yemen is noticeable as just a decade ago, sectarian identity had limited relevance in Yemen. However, now references to sectarian identity are becoming more commonplace. The Houthis are increasingly using sectarian language and symbolism (al-Muslimi 2015; Valbjørn 2018).

This process has been facilitated by the official Saudi Arabian approach to mobilize sectarian discourse by playing up the Houthis' Shi'ite affinity, confusing the existence of nominal difference with a compelling causal story (Yadav 2014). As I have argued elsewhere, critically assessing the validity of the sectarian narrative does not imply rejecting that religious convictions play a role in the Houthi movement and that there has been a rapprochement between Iran and the Houthis (Clausen 2019b). Iran and the Houthis have an ideological commonality and shared opposition to the regional order dominated by the United States and its key allies, most notably Saudi Arabia and Israel.[28] For Iran, the relationship with the Houthis allows them to project power on the Arabian Peninsula on a modest investment, while the Houthis gain access to resources that allow them to continue to strengthen their political and military position in Yemen (Juneau 2016). The relationship is further made possible by Iran's limited interest in domestic Yemeni politics. However, sectarianism is a consequence of the conflict, not a cause of it.

Yemen is not the only place where a deliberate sectarianization of a conflict has been used as a a strategy by Saudi Arabia and Iran in their rivalry. Raymond Hinnebusch has argued that sectarianism helps Saudi Arabia isolate Iran in the Sunni world (Hinnebusch 2016) and Marc Lynch has argued that: 'The Saudi regime, most obviously, systematically uses sectarianism in order to intimidate and control its own Shiite citizens at home and to combat Iranian influence regionally. Saudi leaders might or might not genuinely hate Shiites, but they know that sectarian conflict is a useful strategy' (Lynch 2013). The narrative emphasizes that the Houthis are a tool of Iran as a way of delegitimizing them. The official Saudi narrative suggests that Iran uses sectarian language to promote strife among citizens which undermines national identity and creates conflict. The destabilization of countries and the spread of chaos then allow Iran to interfere in the affairs of other states and thereby grow its influence by working with armed non-state actors.

Saudi Arabia presents itself as being non-sectarian. In doing this, Saudi Arabia seeks to define what is sectarian and what is not, and who is sectarian and who is not. It has been argued that the labelling of others as being sectarian can be seen as delineating a moral hierarchy in which some deem themselves as superior to others. Superiority comes with the right to judge (Makdisi 2017). In the Saudi case, it is repeatedly argued that the war in Yemen was, as stated by Adel al-Jubeir, 'a war that we didn't want. This is a war that was imposed on us.'[29] In this way, the narrative of Saudi Arabia as a friend of Yemen is tied to the image of the Houthis as an Iranian proxy seeking to destabilize Yemen and in the process being responsible for the war and its consequences.

Conclusion

The chapter has argued that the Saudi justification for the military intervention into Yemen can be understood as building on two overall components that refer to a distinction between friend and enemy in politics. The chapter has sought to show, first, how Saudi Arabia has used the position of 'Abd Rabbuh Mansour Hadi as the legitimate president of Yemen, being threatened by an illegitimate Iran-backed militia, to position itself as a friend of Hadi and by extension a friend of the Yemeni people. And second, how Iran is positioned as an enemy of Saudi Arabia and the international community through its perceived disregard for international law and norms of non-interference and the Houthis as a proxy to Iran, a link that is often made by labelling the Houthis as Shi'a although it seems that ideology and world view are more important than religion in the relationship between the Houthis and Iran.

This chapter has not sought to unravel the true extent of the relationship between Iran and the Houthis, nor does it evaluate the accuracy of the components that constitute the Saudi narrative to justify the intervention into Yemen. The official Saudi narrative does not discuss whether or not the Houthis are an Iranian proxy but presents it as a fact. When seeing the proxy concept as an essentially contested concept, the crux of the investigation moves from focusing on whether something is an accurate depiction, to accepting that the contested nature of the proxy concept itself means that the application of the concept tells us little about the relationship between the Houthis and Iran. What is more, by approaching the proxy concept as an essentially contested concept, it is possible to investigate the normative components of the concept as well as how its definition is adjusted in the specific context of the Saudi-led intervention in Yemen. The normative aspect is evident in this chapter's investigation of the official Saudi narrative, specifically how the dichotomy between Iran, as the sectarian enemy and supporter of an illegitimate militia, and Saudi Arabia, as a friend and upholder of international and humanitarian law, is constructed rhetorically.

The conflict in Yemen is taking place in the backdrop of increased fragmentation in the Middle East following the Arab Uprisings. Iran has been the main benefactor of the resulting increased instability and has not hesitated to take advantage of the events in Yemen while denying any role in the conflict as it calls for Yemeni-Yemeni negotiations to end the conflict, in the process positioning itself as a state looking out for the interest of the Yemeni. The battle over the narrative of the conflict in Yemen has reflected existing understandings of what define the rivalry between Iran and Saudi Arabia. This has aggravated sectarianism in Yemen. While the sectarian narrative was initially considered foreign to Yemen, and largely found on the fringes of political debate, the conflict has changed this. As the future of the Yemeni state remains undecided, it is difficult to predict whether and in what ways sectarianism will become part of post-war Yemen.

Notes

1 The United Nations Official Document System (ODS) database can be accessed through the UN website, un.org. The database holds selected scanned documents from before 1993 and is fully updated from 1993 onwards.
2 National Dialogue Conference Outcomes Document, 2014, file:///C:/Users/mlcl/Downloads/YE_140124_NDC_National%20Conference%20Outcomes%20Document_EN.pdf
3 United Nations Security Council, 14 April 2015, resolution 2216.
4 Agreement on the implementation mechanism for the transition process in Yemen in accordance with the initiative of the Gulf Cooperation Council (GCC). Available online: https://peacemaker.un.org/sites/peacemaker.un.org/files/YE_111205_Agreement%20on%20the%20implementation%20mechanism%20for%20the%20transition.pdf (last accessed 15 November 2019).
5 Video: Saudi ambassador in U.S. speaks on military campaign in Yemen, 26 March 2015. Available online: http://english.alarabiya.net/en/webtv/reports/2015/03/26/Video-Saudi-ambassador-in-U-S-speaks-on-military-campaign-in-Yemen.html (last accessed on 15 November 2019).
6 UN Security Council, S/2015/238 (https://undocs.org/en/S/2015/238).
7 Pact of the League of Arab States, 22 March 1945, article 6, and article 51 of the United Nations Charter.
8 Saudi Press Agency, 25 September 2019. Available online: https://www.spa.gov.sa/viewstory.php?lang=en&newsid=1974223 (last accessed 15 November 2019).
9 There are numerous examples where parties to the conflict have declined participation, rejected results or insisted on carrying out their own investigations (see, for example, this report to the Human Rights Council on violations by parties to the conflict in Yemen, A/HRC/42/CRP.1: https://www.ohchr.org/Documents/HRBodies/HRCouncil/GEE-Yemen/A_HRC_42_CRP_1.PDF).

10 Saudi Gazette, Griffiths congratulates Crown Prince on Riyadh Agreement, 8 November 2019. Available online: http://saudigazette.com.sa/article/582027/SAUDI-ARABIA/Griffiths-congratulates-Crown-Prince-on-Riyadh-Agreement (last accessed 15 November 2019).
11 Data from the KSrelief homepage. Available online: https://www.ksrelief.org/ (last accessed 15 November 2019).
12 Data from Financial Tracking Service home page. Available online: https://fts.unocha.org/data-search/results/outgoing?usageYears=2015%2C2016%2C2017%2C2018%2C2019&locations=196&f%5B0%5D=destinationLocationIdName%3A%22248%3AYemen%22&search_type=directional (last accessed 15 November 2019).
13 Saudi Press Agency, 25 September 2019. Available online: https://www.spa.gov.sa/viewstory.php?lang=en&newsid=1974223 (last accessed 15 November 2019).
14 Chatham House, Saudi Arabia's foreign policy priorities, 21 October 2019. Available online: https://www.chathamhouse.org/event/saudi-arabias-foreign-policy-priorities (last accessed 10 November 2019).
15 https://www.cnbc.com/2019/09/22/cnbc-transcript-adel-al-jubeir-saudi-minister-of-state-for-foreign-affairs.html.
16 United Nations Security Council, 21 December 2015, S/2015/954.
17 Saudi Press Agency, 20 October 2019. Available online: https://www.spa.gov.sa/viewstory.php?lang=en&newsid=1984616 (last accessed 15 November 2019).
18 Saudi Press Agency, 2 June 2022. Available online: https://www.spa.gov.sa/viewstory.php?lang=en&newsid=2359476 (last accessed 1 November 2022).
19 Saudi Press Agency, 25 September 2019. Available online: https://www.spa.gov.sa/viewstory.php?lang=en&newsid=1974223 (last accessed 15 November 2019).
20 https://www.spa.gov.sa/viewstory.php?lang=en&newsid=1976876.
21 See, for example, Michael Knights for an account that emphasizes the importance of the link between Iran and the Houthis, although the conclusion remains that Iran does not appear to control the Houthis (Knights 2018).
22 Final report of the Panel of Experts, in accordance with paragraph 6 of resolution 2456 (2019), 27 January 2020 (last accessed 20 March 2020).
23 UN Security Council, Final Report of the Panel of Experts, 2018, p. 33: https://www.undocs.org/S/2018/193 (last accessed 15 November 2019).
24 Ibid.: 34.
25 See, for example, United Nations Security Council, 29 March 2018 (S/2018/278).
26 See UN Security Council, 15 November 2017 (S/2017/937), UN Security Council, 16 September 2016 (S/2016/786), UN Security Council, 26 December 2017 (S/2017/1133), UN Security Council, 23 January 2018 (S/2018/55), UN Security Council, 27 March 2018 (S/2018/266), UN Security Council, 16 April 2018 (S/2018/337), UN Security Council 11 May (S/2018/448). Last accessed 15 November 2019.
27 Al-Jubeir, Adel bin Ahmed (2016), Can Iran Change?, *New York Times*, 19 January 2016.
28 See Shiban, Baraa (2018), Brothers in Arms – Dissecting Iran-Houthi Ties, *The Brief*, 2 November 2018, which points to the importance of politics as key to understand the relationship between the Houthis and Iran.
29 Council of Foreign Relations, A Conversation with Adel al-Jubeir, Wednesday, 26 September 2018. Available online: https://www.cfr.org/event/conversation-adel-al-jubeir (last accessed 15 November 2019).

References

al-Muslimi, F. (2015), 'How Sunni-Shia Sectarianism Is Poisoning Yemen', *Diwan*. Available online: https://carnegie-mec.org/diwan/62375.
Albloshi, H. H. (2016), 'Ideological Roots of the Ḥūthī Movement in Yemen', *Journal of Arabian Studies*, 6: 143–62.
Ardemagni, E. (2022), 'Yemen's Post-Hybrid Balance: The New Presidential Council', *Carnegie Endowment for International Peace*, 9 June 2022. https://carnegieendowment.org/sada/87301.
Berenskoetter, F. (2007), 'Friends, There Are No Friends? An Intimate Reframing of the International', *Millennium – Journal of International Studies*, 35: 647–76.
Brandt, M. (2017), *Tribes and Politics in Yemen. A History of the Houthi Conflict*, London: Hurst.
Campbell, D. (1998), *Writing Security, United States Foreign Policy and the Politics of Identity*, Manchester: Manchester University Press.
Clausen, M.-L. (2018), 'Can Federalism Save the Yemeni State?', in Marie-Christine Heinze (ed.), *Yemen and the Search for Stability: Power, Politics and Society after the Arab Spring*, Croydon: I.B. Tauris, 306–26.
Clausen, M.-L. (2019a), 'Justifying Military Intervention: Yemen as a Failed State', *Third World Quarterly*, 40: 488–502.
Clausen, M.-L. (2019b), 'Sectarianisation of a Multidimensional Conflict: A Reply to Durac', *Global Discourse*, 9: 675–77.
Collier, D., Hidalgo, F. D., and Maciuceanu, A. O. (2006), 'Essentially Contested Concepts: Debates and Applications', *Journal of Political Ideologies*, 11: 211.
Connolly, W. E. (2002), *Identity/Difference, Democratic Negotiations of Political Paradox*, Minneapolis: University of Minnesota Press.
Doty, R. L. (1996), *Imperial Encounters: The Politics of Representation in North-South Relations*, Minneapolis: University of Minnesota Press.
Gallie, W. B. (1956), 'Essentially Contested Concepts', *Aristotelian Society, Proceedings*, 56: 167.
Gause, F. (2014), 'Beyond Sectarianism: The New Middle East Cold War', in *Brookings Doha Center Analysis Paper*. Available online: https://www.brookings.edu/wp-content/uploads/2016/06/English-PDF-1.pdf.
Groh, T. L. (2019), *Proxy War: The Least Bad Option*, Redwood City: Stanford University Press.
Hansen, L. (2006), *Security as Practice: Discourse Analysis and the Bosnian War*, New York: Routledge.
Hinnebusch, R. (2016), 'The Sectarian Revolution in the Middle East', *R/evolutions: Global Trends & Regional Issues*, 4: 120–52.
Hughes, G. (2012), *My Enemy's Enemy: Proxy Warfare in International Politics*, Portland, OR: Sussex Academic Press.
Juneau, T. (2016), 'Iran's Policy towards the Houthis in Yemen: A Limited Return on a Modest Investment', *International Affairs*, 92: 647–63.
Kendall, E. (2017), 'Iran's Fingerprints in Yemen. Real or Imagined?', *Atlantic Council, Issue Brief*, 1–11. Available online: https://www.atlanticcouncil.org/wp-content/uploads/2017/10/Irans_Fingerprints_in_Yemen_web_1019.pdf.
Knights, M. (2018), 'The Houthi War Machine: From Guerrilla War to State Capture', *CTC Sentinel*, 11 (8): 15–23.

Lynch, M. (2013), 'The Entrepreneurs of Cynical Sectarianism', *Foreign Policy*. Available online: https://foreignpolicy.com/2013/11/13/the-entrepreneurs-of-cynical-sectarianism/.

Makdisi, U. (2017), 'The Mythology of the Sectarian Middle East'. In Center for the Middle East, Rice University's Baker Institute for Public Policy.

Morozov, V., and Rumelili, B. (2012), 'The External Constitution of European Identity: Russia and Turkey as Europe-Makers', *Cooperation and Conflict*, 47: 28–48.

Mumford, A. (2013), 'Proxy Warfare and the Future of Conflict', *RUSI Journal*, 158: 40–6.

Perkins, B. M. (2019), 'US-Iran Tensions Overshadow Houthi Agenda in War in Yemen', *Terrorism Monitor*, 17 (13): 7–8.

Rageh, M., Nasser, A. and al-Muslimi, F. (2016), *Yemen without a Functioning Central Bank: The Loss of Basic Economic Stabilization and Accelerating Famine*, Yemen, Sanaa: Sanaa Center for Strategic Studies.

Ruys, T., and Ferro, L. (2016), 'Weathering the Storm: Legality and Legal Implications of the Saudi-Led Military Intervention in Yemen', *International and Comparative Law Quarterly*, 65: 61–98.

Salisbury, P. (2015), *Yemen and the Saudi – Iranian 'Cold War'*, London: Chatham House.

Strömbom, L. (2012), 'Thick Recognition: Advancing Theory on Identity Change in Intractable Conflicts', *European Journal of International Relations*, 20: 168–91.

Valbjørn, M. (2018), 'Unpacking a Puzzling Case: On How the Yemeni Conflict Became Sectarianised', *Orients – German Journal for Politics, Economics and Culture of the Middle East*, 59: 65–73.

Vatanka, A. (2020), 'Iran's Role in the Yemen Crisis', in Stephen W. Day and Noel Brehony (eds), *Global, Regional, and Local Dynamics in the Yemen Crisis*, Cham: Springer International Publishing, 149–64.

Yadav, S. P. (2014), 'The Limits of the "Sectarian" Framing in Yemen', *Monkey Cage*, 25 September 2014. Available online: https://www.washingtonpost.com/news/monkey-cage/wp/2014/09/25/the-limits-of-the-sectarian-framing-in-yemen/.

Zhukova, E. (2017), 'Foreign Aid and Identity after the Chernobyl Nuclear Disaster: How Belarus Shapes Relations with Germany, Europe, Russia, and Japan', *Cooperation and Conflict*, 52: 485–501.

Chapter 8

SECTARIANISM AND CIVIL WARS IN THE MENA REGION

Francesco Belcastro

Introduction

This chapter looks at the relation between sectarianism and civil wars in the Middle East and North Africa (MENA) region. It focuses on how states exploit sectarianism to influence the development and outcome of civil wars. Sectarianism is often indicated as a cause of conflict and instability in the region. The narrative of the 'ancient Shia–Sunni hatred' as the defining factor in MENA politics, in particular, has been predominant. This chapter argues that while the presence of sectarian divides does affect civil wars, this process has to be understood through the role of actors, and particularly states. The role of states in this analysis is twofold. Firstly, states exploit the presence of sectarian divides to mobilize, recruit and organize foreign fighters in civil wars. Foreign fighters represent useful 'tools' for states willing to influence the development and outcome of a civil war according to their own goals. The relevance of states, however, goes beyond the use of foreign fighters. By manipulating sectarian identities, states become actors in the broader process of sectarianization of civil wars. States do not only exploit pre-existing divides, but are also part of the process that shapes, reinforces and strengthens these sectarian divides. As foreign fighters' participation in conflict is a transnational process, this chapter seeks to contribute to the *Regional Dynamics and Proxies* section of the volume. Moreover, this chapter argues that the collapse of central authority and 'return of primordial identities' narrative often associated with civil wars represents unique conditions to engage with 'contemporary manifestations of sectarianism', the broad theme underpinning this volume.

In order to analyse this process, the chapter engages with the debate on ethno-sectarianism and identities as well as with the literature on civil wars. Several recent studies (such as that of Hashemi and Postel 2017) have challenged a simplistic explanation of sectarianism as a source of conflict in the region, pointing out how authoritarian regimes use sectarianism in order to increase their legitimacy and remain in power. This debate is particularly salient to the topic of civil wars, as it addresses the issue of when and how the presence of sectarian divides leads to violence and conflict.

This analysis will focus specifically on the MENA region. While the debate on ethno-sectarianism is not unique to the region, the study of this aspect is particularly central to the MENA region because of the relevance of transnational identities in regional politics. Furthermore, civil wars that took place in the MENA region in recent decades saw strikingly different levels of participation by foreign fighters, ranging from the tens of thousands of fighters involved in the Syrian conflict to the low numbers of foreign fighters in the Algerian civil war. This chapter is composed of five sections. Part I provides the theoretical framework for the analysis and also discusses the relevant literature, aims and limitations of the chapter. Section two looks at how states exploit sectarianism to favour the flow of foreign fighters to civil war scenarios. Section three focuses on states as actors in the sectarianization process. Section four develops the case of the Syrian civil war. The case study of a 'semi-sectarian' civil war (Philipps 2015) will provide an insight into the process of sectarianization and the role that domestic and external actors play in it. Section five contains some final remarks and discusses the potential for further research in this area.

Sectarianism and regional involvement in civil wars: An overview

This research draws on two bodies of literature. The first is the literature on sectarianism and sectarian identities, their 'creation' and their role in Middle Eastern politics. The second is the literature on civil wars, external involvement and ethno-sectarian conflict. The sectarianism literature stems, at least partially, from the rich debate among scholars studying identity. This debate has in recent years become more central to analysis of regional politics, and has attracted the attention of public intellectuals as well as academics (Bishara 2022). Within this debate, the term sectarianism has been used with two different meanings: one is 'neutral' and refers to the presence of different sects in a state, while the other refers to 'discrimination, hate or tension' based on the presence of different sects (Haddad 2011: 31). Clearly, the distinction is not just a matter of semantics, for the issue of how the first sectarianism (the presence of sects) turns into 'malign' sectarianism has been central to the whole debate. Based on the concept of sectarianism, Hashemi and Postel define sectarianization as 'a process shaped by political actors operating within specific contexts, pursuing political goals that involve popular mobilization around (religious) identity markers' (2017: 3). The concept of sectarianization emphasizes agency. The centrality of sectarianism in the Middle East is therefore not a consequence of ancient and immutable hatreds, but rather the result of processes that took place in the last decades. States and particularly authoritarian regimes are central to this argument. Unable to address their population's demands for 'greater inclusion, rights, recognition and representation' (Hashemi and Postel 2017: 10), Arab regimes use sectarianism to boost their domestic legitimacy. Particularly relevant are 'sectarian symbols' such as religious sites or places of relevance to one or more religious groups. In the last few years, several scholars sought to contribute to this debate and to develop theoretical tools to address key questions in different areas of Middle Eastern politics. Recent examples include the work of Valbjorn and Hinnebusch (2018) on sectarianism and authoritarian regimes in the wake of the Arab Spring or that of Kasbarian and Mabon (2017) on sectarianism and post-uprising Bahrain. Particularly relevant to this study is the work of Philipps and Valbjorn (2018) on how different identities relate to proxy wars and Philipps's (2015) work on the sectarian nature of the Syrian civil war. Building on this growing literature, this chapter uses the neutral term 'sectarian divide' to refer to the existence of groups with different religious identities and affiliations among those fighting in the civil war.

What constitutes a civil war (and how it is different from a war) has been a controversial point. This study uses the definition provided by Kalyvas (2006: 14): 'Armed combat within the boundaries of a recognized sovereign entity between parties subject to a common authority at the outset of the hostilities.' As several cases from the MENA region show, the distinction between civil wars and wars is often not straightforward. Several regional conflicts straddle the line between civil wars and wars, presenting elements of both. This undoubtedly adds a further level of complexity to the analysis. The Syrian conflict (the case study in this chapter) in its initial stages fits in with the definition of civil wars provided here. However, as the involvement of external actors became more prevalent, the conflict became a regional and global one as well as a civil war.

The literature on external involvement is less developed and focuses on issues such as whether intervention increases or shortens the length of the conflicts (Regan 2002) or on neighbouring countries' involvement in civil wars (Kathman 2010). A few studies focus on states and ethnic-based conflict. Akhaba et al. (2008) analyse why ethnic conflicts attract external support from states. The authors focus on whether discrimination of minorities plays a role in increasing external intervention. Carment and James (2004) analyse which kind of states are more likely to get involved in ethnic strife: they conclude that those with low domestic constraints and ethnic uniformity tend to be more belligerent. Huibregtse looks at how the ethnic make-up of states affects the potential for intervention in state conflict (2014). The author concludes that 'ethnically fractionalized states dominated by a large ethnic group have the highest probability of intervening in an internal ethnic conflict' (Huibregtse 2014: 287). Kaufman's work (2001) focuses specifically on ethnic conflict. The author argues that in multi-ethnic states, conflict is not the norm, but it is rather an overlapping of short- and long-term causes that leads to conflict. The presence of 'ancient' hatreds per se does not lead to conflict, but it does so when it is coupled with short-term factors such as the presence of political opportunities to mobilize (Kaufman 2003). This chapter will build on insights from both bodies of literature to develop the nexus between sectarianism and civil wars.

Aims and limitations

This chapter looks at the relation between sectarianism and civil wars. It seeks to contribute to two bodies of literature. The first is the debate on sectarianism in the MENA region. Civil wars provide a unique insight into this debate, and a better understanding of how sectarianization works in the context of these conflicts can contribute to a better understanding of the broader issue of sectarianism. This chapter also seeks to contribute to the literature on foreign fighters' involvement by focusing specifically on the effect of sectarianism and the related role of state actors – an important yet understudied issue.

This study does not seek to build a systemic analysis of external involvement in civil wars. Furthermore, the focus here is exclusively on sectarianism and therefore on religion-based identity politics. It is, however, important to recognize how the Middle East is characterized by the presence of overlapping and often competing identities. Reflecting on this multi-layered system, Hinnebusch underlines how the nation-building process in the region led to 'an incongruence between identity and territory' (2016: 159). The sectarian dimension will often be present (and in some cases compete) with other identities, whether ethnic, tribal, local or of other nature. Finally, the focus of this chapter will be on state actors and their 'use' of sectarianism. The chapter will therefore not engage with individual fighters' motivations for taking part in the conflict. It is, however, important to note the existence of a vast literature on fighters' motivations that complements the topic of this study (see, for example, Kundnani 2012; Spalek 2007).

Sectarianism, states and foreign fighters

This section will explore the relation between foreign fighters' involvement in civil wars and sectarianism. It will argue that the process of foreign fighters' participation in these conflicts is often not 'neutral' as it is driven by actors (particularly states) that seek to exploit such conflicts for their own aims. The term 'foreign fighter' broadly indicates individuals or groups that leave their country of origins to join a conflict in a different country. Foreign fighters' main motivation to take part in the conflict is 'religion, kinship, and/or ideology rather than pecuniary reward' (Moore and Tumelty 2008: 422). This aspect separates foreign fighters from mercenaries – professionals who are hired by state or non-state actors to fight on their behalf. However, foreign fighters themselves often receive pecuniary rewards, with the distinction between the two categories based on the (often hard to establish) point of whether money or ideology/religion represents the primary reason for joining the conflict. Foreign fighters have been central actors in several civil wars in the MENA and in other regions. The rise of groups such as ISIS in Iraq and Syria has shown how foreign fighters can pose severe threats to states. Most of the literature on this topic has focused on jihadi groups, looking at issues such as how insurgent groups recruit foreign fighters (Malet 2010) and particularly how radicalization works (Dawson and

Amarasingam 2017; Nilsson 2015). Despite the emphasis on non-state actors, states are in several cases central to the involvement of foreign fighters in civil wars. As Byman (2018) explains, the presence and effectiveness of foreign fighters often depends on states themselves. States in fact facilitate, tolerate and in some cases organize the flow of foreign fighters as these represent tools to 'bolster allied regimes, weaken rivals, and placate opinion at home' (Byman 2018: 931). States can therefore 'use' foreign fighters to influence civil wars according to their agendas and interests.

The occurrence of a civil war presents threats and/or opportunities to regional and international actors. The literature on civil wars, briefly discussed in the previous section, shows how states can decide to intervene in civil wars for a broad range of reasons. States can intervene in support of one or more of the warring parties, seek to facilitate a negotiated outcome or act to increase or reduce the duration of the conflict. Regardless of what their motives and aims are, states seeking to influence the outcome of a civil war have a variety of tools at their disposal. These range from providing economic support for one or more of the warring parties to direct military intervention. The use of foreign fighters represents one of the options available to states and, in some circumstances, one of the most cost-effective as well as less politically risky. Byman sees the use of foreign fighters as a spectrum ranging from 'regime efforts to use foreigners as auxiliaries for a state's army to toleration of foreign fighters' activity' (2018: 932). The latter option provides the advantage of allowing states the possibility to deny direct responsibility (Byman 2018: 935). The involvement of foreign fighters can be divided into different stages, all of which can see states playing a significant role. States can, through formal or informal networks, participate in the recruitment of foreign fighters. This typically takes place in the foreign fighters' countries of origin. This is the case of the Soviet Union during the Spanish civil war. Through its sister parties in Europe and beyond, Moscow played a fundamental role in the recruitment of volunteers to fight against Franco's army. It is estimated that the International Brigades provided up to 50,000 fighters throughout the civil war (Thomas 2001: 430–1). Through the same or different networks, states can facilitate or finance the travel to the country where the civil war is taking place. States that border the country where the civil war occurs typically play a key role, particularly when the features of the border make access to the country and the area where the fighting is taking place easy. Finally, states can coordinate the training and enrolment of foreign fighters once they reach the country where the civil war is taking place. This is the case of Iran and Hezbollah (itself a militia) in Syria. Tehran and its Lebanese client showed a remarkable ability to train and organize a large number of recruits (Byman 2018: 988). States can be involved in any or all of these stages. It is worth noting how the use of foreign fighters can also present risks for states that recruit and mobilize them. States can often exercise only a very limited degree of control over the foreign fighters. As a result, fighters can 'turn against' the state that initially facilitated their involvement in the civil wars. This is the case of the Jihadis involved in the fight against American forces in post-2003 Iraq. Their involvement was tolerated and even encouraged by the Al-Assad regime.

However, some of the same fighters were later involved in the post-2011 conflict against the regime (Scarborough 2013).

States and foreign fighters

How do states favour the flow of foreign fighters? As mentioned before, the main reasons that drive foreign fighters to join civil wars are not material rewards but ideological, sectarian and ethnic factors. This however does not mean that states, directly or through other agents, do not provide foreign fighters with different kinds of rewards. Monetary benefits such as salaries or lump-sum payments represent a major incentive. During the 1979–89 Afghanistan war, Saudi Arabia (as well as other powers) paid significant sums to fighters joining the war against the USSR and its allies. Robert Riedel maintains that the regime not only contributed with significant public funds, but was also central in channelling 'private' donations that at the peak amounted to approximately 20 million USD per year (Riedel 2014). While Saudi Arabia and the United States provided most of the funding, it was Pakistan that in this case trained the fighters (Riedel 2014). Other benefits include non-monetary rewards for fighters or their family members. Iranian permanent residencies were allegedly offered (together with a salary) to Afghan Shias recruited to fight in Syria (Rasmussen and Nader 2016).

While these material incentives are undoubtedly relevant, even a cursory look at the conflicts mentioned earlier confirms that foreign fighters do not join (civil wars especially) with the primary motivation of pursuing material rewards. The possibility to fight for a just cause represented one of the driving forces behind the involvement of foreign fighters in the Spanish Civil War (1936–9). Young leftist militants joined the civil war from all of Europe and beyond to defend the Spanish government fighting against General Franco and his sponsors Mussolini and Hitler. The Soviet Union, due to its well-established transnational network of parties and organizations, was able to channel and exploit the flow of foreign fighters (Malet 2010) Similarly, being able to defend 'Muslim land' against an invading superpower was a driving factor behind the flow of foreign fighters in Afghanistan. The presence of ideological, ethnic or sectarian divides at play in the conflict therefore represents an important tool available to states in order to mobilize, recruit and organize foreign fighters. States can use these divides as recruitment and organizational tools. States, whether directly or through their agents, can emphasize the possibility to fight in order to defend a 'just cause' by using ideology or identity. These can also provide an important motivational tool once fighters are involved in the conflict.

Sectarianism has been used as an effective tool in several MENA conflicts. The prevalent narrative of a region inflamed by Shia–Sunni tensions creates the ideal conditions for exploiting these sectarian divides. As the section on the Syrian civil war will discuss, states on both sides of the conflict can exploit a sectarian narrative of the conflict to favour the flow of fighters to the country. For this to happen, the civil war has to 'fit' within the sectarian discourse: it needs in other words to present some sort of sectarian cleavages that can reasonably be represented within the Shia–Sunni divide. Civil wars such as the Algerian one, fought in countries where almost the entire population is Sunni, clearly do not present a sectarian dimension that can be exploited by external or domestic actors.[1] In cases where these sectarian divides exist, several actors can seek to exploit them. This includes regional states and in cases (such as Syria) where the civil war features an incumbent regime among the warring parties, the regime itself. Furthermore, states are not the only actors that can play the sectarian card to favour the flow of external fighters to fight on their side. Different factions involved in the war can seek to use sectarian divides for this purpose. What separates the role of states is usually their ability to play an important logistic role (whether directly or through other agencies) in the recruitment and deployment of foreign fighters.

While reliable statistics on the involvement of fighters and particularly on their 'real' motivations to join a conflict are hard to obtain, it is reasonable to expect that the presence of sectarian divides will in fact increase the number of fighters taking part in a civil war, particularly when states are able to exploit these sectarian divides. A systemic analysis of civil wars, state involvement and sectarianism would provide an important contribution but is beyond the scope of this chapter. This chapter will focus instead on the broader relations between sectarianism and civil wars. By recruiting 'sectarian' foreign fighters, deploying them using sectarian symbols and more generally manipulating sectarianism, states also become actors in the sectarianization process. The next section will discuss the implication of states' roles in order to understand what this means for civil wars and regions, more broadly, before turning to the analysis of the Syrian case.

Sectarianism, civil wars and regions

The previous section discussed how states exploit sectarian divides to recruit, mobilize and organize foreign fighters. This section looks at states as actors in the sectarianization of civil wars. It argues that by manipulating sectarian identities, states become part of the process of sectarianization. This aspect brings the analysis back to the central point in the debate on ethno-sectarianism, the one over the 'nature' of sectarian (and ethnic) identities. Are these identities pre-existing and fixed, and get 're-activated' under some conditions, as suggested by primordialist interpretations? Or are they rather more fluid and can be created, modified and exploited, as suggested by instrumentalists? With particular reference to the issue of civil wars, do state actors contribute to the sectarianization of conflicts, or do they simply exploit the re-emergence of dormant identities? Civil wars provide interesting insights into the ethno-sectarian debate. They are characterized by a partial or total collapse of central authority and the occurrence of 'micro-fighting' that often significantly impacts the local population. As the state no longer functions, or functions in a limited way (i.e. only in some parts of the territory, or in all of the territory but with severe restrictions), there are more possibilities for groups to mobilize and get organized (Kaufman 2001: 32). Civil wars are often described as brutal and senseless acts of violence, something akin to a return to the state of nature. This idea is rooted in the work of classical authors, but is also present in several contemporary accounts of civil wars (Armitage 2017). Because of their nature, civil wars provide ideal conditions for a return of 'primordial identities', divides that were present in the society but previously subdued. According to a prevalent narrative (in public opinion discourse if not in academia), civil wars in countries with a heterogeneous population are 'sectarian by default'. This aspect seems to be omnipresent in explanations of Middle Eastern conflicts, often analysed through the lenses of Shia–Sunni differences that were kept under control by authoritarian regimes but emerged again once the opportunity arose (Hashemi and Postel 2017).

Both the literature on civil wars and the literature on ethno-sectarianism, however, suggest a more nuanced approach to the issue. Other conditions have to subsist together with the presence of ethnic or sectarian divides, drawing attention particularly to the agency of actors involved in the sectarianization process. Kalyvas's seminal study (2006) exposes the flaws in the 'irrational violence' argument by looking at violence carried out against non-combatants. While his analysis focuses specifically on violence against civilians, Kalyvas's work clearly challenges the traditional representation of violence in civil wars more broadly. One aspect underlined by his study (2006: 389) is particularly relevant to this analysis: 'War is a transformative phenomenon, and civil war even more so. The advent of war transforms individual preferences, choices, behaviours and identities-and the main way in which war exercises its transformative function is through violence.' Civil wars are therefore not 'rigid' processes where predetermined identities are frozen and unmodifiable, but rather, they are dynamic scenarios during which actors can readjust their position and switch their allegiances. This transformative nature of violence in civil wars provides political opportunities for different actors to exploit cleavages in society, including sectarian ones. This, however, does not happen in all civil wars, or at least not on the same scale. Scholars of ethno-sectarian conflict have widely debated the conditions under which domestic sectarian divides lead to the occurrence of violence. Kaufman (2001) discussed different explanations of why ethnic conflict occurs, ranging from the presence of economic rivalry among groups to the genuine fear of extinction and the role of elites seeking to manipulate ethno-sectarian divides for their purposes. Dodge (2005), in his study on Iraq, shows how the collapse of the central state created opportunities for actors willing to exploit sectarian identities. He focuses on how domestic 'sectarian entrepreneurs' exploit Shia–Sunni divides (Dodge 2012: 34). Sudden structural changes provoked by the US-led intervention and subsequent collapse of the central state created a power vacuum that was filled by actors providing 'a degree of stability and certainty' (Dodge 2012: 35).

The works analysed so far focus on the role of domestic actors and the societal level in the sectarianization process. Domestic actors are in fact the ones vying for consensus and legitimacy amid the chaos created by the civil war. However, the same conditions provide opportunities for state actors to manipulate existing identities.[2] The role of external actors is particularly relevant in the MENA region, where transnational identities are prevalent and networks often straddle across borders. These ties in fact provide channels for state actors to manipulate sectarian identities. How do states partake in this 'sectarianization process'? The previous section has described how these actors exploit sectarian divides to favour the flow of foreign fighters in civil wars. By supporting or even organizing the flow of 'sectarian fighters', states also contribute to the sectarianization of the conflict itself. The presence of fighters who join the conflict with a sectarian agenda is in fact likely to alter the dynamics of the conflict itself and does so in the direction of a more pronounced sectarianization. The role of states in the 'sectarianization process' is not however limited to foreign fighters. States can also support pre-existing domestic actors with sectarian make-up or agendas. These include both 'political' factions and (crucially) militias or other groups taking part directly in the fighting. By supporting, financing and sponsoring 'sectarian forces' (often over factions that have more secular or nationalist agendas), states contribute to the sectarianization of the conflict. Furthermore, as the Syrian case will show, the use of sectarian rhetoric itself contributes to a sectarian narrative of the conflict. Through the media they own or control or directly through their representatives, states can pander to a narrative of sectarian conflict. By emphasizing the sectarian nature of civil wars, the actors involved as representative of a religious group and the defence of religious identity as at stake in the conflict, states contribute to a narrative of 'sectarianization' of the civil war itself.

The 'transnational' nature of ethno-sectarian identities also leads to some considerations regarding the relation between sectarianism in a civil war and broader regional dynamics. In a region like the Middle East, where ties among (Arab) countries and public opinions are very strong, the relation between domestic developments and regional trends is likely to be a very close one. In other words, it is useful to think of the country where the civil war is taking place as part of a broader system. Within this system, the manipulation of sectarian identities and/or the sectarianization of a civil war in one country has repercussions at the regional level. The occurrence of a 'sectarian' civil war is in fact likely to further inflame regional tensions along sectarian lines. The nexus between civil wars and broader regional dynamics is not, however, unidirectional. As discussed in the previous section, sectarian cleavages have to be present in the conflict for states to be able to exploit them to recruit and mobilize foreign fighters. States cannot use sectarianism in domestic or regional contexts where sectarian divides are non-existent or not an issue. The relation between sectarianism and the state's role in civil wars can be conceptualized as 'circular'. States exploit sectarian divides to favour the flow of foreign fighters. States' actions, and particularly the flow of 'sectarian' foreign fighters that they favour, increase the sectarianization of the conflict. In turn, the presence of a sectarian conflict (or the sectarianization of a previously less sectarian conflict) increases sectarian divides and tensions in the region.

Sectarianism and civil wars: The case of Syria

The Syrian civil war is an excellent case study for analysis of the relation between civil wars and sectarianism. This section will discuss the 'sectarian' nature of the civil war before turning to the role of state actors in the sectarianization process. The Syrian conflict is routinely described by commentators as a sectarian war that pits an Alawite regime (supported by Shia Iran) against a Sunni insurgency sponsored by Sunni powers – namely, Saudi Arabia, Qatar and Turkey. According to this explanation, sectarian hatred has always existed (albeit it was dormant) in the country. The occurrence of the civil war, with the collapse of the state's central authority and the occurrence of widespread violence, would have simply reactivated these pre-existing cleavages. The civil war itself would be an expression of ancient ethnic and sectarian hatreds that had been suppressed by successive authoritarian regimes. This view of the Syrian conflict is so prevalent that even former president Barack Obama in a frequently cited speech made in the summer of 2013 explained the Syrian civil war in terms of the 'presence of ancient sectarian differences' (Obama 2013).

The Syrian polity

The making of the Syrian polity provides the basis for this primordialist interpretation of the country's politics and more specifically of the civil war. Syria is in fact a heterogeneous country where ethno-sectarian differences have undoubtedly been an important factor. Furthermore, the Syrian civil war did present several instances of sectarian-based violence, some of these taking place in the early phases of the conflict. Groups and militias formed on the basis of sectarian identities mushroomed as the conflict developed, gradually replacing forces with a more 'national' agenda. All these factors together led many analysts to adopt a primordialist view of the conflict. However, a closer scrutiny shows an undoubtedly more complex picture. While sectarianism has been an important aspect in the Syrian polity, the role of political actors in manipulating identities is clear. Ethnic and sectarian cleavages have in fact historically been exploited by ruling elites. Both external powers such as France and later on domestic elites sought to manipulate the heterogeneous nature of Syria's population to their advantage. White (2011) traces the emergence of minorities (and therefore sect) as a political concept to the French Mandate era. Two factors led to this emergence: the policies put in place by the French and the transition towards the nation-state (White 2011: 44). While several analyses concentrate on the 'divide and rule' strategy pursued by the colonial power, White's analysis focuses on a more complex process that sees the 'emergence of minorities' in parallel to the development of the nation state model in Syria. This process had significant consequences in the post-independence phase. The polity that emerged after a bloody struggle against French occupation lacked legitimacy and was marred by instability. This was partially because the country that emerged was a reduced version of the historical Bilad Ash-Sham (Hinnebusch 2001: 18). Arabism provided a unifying ideology that brought most Syrians together (the notable exclusion being Syria's significant Kurdish population in the north), but it had to compete with rival identities such as a pan-Syrian one. In this context, minority politics maintained an important if often not so visible relevance. The urban upper class that led the country to its independence and through the post-independence years was largely Sunni. The two forces that would dominate Syrian politics from the 1960s onwards – the army and the Ba'th party – saw from their onset an over-representation of minorities (Hinnebusch 2001: 22–7). The long-discriminated Alawite community gradually acquired a dominant position in the army and a central one in the party. Two institutions that were openly nationalist (although at least in the case of the Ba'th party, the ideology was Arab nationalist rather than Syrian nationalist) therefore also became 'sectarian'.

This tension was exploited to the fullest by Hafiz Al-Assad, the strongman who took over power in the country in 1970. The Syrian president carried out a strategy of identity construction based on a substantial use of Syrian national symbols. However, he also used his sectarian ties to the Alawite community (and particularly to his tribe and larger family group) to shore up his position (Hinnebusch 2001). This strategy, together with the co-optation of different groups and particularly of key sectors of the Sunni majority, gave the regime a 'complex sectarian' identity, one where sectarianism was not openly addressed or discussed but where sectarian ties provided an important power tool. After the president's death in 2000, his son Bashar Al-Assad inherited the country. The Bashar years were characterized by a gradual 'retreat of the state' caused by a reduction in the size of institutions such as the Ba'th party and workers' unions (Hinnebusch 2012). This retreat left more room for ethnic and sectarian actors such as religious leaders and organizations, often supported by the regime, to expand their role and influence. Under Bashar, the regime also attempted to embrace a more openly religious identity, seeking to exploit it as a consensus tool. Religious charities, schools and other institutions were therefore encouraged to operate as an alternative to more 'malign' forms of Islamism as well as to secular opposition (Hinnebusch 2012: 104). While these groups were arguably not directly responsible for the sectarianization of the country, they did contribute to a more central role of religion in Syria (Philipps 2015). At the same time, the economic changes that took place in the country created an overlapping of social and ethnic tension. The push towards a crony capitalism economic model benefited mostly members of the Alawite community close to the president. The 'losers' in this phase were often farmers and more generally the rural population, who often tended to be Sunni.

The civil war

A primordialist interpretation of the development of the civil war also presents several problems. Despite a long history of the use of sectarianism as a political tool described in the previous section, the protests that took place in the country as part of the Arab spring were initially 'non-sectarian' in nature (Philipps 2012). Protesters who took to the streets to demonstrate against the regime used mostly national symbols. Initially, both the regime and the opposition referred to Syrian national identity rather than ethnic and sectarian ones. Islamist forces such as the

Muslim Brotherhood were caught by surprise by the development of the protests and managed to get a foothold in the protest movement only in the second phase. Similar to what happened in other Arab countries, the discontent that led to the protests had social and economic roots. Furthermore, it was the heavy handling of the protests by the regime, exemplified by the famous episode of the arrest of the schoolboys in Dera'a, that led to an increase in the opposition to the regime and, later, to a militarization of protestors (Lesch 2013).

Despite the initially 'non-sectarian' nature of the protests, several actors pursuing ethno-sectarian goals soon emerged. Philipps (2015) shows how the process of sectarianization was gradual and took place in parallel to the militarization of the crisis. What led to the sectarianization of the conflict? The Syrian civil war presented all the conditions for ethnic conflict indicated by Kaufman. The first is the presence of 'myths justifying ethnic hostility' (Philipps 2015:30). These myths can be based on aspects such as the legitimacy of the use of violence to defend the ancestral home of a group or the historical oppression of a minority group in a particular region. These myths were particularly present in the discourse on Sunni–Shia relations at the start of the Syrian civil war. Related to this first aspect is a second, the presence of ethnic fears – that is, when one or more groups fear that their existence is at risk (Philipps 2015: 31). These fears can in some cases be largely exaggerated, but what matters is that they are believed within the group (however, in the Syrian case, it can be argued that the involvement of radical jihadis and the growth of groups such as Al Nusra or ISIS later gave minorities tangible reasons to be concerned). Myths provided different groups, and particularly minorities, with grounds to fear for their security. Finally, the opportunity to mobilize (Philipps 2015: 33) represents another key factor. In the Syrian case, the retreat (and, in some cases, the collapse) of the central state in vast parts of the country provided this opportunity to a wide range of groups.

These conditions allowed the Syrian crisis to slide towards ethnic conflict and violence; however, this process was 'driven' by the role of what Dodge (2012) calls sectarian entrepreneurs. The Syrian regime, in particular, was central to the process. As outlined previously, the Al-Assad regime in fact sought to exploit sectarian divides to strengthen its position. When faced with the unrests, the regime soon played the 'sectarian card' by portraying itself as the defender of Syria's minorities (as well as Syria's secular Sunnis) against an Islamist opposition (Philipps and Vabjorn 2018). By building on this narrative, the regime clearly played on minority fears of an Islamist dominated country. The regime also actively operated to eradicate secular opposition in order to create the dichotomy between a secular regime and an Islamist opposition. When it succeeded in doing so, the regime could portray itself as 'the only alternative to Islamists', therefore forcing minority groups to choose on the basis of their (in many cases legitimate) sectarian fears. From 2012 onwards, the regime also used sectarianism to address its chronic manpower shortage amidst significant losses of territory. The regime encouraged the creation of local 'sectarian' militias, often entrusted with defending the local population and controlling the territory on behalf of the regime (Philipps 2015: 369). So the defence of Suwayda, the Syrian city with the largest Druze community, was delegated to Druze militias such as Jaysh al-Muwahhideen or Dir' Al-Watan. The Druze community had been a victim of several attacks by radical Islamist actors such as Nusra, including the massacre of an unarmed population in the village of Qalb Lawzah in the Idlib province in the summer of 2014 (Al-Assil and Slim 2015). The regime was therefore able to use the fears of an 'Islamist threat' for its own goals.

While the regime was central to the sectarianization of the civil war, other regional states involved in the conflict also played an important role. The Syrian civil war saw from the onset a high degree of involvement by external actors (Philipps 2016). Due to the country's geopolitical centrality, several regional powers had a stake in the development and outcome of the unrest in the Levantine country. Allies and foes of the regime influenced the conflict through different means, ranging from diplomatic support to direct intervention on the ground. Among the different typologies of support, the recruitment, training and organization of foreign fighters are particularly relevant given the topic of this volume. Foreign fighters were in fact often not only recruited 'along sectarian lines' but also enlisted and trained through the use of sectarian symbols.

Long-term allies Iran and Russia intervened heavily on the side of the regime. The two powers were central to the regime's survival in the face of growing pressure by the armed opposition. Iran and Russia were also largely responsible for the regime's substantial recovery of territory from 2016 onwards. While Russia shored up the regime with its air campaign, it was Iran that provided the troops needed to overcome the Syrian regime's manpower shortage. Iran's intervention was largely carried out through the use of proxies and militias rather than directly by the national army (which, however, played an important organizational and logistic role). These militias were largely recruited among the Shia population, mostly in Pakistan, Afghanistan and neighbouring Iraq. Several reports show that the use of sectarian propaganda was part of Iran's effort to recruit Shia fighters to be deployed in Syria, together with the promise of economic rewards (Moslih 2016). This is particularly clear in the first phase, the recruitment of foreign fighters in the countries of origin. It is also evident later on in the process, in acts such as the deployment of militias formed of foreign fighters under clearly sectarian symbols (such as brigade or unit names or banners). An example is provided by the Liwa Zainebiyoun, a Shia militia composed mostly of Pakistani fighters (and trained by Iran's Revolutionary Guards) whose name and symbols refer to Zaynab, daughter of Ali. The militia was initially formed with the goal of defending the mosque and grave of Zaynab, located in the outskirts of Damascus (Zahid 2016). Another important asset to the regime was the Shia Lebanese militia Hezbollah. Led by charismatic leader Hassan Nasrallah and ideologically aligned to Tehran, Hezbollah intervened to prop up its ally in Damascus and proved to be one of the most effective fighting forces in the conflict.

Regional powers Qatar and Turkey initially attempted to exploit their positive relations with the Syrian regime to mediate a solution to the conflict. Unable to exercise any leverage over the Al-Assad regime, the two countries together with Saudi Arabia threw their weight behind the rising Syrian opposition. In doing so, these countries also contributed to the sectarianization of the conflict. Firstly, the three powers supported domestic militias with clearly sectarian agendas. While officially supporting the 'national' Free Syrian army, the three countries all cultivated links with other (Islamist) groups on the ground. Qatar threw its weight behind groups ideologically aligned to the Muslim Brotherhood, while Saudi Arabia exploited its broader network of contacts that largely consisted of different Islamist actors (Hokayem 2014). These groups eventually replaced and cannibalized more secular militias. Furthermore, these powers favoured (and in some cases organized) the flow of 'sectarian' foreign fighters. Turkey's role was particularly important, as the long border with Syria was the point of entry for many fighters as well as weapons and other tools. Several sources maintain that Turkey did more than acquiescing to the passage of jihadis, coordinating the logistics of fighters' entry into Syria and providing weapons and funds (Uslu 2016).[3] These groups gradually defeated and absorbed more secular groups, contributing to the sectarianization of the conflict. Finally, the Gulf countries, and Saudi Arabia in particular, pushed a heavy anti-Alawite narrative through the TV channels and other media they controlled, often using religious authorities close to the Kingdom.

Conclusion: Civil wars and the sectarianism debate

This chapter analysed the relation between sectarianism and civil wars by focusing on two aspects: states' use of sectarianism to favour the flow of foreign fighters and their role in the 'broader' sectarianization of the civil wars as they progressed. The first section focused on how states exploit the presence of sectarian divides to influence the development and outcome of civil wars. States do so by tolerating, favouring or supporting the flow of foreign fighters to the countries where civil wars are taking place. Sectarian divides provide states with an important tool that can be used to recruit fighters, but also to organize and motivate them once they have already been recruited. However, states not only exploit existing sectarian identities, but are also actors in the sectarianization of civil wars. By manipulating identities to pursue their own goals, states also contribute to the sectarianization of conflicts. States mobilize 'sectarian' foreign fighters, increasing the sectarian nature of the conflict itself. Furthermore, states can often support militias and groups with sectarian agendas over more secular ones. Finally, states can reproduce sectarian narratives of civil wars through their representatives, the media they control or other channels.

The analysis has also raised some interesting points on the relation between the sectarianization of civil wars and broader regional dynamics. This represents an important contribution to the theme of this section, *Regional dynamics and proxies*. The case analysed in this chapter presents an interesting interaction between regional power balancing and sectarianism, and shares in this extent some of the features outlined by Chapters 6 and 7 of this volume. In particular, the same pattern of Iranian-Saudi competition that is analysed in the previous chapter in the context of the Yemeni civil war was one of the key factors influencing the development of the Syrian conflict. In this sense, it is clear that civil wars and the countries where they take place are not 'closed environments' but rather parts of bigger regional systems. This aspect will be particularly relevant in regions such as the Middle East, where transnational ties are strong and long established. While states use sectarianism as a tool to influence civil wars according to their own goals and agendas, the effects of this process extend beyond the country where the civil war is taking place. The occurrence of a strongly 'sectarianized' civil war is likely, in turn, to increase sectarian tensions existing at the regional level. Further research on this aspect would undoubtedly contribute to both the debate on ethno-sectarian identities and the literature on external involvement in civil wars.

The case of the Syrian civil war provided an interesting case study for this analysis. The Syrian regime as well as external states have exploited the existence of sectarian divides in the country and in the broader region. In the case of this civil war, the regime was the main 'sectarianizing' actor. The Al-Assad regimes had a long history of manipulating sectarian identities for their own benefits. While building a Syrian 'national' identity, Hafiz Al-Assad also relied on sectarian ties to shore up his position of power. As a result, the Ba'thist state was in its rhetoric both pan-Arab and 'national Syrian', but sectarian identities played an important if often unspoken role. The economic changes that started during Hafiz's era but increased significantly during Bashar's years also increased inter-sectarian tensions. The post-liberalization era was dominated by crony capitalism, and most (although significantly not all) of the beneficiaries were Alawites close to the president. However, when protests started as part of the Arab Spring, sectarianism was clearly not the defining aspect. From the onset of the crisis, the regime sought to portray itself as the protector of Syrian minorities against an Islamist insurgency. Furthermore, the regime addressed its manpower shortage by delegating the control and defence of part of the territory to 'sectarian' militias. The regime's key ally Iran used its networks to recruit Shia fighters from countries such as Afghanistan and Pakistan. These forces, together with the Lebanese Shia militia Hezbollah, were crucial in preventing the collapse of the regime amidst significant pressure by the opposition. The regime and its allies were, however, not the only ones to exploit sectarian divides. The main opposition supporters Qatar, Saudi Arabia and Turkey all supported sectarian militias on the ground, as well as favouring the flow of jihadis in the attempt to topple the Syrian regime. Finally, it is difficult to assess the long-term impact of the Syrian conflict on regional processes of sectarianization (or de-sectarianization). It is however realistic to expect that the conflict would have contributed to creating a more sectarian (and sectarianized) region, representing therefore an obstacle to potential future de-sectarianization attempts.

The chapter has built on a growing literature that has revisited the traditional debate on sectarianism in the Middle East. Given the prevalence of the narrative of ancient hatreds in many accounts of regional politics, the debate on ethno-sectarianism provides a much-needed reflection on the role of identity (or rather identities) in regional politics. Recent studies (Philipps and Valbjorn 2018) have shown how civil wars provide fruitful cases to analyse the processes of sectarianization in the region. Civil wars are characterized by a collapse of the central authority and diffused violence and should therefore provide the perfect conditions for a 'return to basic identities' such as sectarian ones. However, both the literature on civil wars and the literature on ethno-sectarianism challenge this understanding of civil wars, underlining how a combination of factors and particularly the role of actors shapes the sectarianization process. Among these actors, states play a crucial role by both exploiting the presence of sectarian divides for their own goals and partaking of the 'broader' sectarianization of civil wars.

Notes

1 Algeria does have a significant ethnic minority group, the Berbers. Despite a long history of unrest and struggle for autonomy or independence, the Berber population was not significantly involved in the Algerian civil war (Roberts 2003).
2 These include external states but also, in cases when the central authority does not collapse completely, the regime in power at the beginning of the civil war.
3 This policy was partially reverted later on, due also to pressure from Western allies and public opinion.

References

Akhaba, Y., and James, D. l. (2008), 'The "Chicken or the Egg"? External Support and Rebellion in Ethnopolitics', in S. Saideman (ed.), *Intra-State Conflict, Government and Security*, London: Routledge, 161–81.
Al-Assil, I., and Slim, R. (2015), 'The Syrian Druze at a Crossroad', *Middle East Institute Online Edition*, 13 June 2018.
Armitage, D. (2017), *Civil Wars: A History in Ideas*, New Haven, CT: Yale University Press.
Byman, D. (2018), 'How States Exploit Jihadist Foreign Fighters', *Studies in Conflict & Terrorism*, 41 (12): 931–45.
Bishara, A. (2021), *Sectarianism without Sects*, London: Hurst Publisher.
Carment, D. and James, P. (2004), 'Third-Party States in Ethnic Conflict: Identifying the Domestic Determinants of Intervention', in S. Lobell and P. Mauceri (eds), *Ethnic Conflict and International Politics: Explaining Diffusion and Escalation*, New Yok: Palgrave Macmillan, 11–24.
Dawson L. L., and Amarasingam A. (2017), 'Talking to Foreign Fighters: Insights into the Motivations for Hijrah to Syria and Iraq', *Studies in Conflict & Terrorism*, 40 (3): 191–210.
Dodge, T. (2005), *Inventing Iraq: The Failure of Nation Building and a History Denied*, London: Columbia University Press.
Dodge, T. (2012), *Iraq: From War to a New Authoritarianism*, London: International Institute for Strategic Studies.
Haddad, F. (2011), *Sectarianism in Iraq: Antagonistic Visions of Unity*, London: C. Hurst.

Hashemi, N. (2016), 'Toward a Political Theory of Sectarianism in the Middle East: The Salience of Authoritarianism over Theology', *Journal of Islamic and Muslim Studies*, 1 (1): 65–76.
Hashemi, N., and Postel, D. (2017). 'Sectarianization: Mapping the New Politics of the Middle East', *Review of Faith & International Affairs*, 15 (3): 1–13.
Hinnebusch, R. (2001), *Syria. Revolution from Above*, London: Routledge.
Hinnebusch, R. (2012), 'Syria: From "Authoritarian Upgrading" to Revolution?' *International Affairs*, 88 (1): 95–113.
Hinnebusch, R. (2016) 'The Politics of Identity in Middle East International Relations' in L. Fawcett (ed.), *The International Relations of the Middle East*, 5th edition, Oxord: Oxford University Press, 155–75.
Hokayem, E. (2014), 'Iran, the Gulf States and the Syrian Civil War', *Survival*, 56 (6): 59–86.
Huibregtse, A. (2014), 'External Intervention in Ethnic Conflict', *International Interactions*, 36 (3): 265–93.
Kalyvas, S. (2006), *The Logic of Violence in Civil Wars*, Cambridge: Cambridge University Press.
Kasbarian, S., and Mabon, S. P. (2017), 'Contested Spaces and Sectarian Narratives in Post: Uprising Bahrain', *Global Discourse*, 6 (4): 677–96.
Kathman, J. (2010) 'Civil War Contagion and Neighboring Interventions', *International Studies Quarterly*, 54 (4): 989–1012.
Kaufman, S. J. (2001), *Modern Hatreds: The Symbolic Politics of Ethnic War*, New York: Cornell University Press, 2001.
Kundnani, A. (2012), 'Radicalisation: The Journey of a Concept', *Race and Class*, 54 (2), 3–25.
Lesch, D. (2013), *Syria: The Fall of the House of Assad*, New York: Yale University Press.
Malet, D. (2010), 'Why Foreign Fighters? Historical Perspectives and Solutions', *Orbis*, 54 (1): 97–114.
Malet, D. (2015), 'Foreign Fighter Mobilization and Persistence in a Global Context', *Terrorism and Political Violence*, 27 (3): 454–73.
Moore, C., and Tumelty, P. (2008), 'Foreign Fighters and the Case of Chechnya: A Critical Assessment', *Studies in Conflict and Terrorism*, 31 (5): 412–33.
Moslih, H. (2016) Iran 'foreign legion' leans on Afghan Shia in Syria war, *Al Jazeera Online Edition*, 22 June 2016. Available online: https://www.aljazeera.com/news/2016/1/22/iran-foreign-legion-leans-on-afghan-shia-in-syria-war#:~:text=Iran%20is%20recruiting%20Afghan%20Shia,of%20President%20Bashar%20al%2DAssad.
Nilsson, N. (2015), 'Foreign Fighters and the Radicalization of Local Jihad: Interview Evidence from Swedish Jihadists', *Studies in Conflict and Terrorism*, 38 (5): 343–58.
Obama, B. (2013), *Speech to the American Press*, 31 August 2013.
Phillips, C. (2015), 'Sectarianism and Conflict in Syria', *Third World Quarterly*, 36 (2): 357–76.
Philipps, C. (2016), 'The Battle for Syria', *International Rivalry in the New Middle East*, New Haven, CT: Yale University Press.
Phillips, C., and Valbjørn, M. (2018), 'What Is in a Name? The Role of (Different) Identities in the Multiple Proxy Wars in Syria', *Small Wars & Insurgencies*, 29 (3): 414–33.
Rasmussen, S. E., and Nader, Z. (2016), 'Iran Covertly Recruits Afghan Shias to Fight in Syria', *The Guardian Online Edition*, 30 June 2016. Available online: https://www.theguardian.com/world/2016/jun/30/iran-covertly-recruits-afghan-soldiers-to-fight-in-syria.

Regan, P. (2002), 'Third-party Interventions and the Duration of Intrastate Conflicts', *Journal of Conflict Resolution*, 46 (1), 55–73.
Riedel, B. (2014), *What We Won: America's Secret War in Afghanistan, 1979–89*, Washington, DC: Brookings Institution Press.
Roberts, H. (2003), *The Battlefield: Algeria 1988–2002, Studies in a Broken Polity*, London: Verso Books.
Salloukh, B. (2017), 'The Sectarianization of Geopolitics in the Middle East', in N. Hashemi and D. Postel (eds), *Sectarianization: Mapping the New Politics of the Middle East*, London: Hurst, 35–52.
Scarborough, R. (2013), 'Al Qaeda "Rat Line" from Syria to Iraq Turns Back against Assad', *The Washington Times*, 19 August. Available online: http://www.washingtontimes.com/news/2013/aug/19/al-qaeda-rat-line-from-syria-to-iraq-turns-back-ag/.
Spalek, B. (2007), 'Disconnection and Exclusion: Pathways to Radicalisation?' in T. Abbas (ed.), *Islamic Political Radicalism: A European Perspective*, Edinburgh: University of Edinburgh Press, 192–206.
Thomas, H. (2001), *The Spanish Civil War*, New York: The Modern Library.
Uslu, E. (2016) 'Jihadist Highway to Jihadist Haven: Turkey's Jihadi Policies and Western Security', *Studies in Conflict & Terrorism*, 39 (9): 781–802.
Valbjorn, M., and Hinnebusch, R. (2018), 'Playing "The Sectarian Card" in a Sectarianized New Middle East', *Babylon: Nordisk Tidsskrift for Midtøstenstudier*, 2: 42–55.
White, B. T. (2011), *The Emergence of Minorities in the Middle East: The Politics of Community in French Mandate Syria*, Edinburgh: Edinburgh University Press.
Zahid, F. (2016), 'The Zainabiyoun Brigade: A Pakistani Shiite Militia Amid the Syrian Conflict', *Terrorism Monitor*, 14 (11): 5–6.

Part III

DE-SECTARIANIZATION

Chapter 9

IRAN'S SOFT POWER IN THE GULF FROM THE ISLAMIC REVOLUTION TO POST-INTRA-GULF CRISIS AND PROSPECTS FOR DE-SECTARIANIZATION IN THE GULF

Nesibe Hicret Battaloglu

Introduction

Iran has long been an aspirant player to project its power through its surrounding neighbours, including the Gulf region. Both material and ideational capabilities alongside with willingness to perform a regional power behaviour render Tehran to pursue its interests mostly through soft power means in the Gulf. This study examines Iran's soft power sources, policies and impacts in the Gulf region since the Islamic Revolution of 1979. Methodologically, capitalizing on available public opinion surveys, this research underlines driving factors in the public opinion of Gulf people towards Tehran to draw a comprehensive and broader picture of the soft power policies of this non-Sunni, non-Arab state within the light of domestic and regional developments. Personal interviews with Iranian officials and scholars are also articulated to understand how Iran frames its soft power strategies towards the Gulf region.

The results of this research suggest that the geopolitics of the region and domestic developments in both Iran and the Gulf monarchies are determinants in Iran's image and reach to the Gulf region via soft power means. Iran has long enjoyed positive public opinion in the Gulf states as an independent, multilateral and self-sustained state that is vocal in Muslim causes and an Islamic republican state. The geopolitical developments since Arab uprisings have altered the regional material and ideological balance of power and have led to the mushrooming of weak states with divided societies along confessional and ethnic lines in the Middle East. When coupled with regime survival concerns of the Gulf monarchies, sectarianization of regional politics has both enabled and curbed Iran's reach via soft power means into the region. While Tehran has enhanced and enlarged its constituency by aiding mostly Shia and non-state allies within other states in the Middle East, its image has deteriorated in the Gulf: Iran has been labelled as having an expansionist agenda and framed as not having the capacity and desire to unite Muslim countries or in fighting against Israel (Saouli 2020).Yet, more recently, the increasing assertiveness of Gulf monarchies in regional politics, intra-Gulf disputes between Qatar and the Saudi Arabia-the United Arab Emirates-Bahrain axis, and historic peace deals between Israel and some Gulf states altered the political agenda of the Gulf public space. Amidst these developments Iran seems to appear as a lesser evil and Tehran would capitalize on the momentum to boost its damaged image through soft-power means in a divided Gulf political and public sphere.

The overall picture of Iran's image in the Gulf highlights important points to be addressed on theoretical and analytical fronts. The findings of the research reflect upon the non-static nature of Iranian soft power in the midst of regional and domestic developments in the Gulf. The fluctuations of Iran's image in the region show that a context-specific interpretation of the sectarianization debate is necessary and focusing on attitudes towards Iran in the Gulf would offer an alternative conceptual framework beyond rigid binaries of primordialism and instrumentalism. The anti-Iranian attitudes in the Gulf are neither ancient nor solely dependent on the Gulf regimes' securitization strategies. Rather, Iran's image is dependent upon Iran's domestic and regional policies, alongside with Gulf monarchies' domestic concerns and geopolitical aims operating in broader regional settings.

Focusing on Iran's experience with soft power policies towards the GCC states would also contribute a nuanced understanding of de-sectarianization in the Gulf. A context-sensitive approach to de-sectarianization logic would capitalize on soft power as a conceptual framework to achieve normalization of inter-state relations in the Gulf. Under convenient domestic and regional circumstances, Iran's soft power resources and willingness to enhance its image in the Gulf would contribute to ease the inter-state rivalry between Gulf monarchies and Iran, which is one of the most important external factors in sectarianization of regional politics, for a gradual yet sustained de-sectarianization (Mabon 2019).

Soft power: Its definition, sources and limitations

In 1990, Nye introduced the notion of 'soft power' as a different type of power in international relations amidst declining US power in the post–Cold War era and increasing limitations on the traditional concept of military balance of power. According to Nye 'a state may achieve the outcomes it prefers in world politics because other states want to follow it or have agreed to a situation in world politics as to get others to change in particular cases', which refers to 'co-optive or soft power in contrast with the hard and command power of *ordering* others to do what it wants' (Nye 1990: 166). By definition, soft power differs from hard power in certain ways. It operates through agenda setting, persuasion and attraction, not through coercion, use of force or paying to change others' preferences. There are three main areas that one should consider: culture, political values and foreign policies (Nye 2004). When compared to hard power, soft power sources appear less clear, less tangible and more difficult to control; as Nye perfectly describes, 'soft power may appear less risky than economic or military power, but it is often hard to use, easy to lose and costly to reestablish' (2011: 83). In terms of measurement 'public opinion polls' and 'careful content analyses' appear as useful tools to make 'first estimations' about one state's soft power over another (Nye 2011: 94–5). Here, public opinion is framed as an important factor affecting decision making at the top level of the states. If one takes soft power as the 'ability to attract' and if 'attraction often leads to acquiescence', creating a positive public opinion via attraction is a key dimension for wielding soft power. Nye also lists certain limitations and challenges (2007):

1. Soft power resources are diffused among different agencies and departments
2. It takes a long time to bear the fruits of soft power and more patience is needed.
3. Soft power investments are not under the monopoly of governments, 'while governments control policy, culture and values are embedded in civil societies' (171).
4. Soft power rests upon credibility and governments should avoid being perceived as manipulative, because when 'information is perceived as propaganda and indoctrination, credibility is destroyed' (171).
5. Soft power is not a magical power to have absolute 'leverage' in certain cases (i.e. dispute over North Korea's nuclear weapons)

Wielding soft power may face cultural obstacles as well. To put it clearly, as the effectiveness of soft power depends on how it is perceived by others, the same sources of soft power of a particular state can reach the audience differently through the filters of cultures. Therefore, states cannot fully control the 'perceptions' in different cultural settings (Nye 2011).

The rationale of studying Iran's soft power in the Gulf

The soft power approach opens a discussion for the capabilities of middle powers beyond their mere material competences in the multipolar international and regional politics. Although Nye's concept of soft power has been developed around the argument of the US's declining influence in the world and tries to offer solutions for this, Nye (2004) himself notes that 'soft power is available to all countries, and many invest in ways to use soft-power resources to 'punch above their weight' in international politics (89). Given their limited overall power resources vis-à-vis the great powers, the soft power policies enable middle-sized states, including Iran, to create a greater impact and may catalyse the process of achieving their national interests under certain conditions. With material and ideational resources, willingness and interest, means and capacity to project power, and the ability to affect regional powers' behaviours, Iran certainly fits into the 'middle power' definition (Saouli 2020) and the soft power framework is useful to capitalize when studying Iran–GCC relations over the last four decades.

Another factor to focus on regarding Iranian soft power is that Iran has not initiated any military offensive towards the GCC countries except for the dispute over three islands in the Gulf between Iran and the United Arab Emirates in 1971 and Iranian support for the Sultan of Oman to suppress the socialist Dhofar rebellion[1]. Tehran rarely implemented hard power instruments against the GCC countries. On the contrary, since the beginning of 1980, soft power policies such as images, rhetoric, values and economic cooperation, and in some cases the goodwill of Iran, have been used to target their audiences in the GCC. Iran opted for soft means to deliver its message, even when Tehran adopted a hard rhetoric towards the Gulf monarchies. The soft power approach serves the interests of Iran in its foreign policies towards the GCC, and Tehran wielded its soft power tools of persuasion, agenda setting and attraction in the immediate aftermath of the Islamic Revolution. Under the charismatic leadership of Ayatollah Khomeini, Iran had tried to articulate the legitimacy of the revolution and used persuasion, attractiveness and justness of the Islamic revolution to encourage people living in the Gulf against oppressive rulers. After the death of Ayatollah Khomeini, the reformist governments of President Rafsanjani and Khatami shifted Iran's foreign policy, and soft power become even more important in facilitating the relations with the GCC countries to break Iran's regional isolation and boost its economic opportunities.

Soft power policies also became a part and parcel of Iran's foreign policy in the midst of increasing regional rivalry, which manifested itself mostly along a Sunni–Shia divide following the Arab Uprisings of 2011. On the offensive side, widespread protests and the downfall of pro-Western regimes in some Arab countries were cautiously welcomed by Tehran, and Iran tried to portray such upheavals as 'Iranian inspired' (Parsi and Marashi 2011). Yielding soft power, in this sense, has become the most reliable policy option, as 'Iran's self-perception of regional leadership is not based on military superiority, but rather on its political and financial investment in various regional movements and its ability to exploit popular frustration over domestic political issues and injustices in the region' (ibid.). Yet the dual effect of Iraninan soft power strategies mostly constrained Tehran's ability to garner support from the Gulf public. Since 2011, Iran's sponsorship of mainly Shia factions in Syria, Yemen, Iraq and Lebanon has enabled Iran to penetrate into more Arab states and garner constituencies. Yet the same strategy also stirred a broad distrust of Tehran's geopolitical intentions (Watkins 2020), especially among GCC states, and served Saudi Arabia's strategy to frame Iran's policies from securitized and sectarianized lenses.

On the defensive side, Iran also pursues soft power strategies to counter what Tehran labels as 'soft war' orchestrated by the United States and its allies for a regime change in Iran (Price 2012). The term 'soft war' became an important strand of Iran's foreign policy during Ahmadinejad's presidency, and Iran gained significant popularity among the Arab and Muslim worlds, including the Gulf region, through the means of 'soft war' strategies, such as pursuing a nuclear enrichment programme and a defiant foreign policy against the US and Israel. The concept of 'soft war', therefore, indicates that ideas, means and policies of soft power have certainly become an important element of foreign policymaking in Iran (Wastnidge 2015).

Integrating the soft power framework into sectarianization and de-sectarianization debates also contributes to enlarging the analytical horizon of this approach. In the sectarianization thesis, Nader Hashemi and Danny Postel (2017) argue that sectarianization is 'an active process shaped by political actors operating within specific contexts, pursuing political goals that involve the mobilization of popular sentiments around particular identity markers' (Hashemi and Postel 2017: 3). While it elaborates on actors and factors that constitute the sectarianization process, it largely ignores how the constituency responds to sectarianization. Tracking public opinion towards Iran at different times would enable an alternative reading, from the public side, of sectarianization. Also, Iran's soft power policies since the revolution towards the Gulf region and its repercussions on bilateral relations between Saudi Arabia and Iran can provide valuable insights into understanding de-sectarianization of inter-state rivalries.

Iran's soft power resources, currencies, motivations and application in the Gulf region

Nye (2011) mentions that culture, political values and foreign policies are the three main soft power resources of a given country. Yet, a perspective focusing on fixed resources appears to be inadequate and misleading to analyse a country's soft power in a complex and ever-shifting regional environment that filters those given resources through the lens of particular cultural settings and domestic politics. Further, depending on the context, hard power resources of a given state such as economic and military strength can generate soft power, which is clearly the case for Iran's soft power in the Gulf region.

According to Vuving (2009), power is not identical with its resources, and 'a typical soft power resource' such as a moral value can be used both to persuade someone, when the person privately agrees with it, and force another, when it is used to build social pressure' (4). In order to answer how soft power actually works, Vuving (2009) addresses three 'generic power currencies' of beauty, brilliance and benignity. Benignity is one of the most crucial aspects to generate soft power over other states. According to Vuving this concept has a range of meanings from 'no harm to others' to 'actively protecting and supporting others', and it operates through producing 'gratitude and sympathy' (2009: 9). Brilliance, which is associated with strength and advancement in hard and soft power sources, can articulate soft power through attraction, creating myths of invincibility and inevitability (Vuving 2009: 10). Beauty in international relations refers to the exchange of sympathy between actors, stemming from shared ideals, values, causes or visions.

Cultural assets are one of the main pillars of Iranian soft power in the Gulf region. The Iranian culture, in its broadest sense, corresponds to both Nye's categorization and Vuving's concept of beauty. The former deputy foreign minister of Iran from 1988 to 1997, Abbas Maleki, highlighted in an exclusive interview that Iran's cultural presence with art, language, literature and architecture and interaction with the Arab Gulf is one of the most important assets of Iran's potential soft power in the region. He said, 'Today many logos and symbols of institutions in the GCC are *Badgirs*, the wind towers of Iranian style of ventilation from 2000 years ago. Or the word of *Bandar* is a Persian word used for port is very widely used in the region' (Maleki 2016). Tehran's self-projected image of greatness based on its culture, religion, ethics and beliefs constitutes the main ideological incentives for wielding soft power towards Gulf states. According to Manoucher Mohammadi (2008), former Iranian deputy foreign minister for Education, the soft power of Iran stems from its national character and asserts that this power 'outshines and overcomes hard power in a sphere in which the power is derived from spiritual sources and mainly rooted in divine and religious faiths and beliefs' (Mohammadi 2008: 6).

An interviewee from Qom (Iran), who prefers to remain anonymous, also mentioned that Iran's soft power has its roots in the psychological and social structure of Iranian society that has been shaped around the norms of the Islamic revolution; he adds, 'the soft power of Iran is not about convincing others, it is rather the realization of Iranian identity' (Interviewee, 13 March 2016). The soft power motive taking its essence from cultural identity, therefore, has become an important and inseparable part of the exporting revolution during the early years of the Islamic republic as Khomeini attempted to develop a 'universally acceptable model' to enhance Iran's popularity in the Gulf region (Feizi and Talebi 2012).

Economic and military strength is another source, which articulates the power currency of brilliance in yielding Iranian soft power in the region. Although they first appear as hard power tools, technological advancement, the self-sustaining economy and military capabilities of Iran would act as soft power sources because 'a successful economy is an important source of attraction' (Nye 2007: 165) and 'some people are generally attracted to strength' (ibid: 167). Iran's nuclear programme has long been an asset that produced admiration in the eyes of people in the Gulf region. Lawrence Rubin (2010) says that Iran's nuclear capability provides a 'symbolic benefit' in terms of soft power assets and notes, 'First, the technological advances made communicate that Iran is an advanced and modern nation, and is on its way to joining an elite club. Second, Tehran's defiance of Western demands for more intrusive inspections demonstrates its independence in pursuit of its own interests' (2010: 13). In fact, as the results of a survey in 2008 show, a plurality of Arab people (67 per cent) stated that Iran has a right to its nuclear programme and the international pressure should cease (Telhami 2008). In Saudi Arabia 73 per cent of people indicated that they were expecting a positive outcome in the Middle East if Iran acquired nuclear weapons (ibid.).

Political ideas, norms, values and actions as soft power resources become soft power currencies in the form of *beauty*, which gives actors a sense of warmth and security, hope and self-extension, identity and community, and vindication and praise. Actors can discover this beauty when they are jointly pursuing their 'shared ideals, values, causes, or visions' (Vuving 2009:11). Iran has had considerable political assets, which articulated soft power in the eyes of many people in the Gulf. The Islamic Revolution in 1979 was one of the turning points with regard to the ideological aspect of soft power. During the early years of the revolution, Iran emerged as an Islamic state that stood against imperialism, communism, any foreign domination and repression, which resonated with many people in the Gulf. The charismatic supreme leader Ayatollah Khomeini called for exporting revolution abroad against repressive rulers. Khomeini, in a speech in Radio Tehran in 1980, said,

> We should try hard to export our revolution to the world, and should set aside the thought that we do not export our revolution, because Islam does not regard various Islamic countries differently and is the supporter of all the oppressed people of the world. On the other hand, all the superpowers and all the powers have risen to destroy us. If we remain in an enclosed environment we shall definitely face defeat. We should clearly settle our accounts with the powers and superpowers and should demonstrate to them that, despite all the grave difficulties that we have, we shall confront the world with our ideology.

During the early phase of the Islamic Republic, adopting 'isolationism with a universal message' approach, Iran emerged as an influential actor supporting Muslims across the globe. Although the ruling elite in the Gulf perceived the message of Iran as a deadly threat to the survival of their monarchical rules, the idea of resistance to and reaction against the oppressors appealed to many people in the region.

Following the reformist presidents like Rafsanjani, Khatami and then Rouhani have been very much aware of their limitations stemming from Iran's revolutionary image on its soft power and its reach in the Arab world. In fact, the Iranian leadership has effectively given up the idea of promoting revolution in the Arab world. Rather, geo-economic concerns and foreign policy interests motivated Tehran to pursue a soft power strategy based on cultural diplomacy initiatives. The new approach with regard to the oil policy of Tehran, which was based on relaxed energy policies and increase in oil production, during the 1990s under the presidency of Akbar Hashemi Rafsanjani and then Mohammad Khatami led Iran to seek greater cooperation with Saudi Arabia and other GCC countries under the umbrella of OPEC and bilateral arrangements (Ramazani 1992). Ramazani (1992) notes, 'This new realism in economics, as in domestic politics and foreign policy, results from the emphasis of the dual leadership on reasons of state as opposed to on a chiliastic ideological crusade. The export of the revolution by coercive means is being largely replaced by the projection of an Irano-Islamic role model by peaceful means' (p.395).

During the interviews, it is frequently mentioned that Iran has economic interests and motivations in the Gulf region that can be achieved through soft power policies and more reconciliatory attitudes in relation to the GCC countries. Professor Shahram Akbarzadeh commented, 'The overall soft power goal of Iran is normalizing relations between Iran and its neighbours; and benefiting from economic dividends of normal relations. Iran is very much a rational state which means if there are steps, measures, processes that undermines and contradicts

Iran's national interest then Iran would not be very much following the past' (Akbarzadeh, personal interview, 13 March 2016).

Similarly, former deputy foreign minister of Iran Maleki (personal interview, 13 March 2016) noted that one of the main interests of Iran in the GCC region through soft power has been the 'stability and calmness in the Persian Gulf and Strait of Hormuz', as the most important and strategic waterway in the world, and enhancing 'economic cooperation among Iran UAE, Qatar, Oman and even with Saudi Arabia and Kuwait'.

Given the motivations above, under President Khatami, Iran enhanced its international image through demonstrative effect, public diplomacy tools and foreign policy initiatives. One of the main aspects of wielding soft power is the so-called leading by example or demonstrative effect. During the presidency of Khatami, the dual attempt of strengthening civil society and rights domestically and initiating détente with the neighbouring states can be considered as consistency and leading by example in that respect. Edward Wastnidge (2015) argues, 'Such attempts fit in with Nye's views on political values being important to a country's soft power capabilities. While the Islamic Republic cannot be seen as having any major clout historically in this regard, Khatami's attempts at promoting reformist, modern Islamic politics did have a positive effect on its international image' (p.369).

The foreign policy initiatives of Iran have been important tools to project soft power in the GCC region. The foreign policies of both states have changed depending on the domestic and international conditions and have evoked positive reactions at different times and among different segments within different GCC countries. The foreign policy initiatives of multilateralism, diplomatic support and adherence to international norms as well as the resistance, assertive foreign policy and rhetoric of charismatic leaders of both states have been presented as soft power tools of Iran in the GCC countries.

Iranian President Khatami initiated 'Dialogue among Civilizations' as a foreign policy priority for improving Iran's international standing and further restoring its relations with the neighbouring states. The Organization of Islamic Countries (OIC) summit in Tehran in 1997 took place within this new aura in Iran's foreign policy, supporting dialogue, peace promotion and multilateralism. The outcome was positive for Iran in restoring its image: the then Crown Prince Abdullah of Saudi Arabia, 'the most senior Saudi visitor to Iran since the 1979 revolution', attended the conference (Molavi 2015); the positive repercussions on Iran–GCC relations were reported in GCC media outlets (Fas.org 1997); and frequent ministerial visits took place between Iran and the GCC states (Clawson et al. 1998).

Albeit with a different tone and through different means, Iran continues to capitalize on soft power approaches to boost its regional standing and image. The interviewees[2] mentioned that Iranian foreign policy under President Ahmadinejad was successful in creating soft power. If one analyses the first term (2005–2009) of Ahmadinejad's foreign policy, a return to the revolutionary discourse, confrontational rhetoric with the West over Tehran's nuclear programme and stance against Israel can be highlighted as the milestones that enhanced Iran's image in the Arab streets. In 2005, during his speech in The World Without Zionism in Tehran, Ahmadinejad was quoted, 'The Imam said this regime occupying Jerusalem must vanish from the page of time' (Norouzi 2007). However, many mainstream international media have reported a different translation of Ahmadinejad saying, 'As the Imam [Ayatollah Khomeini] said, Israel must be wiped off the map' (McGreal and McAskill, 26 October 2005). President Ahmadinejad also called the Holocaust (the Nazi genocide of 6 million Jews in the second world war) a myth during a live broadcast on Iranian television with wide publicity (Tait and Harding, 15 December 2005). Trita Parsi (2006) argues that Ahmedinejad's anti-Israel rhetoric is determined within geostrategic rivalry between the two, rather than ideological collision. Parsi (2006) notes that 'Iran started to translate its rhetoric on Israel into actual policy in order to sabotage the peace process – deemed to be the weakest link in the US-Israeli effort to create an Israel-centric order in the region based on Iran's prolonged isolation' (8). Despite the geostrategic calculations of Iran, President Ahmadinejad's rhetoric resonated in the Arab streets (Soghom 2008). In the aftermath of the 2006 war between Israel and Iran's main ally Hezbollah in Lebanon, Hezbollah leader Nasrallah has been the most admired leader in the Arab world followed by Syria's Bashar Essad and Iranian president Ahmadinejad (Telhami 2008).

Under the reformist presidency of Rouhani, Iran also deployed soft power means to reach audiences in the GCC states. Op-ed articles written by prominent political figures are an acceptable way of conveying messages to targeted audiences. An article by the Iranian Foreign Minister Zarif appeared in the English edition of Saudi Arabia's *Alsharq Al-Awsat* in 2013. In the article titled 'Our neighbors are our priority' Zarif conveys important messages to portray Iran's benignity as a soft power currency towards its 'southern neighbours' at a time when the tensions between Iran and GCC countries were high: 'We recognize that we cannot promote our interests at the expense of others. This is particularly the case in relation to counterparts so close to us that their security and stability are intertwined with ours' (parag.2). Zarif adds, 'Iran, content with its size, geography, and human and natural resources, and enjoying common bonds of religion, history and culture with its neighbors, has not attacked anyone in nearly three centuries. We extend our hand in friendship and Islamic solidarity to our neighbors, assuring them that they can count on us as a reliable partner' (parag.17).

As discussed in more detail below, the geopolitics of sectarianization following the Arab Spring, regime survival concerns of GCC monarchies, the rise of civil conflicts in the region and Iran's own policy preferences and actions undermined Iran's soft power efforts toward the Gulf region. Iran's positive image declined considerably after 2009 and further declined after the Arab Uprisings.

Measuring soft power: Gulf public opinion towards Iran

Equating soft power of a given state only with sources and motivations can be an incomplete assessment as the other side of the soft power equation is about how others perceive this state. Public opinion surveys and expert interviews are the most useful tool for collecting data on the impact of the soft power policies of Iran in the eyes of Gulf people.

Marking the Iranian Revolution as a starting point, early estimations on Iran's soft power in the Gulf are collected via interviews. It seems convenient to say that Iran's image in the eyes of the Gulf public was enhanced due to the appealing model and messages of the Islamic Revolution but at the expense of bilateral interstate relations. Ibrahim Fraihat, the Deputy Director of Brookings Doha, noted, 'In early 1980s Iran's soft power was at its peak because of rising anti-colonialism, anti-imperialism or Islamic liberation. They found a huge audience in the region, including the Gulf' (Fraihat Interview 2016).

Yet Iran's image in the eyes of the GCC ruling elite improved under moderate President Rafsanjani and President Khatami during the 1990s. The Middle East Contemporary Survey notes that most of the GCC states, including Bahrain, were quick to seek a rapprochement with Iran following the invasion of Kuwait, and there was positive media coverage towards Iran's increasing integration in the region (Ayalon 1992: 308–9). Tehran expanded its foreign relations, projecting an image of reliability and stability (ibid.: 369). In 1991, the rapprochement between Saudi Arabia and Iran bore fruit, and the two reached an agreement with the help of Omani mediation on the return of Iranian pilgrims and a rally in Mecca to convey supreme leader Khamenei's message (Kramer 1993).

Reliable and online public opinion polls on GCC perceptions towards Iran date back to the early 2000s. In 2002, the poll titled 'Arabs: What They Believe and What They Value Most' by Zogby International finds that Iran received highly favourable reviews in Saudi Arabia and Kuwait – 66 per cent and 79 per cent, respectively, and 38 percent in the UAE (Zogby International 2002). The poll was conducted with 3200 Arab adults from eight countries (Egypt, Israel, Jordan, Lebanon, Kuwait, Morocco, the United Arab Emirates and Saudi Arabia) and provides important insights into Iran's favourability in the three Gulf states in the early 2000s.

'Looking at Iran' by Zogby International (2013) shows that Iran's image in the GCC (Saudi Arabia and the UAE included) countries was positive until 2009, and attitudes towards Iran saw a sharp decline after that (see Figure 9.1). While 85 per cent of the Saudi and 68 per cent of the Emirati respondents had favourable attitudes towards Iran in 2006, this dropped to 35 per cent for Saudi Arabia and 13 per cent for the UAE in 2009.

The same survey included all six GCC countries (Saudi Arabia, Qatar, Kuwait, Bahrain, the UAE and Oman) and eleven other Arab countries' general attitudes towards Iran and the Iranian Revolution, Iranian people and culture and Iran's nuclear activities to present an extensive picture in 2012. As of 2012, Iran was relatively favourable only in Kuwait out of the six GCC countries, with 50 per cent. In the rest of the GCC countries, the majority of respondents' attitudes towards Iran were classified as unfavourable. Unfavourable attitudes are reported as highest in Saudi Arabia (84 per cent) and Qatar (79 per cent) (see Figure 9.2).

The respondents in the GCC viewed Iran's role as negative in Iraq, Lebanon, Syria, Bahrain and the Arab Gulf region: 'In each case, about 50% of respondents

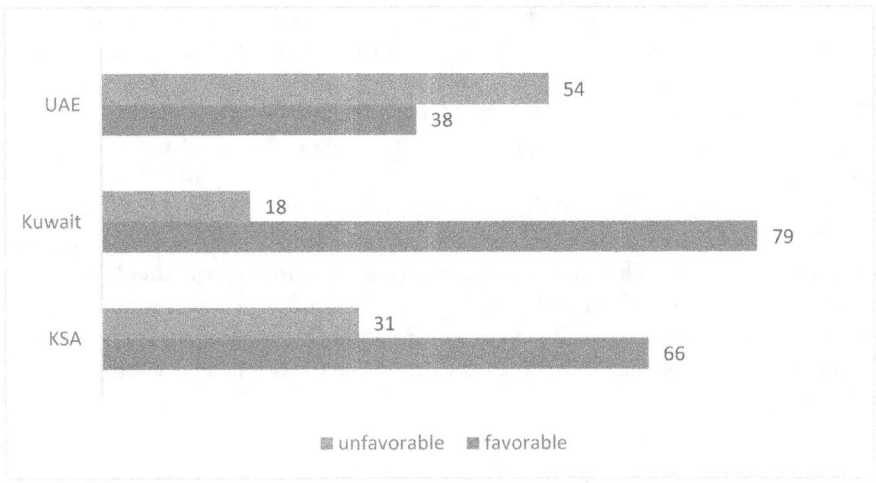

Figure 9.1 How GCC states viewed Iran in 2002.

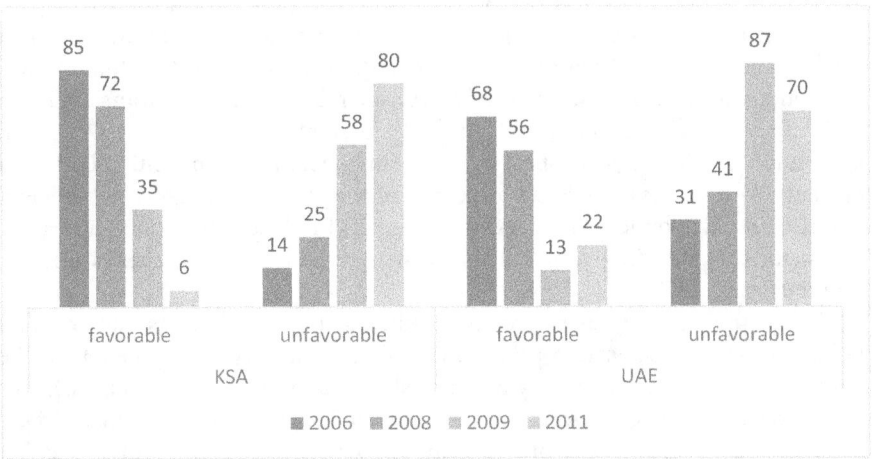

Figure 9.2 Perception towards Iran.

in Kuwait and Bahrain say Iran's role is negative, while about two-thirds of respondents in Oman and UAE see Iran as playing a negative role in each country and the region. Saudi and Qatari respondents are the most negative, with about three-quarters of these respondents saying Iran plays a negative role' (Zogby 2013: 15). When asked whether they agreed or disagreed with the statement, 'Iran is a role model for my country', the majority of the respondents in all GCC countries stated that they disagreed (Kuwait 53 per cent, Bahrain 58 per cent, Qatar 78 per cent, UAE 62 per cent, KSA 84 per cent and Oman 57 per cent).

The poll 'Today's Middle East: Pressures and Challenges', conducted by Zogby Research Services (2014) for Sir Bani Yas Forum, included the two GCC states Saudi Arabia and the UAE. Poll results show that the majority of respondents from Arab Gulf countries continue to perceive Iran's role in Syria, Lebanon, Iraq, Bahrain and Yemen as negative (Saudi Arabia 66 per cent and the UAE 52 per cent).

Another crucial finding of the poll (Zogby Research Services 2014) is that the election of a moderate president in Iran has not contributed to enhancing Iran's image in the region. When the respondents were asked to state whether they agreed or disagreed with the statement, 'During the presidency of Hassan Rouhani, Iran's behaviour in the region has moved in a more positive direction', most respondents from GCC countries stated that they disagreed (Saudi Arabia 47 per cent, the UAE 65 per cent).

Assessments on Iran's soft power in the GCC countries: From the Green Movement to the Arab Spring

The survey results, first and foremost, show that soft power or the positive image of a given country over other countries is neither static nor permanent. When Iran's image in the GCC countries is considered, the poll results show that positive perceptions towards Iran have declined considerably since 2009. Iran's ability to maintain a positive outlook in the GCC was mainly due to its cultural, political and military/technological appeal in the region where Islamism, anti-colonialism and anti-Western ideas were still present. Iran was able to manage a self-sufficient political and economic system and to champion the Palestinian cause at least at the rhetorical level. Yet Tehran failed to sustain its allure for a number of reasons, especially since 2009.

Firstly, the unbridgeable perceived contradictions in Tehran's rhetoric and policies started in 2009. Iran gained increasing popularity among people in the neighbouring states, particularly in the Arab world even after the US invasion of Iraq, and Iran increased its soft power reach during the first term of Ahmadinejad's presidency through its aims of defending the rights of Muslims worldwide. Yet the controversial presidential victory of Ahmadinejad in his second term changed Iran's image in the eyes of the people. The Green Movement in 2009 and the Iranian regime's repressive response against popular uprisings was covered widely by international media (Al Jazeera English 2009; Freeman and Blair 2009; Jeffrey 2009; Rothberg 2010; and Makhmalbaf 2009) and exposed the contradictions in Iran's championing of populations against repressive regimes since the revolution and the domestic responses to popular demands. The Zogby Research poll of 2012 shows that the majority of the respondents in all six GCC countries identified themselves with the Green Movement rather than the Iranian government (70 per cent in Kuwait, 53 per cent in Bahrain, 73 per cent in Qatar, 68 per cent in the UAE, 62 per cent in KSA and 61 per cent in Oman). The perceived contradictions in Iran's policies were also revealed after the Arab Spring.

Tehran's support for the Syrian regime, against popular demands, contributed to credibility and legitimacy problems for Iran during the Arab Spring. In fact, there were two different perceptions among the Iranian political elite towards the uprisings: the first camp around the supreme leader framed it as an Iranian-inspired Islamic awakening and advocated support for the uprisings; yet the second camp around the president Ahmadinejad perceived the developments in the Middle East as a US–Israeli conspiracy, and they took a cautious stance and supported establishing diplomatic relations with those states (Haji-Yousefi 2012). However, Iran's outspoken rhetoric praising the demands of people in other parts of the Arab world, on the one hand, and Tehran's overall support for the Assad regime, on the other hand, damaged the image of Iran in the eyes of many people in the Arab Gulf region. Poll findings demonstrate that following the Arab Uprisings, Iran's engagement in Syria to reinstate the Assad government has resulted in the erosion of its self-proclaimed status as a resistance state opposing oppressive forces, while concurrently diminishing its positive image for a regional leadership.

Secondly, regional developments sharpened threat perceptions, and the increased sectarianization and counter-revolutionary efforts of some GCC countries after the Arab Spring apparently played an important role in torpedoing Iran's image in the GCC region. This can be evaluated in the context of the geopolitical conditions under which Iran and the GCC states are operating. Sectarianization of conflicts not only in Iraq and Syria, but also in Bahrain and Yemen challenged Iran's ability to project soft power in the region. On this issue, Professor Akbarzadeh noted in a personal interview:

> 'The sectarian war in the region has meant that Iran is now labeled as a Shia state. It is perceived as a purely sectarian state because Iran's allies in the region are Shia partners, Syria and Hezbollah in Lebanon. Once Iran is seen as a sectarian Shia state, it is very hard to break out of that box. Everything Iran says and does is interpreted from that point of view. That really undermines Iran's ability to reach out to the region' (Akbarzadeh 2016).

GCC countries' counter-revolutionary efforts also succeeded in widening the region's sectarian divide and filtered regional events through sectarian lenses (Kamrava 2012). In 2011, the Saudi-led forces suppressed popular uprisings in Bahrain, and Iran was accused of being responsible for the upheavals. Since then, the Bahraini and Saudi governments have very successfully framed popular discontents from sectarian perspectives and reduced Iran's ability to reach the GCC states as a benign power.

Factions within the Iranian regime, especially the Revolutionary Guards (IRGC) and hardliners in the media, can be highlighted as factors undermining the soft power efforts of Iran in the GCC region at a time when sectarianization has been on the rise. It also shows that the Iranian government has no monopoly over the media tools, and it is extremely difficult to project one image. While Zarif expressed Iran's intentions to reach out to the GCC public and seek rapprochement with GCC governments, Major General Mohammad Ali Jafari, then commander of the Islamic Revolutionary Guards Corps (IRGC), was quoted in 2015 as saying that 'The Islamic revolution is advancing with good speed, its example being the ever-increasing export of the revolution', 'Today, not only Palestine and Lebanon acknowledge the influential role of the Islamic republic but so do the people of Iraq and Syria' and '… the phase of the export of the revolution has entered a new chapter' (Alabbasi 2015). Similarly, Tehran city representative Ali Reza Zekani was quoted as saying, 'the Yemeni revolution will not be confined to Yemen alone,' adding that it would extend to Saudi Arabia as well (Nakhoul 2015). In the information age, the different messages from Tehran can easily reach the GCC and it would be argued that such statements from Iran reinforce negative images of Iran and enhance GCC governments' counter-revolution efforts in the region.

Gulf assertiveness, Gulf crisis and Iran as a lesser evil?

The post–Arab Spring environment has significantly altered the sub-regional balance of power, and differing threat perceptions further sharpened regional rivalries in the Gulf. The events that unfolded after 2011 revealed intra-GCC disagreements more than ever before. The fragility of the GCC and the policy divergences among its member states came to the front when in May 2017, the Saudi-led block severed diplomatic ties with Doha accusing Qatar of supporting terrorism, having friendly relations with Iran and interfering in their domestic affairs (Al Jazeera 5 December 2017). Diplomatic spats followed, with borders being closed and sea and airspace being restricted for Qatar-bound traffic. Among thirteen demands that the blockading countries imposed on Qatar to end the embargo, the first point clearly targeted relations with Iran: 'Curb diplomatic ties with Iran and close its diplomatic missions there. Expel members of Iran's Revolutionary Guard from Qatar and cut off any joint military cooperation with Iran. Only trade and commerce with Iran that complies with US and international sanctions will be permitted' (Gulf News 2017).

The aggressive foreign policy choices of certain Gulf states started to shape the regional politics with significant international concern. Coupled with initiating severe blockade over their Qatari brethren, Saudi (and to some extent Emirati) assertiveness raised eyebrows among the regional and international public. The murder of journalist Jamal Khashoggi in Consulate of Saudi Arabia in Istanbul and killings of thousands of civilians in Yemen by airstrikes have certainly torpedoed those Gulf states' image (Almutawakel and Alfaqih 2018).

Also, post-2011 reordering of regional politics has brought the Saudi–UAE bloc and Israel closer as both parties have significantly agreed that Iran and Islamist movements pose the greatest threat to security and stability in the region (Ulrichsen 2018). In 2018, during a meeting with Jewish leaders in New York, Saudi Crown Prince Mohammed bin Salman reportedly asserted that 'it's about time that the Palestinians accept the offers, and agree to come to the negotiating table – or they should shut up and stop complaining,' and elaborating 'the Palestinian issue is not at the top of the Saudi government's agenda. There are much more urgent and more important issues to deal with – such as Iran' (Times of Israel 29 April 2018). However, the Gulf–Israeli rapprochement (albeit unofficial) comes against the fact that the Palestinian issue maintains its importance in the eyes of the Arab public. According to the 2017–2018 Arab Opinion Index, 90 per cent of respondents believe that Israel poses a threat to the security and stability of the region and 80 per cent of Saudi participants stated, 'Palestinian cause concerns all Arabs, not just Palestinians alone' (Arab Opinion Index 2018: 30). In September 2020, the UAE and Bahrain formalized their relationship with Israel in a strategic alignment against Iran.

From the Iranian perspective, the Gulf spat is another crack on the GCC bloc that Tehran would seize to capitalize on and exert its soft power influence through the region as the only option to build its regional policy amidst increasing sectarianization and anti-Iranian sentiments in the GCC states. Tehran was quick to side with Doha in the crisis, calling for easing of escalation and offered food shipment and open-air routes for Qatar-bound traffic (Regencia 2017). In return, in August 2017, Qatar restored full diplomatic relations with Iran, which had deteriorated when the emirate recalled its ambassador in 2016 when Saudi diplomatic missions in Iran were attacked after Saudi Arabia executed a leading Shia Muslim cleric (BBC.com 2017). Yet when the historical track of Qatar–Iran relations is examined, the post–Gulf war situation is neither surprising nor substantial, but rather instrumental (Kamrava 2017). Both states have managed to pursue a 'mutual accommodation' approach throughout the years before and after the Iranian revolution and continued diplomatic relations. While Qatar sees relations with Iran as a key asset in its foreign policy to balance Saudi Arabia, for Iran, Qatar is an Arab partner in the Gulf with whom ideological, territorial and strategic competition is contained (ibid.).

In the post–Arab spring regional environment, where Saudi Arabia and the UAE resort to more and more hard power tools to form their foreign policy, Iran would be classified as a lesser evil than before. At least Iran would share the burden of blame for causing instability and violence in Yemen and elsewhere. A survey conducted by Zogby Research Services in 2018 reveals that for all surveyed countries including Saudi Arabia and the UAE, the respondents think that the most important concern is the humanitarian crisis in the ongoing conflict in Yemen (Zogby Research Services 2019: 327). In parallel, the concerns over the Iranian interference in Yemen declined in Saudi Arabia from 35 per cent in 2017 to 25 per cent in 2018 and the UAE from 41 to 15 per cent over the same period. (ibid.)

Indeed, according to the Arab Opinion Index, the percentage of respondents who said Iran is certainly a threat has reduced from 52 per cent in 2016 to 47 per cent in 2018 (Arab Opinion Index, 2018). Also, a survey conducted by Justing Gengler in 2016–17 on state and non-state threat perception among Gulf nationals supports the Arab Opinion Index results. The survey asked participants to identify the 'greatest challenge to the security and stability of the Gulf countries' from among the following options: 'the spread of terrorist groups such as Daesh [the

Islamic State] and al-Qaeda'; 'the Iranian nuclear program'; 'economic problems due to low oil prices' and 'interference from Western countries'. The poll results show that Iran was perceived as a distant second threat in Kuwait, Qatar and Saudi Arabia and the third most-cited threat in Oman (Gengler 2017).

According to the 2019–20 Arab Opinion Index results, 27 per cent of the Arab Gulf region respondents (KSA, Kuwait and Qatar) stated that Iran is the first threat to their countries, highest among other Arab sub-regions. However, on a country basis only 9 per cent of Qataris marked Iran as the most threatening country, and 55 per cent of Qataris believed that the neighbouring Arab countries posed the greatest threat to their country (Doha Institute 2020). When asked 'Which state poses the greatest threat to the Arab world's security' Gulf countries responded with 41.4 per cent Israel, 24.2 per cent United States and 3.9 per cent Iran as the greatest threat (ibid.).

The poll results show that sectarianization efforts of Gulf monarchies have lost their momentum and the Gulf public have prioritized other countries and issues as the most threatening factors to their security. Particularly for Qatar, after the blockade, Qatari people believe that their Arab neighbours are much more detrimental to their security than Iran. It is still premature to assume that Iran has garnered a favourable image in the Gulf, yet the overall picture shows that the intra-GCC dispute and regional developments since 2017 have changed the almost completely negative image of Iran following a few years of Arab Uprisings. As the Gulf crisis in 2017 showed, in addition to Qatar, Oman and Kuwait saw the depth and the scope of Saudi-Emirati assertiveness and understood the importance of maintaining working relations with Iran (Bianco 2020).

Iran's soft power and possibilities for de-sectarianization of the Gulf region

Iran's soft power reach in the Gulf is closely linked to sectarianization of the region. The rivalry between Saudi Arabia and Iran has significantly curbed Iran's image in the eyes of the Gulf people. Indeed, according to Mehran Kamrava, after the Arab Spring, people in the GCC countries are evaluating the events through sectarian lenses. Kamrava also notes,

> After Iran's stance in Syria and the rise of sectarianism, the Bahraini and Saudi governments have very successfully framed popular uprisings in a sectarian perspective and Iran's soft power declined rapidly. (Kamrava, personal interview, 5 April 2016)

The sectarianization thesis argues that sectarianization is 'an active process shaped by political actors operating within specific contexts, pursuing political goals that involve the mobilization of popular sentiments around particular identity markers' (Hashemi and Postel 2017: 3). This process is dependent upon the interplay between domestic and external factors such as political authoritarianism, class dynamics and geopolitical rivalries (ibid.). It gives agency to political actors in the process – Madawi Al-Rasheed (2017) labelled those actors as 'sectarian entrepreneurs'. The sectarianization framework, thus, enables scholars to track and explain the reasons and tools of such actors in (sectarian) identity mobilization processes. Focusing on Iran's soft power and Tehran's image in the Gulf region over decades opens the space to identify specific contexts where sectarianization operates. A closer reading of Iran's changing image in the Gulf region would explain why the sectarianization process after 2009, not in 2005, further intensified following the Arab Uprisings and then lost its momentum since 2017 in the eyes of the Gulf people.

Most importantly, the sectarianization framework logically makes arguments about de-sectarianization possible, and Iran's soft power goals, application and image in the Gulf region would offer a way to achieve it. 'Precisely because of the social construction of sectarianization, it can be deconstructed,' notes Simon Mabon (2019) when he offers areas to consider for de-sectarianization of regional politics. According to Mabon, geopolitical rivalries, especially the one between Tehran and Riyadh, significantly contribute to sectarianization in the region and 'addressing the rivalry between Saudi Arabia and Iran will be key in any long-term desectarianization' (Mabon 2019: 32).

Any prospects on de-sectarianization appear to be in the long term. Yet, a poll conducted in 2018 asked Arab public 'is it possible for Iran and the Arab world to live in peace?' and for majority of the surveyed countries it is 'very possible' or 'somewhat possible' to live in peace with Iran (Zogby Research Services 2019). It is particularly promising for a de-sectarianization agenda that a total of 65 and 58 per cent of the respondents in Saudi Arabia and the UAE respectively indicated that peaceful co-existence is very possible or somehow possible (ibid.:330).

This research tries to show, capitalizing on soft power sources and tools may be a good way to alleviate inter-state and inter-communal hostilities between Iran and its neighbours in the Gulf. As history has shown, Iran had enjoyed favourable public opinion in the Gulf for quite a while and cordial relations between Iran and the GCC states prevailed following the Iran–Iraq War until the US invasion of Iraq in 2003 (Keynoush 2016). Indeed, as poll results show, Iran had enjoyed quite favourable views until 2009.

The end of the Cold War created an opportunity for Iran to pursue a more independent and pragmatic foreign policy in a similar manner with its neighbour, Turkey. Saddam's invasion of Kuwait came against this background, and Tehran opted to side with Western powers and Gulf Monarchies in supporting Kuwait's territorial integrity and sovereignty of the ruling family (Etheshami and Zweiri 2007). Tehran soon reaped the fruits of this pragmatic approach, and as Ehteshami (2002) noted,

> Neutrality in this conflict gave Tehran a large measure of flexibility in its foreign relations. It gave it scope to deal with Iraq as well as the antiwar Arab forces, while its insistence on the reversal of the aggression and an unconditional Iraqi pullout brought it closer to the anti-Iraq Gulf monarchies. Its restraint and neutrality also obtained for Iran renewed diplomatic relations with Jordan,

Tunisia, and Saudi Arabia, and some constructive contacts with Egypt and Morocco (2002:301).

Iran's position in the Kuwait invasion and foreign policy efforts of President Rafsanjani facilitated Iran–GCC relations at least in the economic realms. Afshin Molavi (2015) notes, 'Rasfanjani's position did alter GCC perceptions of Iran. Trade increased. Direct flight links were restored. And money began flowing more freely across borders. The Rafsanjani era offered Iran and the region a soft landing from the war's ravages and the revolution's zealotry' (para. 13).

Through the end of the decade, Iran's foreign policy under President Mohammed Khatami in 1997 came under 'moderate' track. The new discourse in Iran's foreign policy such as 'détente', 'stability' and 'dialogue among civilizations' were some of the foremost characteristics. Soft power tools and a charm offensive in diplomacy marked the beginning of the Khatami period in Tehran's relations with the Arab Gulf region (Clawson et al. 1998). The presence of the then Saudi Crown Prince Abdullah in the Organization of Islamic Countries (OIC) summit in 1997 in Tehran was a clear sign of the changing nature of relations. In an attempt to break Tehran's decades-long isolation in the region, President Khatami visited Saudi Arabia, Qatar and some other Arab countries in 1999, which was an 'historic' moment in the relations with the GCC countries since the revolution in 1979 (Jehl 1999). The rapprochement between Iran and GCC lasted for a considerable time. In 2004, then Iranian Defense Minister Ali Shamkhani, received Saudi Arabia's highest honour, the Order of Abdel-Aziz Al Saud, 'for his efforts in defusing tensions between Iran and the Arab states' (Kinninmont 2015).

At first sight, the geopolitical context after the Arab Spring and intense sectarianization of Gulf politics does not appear to be conducive for trust building between Iran and GCC members through soft power initiatives, like the period in the 1990s. Yet as argued in the previous part, perceptions of 'Iran as a threat' are in decline in the Middle East, and Iran has become a distant threat to their security and stability in Qatar, Kuwait, Saudi Arabia and Oman (Gengler 2017). Further, the intra-GCC crisis has led some members of the block to develop even more cordial relations with Iran bilaterally. In this sense, Iran can articulate Vuving's (2009) soft power currency of 'benignity'.

Against the increased assertiveness of Saudi Arabia and the UAE in the Gulf, Tehran has the opportunity to portray itself as a harmless neighbour and can actively protect and support other GCC states, as in the case of the Qatari crisis. Further, a closer examination of a near history shows that Iran appeared as supporter at the time of existential crisis that some Gulf monarchies faced. Supporting Oman in 1973 during Dhofar Rebellion, standing with Kuwait against Iraq in 1991 and siding with Qatar in the 2017 Gulf crisis create an historical track on Iranian image as a 'reliable neighbor'.

Demographically speaking, Iranian aspirations to lead the Sunni majority (85%) Muslim world limits Tehran's reliance on explicit sectarian discourse (Hashemi and Postel 2017). Considering that Shia populations are minorities in the GCC states (except Bahrain), Iran has incentives to invest in all-embracing, non-sectarian soft power strategies to reach out to people in the Gulf. Within this geopolitical and demographical setting, Iran's reliance on soft power tools, assets and policies based on culture in a unified, sustained and consistent manner could help in de-sectarianization of the region in the long term.

Conclusion

The Gulf region has entered into a reconciliation phase as the GCC states signed Al-Ula statement, aka the 'solidarity and stability agreement', ending the boycott on Qatar in January 2021. Arguably, the agreement also played a facilitating role in de-escalation among bitter enemies of Iran and Saudi-Emirati block after a period of highly securitized identities in the region (Battaloglu 2021). In August 2022, the UAE and Kuwait decided to send ambassadors to Tehran after more than six years of downgraded diplomatic relations with Iran (Yeranian August 2022). The fifth round of Saudi-Iranian talks for rapprochement took place in Iraq and reportedly, Saudi Arabia is ready to move reconciliation to political and public levels (Al Monitor July 2022). The regional dynamics once again seems to be an important determinant for Iran to exert soft power over the Gulf monarchies to achieve regional foreign policy goals under President Ebrahim Raisi.

The overall picture of Iran's image in recent years in the Gulf highlights important points to be addressed on theoretical and analytical fronts. First, the poll results demonstrate that when compared with other state and non-state actors (i.e. Israel, the United States, ISIS etc.), Iran as a neighbouring state is perceived as less of a threat to the Arab public in general and the Gulf public in particular than in recent years. However, when asked for their opinion regarding Iran as a single country, Tehran and its regional allies scored remarkably low in positive views. Although Iran is viewed as a lesser evil, it is still evil. As Nye puts it correctly, soft power is 'often hard to use, easy to lose and costly to reestablish' (2011: 83), and for Iran, it seems difficult to restore its previous positive image because it has been tarnished to a great extent.

Further, the tentative and relative improvement of Iran's image in the Gulf region reflects public opinions towards state-sponsored anti-Iranian campaigns in the region as well. To put it more clearly, the Gulf public has not been taking the pure conspiracy rhetoric on Iranian expansion and Shiite empowerment for granted and have developed an awareness of other regional dynamics, threats and developments since 2011. Rather, as Gengler argues, 'ordinary citizens appear much more concerned with the tangible aspects of their everyday lives, including in some countries the real threat of terrorist violence, economic insecurity due to a shrinking social safety net, and the presence of Western military forces' (Gengler 2017: para. 15). This point is especially conceptually important on the grounds that soft power (or soft war) loses its credibility if it is perceived as propaganda or false news. The effectiveness of the soft power and counter-policies lies in the consistency and reliability of actions and rhetoric.

On the theoretical front, tracking changes in Iran's soft power in the Gulf might also contribute to the sectarianism debate in the Middle East from a broader perspective. The rise and fall of Iran's image in the region requires a context-specific interpretation of soft power and the sectarianism/sectarianization debate and would offer a conceptual framework that is an alternative between the rigid binaries of primordialism and instrumentalism. In this regard, further studies on Iran's soft power and its image in the region would contribute to develop 'beyond strategies' on the sectarianism debate by bringing ideational-material, agency-structure, domestic-international dimensions together in an eclectic way (Valbjørn 2018).

Iran's soft power initiatives can also contribute to de-sectarianization of the Gulf region, especially in addressing regional rivalry between Iran and Saudi Arabia. Given the inherent nature of de-sectarianization prospects and the operational principles of soft power, Tehran's investment in soft power policies should be a long-term project to bear fruit.

Notes

1 Dhofar rebellion took place between 1962 and 1976, launched by Marxist-Leninist guerilla against the Sultan of Oman. In 1973, Iranian Special Forces arrived to Oman to aid suppressing the rebellion (Mc Keown 1981).
2 Professor Shahram Akbarzadeh, Professor Mehran Kamrava, Dr. Ibrahim Fraihat and Dr. Mahdi Ahouie referred this point during personal interviews.

References

Akbarzadeh, S. (2016), Face to face interview with Hicret Battaloglu, 13 March.
Alabbasi, M. (2015), *Iran Continues to Boast of Its Regional Reach*. Available online: http://www.middleeasteye.net/news/iran-continues-boast-regional-reach-944755422 (accessed 29 April 2016).
Aljazeera English (2009), Poll results prompt Iran protests. Retrieved 24 April 2016, from http://www.aljazeera.com/news/middleeast/2009/06/20096131721 30303995.html.
Aljazeera English (2017), *Qatar-Gulf Crisis: Your Question Answered*. Available at: https://www.aljazeera.com/indepth/features/2017/06/atar-gulf-crisis-questions-answered-170606103033599.html (accessed 27 May 2019).
Almutawakel, R., and Alfaqih, A. (2018), *Saudi Arabia and the United Arab Emirates Are Starving Yemenis to Death*. Available online: https://foreignpolicy.com/2018/11/08/saudi-arabia-and-the-united-arab-emirates-are-starving-yemenis-to-death-mbs-khashoggi-famine-yemen-blockade-houthis/ (accessed 30 October 2019).
Al-Rasheed, M. (2017), "Sectarianism as Counter-revolution: Saudi Responses to the Arab Spring." In Sectarianization: Mapping the New Politics of the Middle East, edited by Nader Hashemi and Danny Postel. New York: Oxford University Press, 143–58.
Arab Opinion Index (2018), *The 2017–2018 Arab Opinion Index: Main Results in Brief*. Available online: https://www.dohainstitute.org/en/Lists/ACRPS-PDFDocumentLibr

ary/2017-2018%20Arab%20Opinion%20Index%20Main%20Results%20in%20Br ief%20-%20final%20(002).pdf (accessed 27 May 2019).

Ayalon, A. (ed.) (1992), *Middle East Contemporary Survey: 1990*, Vol. 14, New York: The Moshe Dayan Center.

Battaloglu, N. H. (2021) Al-UlaDeclaration: A Window of Opportunity for Wider Regional Reconciliation?. Gulf Insights No:50 Available at: http://www.qu.edu.qa/static_file/qu/research/Gulf%20Studies/documents/Gulf%20Insights%2050.pdf.

BBC (2017), 'Qatar Restores Diplomatic Ties with Iran amid Gulf Crisis'. Available online: https://www.bbc.com/news/world-middle-east-41035672 (accessed 27 May 2019).

Bianco, C. (2020). 'The GCC monarchies: Perceptions of the Iranian threat amid shifting geopolitics'. *The International Spectator*, 55 (2): 92–107.

Bilgin, P., and Elis, B. (2008), Hard power, Soft power: Toward a more realistic power analysis. *Insight Turkey*, 10 (2), 5–20.

Clawson, P., Eisenstadt, M. and Menashri, D. (1998), 'Iran Under Khatami'. Retrieved 26 April 2016, from http://www.washingtoninstitute.org/policy-analysis/view/iran-under-khatami-a-political-economic-and-military-assessment.

Ehteshami, A., and Zweiri, M. (2007), *Iran and the Rise of Its Neoconservatives: The Politics of Tehran's Silent Revolution*, London: I.B. Tauris.

Ehteshami, A. (2002), 'The Foreign Policy of Iran', in R. A. Hinnebusch and A. Ehteshami (eds), *The Foreign Policies of Middle East States*, Boulder Lynne Rienner, 261–88.

Feizi, H., and Talebi, B. (2012), 'Iran's Soft Power Borne of Necessity and Complexity of Its Multi-dimensional Audience', *Exchange: The Journal of Public Diplomacy*, 3 (1): 6.

Finnemore, M., and Goldstein, J. (Eds). (2013), *Back to Basics: State Power in a Contemporary World*, Oxford: Oxford University Press.

Fraihat, I. (2016), Face to face interview with Hicret Battaloglu, 31 March.

Freeman, C., and Blair, D. (2009), *Defeated Iranian Reformist Mir-Hossein Mousavi Calls for More Protest against Mahmoud Ahmadinejad*. Available online: http://www.telegraph.co.uk/news/worldnews/middleeast/iran/5533782/Defeated-Iranian-reformist-Mir-Hossein-Mousavi-calls-for-more-protest-against-Mahmoud-Ahmadinejad.html (accessed 24 April 2016).

Gengler, J. (2017), How Gulf Citizens View Iran. Available online: https://www.foreignaffairs.com/articles/persian-gulf/2017-10-02/how-gulf-citizens-view-iran (accessed 30 October 2019).

Gozaydin, I. (2010), *Religion as Soft Power in the International Relations of Turkey. Political Studies Association*, available online at: http://www. psa. ac. uk/journals/pdf/5/2010/1365_1228. pdf

Gulf News. (2017), *What Are the 13 Demands Given to Qatar?*, available at: https://gulfnews.com/world/gulf/qatar/what-are-the-13-demands-given-to-qatar-1.2048118

Haddad, F. (2017), 'Sectarianism'and Its Discontents in the Study of the Middle East', *The Middle East Journal*, 71(3): 363–82.

Haji-Yousefi, A. M. (2012), 'Iran and the 2011 Arab Revolutions: Perceptions and Actions', *Discourse: An Iranian Quarterly*, 10 (1–2): 23–60.

Hashemi, N., and Postel, D. (2017), 'Sectarianization: Mapping the New Politics of the Middle East', *Review of Faith & International Affairs*, 15 (3): 1–13.

Jeffery, S. (2009), 'Iran Election Protests: The Dead, Jailed and Missing'. Available online: http://www.theguardian.com/world/blog/2009/jul/29/iran-election-protest-dead-missing (accessed 24 April 2016).

Jehl, D. (1999), 'On Trip to Mend Ties, Iran's President Meets Saudi Prince'. Retrieved 6 March 2016, from http://www.nytimes.com/1999/05/17/world/on-trip-to-mend-ties-iran-s-president-meets-saudi-prince.html.

Kamrava, M. (2012), 'The Arab Spring and the Saudi-led Counterrevolution', *Orbis*, 56 (1): 96–104.

Kamrava, M. (2016, 5 April). [Personal interview].

Kamrava, M. (2017), 'Iran-Qatar Relations', in A. Ehteshami, N. Quilliam and B. Gawdat (eds), *Security and Bilateral Issues between Iran and Its Arab Neighbours*, Cham: Palgrave Macmillan, 167–87.

Keynoush, B. (2016), *Saudi Arabia and Iran: Friends or Foes?* New York: Springer.

Kinninmont, J. (2015), *Iran and the GCC: Unnecessary Insecurity*, Chatham House for the Royal Institute of International Affairs.

Kramer, M. (1993), 'Islam in the New World Order', in A. Ayalon (ed.), *Middle East Contemporary Survey 1991*, New York: The Moshe Dayan Center, 172–205.

Mabon, S. (2019), 'Desectarianization: Looking Beyond the Sectarianization of Middle Eastern Politics', *Review of Faith & International Affairs*, 17 (4): 23–35.

Makhmalbaf, M. (2009), 'I Speak for Mousavi. And Iran | Mohsen Makhmalbaf'. Available online: http://www.theguardian.com/commentisfree/2009/jun/19/iran-election-mousavi-ahmadinejad (accessed 24 April 2016).

Maleki, A. (2016), Face to face interview with Hicret Battaloglu, 14 March.

Mattern, J. B. (2005), 'Why Soft Power Isn't So Soft: Representational Force and the Sociolinguistic Construction of Attraction in World Politics', *Millennium-Journal of International Studies*, 33 (3): 583–612.

Mohammadi, M. (2008), 'Sources of Power in Islamic Republic of Iran', *The Iranian Journal of International Affairs*, 20 (3): 2–21.

Molavi, A. (2015), 'The Iran Primer'. Retrieved, from http://iranprimer.usip.org/resource/iran-and-gulf-states (accessed 19 April 2016).

Nakhoul, S. (2015), 'Iran Expands Regional "Empire" Ahead of Nuclear Deal'. Available online: http://www.reuters.com/article/us-mideast-iran-region-insight-idUSKBN0MJ1G520150323 (accessed 24 April 2016).

Norouzi, A. (2007), '"Wiped off the map"-The Rumour of the Century', *The Mossadegh Project*. Available online: https://mohammadmossadegh.com/news/rumor-of-the-century/ (accessed 11 June 2023).

Nye, J. S. (1990), *Soft Power. Foreign Policy*, Washington, DC: The FP Group.

Nye, J. S. (2004), *Soft Power: The Means to Success in World Politics*, Cambridge: Public Affairs.

Nye, J. S. (2007), 'Notes for a Soft Power Research Agenda', in F. Berenskoetter and M. J. Williams (eds), *Power in World Politics*, Oxford: Routledge, 162–72.

Nye, J. S. (2011), *The Future of Power*, Cambridge: Public Affairs.

Parsi, T. (2006), 'Ahmadinejad's rethoric and the essence of the Israeli-Iranian Clash.' *Vaseteh-Journal of the European Society for Iranian Studies*, 1(1), 7–10.

Parsi, T., and Marashi, R. (2011), 'Arab Spring Seen from Tehran', *Cairo Review*, 2: 98–112.

Pollock, D. (2017), *Survey: Qatari Public Wants Compromise, Not Iran's Help*. Available at: https://www.washingtoninstitute.org/policy-analysis/view/survey-qatari-public-wants-compromise-not-irans-help (accessed 27 May 2019).

Pollock, D. (2018), *UAE Public Privately Split on Key Issues, New Poll Reveals*. Available at: https://www.washingtoninstitute.org/fikraforum/view/in-private-uae-public-split-on-key-issues-new-poll-reveals (accessed 27 May 27 2019).

Price, M. (2012), 'Iran and the Soft war', *International Journal of Communication*, 6 (19): 2397–2415.
Ramazani, R. K. (1992), 'Iran's foreign policy: Both North and South.' *Middle East Journal*, 46 (3): 393–412.
Al-Rasheed, M. (2017), 'Sectarianism as Counter-revolution: Saudi Responses to the Arab Spring', in Nader Hashemi and Danny Postel (eds), *Sectarianization: Mapping the New Politics of the Middle East*, New York: Oxford University Press, 143–58.
Regencia, T. (2017), 'Qatar-Gulf Rift: The Iran Factor'. Available online: https://www.aljazeera.com/indepth/features/2017/06/qatar-gulf-rift-iran-factor-170605102522955.html (accessed 27 May 2019).
Rothberg, P. (2010), 'Protests in Iran'. Available online: http://www.thenation.com/article/protests-iran/ (accessed 24 April 2016).
Rubin, L. (2010), 'A Typology of Soft Powers in Middle East Politics', *The Dubai Initiative. Working Paper*, 5:1–20.
Saouli, A. (ed.) (2020), *Unfulfilled aspirations: Middle power politics in the Middle East*. London: Hurst.
Soghom, M. (2008), 'Iran's President And The Arab Street.' Retrieved 27 April 2016, from http://www.rferl.org/content/Iran_President_Battle_Arab/1293381.html.
Telhami, S. (2008), '2008 Annual Arab Public Opinion Poll'. Available online: http://www.brookings.edu/~/media/events/2008/4/14 middle east/0414_middle_east_telhami (accessed 3 April 2016).
Times of Israel (2018), 'Palestinians Must Make Peace or Shut Up, Saudi Crown Prince Said to Tell US Jews'. Available online: https://www.timesofisrael.com/palestinians-must-make-peace-or-shut-up-saudi-crown-prince-said-to-tell-us-jews/ (accessed 27 May 2019).
Ulrichsen, K. C. (2018), 'Palestinians Sidelined in Saudi-Emirati Rapprochement with Israel', *Journal of Palestine Studies*, 47 (4): 79–89.
Valbjørn, M. (2018), 'Studying Sectarianism while Beating Dead Horses and Searching for Third Ways'. Available online: https://blogs.lse.ac.uk/mec/2018/09/17/studying-sectarianism-while-beating-dead-horses-and-searching-for-third-ways/ (accessed 27 May 2019).
Vuving, A. (2009), *How Soft Power Works*. Available at SSRN 1466220.
Wastnidge, E. (2015), 'The Modalities of Iranian Soft Power: From Cultural Diplomacy to Soft War', *Politics*, 35 (3–4): 364–77.
Watkins, J. (2020) 'Iran in Iraq: The Limits of "Smart Power" Amidst Public Protest', LSE Middle East Centre Paper Series 37.
Zogby International (2002), 'Arabs: What They Believe and What They Value Most'. Available online: https://d3n8a8pro7vhmx.cloudfront.net/aai/pages/9767/attachments/original/1438878620/Arab_Opinion_2002.pdf?1438878620 (accessed 8 June 2016).
Zogby Research Services (2014), 'Today's Middle East Pressures & Challenges'. Available online: http://b.3cdn.net/aai/a6466ad6476c08d752_bum6b4j6l.pdf (accessed 8 June 2016).
Zogby, J. (2013), 'Looking at Iran: How 20 Arab and Muslim Nations View Iran and Its Policies', *Zogby Research Services*, available at: iranpollfindingspresenation.pdf (wilsoncenter.org) (accessed 17 July 2023).

Chapter 10

POLITICAL AND DISCURSIVE DE-SECTARIANIZATION: RE-ORDERING SAUDI FOREIGN AND DOMESTIC POLICY-MAKING

Umer Karim

Saudi Arabian political fold has taken a significant turn since the ascension of King Salman and the emergence of his son Crown Prince Mohammad Bin Salman as the ultimate power broker after the king. This change within Saudi power structures and decision-making patterns has been manifest in the Kingdom's foreign policy outlook, most notably in the form of the military intervention in Yemen and the boycott of Qatar alongside its allies (Karim 2017). However, processes of social and economic liberalization on the one hand and considerable reduction in the political capital of religious establishment on the other hand need to be contextualized in the larger scheme of things. This flux within Saudi domestic political variables is impacting upon the Saudi society and polity in a unique manner and within the discursive fold contributing towards a de-sectarianization of its national identity and polity, with a markedly lesser emphasis on the religious identity markers and a relatively greater focus on the country's geographical signposts. This trend has implications for the sectarianized state–society relationship inside the Kingdom but is also reminiscent in the events unfolding within the foreign policy domain, specifically Saudi engagement with Iraq and an appreciation of new political challenges from Sunni polities like Turkey. In this manner political developments heralded by the rise of Saudi Crown Prince Mohammad Bin Salman are having an impact on the manner in which sectarian relations and discourse are being framed within the Kingdom while also informing the nature of 'nationalism'. Linked to these transitions within Saudi Arabia are openings within Saudi foreign policy approach which indicates a change in Saudi leadership threat perception.

This research builds upon the recent works (Al-Rasheed 2017; Alhussein 2019a; Mabon 2019; Freer 2019; Wehrey 2016) dealing with state–society relations in Saudi Arabia whether between the rulers and religious elites or the state with its Shi'ite population and attempts at contributing towards literature on the evolving state–society relations, intra-societal relations and a rather regulated de-sectarianization of the discursive field in a Saudi context. This research will start with situating the sectarian nature of Saudi political identity and the Saudi state's relationship with its Shi'ite citizenry throughout its modern political history. After delving into Saudi Arabia's political history and understanding the construction of sectarianized political identities, the researcher will try to understand the emergence of a politically patronized discourse of Saudi nationalism. Focus of attention will be its impact on the prevailing nature of sectarianized political debates and the discursive silence or acquiescence on the part of Saudi religious establishment, an entity that has remained one of the principal determinants of Saudi national identity in the past. This will be followed by a discussion of the de-sectarianization trends within Saudi foreign policy. In particular, the focus will be on Saudi decision-makers' approach towards Iraq and attempts upon political engagement to normalize bilateral relationships. The study will also touch upon the growing unease in the Saudi-Turkey relationship and explore the variables driving this trend.

Conceptual framework

The purpose of this work is not to explore the complexity of Saudi Shi'ite identity but to dissect the Saudi state's sectarian outlook both at the national and transnational levels. This can be understood by observing the state's engagement with its Shi'ite citizenry and the implications of Saudi nationalism on this relationship in a discursive but also more practical manner. It is here that this work will try to de-construct the political and discursive formations that have impacted sectarian identities within Saudi Arabia and how these formations have been politically and religiously regulated and manipulated by the Saudi state.

Focus on the shared 'Arab' and not the 'other Shi'ite' identity drives the de-sectarianization trend within Saudi foreign policy domain. It will also be vital to locate the patrons of this transformation and the factors compelling them to patronize these processes. Eventually, the study aims to uncover whether this de-sectarianization should be considered an ideational change at the level of Saudi rulers and its religious elites or one that remains an indirect consequence of the evolving nature of Saudi state's relationship with its sub-national elites, and if this new state of affairs fits well into the Saudi decision-makers' rather tacit attempts to exploit opportunities on the external front.

As we are trying to encompass the nature of change in the sectarian vector point within the Kingdom's domestic and foreign policy, we need to develop a rather holistic framework that can connect all these relevant and interlinked domains. The conceptual structure of this enterprise relies on the dialectics of Fanar Haddad vis-à-vis 'sectarianism' and the idea of 'sectarianization' and its treatment as a procedural construct coined by Hashemi and Postel. Haddad argues for the development of an integrated analytical approach cutting across the local, national, transnational and religious domains to better understand the processes of sectarianization or in this particular case de-sectarianization.

Haddad starts his argumentation by discarding sectarianism as an epistemological construct often utilized by political scientists to approach the geopolitics or domestic politics of the Middle Eastern states. Haddad postulates an academic approach that goes beyond the debates of primordialist and instrumentalist while studying sectarianism. The focus rather seems to be upon the centrality of sectarian identities which not only chart out a trajectory for state–society relations but also impact the state's ideational and political projection particularly in the foreign policy domain. Haddad argues the need for adoption of a multilayered framework to better understand sectarian identity and sectarian relations. For this purpose we need to understand the interplay of sectarian discourses on religious/doctrinal, national, sub-national and finally transnational levels (Hadad 2018). Hadad's argumentation rhymes well on a methodological level with Foucauldian conceptualization of discursive formations and the regularities that condition their existence. It is also relevant as this research focuses on the formation and evolution of Saudi national discourses. The evolution of sectarianized discursive formations within Saudi Arabia indeed needs to be analysed at both political and societal levels to dissect and uncover what Foucault calls both the conditions of unity and disunity leading to the emergence of (in this case) sectarianized discursive constructions impacting upon the identities of citizens but also state. These concepts, themes and contexts have been constructed in an environment where political and religious actors have operated together and in unison but often have differed in their strategies and goals. Thereby, even ordered discursive formations on matters of national identity and state–society relations do have discontinuities not only due to the varying agencies of different stakeholders but also because of their relative power. This debate in the Saudi context further pushes us to unveil *discursive regularities*[1] or these actors or norms with the potential to regulate such formulations (Foucault 1972: 37–38). Thereby, these regimes of sectarianization or de-sectarianization are regulated by Saudi decision-makers. This then pushes us to understand the nature of political system within the Kingdom and that of its decision-makers.

The theorization developed by Hashemi and Postel (2017: 4–8) focuses on 'sectarianization' and stresses upon understanding the specific context in which political actors pursuing their political goals push for popular mobilization around specific religious markers. For Hashemi and Postel, the authoritarian character of Middle Eastern politics remains a key point in understanding processes of sectarianization. Authoritarian rulers manipulate and incite sectarian identities to curb and deflect away from the demands of political reform and change particularly in societies that have a multiplicity of sects or religious groupings (Hashemi and Postel 2017: 4–5). If Haddad's argument to study sectarian discourses across different political levels is important, Hashemi and Postel's focus on authoritarian manipulation of sectarian identities is particularly relevant for a country like Saudi Arabia where all the aspects of the political, religious, social and economic life are directly or indirectly connected with the Saudi Royal family.

This framework of Haddad alongside the sectarianization[2] hypothesis of Hashemi and Postel needs to be integrated in the Saudi-specific political and religious context. It also needs to be applied on the focal point of this study which is to explore the evolution in Saudi national discourse and its gravitation away from a religious pan-Islamic-oriented one to a more geographical epitome, factors and actors responsible for this change, its impact on subsequent state–society relations and impact on Saudi Arabia's external outlook.

Structural variables impacting upon the sectarian outlook

In order to understand the emergence of these new *discursive formations* across the domestic/national and external/transnational divides, we need to identify the *discursive regularities*[3] critical in this regard.

1- The first variable crucial to studying any political occurrence within current-day Saudi Arabia is the momentous shift in the power hierarchy and the decision-making patterns putting King Salman and his son Crown Prince Mohammad Bin Salman in an all-powerful position, markedly different from the traditional de-centralized form of decision-making (Mabon 2018a). Though Haddad advocates for going beyond top-down or bottom-up approaches, sectarianization processes in a system like Saudi Arabia do happen to be regularized from top to bottom and impact upon all the multilayers that Haddad emphasizes to focus upon (Gause III 2020: 13). Yet the narratives building up at the bottom cannot also be simply ignored as they can be at times classified as reactionary. Sometimes these reactions are discursive formations resisting the ones delegated from the top or improvising on their own or simply discursive silences. Focusing on these discursive formations will also help us to explore the political expedience factor for Saudi decision-makers within these processes.

2- Within the domestic sphere, sub-national elites act as discursive entrepreneurs that can disseminate a message within the broader social sphere. Dodge considers these elite actors important as a state can manipulate them to promote the activities of a certain group while blocking or restricting others (Dodge 2016). In Saudi Arabia a new societal segment – 'the discursive entrepreneurial class' – has risen and become torch bearers of this drive emanating in the form of a *hyper-nationalist* discourse. These social actors are creating discursive regularities in their own right that promote discursive formations that remain nationalistic and sect-inclusive while also sanctioning narratives bearing pan-Islamic or sectarian themes emanated by the scholars of Sahwa movement or those affiliated with the Saudi religious establishment. The state itself has also restricted discursive fields for religious agents which once enjoyed a near hegemony in this arena (Al-Rasheed 2020).

3- The projection of this de-sectarianization trend within the Saudi foreign policy can be better examined by emphasizing on the external or, in structural realist language, the systemic environment. In the Saudi case post-Islamic State of Iraq and Syria (ISIS) Iraqi political sphere and the rise of nationalist Shi'ite polities challenging the Iranian influence over Iraqi politics

has been one reason for Saudi attempts to enhance its engagement with Iraq (International Crisis Group 2018).
4- The other factor at play is a gradual transformation within what Mabon has called the internal security dilemma of Saudi Arabia that has been informing Saudi position towards Iran (Mabon 2018b). Such a perception of the Saudi state has meant that Saudi Shi'ites and ones residing in the Eastern Province of the Kingdom have been seen with suspicion and considered a possible fifth column (Matthiesen 2014). As argued by Gause in the post-Arab Spring political order, the perceived threat to Saudi regime is increasingly originating from the Salafi Jihadists and Muslim Brotherhood networks, leading to the sanctioning of these groups both in the discursive and practical fold within Saudi Arabia under Mohammad Bin Salman while on the other hand Saudi Shi'ites don't qualify to that degree of threat for the Saudi state anymore (Gause III 2020: 15). This change in the threat emanating from Iran into a *balance of power threat* towards Saudi Arabia in a more structural realist sense rather than an *ideological* one has impacted the nature of discourse internally within Saudi Arabia and the State's external outlook and regional threat perceptions.
5- Then comes the question why these processes of de-sectarianization only remain discursive. As highlighted by Gause, Saudi Arabia's official policy at least since the emergence of ISIS and the emergence of transnational Salafi Jihadism has been one of denouncing sectarianism and non-state actors involved in such activities. Yet it has been highlighted that this sectarian violence and mobilization has found adherents within the Kingdom and therefore when it comes to the religious field within Saudi Arabia there remain challenges for this de-sectarianization, one that can lead to an alteration of intra-societal engagement once it is truly internalized (Gause III 2020: 16).

This work will now use Haddad's approach to elaborate sect-based discourses and their transformation across the religious, subnational and external domains, and the arguments outlined above will be used to de-construct these processes in every respective domain. This will be helpful in developing a rather wholistic picture of this 'discursive de-sectarianization' at play while also understanding the politics associated with it and whether these discursive occurrences will also translate into new sociopolitical realities or the hitherto repressed sectarian discourses will appear again.

'From sectarian to sectarianization': A regime strategy or a state's ethos?

The first Saudi state that emerged in the middle of the eighteenth century under the leadership of Mohammad Ibn Saud was basically a political enterprise but with an unparalleled level of religious intensity and zeal turning the head of this project into an Imam (Vassiliev 2013: 161). The socio-religious wing of this new project was led by the charismatic preacher Mohammad Ibn Abdal Wahhab. This made the religious and political thoughts of Ibn Abdal Wahhab the guiding stone of this newly formed political entity. Therefore, on the dogmatic front teachings of Ibn Abdal Wahhab also sometimes referred to as Wahhabism have remained a central pillar of subsequent Saudi states (Mouline 2015: 48). The first Saudi state was inherently a politico-religious enterprise that strongly snubbed the presence and exclamation of other theological viewpoints. The forces of the first Saudi state did not have an exactly positive engagement with the Shi'ite regions of Mesopotamia. They had raided the city of Karbala in 1802 and sacked the shrine of the Prophet's (PBUH) grandson Hussain Bin Ali, one of the holiest places for Shi'ite Islam. Although these incursions did have a financial angle to them as the areas raided by the Saudi forces were much richer, it would be wrong to ignore the religious zeal involved in these campaigns, something that has been different when it came to the decision-makers in the third Saudi state. These attacks on Shi'ite holy places did create anger within the local populace, eventually resulting in the murder of the Saudi Emir Abdul Aziz Ibn Mohammad in 1803 by a Shi'ite assassin in the mosque of Diriya (Al-Rasheed 2010: 21). It can thus be argued that the first Saudi state was a sectarian political entity and although various other motives can be associated with its actions, the ideological factors driving pushing or providing legitimacy to these activities were religious and not political.

The interaction between the third Saudi state with Shi'ite citizenry only started once the eastern parts of Arabian Peninsula with a significant Shi'ite population was brought into its fold. The outlook of the third Saudi state was far less hostile towards its new subjects of different doctrinal inclinations, and it dealt with them in a rather political manner. The new subjects of the Saudi state did suffer on economic grounds owing to confiscation of arable land and high levels of taxation, but in return for their political submission they got concessions within the religious domain and were allowed to hold their own courts run by Shi'ite theologians trained in Najaf. At that moment the Saudi rulers didn't consider Shi'ism as an ideological threat to the process of state formation and once the petroleum industry started to establish within the Eastern Province of the Kingdom Shi'ite citizens who were local inhabitants were integrated within it as workforce. This also shows that the leadership of the third Saudi state was a product of its own times, and although the sectarian differences between the Saudi rulers and their new citizens were quite similar to the ones that existed during the first Saudi state, this time the state's relationship with this portion of society was more influenced by politics than religious differences. Thereby, the state's political relationship with its Shi'ite citizens was affected by the agency of the rulers but it wasn't driven primarily by these religious differences (Louër and Rundell 2020: 154–8). Politically, Saudi Shi'ites were not a threat for this nascent state. The first threats which the state had to encounter came from its very own fold in the form of the radical 'Ikhwan' Bedouins who challenged the authority of King Abdul Aziz and afterwards from Nasserite Egypt and Arab nationalism (F. G. Gause III 2003).

Even though things were calmer at the political front vis-à-vis Saudi Shi'ites this never meant that they had been accommodated within the religious rhetoric of the

Saudi religious establishment. For a state like Saudi Arabia, where the religious establishment acted as a strong pillar of the state and had total monopoly over the state's religious discourse and infrastructure a confrontation with Shi'ism was only a matter of time (Alsaif 2013: 377). This meant that the discourses framed at the political and religious levels did have their divergences (or what Foucault calls discontinuities) but the proximity between the two stratas also meant a possibility of convergence. Yet, this scenario only came into play once regional political realities transformed, upending the established political order of the Middle East.

Islamic revolution in Iran and politicization of Saudi Shi'ite identity

With Islamic revolution in Iran, the secular regime of Reza Shah Pahlavi was replaced by a government led by a Shi'ite cleric Imam Khomeini. The new regime in Iran was at political loggerheads with the Arab Gulf monarchies and propagated a discourse of exporting the revolution in Iran to its regional neighbours. This seismic political change also transformed the hitherto slow and under-the-surface current of Shi'ite Islamism within Saudi Arabia and mainly in the Qatif region in its Eastern Province, leading to the events of Intifada of Muharram 1400 AH.[4] These Muharram processions had a distinct political outlook, with crowds chanting slogans against the Saudi rulers and their American allies while brandishing images of the leader of Iranian Revolution Imam Khomeini. The political product of these events was the formation of the Organization for Islamic Revolution in the Arabian Peninsula by the Shirazi strand of Saudi Shi'ite Islamists (Louër 2016). Thus, in 1979 the domestic and regional political variables eventually aligned on the question of Saudi Shi'ites and the processes of 'Sectarianization' started on the official level. The Saudi regime had to cater for the domestic domain where its religious establishment pushed for a stricter stance on the matter. The security implications of the presence of elements hostile to the state in the oil producing region of the Kingdom also paved the way for a belligerent approach by the Saudi state. On the external front, the fate of Saudi Shi'ites got linked with the relationship of the Saudi Kingdom with Iran (Teitelbaum 2010: 74). Since then, it is an interplay of these factors that has regulated the political behaviour of the Saudi regime towards its Shi'ite citizens with periods of confrontation and repression followed by those of co-optation. These regime tactics to manage the Shi'ite citizenry under control also serve the purpose to keep the Sunni majority and in particular the Wahhabi establishment in check in order to minimize threats to regime security and stability. This clearly conforms with the thoughts of Hashemi and Postel on sectarianization within authoritarian state environment.

The strategy adopted by the Saudi state to manage its Shi'ite population has been characterized as overtly sectarian and one that has often used the Shi'ite variable to balance out against Islamist opposition in its Sunni heartlands and vice versa. This has meant the state employing discursive formations and rhetoric often similar to that of the wahabi religious elements and inherently sectarian but ones that are also different. The State went hard against Shi'ite activists in the 1980s but as the state encountered the challenge of Sahwa Islamists it opted for a rapprochement with the Shi'ite opposition ranks. Similarly, in the 2000s as Saudi Arabia came under increased Western criticism following 9/11 attacks and faced the challenge of an Al-Qaeda insurgency at home the political front further opened for Saudi Shi'ites who were received by Crown Prince Abdullah and were part and parcel of the Saudi national dialogue (Hammond 2013: 5). These political steps also were aligned with the changing political atmosphere in the region. During the 1990s a phase of rapprochement started between Saudi Arabia and Iran. However, it eventually ended in the late 2000s. The American invasion of Iraq and empowerment of Iraqi Shi'ites created a new threat variable for Saudi regime and compelled decision-makers to move swiftly to counter its impact within the Shi'ite political spectrum in the Kingdom. Yet, this positive engagement of Saudi state with Shi'ites didn't go down well with the Wahhabi religious cadres whether it was the official clergy or Sahwa clerics. For these figures the events unfolding in Iraq merited a stronger Saudi response in defence of the Iraqi Sunnis. This prompted a balancing act from the Saudi government and anti-Shi'ite sectarian discourses gradually started emerging and proliferating in the national discourse (Wehrey 2016: 157–8).

Sectarian and regional fault lines within Saudi politics

Therefore, sectarianism emerged as a classical regime tactic within Saudi Arabia to play upon the underlying societal fears and divisions among different groupings and use it to ensure regime security. The Saudi regime successfully deployed this strategy at the start of the Arab Spring protests to contain political mobilization and any sliver of a collective national action. At one end the spectre of a Shi'ite crescent in the Middle East unnerved Saudi religious circles and compelled them to support Saudi rulers entirely. But this sectarian dynamic and the possibility of a regional political order dominated by Shi'ites forces was dreadful enough even for Sunni Islamists who held significant grievances against the government and advocated for political reforms. The Saudi state was also successful in influencing the liberal fold within the country that could have acted as a bulwark against conservative forces and had offered a political platform to Saudi Shi'ites alongside their Sunni compatriots (Al-Rasheed 2017: 153).

On the other hand, strong regional identities, a functional outcome of Saudi state building and evolution, have further helped the State apparatus to frame the protest movement in the Qatif region according to a narrative of its choice. In the wake of Arab Spring the protest movement in Qatif though was led by firebrand Shi'ite clerics like Sheikh Nimr Al-Nimr yet this mobilization was also an outcome of the long-standing structural patterns of geographical and economic discrimination faced by the town of Qatif and not simply the outcome of its unique sect-based identity (Sultan 2018: 100). In this manner the discursive tools, agents and platforms were always within the purview of the Saudi state to utilize sectarianism as a strategy in its statecraft where necessary but also to frame regional political events as overtly sectarian to further reduce possibility of any collective national action challenging its grip on power. The monopolization of the Iraqi political field by Shi'ite parties and the ever-increasing footprint of Iran further cemented this equation.

Changes in Saudi system: Centralization of political power and marginalization of religious forces

The Saudi state's engagement with its Shi'ite citizenry has taken several turns over a period of several years from repressive to accommodative. The nature of the state's outlook has often been determined by a combination of domestic and external variables and their linkage with regime security. It would not be wrong to label the behaviour of the Saudi regime as pragmatic and one purely driven by political interests rather than ideological zeal as also argued by Hashemi and Postel (2017). Although this ruling model has continued with modifications, yet the agency of the sovereign and his interpretation of the political challenges both internally and externally has impacted the state of affairs significantly.

Rather prophetically, Wehrey in a 2014 essay had indicated that two key variables were to play a major role in transforming, at least on the surface if not intrinsically, the nature of Shi'i–Sunni tensions in the Gulf and in the Saudi case the nature of State–sect relationship. These two factors had been an impending generational change within the royal houses of Gulf countries and secondly the emergent divisions within the Sunni religious fraternity (Wehrey 2014). As we discuss the Saudi case, such changes were to change the political and decision-making system within the country – one that had an impact on both domestic as well as the foreign policy outlook of the regime. The ruling bargain or social contract within the Saudi Kingdom took a new form with the arrival of King Salman at the helm of affairs. This development also heralded the rise of King Salman's young son Mohammad, who was first appointed as the defence minister and then subsequently was promoted to the position of Crown Prince, making him virtually the most powerful person in the Kingdom after his father (Roelants and Aarts 2016: 600–1). This development re-configured the Saudi system of power from a rather de-centralized, horizontal and consensual one to a rather vertical, centralized and swift enterprise (Herb 1999).

The new decision-maker and decision-making system have had direct impact on the second variable highlighted by Wehrey regarding a possible split within Saudi Islamist sphere. This in turn also impacted upon the State's engagement with Shi'ite citizenry. Saudi state's relationship with the conservative cadres of the society has always been an interesting one. The main power groups within this broader constituency include the Saudi official religious establishment and their subsequent patronage networks mostly within government institutions and the Sahwa Sheikhs constituting the Muslim Brotherhood variant of Saudi Arabia. In the third Saudi state the influence of the religious establishment within the political realm has been constantly eroding and this has clearly made it a junior partner to the Saudi regime. Yet this didn't alter the official clergy's resolve to support Saudi rulers and provide them with legitimacy (Mouline 2015: 48–9). The Sahwa figures rose to prominence in this backdrop as they challenged the regime when the official religious establishment approved its actions and garnered political, social and religious capital. The state quickly moved against them and most of the group's notable members were arrested. Most of them were released afterwards and had acquiesced their rather hostile political views or in some instances co-opted by the government (DeLong-Bas 2013: 418–20).

With the rise of Mohammad Bin Salman within Saudi politics both of these religious groupings have come under enormous pressure and have been left with no other option but to resolutely support the measures taken by government both locally and internationally to an extent that this has been called out as the eventual separation of mosque and state in the Kingdom (Theodore 2018). Those who have not fallen in line have since been arrested and silence de jure. This campaign has been complemented by processes of social liberalization of Saudi public life resulting in the Saudi religious police or the Commission for the Promotion of Virtue and Prevention of Vice being stripped off its powers (Bashraheel 2019) and Saudi women given the right to drive. These developments have happened alongside the rise of Saudi nationalism as a political project patronized by Saudi rulers and as a discursive trend marginalizing the religious elements of Saudi national identity (England and Al-Omran 2019). This discourse of Saudi nationalism is not something completely new and has been a lingering theme since the time of King Abdullah. In 2005, the government made national day a public holiday and started promoting it. Under the current Saudi government just like the binary witnessed in the religious sphere between official clergy and Sahwa there remain two strands of nationalism: one that is coming from Saudi elites and the other one more organically rising from the bottom and both rally around the figureheads of King and Crown Prince demanding a strict degree of loyalty towards the Saudi state and not some religious association (Alhussein 2019).

Transformation of state–sect relationship under King Salman

At the start of King Salman's reign, the government militarily intervened in Yemen and generally the anti-Iran discourse prevailed within Saudi Arabia. This brought together religious conservatives of every creed in support of the new Saudi government. The Sahwa preachers who had been critical of the Saudi government outlook towards the Arab Spring in the region undertook a complete discursive shift when it came to Yemen and were full of praise for the Saudi Monarch for acting against the Iranian proxies in Yemen (Matthiesen 2015: 8–9). On the discursive front within the social media domain, anti-Shi'ite discourse saw a spike. Moreover, Saudi clerics like Mohammed al-Arefe, Naser al-Omar, Saud al-Shureem and Abdulaziz al-Tarifi who have large following on Twitter supported the campaign in Yemen and disseminated tweets that were loaded with anti-Shi'ite rhetoric. There was a relatively smaller counter-sectarian trend within Saudi social media sphere after suicide attacks targeted Shi'ite mosques within the Eastern Province in 2015 (Alexandra 2018). Notable also has been the role of a Saudi-based television channel Wesal TV which was suspended in 2014 owing to its anti-Shi'ite inflammatory rhetoric but has been again back online (Aboudi and Evans 2014). The execution of firebrand Shi'ite cleric Sheikh Nimr al-Nimr and subsequent tensions with Iran didn't stabilize the sectarian antagonism. The security operation in Awamiyah and the eventual demolition of its old quarter further complicated the state's engagement with its Shi'ite citizenry (Batrawy 2017).

From securitization to development: Changing governance strategies to manage Shi'ite question

It appears that the political developments within Saudi Arabia, particularly the ultimate elevation of Prince Mohammad Bin Salman to the position of Crown Prince, the uptake in nationalistic rhetoric and state sanctioning of elements within the Wahhabi religious fold, played a major role in changing the discourse towards the Shi'ite question of Saudi Arabia. The Saudi regime that had hitherto approached this file from a securitization perspective now diverted the security lens towards political Islamists and religious fraternity on the other side of the sectarian divide while a discourse of development was introduced vis-à-vis the Eastern Province and Saudi Shi'ites. Both within the political and the discursive sphere there have been occurrences that indicate that there has been some change in the Saudi regime's perception of its Shi'ite citizens (Louër 2017).

From the political perspective, an important development took place when in the backdrop of the Arab League meeting of 2018 in Dhahran in the Eastern Province, Saudi King Salman hosted a reception for local notables that also included prominent Shi'ite leaders Sheikh Hasan Al-Saffar and Sayyid Ali Naser, a Saudi Shi'ite representative of Najaf's Grand Ayatollah Ali Al-Sistani. Similarly, a project to reconstruct the demolished quarter in the town of Awamiyah has been underway and the inauguration ceremony was attended by the governor of the Eastern Province Prince Saud Bin Nayef, showing the state's interest in rebuilding activities in the town that can help revive the local economy (Diwan 2018). In 2013, as Prince Saud was appointed the governor of the Eastern Province the political situation was fragile. It was apparent that King Abdullah the monarch at that time wasn't happy with how the situation had evolved within the province and particularly in its Shi'ite-dominated area of Qatif and wanted a new person to take up the job. Prince Saud had remained a deputy emir of the province in the 1980s, so this gave him some well-needed experience as well for the job (Alsharif and McDowall 2013). For a Saudi researcher hailing from the Eastern Province, this appointment has been the most critical development in the context of local politics. The change showed an admission at the leadership level that a newer governance approach towards the Eastern Province and its people was needed, one that also prioritises trust building and on a personal level has no negative baggage. Since then the governorship under Prince Saud has achieved a reduction in violence and attempted to change the perception of the governor's office, although this change can also be attributed towards the arrests of dissenting Shi'ite leadership in the province and a gradual fatigue within the opposition movement (Researcher 2020).[5] Perhaps, this is one reason that although the governor's brother, former Crown Prince Mohammad Bin Nayef, remains under house arrest and even his associates are being targeted, Prince Saud himself has retained his position.

Controlling discourse: Reducing the discursive monopoly of religious groupings

On the discursive front, this shift has been led directly by the Crown Prince Mohammad Bin Salman with an emphasis on 'moderate Islam' and how after 1979 it was allowed to be hijacked by more extreme elements. More important had been his negation of 'Wahhabism' and the emphasis on the need to consider Saudi Shi'ites as part of the Saudi national fabric and not aliens. This is something that no Saudi ruler had done publicly in such an open manner before (Freer 2019: 103). These words also worked as a signifier for all the discourse regulators whether they were in the print, electronic or social media domain. Under the Crown Prince various groups of Saudi society including Saudi Royals, the Sahwa preachers, liberal activists as well as women rights activists have been detained and their actions have been labelled in various ways against the Saudi national project. There have been arrests of people like Bader Al-Ibrahim who talked about Shi'ite political discourse in Saudi Arabia. The arrests seem to have been state reaction to his activism rather than sectarian identity (Molana-Allen 2019).

The preachers mainly hailing from Sahwa movement have been deemed as 'anti-reform' and 'extremists' in addition to ones that are working on the agenda of foreign powers (Pimodan 2018). The women or liberal activists have been termed as embassy agents since they engaged with foreign diplomatic missions (Alhussein 2019). Yet here one should mention that all of these groups targeted by the state have been targeted in the past as well and these developments also have a political motif mainly to control the discourse and have it centred around the personality of Crown Prince (Ulrichsen and Sheline 2019). Yet, it would also be wrong to suggest that the official clergy has remained unaffected from these changes. From adopting a silent demeanour to supporting steps taken by the government in terms of social liberalization, the clergy has towed the government's line and has also seen its ranks filled with those having a relatively liberal world view (Alhussein 2018).

All these steps have curtailed or significantly reduced the discursive monopoly that the Saudi religious establishment has enjoyed for long. If the discursive focus is upon moderation either the Saudi government has to showcase new faces that don't retain the same baggage or it has to prioritize different discursive strains, for instance, like nationalism. It appears that the Saudi rulers have pushed in both directions. Another spectre of the new Saudi regime has been its control and manipulation of social media. This has enabled it to not only monitor the trends and discussions on the platform but also police them, further constraining discourses the government disallows to propagate (Leber and Abrahams 2019: 248).

Implications for Saudi Shi'ites

For Saudi Shi'ites although indirect these discursive silences imposed on some of their most virulent opponents had a positive effect and there has been appreciation of the reforms taken under the auspices of the Vision 2030 by the Crown Prince to curb 'extremist fundamentalist rhetoric' and in particular the practice of takfir (Al-Mustafa 2018).[6] This is something that has always been advocated by prominent Saudi Shi'ite voices (Alsaif 2013). If there has been rather acceptance and promotion of the Kingdom's Shi'ite citizens, there has also been a censure of anti-Shi'ite hate speech by the proponents of nationalist discourse within social media. As S Ali al-Rabieei, a Saudi cleric with a large following on social media, issued a fatwa prohibiting his followers to commemorate the death of a Kuwaiti Shi'ite actor Abdulhussain Abdulredha, he faced a severe backlash on Twitter for his sectarian rhetoric. A twitter hashtag started trending that demanded him to be held accountable for his viewpoint. Eventually this resulted in him deleting his tweet and then being summoned by the Ministry of Culture and Information for violations of publication laws (Arab 2017). Saudi public prosecution was also quick to react when a social media influencer condemned Shi'ites and asked, 'God not to leave even one Shi'ite on earth, even if they are 99 million.' Not only the person was arrested but the prosecution called on Saudi citizens and residents to display spirit of moderation, citizenship, tolerance, brotherhood and community partnership in their behaviour on social media and other media (Okaz.com 2020). Similarly, another interesting social media campaign of solidarity emerged when the Qatif region in the Eastern Province was put under a lockdown after it had reported its first Covid-19 case. Twitter hashtags 'Qatif in hearts' and 'Qatif is fine' were initiated not only to show support for the people but also to downplay any possible sectarian undertones that the pandemic breakout in Qatif could trigger (Getdaytrends 2020). Many Saudi Shi'ite activists also used the hashtag to express their anger on the discrimination and lack of health facilities in the region.

On the political front the alleged Iranian attacks on Abqaiq–Khurais oil processing facilities of Saudi Aramco have not created a positive impact within the Saudi Shi'ite community. As a large number of Saudi Shi'ites work at Aramco, such an attack has been perceived by many as one directly targeting their livelihood creating a unique negative sentiment towards Iran within these ranks. Furthermore, Saudi Shi'ites have complained about the hate state speech often being disseminated through mosque loud speakers and this has been the case even in the Eastern Province although it has significant clusters of Shi'ite population (Researcher 2020). There has been improvement on this front and the media outlets and mosques have been relatively constrained in the dissemination of condemnation of Shi'ite Muslims. With the most current strain of Shi'ite opposition facing fatigue there has been some internal debate within the Shi'ite intellectual circles on how best they can capitalize with the changes taking place on Saudi social and political front. There have been those who have tried to compare the Shi'ite Islamist opposition to Saudi regime with that of the Sahwa movement and consider this high time for moderate elements within Saudi Shi'ite community to take leadership of their community and engage in the new nationalist project (Al-Omran 2020). The security situation within Qatif has also improved and there remains lesser security presence according to a news report. Saudi Shi'ites feel that the state is now acting against all elements of the society and they're not a scapegoat anymore while accepting the notion that there has been an attempt by the state to be more inclusive. Yet, they remain sceptical as this doesn't mean any organic change in the state of inter-sect relations within Saudi society (Jefferson and Abu-Nasr 2019).

This is the form of discursive de-sectarianization happening within the Saudi Kingdom both from above and below. On the top level a resolve to take stringent measures against the traditional religious classes in order to weaken their politico-social capital alongside an attempt to co-opt the Saudi Shi'ite population has contributed towards it. On the bottom the youth bulge and its adoption of new Saudi nationalism has created a societal revisionism of sorts when it comes to sectarianism. Still it is difficult to say with even a slight degree of certainty whether these trends suggest a transformation of inter-sect relations within Saudi Arabia.

Changing discourses on the foreign policy front

Security considerations have been a major determinant of the foreign policies of Middle Eastern states, and Saudi Arabia is no exception to this trend. Saudi foreign policy in the 1950s and 1960s was oriented around making close relationships with the West to balance against the threats posed by Egypt and the Pan-Arab Movement led by it. After the Iranian Islamic revolution, Iranian Supreme Leader Ayatollah Khomeini questioned the legitimacy of monarchy (Gause III 2003). This was a direct threat not to the Saudi state but to the Saudi regime. Since then both countries have been rivals in regional political order. This competition for regional hegemony is soared further by the number of ideological, cultural and religious differences between the two countries (Berti and Guzansky 2014: 25). In the post-first Gulf war period, both Saudi Arabia and Iran approached each other rather positively and embarked upon an engagement to an effective political rapprochement (Altoraifi 2012).

The American invasion of Iraq opened the strategically locked greater Levant for Iranian influence ending the incentives for Iran from a realistic perspective to continue the status quo vis-à-vis Saudi Arabia. The Saudi Kingdom's counter attempted to utilize its economic muscle in the region, strengthened its ties with other Gulf States and initiated strategic engagement with Turkey to balance against the burgeoning Shi'ite Crescent (Ataman 2012). The political field in the broader Middle East had not stabilized from the effects of the American invasion and in 2011 the Arab Uprisings erupted further complicating and unravelling the balance of power regimes in the region to the detriment of the Saudi Kingdom (Gause III 2011). Saudi Arabia lost its key ally President Hosni Mubarak in Egypt and had to intervene in Bahrain to save another allied regime. If the ruling regime in Bahrain had been ousted the repercussions would have been disastrous for the Saudi and other Gulf rulers (Ulrichsen 2011). The Arab Spring projected Qatar and Turkey as a third pole into the political landscape of Middle East. The two countries openly sided with uprising of 2011 in the region and saw in it a unique opportunity to extend their influence within the region through their linkages with Muslim Brotherhood associated groups (Başkan 2016: 83).

Saudi Arabia responded to such a challenging geopolitical environment by attempting to preserve (in case of Bahrain) or re-establish (in case of Egypt) the regional status quo or to change it into a more favourable political order (in case of Syria). Saudi-led military intervention in Bahrain made it clear that the stability of regimes within the Gulf Cooperation Council (GCC) is its paramount priority and also the threat posed by a Shi'i-led mass movement in Bahrain can quickly tickle across border into the Eastern Province of Saudi Arabia. Presence of Muslim Brotherhood in the power corridors of Egypt was also threatening for the Kingdom (Al-Tamamy 2012). There were two threats for the Kingdom to negotiate on the foreign policy front, one was the 'sectarian other' and the second was the 'ideological other'. Both forces challenged the existing political status quo but also were a threat to Saudi regime security.

In the Egyptian case the status quo got restored after the first elected Egyptian President Mohammad Morsi from the Muslim Brotherhood was removed in a coup led by General Sisi, the head of Egyptian Armed Forces (Hammond 2014). This ostracized Turkey and Qatar from the Egyptian political sphere and re-entrenched the Saudi-led block. Saudi Arabia had a brief fall out with Qatar and bilateral ties with Turkey also got a hit. But owing to the intensity of Syrian Conflict and Gezi Protests within Turkey the political tensions never reached a confrontational stage.

As King Salman came into power the immediate challenge for the new monarch was to counter Iran in the region which was emboldened by the pro-engagement position taken by the Obama administration and had been nearing a nuclear deal with the United States. On the other hand, Iran had been supporting Houthi rebels that had taken over the Yemeni capital Sanaa, creating an active security threat on the southern border of the Kingdom. This drove Riyadh's policy outlook and a rapprochement between Turkey and Saudi Arabia materialized but extended also to other Muslim Brotherhood elements like Hamas. Both sides coordinated their resources in the Syrian theatre and after a year of stalemate rebel forces made significant advances on the battlefield against the Assad regime (Phillips 2020). Turkey and Qatar also supported the Saudi-led military intervention in Yemen and Qatar was even initially part of the campaign against Houthi rebels.

All of this was to change once Saudi Arabia moved against Qatar alongside its allies and initiated a complete boycott/blockade of the Gulf State. This resulted in Turkey deploying its troops in Qatar, effectively impacting upon the established security order of the Arabian Gulf region. This Saudi move in foreign policy domain was followed by arrests of prominent clerics of the Sahwa discussed in detail above. It appeared that the threat perception within Saudi Arabia and its regime that had been centred on Iran had now shifted towards Muslim Brotherhood and its regional patrons Turkey and Qatar. A key factor affecting this change had been Saudi Crown Prince Mohammad Bin Salman's tough stance on Muslim Brotherhood essentially following the policy line of the United Arab Emirates (UAE) vis-à-vis this group (Stancati 2017). Other factors included the special relationship between the Saudi Crown Prince and American President Donald Trump that gave Saudi Crown Prince a considerable degree of confidence and immunity. And also there was an understanding within Saudi Arabia that Iran no longer constituted a domestic security threat through its linkages with Saudi Shi'ite population but rather a threat to the regional balance of power (F. G. Gause III 2020). With the murder of Saudi journalist Jamal Khashoggi in the Saudi consulate in Istanbul and the political clash that ensued this killing, Turkish-Saudi ties were effectively imperilled and bilateral state of affairs had been dubbed as cold war (Tremblay 2020). Discourse emanating from Saudi media enterprises against Muslim Brotherhood, Qatar and Turkey (Al-Rashed 2020) alongside Saudi moves to effectively court all anti-Turkey elements mainly Greece and Cyprus indicated that this opposing pole within the Middle East was dominating Saudi foreign policy agenda and rhymed well with the anti-Ikhwan narrative inside the Kingdom. With the Al-Ulla Accord, a wave of rapprochement has commenced within the political spectrum of Middle East. An economically weakened and politically isolated Turkey and a Saudi Arabia that had lost its close ally President Trump decided to resolve tensions. From the Turkish side suspension of the trial of the murdered Saudi journalist and transferring it to Saudi Arabia was a clear signal that it wants to go ahead with rapprochement (Kucukgocmen 2022). This had been a major Saudi demand vis-à-vis Turkey, and this resulted in the normalization of ties between the two sides and subsequent trips by Turkish and Saudi leadership to each other's capitals. This showed that as the drivers of this Saudi-Turkish discord settled and as the significance of a Muslim Brotherhood political threat to Gulf States diminished, leaderships on both sides were pragmatic enough to mend their ties. Even in this case it is clear that the changing systemic realities on international, regional and subregional levels dictated the statecraft of political leaderships of the region, who seized these opportunities while disregarding their ideological and personal differences.

Rapprochement with Iraq

The regional security regime in the Middle East had remained stabilized in between the troika of Saudi Arabia, Iran and Iraq after the First Gulf War. As Iraq suffered from crippling international sanctions the two other arch-rivals Saudi Arabia and Iran started bilateral engagement that led to a political rapprochement between the two sides. In this manner the three bigger poles of the Middle East were counterbalancing each other but without any armed or political hostility. This political order was completely altered by the American invasion of Iraq. Furthermore, the process of De-Baathification initiated by the Coalition Provisional Authority (CPA) that oversaw Iraqi transition to a new democratic setup meant that virtually all institutions, particularly the military, police and state bureaucracy, collapsed overnight. These left hundreds of thousands jobless and struggling to make both ends meet (Mabon 2019b). These cadres eventually joined ranks of insurgents and terrorist organization fighting against the American forces. The other implication was the rise in the political fortunes of various Shi'ite political forces. Most of these groups and their leaderships had lived in exile within Iran and thereby considered Iran as a natural partner and ally. Iran had given refuge to a number of prominent Shi'ite political figures during the purges of Saddam Hussain and now was ready to capitalize on its links with this Shi'ite polity by influencing different Shi'ite blocks to coalesce and form a government. During the successive governments of Prime Minister Nouri al-Maliki, Iran became the prime player in Iraqi politics and changed the status of Iraq from a foe to a friend (Barzegar 2010: 183).

For Saudi Arabia, this new political environment in Iraq was both a challenge but also one where its choices were increasingly limited. It could not embark upon any campaign to actively confront Iran within Iraq for two main reasons. First had been the Saudi partnership with the United States, and since the United States was a key stakeholder within Iraq any Saudi manoeuvre or Saudi backing of Iraqi Sunnis would have further deteriorated the political and security environment within Iraq. Secondly, it was still actively engaging with Iran and had been reluctant to completely abandon this political process that had been continuing since the 1990s. Saudi Arabia was concerned regarding this growing political influence of Iran but always saw it as a balance of power threat and wanted to roll it back through political push back (Gause, III 2007). The Kingdom had traditionally maintained links with Sunni tribal elites particularly the transnational Shammar tribe. Yet this engagement was never strategic in nature and often too little too late. This didn't change the political fortunes of Iraqi Sunnis (Wehrey and Alrababa'h 2014). Riyadh had practically given up on Iraq and till the departure of Nouri Al-Maliki this dynamic did not change. A prominent Saudi researcher considered this Saudi approach a serious mistake but also pointed out the lack of choices as the Iraqi Shi'ite polity remained fully under the orbit of Iran and didn't want to engage with Saudi Arabia while on the other hand Sunnis also considered it culpable for not providing them with substantial political support and became increasingly fragmented (Scholar 2018).[7]

Political capital above sectarian identity

Under King Salman, one of the most visible foreign policy changes was regarding the Saudi outlook towards Iraq. King Salman and Crown Prince Mohammad Bin Salman had effectively changed Riyadh's past strategies and for the first time attempted to engage with the Iraqi government directly and not with some specific

Sunni political group. This shift only happened once political realities changed within Iraq. The emergence of a rather nationalist Prime Minister Haider Al-Abadi, the menace of ISIS and the rise in anti-Iranian political narratives within Iraq all led to a relative receptive environment within Iraq to any Saudi venture (Economist 2017). This mutual willingness to improve the relationship resulted in Saudi Arabia appointing its first ambassador to Iraq since Saddam's invasion of Kuwait. This was followed by multiple visits of successive Iraqi Prime Ministers Haider Al-Abadi and Adel Abdul-Mehdi and presidents to Saudi Arabia but also of politicians like Qasim Al-Araji whose association with pro-Iran Badr Organization is well established (Coker 2018). Also, the visits were reciprocated from the Saudi side by foreign ministers Adel Al-Jubeir and Faisal Bin Farhan, although the relationship has not been a smooth one and in 2016 Iraqi government asked Saudi Arabia to replace its ambassador in Baghdad after his comments about Iranian involvement in Iraqi affairs (Chmaytelli 2016). For Saudi Arabia, Iraq remains an important vector point in the regional security equation and the current Saudi strategy to engage with Iraq is reminiscent of the prevalent discourses of de-sectarianization in the Saudi domestic fold. The recent Saudi approach revolves around pragmatic political engagement with actors weighed against their political capital rather than sectarian identity. This approach is best described in the words of former Saudi chief of intelligence and envoy to Washington Prince Turki Al-Faisal:

> We've been very much engaged with many Iraqi political groups and we tell them all that we're there for Iraq. We're not there for just one party. In terms of our own security, it's best for us to make ourselves available to all Iraqi political factions as someone they can be friends with. But whether parties like al-Hashd al-Shaabi, which are now represented in the Iraqi parliament, will be open to engaging with Saudi Arabia, I doubt that very much. It will, therefore, be a challenging manoeuvre for Saudi officials. (Rudolf 2020)

Saudi Arabia has understood that it cannot outdo Iran within Iraq if it continues to play the sectarian game, and the Iranian political proxies now have transformed into armed militant factions that gives them additional strength to guard their political turf. Therefore, the Saudi focus has been to reach out to Iraqi Shi'ite leadership that has taken a more nationalistic outlook, while also displaying respect for Najaf-based Shi'ite religious leader Ayatollah Ali Al-Sistani and continuing engagement with tribal elements of both Sunni and Shi'ite denomination (International Crisis Group, Saudi Arabia: Back to Baghdad 2018). The Saudi attempts at engaging with the Iraqi Shi'ite cleric Muqtada Al-Sadr is a notable example of this new Saudi strategy. Al-Sadr's militias have been involved in abuses against Iraqi Sunnis, and in the past, he also threatened to invade Riyadh. Still, this political baggage had been submerged under the waves of nationalism rising both within Iraq and Saudi Arabia. Just like the Saudi Crown Prince has clubbed himself with this nationalist discourse so has Al-Sadr in Iraq where disappointment has been paramount against Shi'ite Islamist politics. Saudi Arabia has also focused on southern Iraq particularly Basra from an economic perspective and has invested in construction of a new Sheraton Hotel and a petrochemical plant. This region fits the bill of Saudi outreach since it is Shi'ite majority but has found itself politically marginalized by governments in Baghdad and has remained a hotbed of anti-government protests and of anti-Iranian sentiment (Mansour 2018). Saudi Arabia and the government in Baghdad have found in the past year another point of agreement and that has been the Turkish ingress and military operations within the Kurdish autonomous region of Iraq. Riyadh issued strongly worded condemnations of these Turkish violations of Iraqi territory (Arab News 2020). This also suggests that Saudi Arabia is keen to project itself as a partner to Iraq that respects its sovereignty and territorial integrity.

This trend within the decision-making corridors of Saudi Arabia has also trickled down to the advisory and research world with a particular focus on searching for nodes of connectivity and bridge building with Iraq. This has led to a host of activities that can make the Saudi policymakers aware of the political and religious complexities of post-Saddam Iraq while also understanding how Iraqis view different regional actors. This author attended one such seminar where a leading expert on Iraqi Shi'ite clergy explained in detail the Shi'ite Marjayyas in Iraq, their outlook towards Saudi Arabia and the linkages with Iran. During this seminar the focus was squarely upon how the Saudi audience can better engage and connect with the Iraqi religious sphere and in this regard for the first time the importance of Saudi Shi'ites has been admitted (Expert 2018).[8]

Conclusion

The emergence of Crown Prince Mohammad Bin Salman has radically altered the political life within the Saudi Kingdom and the political narratives prioritized and patronized by him are apparent within the domestic and foreign political outlook. These discursive expressions may have found favour within the power corridors, but they have not reached a level of new political and societal truths since they pivot around the personality of the crown prince and can very much change once the political threat perceptions change for those in power or there is a change within the decision-making corridors. The processes of sectarianization and actors propagating them have lost a considerable level of power and discourses condemning sectarianism have found favour within the ruling quarters. Yet this does not mean that the sectarian element has disappeared as a marker in sub-national identities and attempts to curtail it show that it has not faded away.

Saudi nationalism indeed for now has a strong societal push and resonates with Saudi youth, yet there have been signs of it becoming a regulator of political correctness in its own right and appropriating, in an unseen manner, some regulating powers that have remained solely the purview of the state. The state has reacted and attempted to rein in these new discursive entrepreneurs of nationalism whenever it notices that they have crossed the threshold (Chopra 2020). On the foreign policy front, the confrontational engagements with Qatar and Turkey were indirectly an extension of the policies adopted in the domestic sphere. As the threat of Muslim Brotherhood has been largely dissipated and as both Turkey and Qatar signalled their intent to resolve political differences with Riyadh, this political dynamic also changed. The Saudi engagement with Iraq is driven by a Saudi resolve to reduce Iranian influence within its northern neighbour to weaken the Iranian regional project. If the current Saudi regime considers this regional political front connected with its own Shi'ite community then any complication within the home turf on the Shi'ite question can jeopardize the whole initiative (Alaaldin 2020). However, if the Saudi regime doesn't consider its Shi'ite community anymore a fifth column and truly believes it to be part of the Saudi nation and its national discourse then the discourses of Iraqi nationalism and Saudi nationalism can align well and progress into a strong political relationship.

Notes

1. Discursive regularities can be categorized as the rules of formation of discourse, which can be objects having discursive value, that is, power holders, forms or debates that influence discursive productions, concepts and ideas.
2. In this particular case first the processes and actors propagating sectarianization in the Saudi political fold will be explored and subsequently those creating and leading the discourses of de-sectarianization will be under focus.
3. Discursive regularities can be categorized as the rules of formation of discourse, which can be objects having discursive value, that is, power holders, forms or debates that influence discursive productions, concepts and ideas.
4. AH, that is, After Hijra, is the standard term used to denote the Islamic Calendar year.
5. The interviewee's name has been kept confidential for safety purposes.
6. It is important to note here that the right appreciating steps taken by Saudi government is also a Saudi Shi'ite but someone who is also considered a liberal in terms of his orientation and does not belong to a more conservative strain of Shi'ism.
7. The interviewee is a notable Saudi scholar but the details are not disclosed for confidentiality reasons.
8. The name of the event and participants is not disclosed for confidentiality reasons.

References

Aboudi, S., and Evans, D. (2014), 'Saudi Arabia Shuts Office of TV Channel for Fomenting Sectarian Tension'. *Reuters.com*. 5 November. https://www.reuters.com/article/us-saudi-television/saudi-arabia-shuts-office-of-tv-channel-for-fomenting-sectarian-tension-idUSKBN0IP1BB20141105 (accessed 7 February 2020).

Alaaldin, R. (2020), 'Iraq's Best Hope Is Developing Stronger Ties to the Gulf — with US help'. *Brookings.com*. 19 August. https://www.brookings.edu/blog/order-from-chaos/2020/08/19/iraqs-best-hope-is-developing-stronger-ties-to-the-gulf-with-us-help/ (accessed 20 August 2020).

Alexandra, S. (2018), 'Twitter Wars: Sunni-Shia Conflict and Cooperation in the Digital Age', in Frederic Wehrey (ed.), *Beyond Sunni and Shia: The Roots of Sectarianism in a Changing Middle East*, New York: Oxford University Press, 157–80.

Alhussein, E. (2018), 'The Enlightened Sheikhs of the New Saudi Arabia'. *Arab Gulf States Institute in Washington*. 27 June. https://agsiw.org/the-enlightened-shei khs-of-the-new-saudi-arabia/ (accessed 10 April 2019).
Alhussein, E. (2019), *Saudi First: How Hyper-Nationalism Is Transforming Saudi Arabia*, Policy Brief, European Council on Foreign Relations London.
Al-Mustafa, H. (2018), 'Saudi Shiites and Their Role in the "New Saudi Arabia"'. *Al-Arabiya.net*. 12 March. https://english.alarabiya.net/en/views/news/mid dle-east/2018/03/12/Saudi-Shiites-and-their-role-in-the-new-Saudi-Arabia-.html (accessed 20 February 2019).
Al-Omran, A. (2020), 'Two Awakenings'. *Riyadh Bureau*. 31 August. https://ahmed.subst ack.com/p/two-awakenings (accessed 31 August 2020).
Al-Rashed, A. R. (2020), 'Erdogan's Bewildering Character'. *Asharq Al-Awast*. 14 June. https://english.aawsat.com/home/article/2333396/abdulrahman-al-rashed/erdo gan%E2%80%99s-bewildering-character (accessed 20 August 2020).
Al-Rasheed, M. (2010), *A History of Saudi Arabia*, Cambridge: Cambridge University Press.
Al-Rasheed, M. (2017), 'Sectarianism as Counter-Revolution: Saudi Responses to the Arab Spring', in Nader Hashemi and Danny Postel (eds), *Sectarianization: Mapping the New Politics of Middle East*, New York: Oxford University Press, 143–59.
Al-Rasheed, M. (2020), *The New Populist Nationalism in Saudi Arabia: Imagined Utopia by Royal Decree*. 5 May. https://blogs.lse.ac.uk/mec/2020/05/05/the-new-populist-nati onalism-in-saudi-arabia-imagined-utopia-by-royal-decree/ (accessed 10 June 2020).
Alsaif, T. (2013), 'Relationship between State and Religion in Saudi Arabia: The Role of Wahabism in Governance', *Contemporary Arab Affairs*, 6 (3): 376–403.
Alsharif, A., and McDowall, A. (2013), 'Saudi King Names New Governor for Restive Oil Region'. *Reuters.com*. 14 January. https://uk.reuters.com/article/uk-saudi-appointment/ saudi-king-names-new-governor-for-restive-oil-region-idUKBRE90D0RN20130114 (accessed 10 June 2019).
Al-Tamamy, S. M. (2012), 'Saudi Arabia and the Arab Spring: Opportunities and Challenges of Security', *Journal of Arabian Studies*, 2 (2): 143–56.
Altoraifi, A. (2012). *Understanding The Role of State Identity in Foreign Policy Decision Making: The Rise and Demise of Saudi–Iranian Rapprochement (1997–2009)*. Thesis, London: The London School of Economics and Political Science.
Arab News. (2020), 'Saudi Arabia Condemns Turkish, Iranian Military Interventions in Iraq'. *Arab News*. 18 June. https://www.arabnews.com/node/1691686/saudi-arabia (accessed 20 August 2020).
Arab, The New. (2017), 'Saudi Arabia Moves to Silence Hate Preacher for Insulting Deceased Kuwaiti Shia Actor'. *The New Arab*. 13 August. https://english.alaraby.co.uk/ english/blog/2017/8/13/riyadh-moves-to-silence-cleric-for-insulting-deceased-actor (accessed 20 February 2019).
Ataman, M. (2012), 'Turkish-Saudi Arabian Relations', *Insight Turkey*, 14 (4): 121–36.
Barzegar, K. (2010), 'Iran's Foreign Policy Strategy after Saddam'. *The Washington Quarterly*, 33 (1): 173–89. https://doi.org/10.1080/01636600903430665.
Bashraheel, A. (2019), 'Rise and Fall of the Saudi Religious Police'. *Arab*. 23 September. https://www.arabnews.com/node/1558176/saudi-arabia (accessed 20 June 2020).
Başkan, B. (2016), *Turkey and Qatar in the tangled Geopolitics of the Middle East*, New York: Palgrave Macmillan.

Batrawy, A. (2017), 'Saudi Demolition of Historic Shiite Homes Stokes Violence', *apnews.com*. 27 June. https://apnews.com/e49d78cdcab64fd28606f20ac1bc029b (accessed 10 April 2020).

Berti, B., and Guzansky, Y. (2014), 'Saudi Arabia's Foreign Policy on Iran and the Proxy War in Syria: Toward a New Chapter?' *Israel Journal of Foreign Affairs*, 8 (3): 25–34. https://doi.org/10.1080/23739770.2014.11446600.

Chmaytelli, M. (2016), 'Iraq Asks Saudi Arabia to Replace Envoy Who Riled Shi'ite Militias'. *Reuters.com*. 26 August. https://www.reuters.com/article/us-mideast-crisis-iraq-saudi/iraq-asks-saudi-arabia-to-replace-envoy-who-riled-shiite-militias-idUSKCN113095 (accessed 17 April 2020).

Chopra, A. (2020), 'Saudi Arabia Seeks to Tame Powerful Cyber Armies'. *Yahoo News*. 7 August. https://news.yahoo.com/saudi-arabia-seeks-tame-powerful-044118605.html?guccounter=1&guce_referrer=aHR0cHM6Ly93d3cuZ29vZ2xlLmNvbS8&guce_referrer_sig=AQAAABGRsxsDLf-a5-aO9Lxhsx1DZatcuS94fXVDTpuHlWACSI1eUVnRmGWglzk3ACIc3y-LbHxwpTu-I8K20kj1-l5rVZqGYVcsdlEpO5L (accessed 7 August 2020).

Coker, M. (2018), 'U.S. Takes a Risk: Old Iraqi Enemies Are Now Allies'. *New York Times*. 11 May. https://www.nytimes.com/2018/05/11/world/middleeast/iraq-iran-election-enemies.html (accessed 20 August 2020).

DeLong-Bas, N. J. (2013), 'Islam and Power in Saudi Arabia', in John L Esposito and Emad El-Din Shahin (eds), *The Oxford Handbook of Islam and Politics*, Oxford: Oxford University Press, 411–22.

Diwan, K. S. (2018), 'Saudi Nationalism Raises Hopes of Greater Shia Inclusion', *Arab Gulf States Institute in Washington*. 3 May. Accessed February 10, 2019. https://agsiw.org/saudi-nationalism-raises-hopes-greater-inclusion-shias/.

Dodge, T. (2016), 'Seeking to Explain the Rise of Sectarianism in the Middle East: The Case Study of Iraq'. *The Gulf's Escalating Sectarianism*. Project on Middle East Political Science (POMEPS).

Economist, The. (2017), 'Saudi Arabia Attempts to Woo Iraq Away from Iran'. *The Economist*. 4 September. http://country.eiu.com/article.aspx?articleid=1304231114&Country=Iraq&topic=Economy&oid=72688991&flid=1585858542 (accessed 20 February 2019).

England, A., and Al-Omran, A. (2019), 'Nationalism on the Rise as Saudi Arabia Seeks Sense of Identity'. *Financial Times*. 7 May. https://www.ft.com/content/31845386-6cb9-11e9-80c7-60ee53e6681d (accessed 10 June 2020).

Expert, Iraq, interview by Umer Karim. (2018), Changes in political and religious power hierarchy in Iraq (August).

Freer, C. (2019), 'The Symbiosis of Sectarianism, Authoritarianism, and Rentierism in Saudi State'. *Studies in Ethnicity and Nationalism*, 19 (1): 88–108.

Gause III, F Gregory (2003), 'Balancing What? Threat Perception and Alliance Choice in the Gulf', *Security Studies*, 13 (2): 273–305.

Gause, III, F Gregory (2007), 'Saudi Arabia: Iraq, Iran, the Regional Power Balance, and the Sectarian Question'. *Strategic Insight*, 6 (2): 1–8.

Gause III, F Gregory (2011), *Saudi Arabia in the New Middle East*. Council Special Report No. 63, New York: Council on Foreign Relations.

Gause III, F Gregory (2020), 'Saudi Arabia and Sectarianism in Middle East International Relations'. *The Project on Middle East Political Science (POMEPS)*. March. https://pomeps.org/saudi-arabia-and-sectarianism-in-middle-east-international-relations (accessed 20 June 2020).

Getdaytrends. (2020), *Getdaytrends*. 8 March. https://getdaytrends.com/saudi-arabia/trend/%23%D8%A7%D9%84%D9%82%D8%B7%D9%8A%D9%81_%D9%81%D9%8A_%D9%82%D9%84%D9%88%D8%A8%D9%86%D8%A7/ (accessed 10 July 2020).

Hadad, F. (2018), *Ontologies of Sectarian Identity: The Many Layers of Sunni–Shi'a Relations.* 18 September. https://blogs.lse.ac.uk/mec/2018/09/16/ontologies-of-sectarian-identity-the-many-layers-of-sunni-shia-relations/ (Accessed 10 September 2019).

Hammond, A. (2013), *The Gulf and sectarianism*, London: Analysis, European Council on Foreign Relations.

Hammond, A. (2014), 'A Very Gulf Coup'. *Turkish Review*, 3 (5): 498–505.

Hashemi, N., and Postel, D. (2017), 'Introduction: The Sectarianization Thesis', in Nader Hashemi and Danny Postel (eds), *Sectarianization: Mapping the New Politics of the Middle East*, New York: Oxford University Press, 1–22.

Herb, M. (1999), *All in the Family: Absolutism, Revolution, and Democracy in the Middle Eastern Monarchies*, Albany: State University of New York Press.

International Crisis Group. (2018), *Saudi Arabia: Back to Baghdad*. Middle East Report Number 186, Brussels: International Crisis Group.

Jefferson, R., and Abu-Nasr, D. (2019), 'Saudi Arabia's Oil Heartland Is Calm. That's Bad News for Iran'. *Bloomberg.com*. 22 November. https://www.bloomberg.com/news/articles/2019-11-22/saudi-arabia-s-oil-heartland-is-calm-that-s-bad-news-for-iran (accessed 23 February 2020.).

Karim, U. (2017), 'The Evolution of Saudi Foreign Policy and the Role of Decision-making Processes and Actors', *The International Spectator*, 52 (2): 71–88. https://doi.org/10.1080/03932729.2017.1308643.

Kucukgocmen, A. (2022), 'Turkish court halts Khashoggi trial, transfers it to Saudi Arabia'. *Reuters*. 7 April. https://www.reuters.com/world/middle-east/turkish-court-halts-khashoggi-trial-transfers-it-saudi-arabia-2022-04-07/

Leber, A., and Abrahams, A. (2019), 'A Storm of Tweets: Social Media Manipulation During the Gulf Crisis', *Review of Middle East Studies*, 53 (2): 241–58. doi: https://doi.org/10.1017/rms.2019.45.

Louër, L. (2016), 'From Revolution to Reform: Shiism and Politics in Saudi Arabia', *Confluences Méditerranée*, 97 (2): 31–41. www.cairn.info/revue-confluences-mediterranee-2016-2-page-31.htm.

Louër, L. (2017), 'The Transformation of Shia Politics in the Gulf Monarchies', *New Analysis of Shia Politics*. Project on Middle Eastern Political Science, 39–42.

Louër, L., and Rundell, E. (2020), *Sunnis and Shi'a: A Political History of Discord*, Princeton, NJ: Princeton University Press.

Mabon, S. (2018a), 'It's a Family Affair: Religion, Geopolitics and the Rise of Mohammed bin Salman', *Insight Turkey*, 20 (2): 51–66. https://www.jstor.org/stable/26390307.

Mabon, S. (2018b), *Saudi Arabia and Iran: Power and Rivalry in the Middle East*, London: Bloomsbury.

Mabon, S. (2019a), 'Desectarianization: Looking beyond the Sectarianization of Middle Eastern Politics', *Review of Faith & International Affairs*, 17 (4): 23–35. https://doi.org/10.1080/15570274.2019.1681776.

Mabon, S. (2019b), 'Saudi Arabia and Iran: Islam and foreign policy in the Middle East', in Shahram Akbarzadehm (eds), *Routledge Handbook of International Relations in the Middle East*, New York: Routledge, 138–52.

Mansour, R. (2018), *Saudi Arabia's New Approach in Iraq*. Analysis Paper, Center for Strategic and International Studies.

Matthiesen, T. (2014), *The Other Saudis: Shiism, Dissent and Sectarianism*, Cambridge: Cambridge University Press.

Matthiesen, T. (2015), *The Domestic Sources of Saudi Foreign Policy: Islamists and the State in the Wake of the Arab Uprisings*. Working Paper, Washington, DC: Brookings Institution.

Molana-Allen, L. (2019), 'Saudi Arabia Arrests Eight Women's Rights Activists in Fresh Crackdown'. *The Telegraph*. 5 April. https://www.telegraph.co.uk/news/2019/04/05/saudi-arabia-arrests-eight-womens-rights-activists-fresh-crackdown/ (accessed 10 June 2020).

Mouline, N. (2015), 'Enforcing and Reinforcing the State's Islam: The Functioning of the Committee of Senior Scholars', in Bernard Haykel, Thomas Hegghammer and Stéphane Lacroix (eds), *Saudi Arabia in Transition: Insights on Social, Political, Economic and Religious Change*, Cambridge: Cambridge University Press, 48–67.

Okaz.com. (2020), 'Public Prosecution Office Directed the Arrest of a Person Who Appeared in a Video Clip Calling for Sectarian Incitement and Sectarian Charging'. *Okaz.com*. 8 August. https://www.okaz.com.sa/news/local/2036333 (accessed 10 August 2020).

Phillips, C. (2020), 'Rivalry amid Systemic Change: Iranian and Saudi Competition in the post-American Middle East'. *Project on the Middle East Political Science*. March. https://pomeps.org/rivalry-amid-systemic-change-iranian-and-saudi-competition-in-the-post-american-middle-east (accessed 20 August 2020).

Pimodan, Q. D. (2018), 'Saudi Islamist Crackdown: A Case Study in Societal Schizophrenia'. *Research Institute for American and European Studies*. 22 September. https://rieas.gr/researchareas/global-issues/middle-east-studies/3025-saudi-islamist-crackdown-a-case-study-of-a-societal-schizophrenia (accessed 12 April 2020).

Researcher, Saudi, interview by Umer Karim. 2020. *Politics of Eastern Province of Saudi Arabia* (January).

Roelants, C., and Aarts, P. (2016), 'The Perils of the Transfer of Power in the Kingdom of Saudi Arabia', *Contemporary Arab Affairs*, 9 (4): 596–606.

Rudolf, I. (2020), 'Interview with Former Saudi Intelligence Chief Turki al-Faisal: "The Ball Is in Iran's Court"'. *Zenith*. 30 January. https://magazine.zenith.me/en/politics/interview-former-saudi-intelligence-chief-turki-al-faisal (accessed 20 August 2020).

Scholar, Saudi, interview by Umer Karim. 2018. *Interview on Saudi Foreign Policy* (August).

Stancati, M. (2017), 'Saudi Crown Prince and U.A.E. Heir Forge Pivotal Ties'. *Wall Street Journal*. 6 August. https://www.wsj.com/articles/saudi-crown-prince-and-u-a-e-heir-forge-pivotal-ties-1502017202 (accessed 20 February 2019).

Sultan, A. (2018), 'Beyond Sectarianism and Ideology: Regionalism and Collective Political Action in Saudi Arabia', in Madawi Al-Rasheed (ed.), *Salman's Legacy: The Dilemmas of a New Era in Saudi Arabia*, New York: Oxford University Press, 97–116.

Teitelbaum, J. (2010), 'The Shiites of Saudi Arabia', *Current Trends in Islamist Ideology*, 10: 73–85. https://www.hudson.org/research/9895-the-shiites-of-saudi-arabia.

Theodore Karasik. (2018), 'The Separation of Mosque and State in Saudi Arabia?' *Center for Global Policy*. 20 March. https://cgpolicy.org/articles/the-separation-of-mosque-and-state-in-saudi-arabia/ (accessed 5 May 2020).

Tremblay, P. (2020), 'Erdogan's Cold War with Saudi Arabia and UAE'. *Al-Monitor*. 5 May. https://www.al-monitor.com/pulse/originals/2020/05/turkey-saudi-arabia-united-arab-emirates-conflict-escalating.html (accessed 5 May 2020).

Ulrichsen, K. C. (2011), 'Repositioning the GCC States in the Changing Global Order', *Journal of Arabian Studies*, 1 (2): 231–47.

Ulrichsen, K. C., and Sheline, A. R. (2019), *Mohammed bin Salman and Religious Authority and Reform in Saudi Arabia*, Issue brief, Houston: Rice University's Baker Institute for Public Policy.

Vassiliev, A. (2013), *The History of Saudi Arabia*, London: Saqi Books.

Wehrey, F. (2016), *Sectarian Politics in the Gulf: From the Iraq War to the Arab Uprisings*, New York: Columbia University Press.

Wehrey, F. (2014), 'The Roots and Future of Sectarianism in the Gulf'. *Project on Middle East Political Science (POMEPS)*. 21 March. https://pomeps.org/the-roots-and-future-of-sectarianism-in-the-gulf (accessed 10 June 2019).

Wehrey, F., and Ala' Alrababa'h. (2014), 'An Elusive Courtship: The Struggle for Iraq's Sunni Arab Tribes'. *Carnegie Middle East Center – DIWAN*. 7 November. https://carnegie-mec.org/diwan/57168 (accessed 10 February 2020).

Chapter 11

INSTITUTIONAL FAITH-BASED DIPLOMACY AND DE-SECTARIANIZATION IN THE MIDDLE EAST: HOW TO UNDERSTAND THE ROLE OF AL-AZHAR IN THE SUNNI–SHIʻI RAPPROCHEMENT?

Hossam Ed-Deen Allam

On 28 February 2017, Shaykh Aḥmad Kabalan, a representative of Lebanon's Shiʻi Higher Council, stated: 'Al-Azhar represents me and represents Qom (in Iran) and Najaf (in Iraq).' The statement was part of a speech that Kabalan delivered at the two-day international interfaith conference on 'Freedom and Citizenship: Diversity and Integration' organized by Al Azhar in Cairo. The Shiʻi official also called for a return of Egypt to its role as 'guide' of the Arab and Muslim world and invited Tehran and Riyadh to talk to each other (Al-Azhar 2017). Such a statement at such a conference embodies one of the manifestations of intra-Islamic dialogue and brings at the forefront the notion of Sunni–Shiʻi rapprochement, especially in light of the violence witnessed in a war-torn country such as Iraq, which is allegedly attributed wholly or partially to Islamic sectarianism.

This chapter is a sincere endeavour that seeks through employing an analytical approach to make a humble contribution towards a better academic understanding of the role of the over one-thousand-year-old Islamic institution of Al-Azhar and its thought in the Sunni–Shiʻi rapprochement and its potential role in de-sectarianization. It is hoped that the chapter will empower academic researchers to develop a better understanding of the nature of the increasing politically sharpened sectarianization of uprisings and conflicts in the Middle East. Additionally, it is hoped that this chapter will provide a stepping stone into embarking on a project that aims to produce conducive de-sectarianization and peace-building strategies. With that in mind, the chapter is structured along this line: Introduction, Early Muslim Scholars' Approach to Differences of Opinion, Tracing the Roots of the Sunni–Shiʻi Rapprochement, Mapping out the Role of Al-Azhar in the Sunni–Shiʻi Rapprochement, Significance of Shaykh Shaltūt's Fatwa on Shiʻi Madhāhib in 1959 AD, Al-Qaradāwi's Declaration of Principles Regarding Sunni–Shiʻi Rapprochement, A Critical Assessment of the Role of Al-Azhar in the Sunni–Shiʻi Rapprochement and De-sectarianization, and Conclusion.

Early Muslim scholars' approach to differences of opinion

Dialogue, deliberations and reconciliation attempts among different Islamic *Madhāhib* (streams of thought) have always been visible within the Muslim intellectual arena since the early centuries. Historically speaking, it is obvious to see what is referred to in Islamic heritage as *Masail ibn al-Azraq* (The Questions of ibn al-Azraq) as a precursor to laying the foundations of intra-Islamic dialogue. Essentially, these texts comprise the debates that took place between the companion 'Abd-Allah ibn Abbas (d. 68 AH) and the head of the khawarij (Outlaws of Islam) Nafi' ibn al-Azraq at the courtyard of the Holy Ka'ba. The questions are documented by the prominent linguist al-Mubarrid (d. 286 AH) in his well-known book entitled *Al-Kamil fi al-Luhga wa al-Adab* (The Sufficient in Language and Literature) (Al-Mubarrid 1998).

Conceivably, it is easy to recognize the status of dialogue and argumentation between the different schools of thought in the early centuries through the intellectual works that tackle dialogue, its premises, bases, rules, etiquettes, approaches, conditions and methods. Moreover, it is highly probable that the vivid intellectual movement among the founders of the various schools of thought was what drove Imam al-Haramain (the leader of the two holy mosques) al-Juwainy (d. 478 AH) to author his book *al-Kafiya fi al-Jadal* (The Adequate in Debates). It also motivated Abu Isḥāq al-Shirāzi (d. 476) to write *al-Mulakhas fil-Jadal fi Usul al-Fiqh* (The Brief in Debate Concerning the Sources of Islamic Jurisprudence), as well as other scholarly works. Further to this, during the fourth century AH several dialogues became notable, such as the debate of the Sunni Imam Abu Bakr Muhammad ibn al-Ṭayyib al-Baqillāni (d. 403 AH) with the prominent Twelver Shia theologian al-Shaykh al-Mufid (d. 413 AH), as well as the debate of the latter with the Imam of al-Mu'tazila, Judge Abd al-Jabbār (d. 415 AH) (Abu Zahra 1943).

Despite the fact that these debates were aimed in the first place to defeat the other party and to show intellectual prevalence, as such, they led to convergence and coming to terms with the opponents. For instance, such dialogues caused rapprochement and similarity between various Madhāhib regarding the terminology of the discipline of Usul al-Fiqh and its applications. In this regard, Shaykh al-Bouty has pointed out that: 'As much as the maxims of Usul al-Fiqh played a significant role over the past in the convergence of the *ijtihad* (independent legal reasoning) exercised within different Madhāhib, and even ending some differences, such maxims stand prominently at the present juncture to serve the same purpose' (Al-Bouty 2011).

Tracing the roots of the Sunni–Shi'i rapprochement

Taqrīb, rapprochement, is a term widely used to identify a broad stream within Islamic thought on the whole, and a movement with a view towards reconciliation between Sunni and Shi'i Muslims more specifically. Long before the current era, calls to bridge the Shi'i–Sunni schism occurred intermittently (Goldziher et al. 1981; Lapidus 2014). These calls took the form of individual initiatives as well as collective efforts from the Sunna and the Shi'a (Al-Qifāry 1993). While Abu Zahra maintains that the call for Taqrīb dates back to the sixth century AH and particularly to the individual efforts of the prominent Persian scholar of the Twelver school of Shi'a, Abu Ja'far Muhammad ibn Hassan al-Tūsi (d. 460 AH), Mahmūd Bassūni contests that it was Faḍl ibn Hassan al-Tabarsi (d. 548 AH) who laid the scholarly foundations of Taqrīb by relying on both Sunni and Shi'i sources in his work on the exegesis of the Qur'an entitled Majma' al-Bayan (The Comprehensive in Interpretation).[1]

However, in addition to the aforementioned scholarly rapprochement, historical sources mention older attempts of rapprochement that occurred during the fifth century AH. The first of them happened in the year 338 AH in the wake of a politically motivated strife that was witnessed for the first time in the history of Baghdad between the Sunna and the Shi'a in 437 AH (Ibn Kathīr 2018). Besides that, there were ruling authority-sponsored rapprochement attempts as well. For instance, the 'Abbasid caliph Al-Ma'mūn (d. 218 AH) appointed the widely Shi'a-supported Ali al-Rida (d. 203 AH) as his successor-to-be. In doing so, the former is reported to have sought to obtain the allegiance of those who believed that the latter was more worthy of being the Khalifa in addition to leaving no room for his opponents to instrumentalize the support for Ahl al-Bayt (the household of the Prophet Muhammad PBUH) to undermine his authority) Al-Musawi 2004(.

Likewise, one of the most remarkable rapprochement attempts on the basis of seeking the truth took place during the twelfth century AH under the auspices of Nader Shah (d. 1160 AH) of Iran. In 1149 AH, following full power assumption, Nader Shah conducted an endeavour for achieving rapprochement by means of an assembly in the city of Najaf that brought together Shi'i scholars (primarily from Iran) and Sunni scholars (primarily from the Hanafi school). This led to an agreement according to which the former consented to renounce the tradition of cursing the first three rightly guided Caliphs and the latter consented to acknowledge Twelver Imams' Shi'ism as a fifth Islamic madhhab, or school of thought (Avery et al. 1991; Kramer 1986; Lapidus 2014).

Mapping out the role of Al-Azhar in the Sunni–Shi'i rapprochement

The quest for rapprochement within Al-Azhar could be traced all the way back at the beginning of the nineteenth century by Shaykh Muhammad 'Abdu (d. 1905 AD), who had an ostensible inclination towards reconciliation between the Islamic Madhāhib. In this regard, 'Abdu was influenced by his teacher Shaykh Jamāl al-Din al-Afghāni (d. 1897 AD), who advocated unity among the various Islamic Madhāhib. Moreover, Shaykh Rashid Rida (d. 1935 AD), editor-in-chief of the Sunni revivalist magazine, al-Manār, met at the General Islamic Congress in Jerusalem in December 1931, with the Iraqi Shi'i jurist Muhammad al-Husain al-Kashif al-Ghita' and articulated his support of rapprochement. Noteworthily, al-Manār served as an open platform to all the schools of Islamic thought.

In the same spirit, during the early twentieth century (1911–36 AD), both the Shaykh of Al-Azhar Salīm al-Bishri al-Maliki and the prominent Shiʻi Twelver scholar ʻAbd al-Husain Sharaf al-Dīn al-Musawi pushed forward the boundaries of rapprochement. In 1331 AH, they had the opportunity to concretize their views on Muslim harmony. Al-Musawi travelled to Egypt and encountered al-Bishri, the Shaykh of Al-Azhar Mosque. The fruit of their exchange of opinions and longtime exchange of letters was the book *al-Murajaʻāt* (The Reviews) which was published in 1936.

The book comprises 112 correspondences between al-Bishri and al-Musawi. The correspondences are primarily focused on the question of Khilafa and Imama from a Shiʻi frame of reference; Sunni and Shiʻi rationales are investigated and critiqued in this book in light of the verses of the Holy Qur'an and the authoritative sources of Sunni hadith compilations (Al-Musawi 2007). The book is written on the basis of mutual respect and away from any discourtesy or contempt. This work is one of the most significant books that presents a well-argued narrative of Shiʻi beliefs, drawing upon sources with a voice that seeks to persuade. The book is also entitled 'al-Munazarāt al-Azhariya wa al-Mubahathāt al-Misriyya' (Debates in Al-Azhar and Discussions in Egypt) (Al-Islam 2019). However, it is worth mentioning that there are certain doubts about the book's authenticity, particularly in light of the fact that the book was only published following the passing away of al-Bishri. Additionally, the son of al-Bishri denied the occurrence of any correspondence between his late father and al-Musawi.

Observably, one of the initiatives that the Shi'i scholar Al-Musawi took to advance Sunni–Shiʻi rapprochement was the choice of the 12th of Rabi' al-Awwal to commemorate the birth of Prophet Muhammad (PBUH) instead of the 17th of Rabi' al-Awwal. He purposefully chose this date since it was the one identified by the Sunni Muslims, and he aspired to foster harmony between all the Shiʻi and Sunni Muslims. Following commemoration of this occasion with his students in his mosque, al-Musawi used to go to the Sunnis to celebrate the event with them. During the pilgrimage season of 1922 (1340 AH), al-Musawi received an invitation from King Hussain, the King of Arabia, to lead the congregational prayers in the Holy Mosque in Mecca, where both Sunni and Shiʻi Muslims were present (Al-Musawi 2007).

The most significant of these endeavours yet was the Jamaʻat al-Taqrīb bayna al-Madhhib al-Islamiyya (The Society for Rapprochement among Islamic Schools of Jurisprudence), which was established in 1947 AD. Its principal professed aim was to bring Sunna and Shiʻa closer together and to eliminate the sectarian tendency in the schools of thought while maintaining the schools themselves. Established and run by a Shi'i Iranian named Muhammad Taqi al-Qummi (d. 1990 AD), it obtained the support of a number of prominent Sunni ʻulama' (scholars) and intellectuals in Egypt and beyond. To wit: two rectors from Al-Azhar University, Shaykh ʻAbd a-Majīd Salīm (d. 1954 AD) and Shaykh Maḥmūd Shaltūt (d. 1963).

In 1949 AD, the Jama'a's journal, Risalat al-Islam, was launched. In that journal, both Shi'i and Sunni writers were provided with the platform to put into words conceptions and points of view in support of *Rapprochement*. Yet, almost all of them shied away from addressing the essential controversial issues between Shi'is and Sunnis. The most noteworthy achievement of the Taqrīb society was the issuance of a fatwa[2] (legal opinion) by Shaykh Maḥmūd Shaltūt on 6 July 1959. The key effect of the fatwa was to confirm that performing acts of worship according to the madhhab of the Twelver Shi'a, Ithna 'Ashariyya, is valid, and the madhhab is fully recognized within the boundaries of Islam.

The significance of Shaykh Shaltūt's fatwa on Shi'a Madhāhib in 1959 AD

In an attempt to situate Shaltūt within the context of recent Muslim scholarship and to identify his contributions in many areas, it is noteworthy that he was the first-ever Shaykh of Al-Azhar to be called *Al-Imam Al-Akbar* (The Grand Shaykh of Al-Azhar). The tendency towards flexibility and tolerance that is apparent in his approach to numerous religious and social questions would seem to stem primarily from an inherent eagerness to make easy for Muslims the practice of their faith-based commitments than from any reported intellectual methodology or framework. As a matter of principle, Shaltūt's literary works and stances reflect him to be a scrupulous scholar, cultivated first and foremost within the parameters prescribed by his traditional religious training at Al-Azhar. Moreover, his scholarly works are permeated by a profound ethical and religious attitude, and the manifestation of this may take precedence over any mere intellectual vindication of his legal opinions (Al-Bayyoumi 2019; Imara 2011; Zebiri 1993).

The significance of Shaltūt's fatwa in question is augmented by the fact that he assumed the position of the Grand Shaykh Al-Azhar. In spite of vicissitudes in the degree of Al-Azhar's independence and funds, it continues to be appreciated as one of the most renowned seats of Sunni authority in the Muslim world. It holds international pan-Islamic conferences, hosts international students and its Fatwa Committee, instituted in 1935, provides answers to the questions of Muslims from across the four corners of the globe (Brown 2011; Dodge 1962).

Maḥmūd Shaltūt became the Grand Shaykh of Al-Azhar at a crucial time for Egyptian affairs in general, and Al-Azhar in particular, from the year 1958 to 1963. In Egypt and elsewhere, it had become clear that the waves of modernization were exceeding the forces of traditionalism, and the influence of the '*ulama*' was no longer what it had been (Hefner 2010; 'Ināyat 1982).[3] As early as 1931, Shaltūt himself was one of a limited number of reform-oriented *ulama who* were expelled by King Fouad from Al-Azhar for their pro-renewal and reform campaigning activities. His appointment could be attributed to his supportive attitude concerning the question of reforming Al-Azhar. Whereas the enforcement of such reforms from outside Al-Azhar by the executive authority under Naser could be interpreted as a form of disrespect to the Azhari scholars, Shaltūt ratified the reforms officially. It could be deduced that this stood as the sole available option for Shaltūt to maintain his position and to deal with critical circumstances. However, Shaltūt must also have discerned that owing to the traditionalist *ulama's* persistent resistance to calls for reform over the preceding decades, they denied themselves the latitude to have their say on the reforms that were ultimately enforced. Besides, whereas certain parts of the reform package could be meant to undermine the independence of Al-Azhar, other parts were in line with the calls of Shaltūt and other Azhari *ulama*. Such parts encompass updating the curricula and the cancellation of the dualism of the educational system, which had escalated between the system of religious schools and colleges on the one hand, and the mostly secular state-run system of education on the other, in addition to the will to end Al-Azhar's isolation and establish ties with other nations and institutions, as well as to provide wider job opportunities for Al-Azhar graduates.

Shaltūt differed from the preceding holders of the banner of reform, such as Muhammad 'Abduh (d. 1905) and Rashid Rida (d. 1935), in being wholly trained in traditional religious education with no study of any foreign language. Therefore, he was more immune to the blunt influence of Western thought.[4] Furthermore, that afforded his works, contrary to some of his counterparts, the value of being free from the requirement to attempt to explain Islamic ordinances in light of prevalent Western values and social patterns (Imara 2011; Smith 1977).

Shaltūt's scholarly works

Shaltūt was a prolific author. His most well-known published works include:[5] *Al-Islam: Aqeeda wa Sharia*, which is dedicated primarily to the Islamic Sharia concerning the sources of Islamic jurisprudence and numerous legal issues; and *Tafsir al-Qur'an al-Karim: al-Ajza' al-'Ashara al-Ola*, a Qur'anic exegesis that treads the path of al-Tafsīr al-Mawdū'i (Thematic Style of Interpretation). Additionally, there exists a specialized treatise on comparative jurisprudence designed as a guidebook for the students of the faculty of Sharia at Al-Azhar University. Additionally, he was a frequent contributor to many Muslim journals, particularly Majallat Al-Azhar, and he regularly conducted interviews with several magazines and newspapers. He also broadcasted radio talks on religious topics, some of which are recorded in his published works. Among his students who have indisputably benefited from him are Shaykh Yusuf al-Qaradāwi (b. 1926) and Muhammad al-Madani. Both are respected Muslim scholars (Imara 2011). Shaltūt himself was a popular Azhari scholar, and his name remains well-known to informed Muslims and academic non-Muslims throughout the world.

Shaltūt's legal opinions represent a genuine endeavour to counter some of the acute concerns confronting Muslims in the age of modernity. Along with exhibiting a deep appreciation of the eternal values of Islam, he was keen to maintain the element of continuity which safeguards the characteristic identity of Muslims. Following in the footsteps of 'Abdu, Shaltūt figured out that it was best to effect reform within the institution. He dedicated much of his time to partaking in bodies that focused on different areas of academic research, reform of Al-Azhar and Muslim welfare. He worked on enhancing the guiding role of the ulama by boosting channels of communication with common Muslims deprived of education. This pursuit manifests itself in his works, which integrate simple phraseology with heart-touching eloquence, not solely regarding general religious writings but in his fatawa and tafsīr as well. One of his most remarkable efforts was resuming the trajectory of 'Abdu and others in the elucidation and popularization of the sharia disciplines. The great demand for this type of guidance may be deduced from the popularity of his book on fatawa (Islamic Legal Opinions), which by 1983 had reached its 12th edition.

Shaltūt's impact on the path of rapprochement

Shaltūt's work is saturated with the earnest keenness to accomplish and maintain Muslim unity. During the last twenty-five years of his lifetime, he was meticulously engaged in the forward-looking activities and works of the aforementioned Taqrīb Society. In his capacity as the Grand Shaykh of Al-Azhar, Shaltūt issued a controversial[6] *fatwa* in 1958 declaring that performing acts of worship according to a Shi'i *madhhab* is as valid as is worship according to a Sunni *madhhab*. Investigative research suggests that Shaltūt did actually issue this fatwa, despite the doubts of senior figures. The text of the fatwa can be found in *Risalat al-Islam* magazine, which was issued by the Taqrīb Society in Cairo. It was entitled *Fatwa Tarikhiyya* (Historic Fatwa). The preface of that issue reads: 'The first page of this issue is dedicated to the historic statement of his Eminence the Grand Shaykh of Al-Azhar, Maḥmūd Shaltūt, the Shaykh of Al-Azhar Mosque, may Allah bless his life and bless the benefiting of the Muslim umma from his knowledge, virtues, and his noble deeds.' Following Shaltūt's clarification concerning the new curricula of the Faculty of Sharia at Al-Azhar University, his fatwa ensued as follows:

His Eminence was asked:
Some individuals maintain that to ensure the validity of one's acts of worship and financial transactions, a Muslim is necessitated to emulate one of the well-known four Madhāhib (Hanafi, Maliki, Shafi'i, and Hanbali), to the exclusion of the madhab of al-Shia al-Imamiyyah as well as that of al-Shi'a al-Zaidiyah. Does Your Eminence support this opinion in every respect? Thus, declaring unlawful following the madhab of al-Shi'a al-Imamiyyah al-Ithna Ashariyyah (i.e., The Twelver Imami Shi'a), for instance?
His Eminence replied:
1) Islam does not oblige a Muslim to adhere to a particular Madhhab. Instead, we say: every Muslim has the right to follow one of the schools of thought, which has been authentically narrated, and its verdicts have been authenticated in its reliable books. Moreover, every individual who is following such Madhāhib can transfer to another school, and there shall be no blame on him or her in doing so.

2) The Ja'fari Madhhab, which is also identified as 'al-Shia al-Imamiyah al-Ithna 'Ashariyah' is a madhab that is permissible and valid to follow regarding acts of worship as are other Sunni Madhāhib.

Muslims are ought to be aware of this and must rid themselves of the unjust partisanship to any specific Madhāhib. Islam and its shari'a were never dependent on or exclusive to a certain madhab. Al-Mujtahidūn (those who are qualified to exercise independent legal reasoning) are accepted in the sight of Almighty Allah, and it is permissible to the non-Mujtahid to act in accordance with what they have established in the jurisprudence be it regarding acts of worship or financial transactions. (Shaltūt 1959)

In reality, the text of this fatwa was initially a verbal statement from Shaykh Shaltūt. During an interview for Al-Hayat newspaper in 1959, Shaltūt announced his intention to effect a rapprochement between the Madhāhib and to incorporate the study of the Shi'i jurisprudence into the new curricula of the Faculty of Shari'a at Al-Azhar University. Henceforth, the representative of Al-Sha'b magazine, Mahmūd Slima, raised that question, and the Shaykh answered as previously mentioned. Afterwards, the Risalat al-Islam magazine reported the statement under the title of Fatwa Tarikhiyya (Historic Fatwa), and later on Al-Azhar magazine published it under the title of *Bayna al-Sunna wa al-Shi'a* (Between the Sunna and the Shi'a). Shortly afterwards, *al-Mujtama' 'al-A'rabi* (The Arab Society) magazine published a dialogue with Shaltūt, which was also fully republished by Al-Azhar magazine, including the following query:

Does the teaching of the Shi'a madhab mean it is valid for application, or is it only meant to enhance the legal capacity of the learners?

Shaltūt replied: At Al-Azhar we are not only interested in theoretical knowledge, but also we are keen on comprehension and acting according to what is proven to be valid. Our legal system has already adopted some of the rulings based on the Shi'i jurisprudence, many of our scholars have approved some of its worship-related rulings, and we, in principle, follow the authority of the Qur'an and the Sunna. Therefore, as long as a given legal opinion does not irreconcilably contradict an explicit authoritative text, it becomes permissible to be followed. This is the aspired rapprochement and the praiseworthy elucidation. (Al-Azhar 1959; Al-Mujtama' 1959)

The fatwa steered many reactions both for and against its juridical value. One of the leading Sunni supporters was Muhammad al-Bahi (d. 1982), who wrote in support of the fatwa an article entitled *Ma'a al-Madhahib al-Islamiyya* (With the Islamic Schools of Thought) (Al-Bahi 1959). In the same issue, Shaykh Mahmūd al-Sharqawi wrote an article entitled *Al-Azhar wa al-Madhahib al-Fiqhiyya* (Al-Azhar and the Schools of Islamic Jurisprudence) (Al-Sharqawi 1959). In the subsequent issue of Risalat al-Islam journal, the Shi'i scholar Muhammad Taqi al-Qumi, secretary general of the Taqrīb society, wrote an article entitled Qissat *al-Taqrīb* (The Story of the Rapprochement), praising the fatwa and Shaltūt's efforts in rapprochement (Al-Qumi 1959). In the same issue, both Shaykh Muhammad al-Madani (d. 1959), the editor-in-chief of Risalat Al-Islam and the dean of Al-Azhar University's Faculty of Sharī'a at the time, as well as Shaykh Muhammad al-Ghazali (d. 1996) wrote in support of Shaltūt's fatwa. While the former wrote an article entitled *Rajjat al-Ba'th fi Kuliyyat al-Shari'a* (The Revival of the Faculty of Sharia) addressing the claims of the opponents of this particular fatwa, the latter wrote an article entitled *'Ala Awal al-Tariq* (The Beginning of the Road) defending the fatwa and discussing the claims of its opponents in his frequent entertaining writing style (Al-Ghazali 1959; Al-Madani 1959).

Within the framework of traditional Islamic scholarship, and not overlooking his seat as head of one of the principal strongholds of that scholarship, Shaltūt could be viewed as forward-thinking regarding his opinions on Muslim rapprochement and unity. He was keen on the circumvention of theological altercation, the inclination to circumscribe the realm of the *haram* (unlawful) and the application of the term *kafir* (disbeliever), and the desire to make Islamic scholarship accessible to all the Muslim communities. Concerning these aspects, he pursued, sustained and advanced the pioneering reform project of Muhammad 'Abdu (d. 1905 AD), his Shaykh Jamal al-Din al-Afghani (d. 1897) and others. Noteworthily, in 2005, Dar al-Iftaa al-Misriyya (Egypt's House of Fatwa) issued a fatwa to the same effect of that by Shaltūt's and even invoked the essence of Shaltūt's ruling as one of the principles on which the subsequent fatwa is based (Dar-al-Iftaa 2011) (see Appendix B).

For political reasons, more than anything else, the Taqrīb Society lost much of its momentum from 1960 onwards. The Iranian Revolution of 1979 and the subsequent disruption of diplomatic relations with the Arab Republic of Egypt marked the end of the joint project once and for all. The Taqrīb Society was dissolved, and its founder, Muhammad Taqi al-Qummi, himself was sent into exile in Paris, where he passed away in 1990 (Brünner 2004). In 2006, however, Al-Azhar reopened the Taqrīb Society. In this regard, Shaykh Maḥmūd 'Ashur (d. 2018), the representative of Al-Azhar, is reported to have stated that

> The mission of this society is to achieve reconciliation and bring together the followers of the one Umma of Islam. The difference between Sunna and Shi'a is primarily of a jurisprudential nature, and it must not cause discord between us. We may differ regarding some issues, but we are in agreement concerning the core principles. We believe in the oneness of Allah, the holiness of the Qur'an, and in Prophet Muhammad (PBUH). The resumption of Sunni-Shi'i dialogue cannot be postponed. If we believe in interfaith dialogue, then how can we neglect dialogue with our Shi'i brothers? (Al-Sharq al-'Awsat 2006)

From that point onwards, the official Al-Azhar institution's degree of engagement in pursuing rapprochement has been in decline. However, there exist notable attempts by Azhari graduates operating outside the institution. One significant example in this context is Shaykh Yusuf al-Qaradāwi.

Al-Qaradāwī's declaration of principles regarding Sunni–Shi'i rapprochement

As a Muslim scholar who graduated from Al-Azhar, al-Qaradāwī (b. 1926) has proven to be very well-known and authoritative all over the Muslim world, which makes his engagement in pursuing Sunni–Shi'i rapprochement noteworthy. He represents a vociferous advocate of *Wasatiyya*[7] (Centrism), a stream of thought that emerged out of the contemporary Islamic reawakening. From its proponent's perspective, it combines *Salafiyya* (a return to ancestral roots) and *Tajdid* (renewal in Muslim thought), and thus embodies a suggested third way forward for the Muslim Umma. It is just intuitive that given his education at Al-Azhar, he should strive to be engaged in such a pivotal issue as the Sunna–Shi'a rapprochement.

Al-Qaradāwī has served as the head of the International Union of Muslim Scholars (IUMS), which was founded in 2004 aiming to conjoin jurisprudential opinions on the main concerns that the Muslim Umma faces, with a view to forewarn them against the dangers that lurk ahead. Al-Qaradāwī's Declaration of Principles for Rapprochement among the jurisprudential schools appears to be an integral part of this endeavour. It can even be said that he presents himself as the representative of Sunni Islam in the eyes of the Muslim Umma including the Shi'a, which obliges him as an influential scholar to take a realistic and flexible stance (IUMS 2015; Skovgaard Petersen and Bettina 2009).

Al-Qaradāwī published a *Declaration of Principles* for dialogue and rapprochement among Islamic jurisprudential schools, leading up to his partaking in the Conference for Rapprochement among the Muslim Jurisprudential Schools, held in Bahrain in 2004. Al-Qaradāwī's principles demonstrate a pragmatic approach that deals with the eventualities of the current Muslim countries, which witness a severe *fitna* (internal discord) between Sunnis and Shi'as, while the Muslim world is threatened by external enemies against whom Muslims must stand united. He fleshed out ten core principles, which once directed the endeavours of Jama'at al-Taqrīb. The ten principles that al-Qaradāwī has itemized are: (1) Proper understanding; (2) Proper consideration; (3) Focus on common grounds; (4) Dialogue over what is disputed; (5) Avoidance of provocation; (6) Abstaining from heretication (*takfir*) of those who testify 'There is no deity worthy of worship except Allah'; (7) Avoidance of religious exaggeration and extremism; (8) Speaking frankly and addressing problems wisely; (9) Cautiousness against the schemes of the external enemy; (10) Solidarity in times of hardship (Al-Qaradāwī 2005).

It is worth noting that al-Qaradāwī views the purpose of rapprochement in much the same way that it is exhibited in the rapprochement literature. He maintains that Sunna and Shi'a do not necessarily have to blend. Rather, the objective is to dissipate the clouds of extreme thinking and mistrust between Sunnis and Shi'a. Additionally, al-Qaradāwī considers Shi'a to be religious innovators, but not kuffar; therefore, it follows in his view that Sunna and Shi'a diverge over 'branches of religion', but not over 'roots of faith'. In this respect, the centrists are completely contrary to the Wahabi thought, which views the Shi'a as being out of the fold of Islam.

A critical assessment of the role of Al-Azhar in the Sunni–Shi'i rapprochement and de-sectarianization

The observer of Al-Azhar's activities, its published literature and the works of its scholars can discern that it possesses an established academic credibility, has an unparalleled history and has been occupying such a renowned status in the Arab and Muslim realms for literally centuries. Additionally, it has been one of the most, if not the first, sought-after Islamic learning centres worldwide, at least as far as Sunni Islam is concerned. Recently, Al-Azhar has been playing a significant role on the global arena, particularly concerning the efforts to dismantle and counter the ramifications of the rise of violent extremism around the globe. The Islamic educational institution has participated in international conferences and has been involved in joint initiatives and programmes to assist the global effort against violence. In April 2019, for instance, at a press conference held at Al-Azhar headquarters in the wake of a meeting with the Grand Imam of Al-Azhar, the UN Secretary General, Guterres, hailed the initiatives taken by Al-Azhar to promote awareness of the true face of Islam and counter the propaganda of violent extremism (UN 2019). Moreover, in February 2019 several global leaders and policymakers praised the '*Document on Human Fraternity for World Peace and Living Together*'. Essentially, it is a joint statement signed by the Grand Imam of Al-Azhar, Prof. Al-Tayyeb, and Pope Francis of the Vatican. The document is the fruit of a brotherly frank dialogue between Francis and Al-Tayyeb, and it is intended to serve as a guide to promote a 'culture of mutual respect and peaceful coexistence'(The Guardian 2019; WOAG 2019).

Clearly, all this activity highlights the potential role of Al-Azhar in de-sectarianization, conflict amelioration, and peace-building. In fact, out of recognition for that potential role, in January 2014, the government of the ex-CAR-President, Catherine Panza, sent an official request to Al-Azhar, among several global actors, to effectuate national reconciliation (Al-Ahram 2015). In response, Al-Azhar dispatched a peace mission to attain that aim (ibid.). Remarkably, in December 2014, Panza paid an official visit to Al-Azhar, during which she discussed with the Grand Imam, Al-Tayyeb, the aspects of cooperation between CAR and Al-Azhar, including increasing the scholarships offered to CAR students to join Al-Azhar (ibid.). While it is true that the activity of Al-Azhar has attracted the global media, this section aims to academically and critically assess specifically the role of Al-Azhar in the Sunni–Shi'i rapprochement and de-sectarianization.

The vision that Al-Azhar stands for, the fatwas that it officially issues and the discourse that it promotes exhibit a high level of rationalization and awareness of the nature of human societies. Overall, its stances seek to maintain a balance between the essential principles of Islam and its major objectives on the one hand, and what the global human community has collectively established as fundamental human necessities and rights on the other. Similar to other major institutions of various faith traditions, Al-Azhar has demonstrated keenness on spreading the values of peaceful coexistence and resorting to constructive dialogue for conflict management and peace-building. At this point of juncture, the voice of Al-Azhar is needed for achieving de-sectarianization in different parts of the world, as well as confronting the rising waves of Islamophobia and violent extremism perpetrated in the name of Islam.

The involvement of Al-Azhar institutionally in pursuing Sunni–Shi'i rapprochement witnessed two major phases; while the first phase was characterized by a tendency to bring together the Sunni Madhāhib and the Ja'fari madhab, the second phase is dominated by a rivalry over who represents the authentic voice of Islam. The condition of Taqrīb today is not at its best due to the intensified political rivalry of who has the upper hand in the Mideast. Moreover, because of the instrumentalization of Al-Azhar to cement the foreign policies of the Egyptian state, the statements of the current Grand Shaykh of Al-Azhar, al-Tayyeb, have been permeated with inconsistency and his stance shifted towards almost a full halt of the activities of Dar al-Taqrīb. His predecessor, Tantawy, had a similar stance as he declined an invitation to attend a conference in Tehran on the importance of intra-Islam dialogue in 2009. In doing so, Tantawy invoked the political conditions between Egypt and Iran on the one hand, and the tense relations with Hezbollah in the wake of arresting a Hezbollah-affiliated cell in Egypt in 2019.

Conclusion

Overall, Al-Azhar's involvement in pursuing Sunni–Shi'i rapprochement stands as a significant example of a faith-based diplomacy[8] approach. Furthermore, the role played by Al-Azhar and in particular the fatwa of Shaykh Shaltūt tends to support a growing literature in IR that challenges the paradigm of 'ancient sectarian animosity' to explain the turmoil in the Middle East. The very fact that the Grand Shaykh of Al-Azhar has issued a fatwa to the effect that the Shia schools of thought are in line with the Sunni ones as far as the essence of Islam is concerned shows that it is not merely a form of sectarianism that stands behind the war-torn Middle East. Rather, it is primarily owing to 'an active process of sectarianization shaped by political actors operating within specific contexts, pursuing political goals that involve the mobilization of popular sentiments around particular identity markers' (Postel et al. 2017: 4). Moreover, the fatwa has created a scope for dialogue within the formal and informal institutions, which in turn can be utilized for meaningful diplomatic engagement.

The one major issue that hurts the reputation of Al-Azhar and undermines its credibility, which it has acquired over the centuries, and the potential game-changing role it could effect in terms of Sunni–Shi'i rapprochement is its political instrumentalization in the context of internal and external disputes. Al-Azhar needs full independence to be in a position to live up to the expectations of both Muslims and non-Muslims worldwide. It needs to have the freedom to exercise its authority over its own affairs and to express its position on the issues and causes that pertain to Muslims and non-Muslims in Egypt and worldwide. However, if the political authority continues to interfere overtly and covertly in the decision-making of Al-Azhar and its scholars, and persists in viewing Al-Azhar as merely a political card to serve its domestic and foreign interests, then the intellectual, spiritual, social and cultural influence of Al-Azhar will keep eroding. Thus, Al-Azhar will eventually seize to hold its credibility in the eyes of the Muslims and will not be able to accomplish the aforementioned aspired role.

Notes

1 However, al-Tabarsi acknowledged that in doing so, he was following al-Tūsi's approach in his exegesis entitled *al-Tebyān* (The Clarification) (Abu Zahra, 2005). Henceforth, al-Tūsi was the forerunner in this regard, and therefore Abu Zahra's opinion is more plausible.
2 A *fatwa* is a non-binding legal opinion, usually in the format of a written question and answer. Technically, a fatwa is defined as clarifying the ruling of God for a legal case based on legal evidence for an inquirer (Abu Zahra, 2001). *Fatwa*s are issued orally or in writing. They constitute such extremely valuable sources for the history of Muslim communities, its living discursive traditions and the religious life of Muslim individuals.
3 In 1952, what is commonly known as 'the Free Officers' Revolution' brought about wide-ranging repercussions for Al-Azhar as well as other Islamic institutions in Egypt. Due to several reasons, the *'ulama'* were largely supportive of the newly born regime and its pro-socialism agenda. From the ruling regime's standpoint, the vivid potency of the Muslim movement posed an existential threat to be reckoned with and represented such a valuable ally to win. When Jamāl Abd al-Nasir (d. 1970 AD) became the president of Egypt, he introduced a series of measures to extend dominance over the Muslim movement in Egypt. Among the primary tactics was the repression of the Ikhwān (Muslim Brotherhood), which posed an ideological threat to the new regime, which the Ikhwān deemed as falling short of being a truly Islamic regime. Further to that, in pursuit of instituting a unified judicial system under state control, new laws were passed to the effect of abolishing the autonomous *Sharia* courts in 1956. Subsequently, in 1961, the military regime found itself in a position to curb Al-Azhar institutionally, and a reformation law was enforced upon it. This infamous law rendered a drastic reorganization of Al-Azhar; with the establishment of a Supreme Council and other new bodies, it was the regime that held the lion's share of power, and the powers of Shaykh Al-Azhar were greatly diminished. This reorganization trailed a persistent campaign of attacks against the *'ulama'*, mainly through regime-controlled journalism.
4 However, this does not mean that he was not aware of the impact of the Western culture particularly on young generations and, actually, when Shaltūt became the Grand Shaykh of Al-Azhar he supervised the introduction of acquiring foreign languages, namely, English and French into the curricula of Al-Azhar (Imara 2011; Shaltūt 2001).
5 For more on Shaltūt's works, see the relevant part in the bibliography.
6 Shaykh Yusuf Al-Qaradāwi, head of the World Union of Muslim Scholars, confirmed that there is no fatwa for Shaykh Shaltūt, the former Shaykh of Al-Azhar, to allow worship according to the Ja'fari madhab. This was during a symposium between al-Qaradāwi and a group of youth attending the training programme of 'Future Scholars' organized by the World Union of Muslim Scholars in Cairo. Towards the end

of the symposium, one of the present journalists asked him 'If Shaykh Shaltūt, may Allah have mercy on him, had really issued a fatwa with the permission to perform the acts of worship on the basis of the Shi'i Ja'fari Madhab.' Al-Qaradāwi answered: 'I tell you: bring me this fatwa … in which of his books it exists? … I have not seen this fatwa! … Can anyone of you say I have seen it in a certain book or magazine?!' (IslamOnline 2018).

7   It should be pointed out that the *Wasatiyya* school of thought spearheaded by al-Qaradāwi is in essence a critique of the performance of al-Azhar over recent years. Its statement of principles, drafted and first published in 1991, reads as follows in this respect: 'We cannot afford to be headless of the lamentable regression in capability exhibited by those institutions [referring to al-Azhar and other religious institutions of education], a regression because of which they are no longer able to fulfil their mission as expected given the new reality of Muslim communities and the entire world.'

8   Faith-based diplomacy refers to incorporating faith-related affairs and concerns into the solution in some of the intricate and identity-based conflicts that exceed the grasp of traditional diplomacy (Johnston 2006).

References

Arabic sources

Abu Zahra, M. (1943), *Tareekh al-Jadal (The History of Debate)*, 1st edn. Cairo: Dar al-Fikr al-Arabi.

Abu Zahra, M. (2001), *Usul al-Fiqh*, 1st edn. Cairo: Dar al-Fikr al-Arabi.

Abu Zahra, M. (2005), *Al-Imam al-Sadiq*, 1st edn. Cairo: Dar al-Fikr al-Arabi.

Al-Ahram (2015). *With the Aim of Confronting Terrorism, Al-Azhar Lights Up the World with "Peace Convoys"*. Issue 46972. 15 July 2015. Available online: https://gate.ahram.org.eg/daily/News/121601/3/414530/%D8%AA%D8%A %D9%82%D9%8A%D9%82%D8%A7%D8%AA/%D8%A8%D9%87%D8%AF%D9%81-%D9%85%D9%88%D8%A7%D8%AC%D9%87%D8%A9-%D8%A7%D9%84%D8%A5%D8%B1%D9%87%D8%A7%D8%A8%D8%A7%D9%84%D8%A3%D8%B2%D9%87%D8%B1-%D9%8A%D8%B6%D9%89%D8%A1-%D8%A7%D9%84%D8%B9%D8%A7%D9%84%D9%85-%D8%A8%D9%80-%C2%AB%D9%82%D9%88%D8%A7%D9%81%D9%84-%D8%A7%D9%84.aspx (accessed 25 July 2023).

Al-Azhar al-Shareef (2017), كلمة أحمد قبلان، ممثل رئيس المجلس الشيعي الأعلى في لبنان خلال مؤتمر الحرية والمواطنة *(The Speech of Ahmad Kabalan, Representative of the Head of Lebanon's Shia Higher Council, during the Conference on 'Freedom and Citizenship'*. 10 February 2017. Available online: https://www.youtube.com/watch?v=BWKfWHi3LLk (accessed 3 April 2019).

Al-Azhar Magazine (1959), vol. 31, Issue no. 2, p. 362, August, Cairo.

Al-Bahi, M. (1959), *Ma'a al-Madhāhib al-Islamia (With the Islamic Schools of Thought)*. *Majalit al-Azhar*, April 1959. 2nd edn, 137–41.

Al-Bayyoumi, M. (2019), *Al-Imam Maḥmūd Shaltūt al-Faqhi al-Muslih al-Mujadid (Imam Maḥmūd Shaltūt Jurisprudent and Reformer*, 1st edn. Cairo: Majlis Hukama al-Muslimeen.

Al-Bouty, M. (2011), *Qawa'id Tafseer al-Nssous wa Atharuha fi al-Taqrīb bayna al-Madhāhib wa al-Firaq (The rules of text interpretation and their imapat on rapprochement between the schools of thought)*. *Majalit al-Taqrīb*, 1st

Release, 60–72. 16 January 2011. Available online: https://www.taghribn
ews.com/ar/news/36978/%D9%82%D9%88%D8%A7%D8%B9%D8%AF-
%D8%AA%D9%81%D8%B3%D9%8A%D8%B1-%D8%A7%D9%84%D9%86%D
8%B5%D9%88%D8%B5-%D9%88%D8%A3%D8%AB%D8%B1%D9%87%D
8%A7-%D9%81%D9%8A-%D8%A7%D9%84%D8%AA%D9%82%D8%B1%D9%8A
%D8%A8-%D8%A8%D9%8A%D9%86-%D8%A7%D9%84%D9%85%D8%B0%D8
%A7%D9%87%D8%A8-%D9%88%D8%A7%D9%84%D9%81%D8%B1%D9%82
(accessed May 2020).
Al-Ghazali, M. (1959), *'Ala Awael al-Tariq (The Beginning of the Road). Risalat al-Islam*,
Issue 4th vol 11, September 1959. 412–16.
Al-Islam. (2019), *Al-Muraja'at*. Available online: https://www.al-islam.org/al-muraj
aat-shii-sunni-dialogue-sharaf-al-din-al-musawi (accessed 2 April 2019).
Al-Madani, M. (1959), *Rajjat Al-Baa'th fi Kulliat al-Sharia (The Revival of the Faculty of
Sharia). Risalat Al-Islam*, Issue 4th, 373–88.
Al-Mubarid, M. (1998), *Al-Kamil fi al-Luhga wa al-Adab*, 1st edn. KSA: Al-Awqaf
al-Saudiya.
Al-Mujtama' al-'Arabi Magazine (1959), Issue No. 32, August.
Al-Musawi, A. (2004), *Al-Mujaz min Hayat A'imat Ahl al-bait (The Brief on the
Biographies of the Imams of the Household of the Prophet)*, 1st edn. Baghdad: Dar
al-Murtada.
Al-Musawi, A. (2007), *Al-Muraja'āt*, 1st edn. Beirut: Dar al-Quari for Publication.
Al-Qaradāwi, Y. (2005), *Mabadi' Fi al-Hiwar wa al-Taqrīb bayna al-Madhāhib
al-Islamiyya*, 1st edn. Cairo: Maktabat Wahba.
Al-Qifary, N. (1993), *Masalit al-Taqrīb bayna Ahl al-Sunna wa al-Shia (The Issue of
Rapprochement between al-Sunna wa al-Shia)*, 2nd edn. Riyadh: Dar Tayba.
Al-Qumi, M. (1959), *Qissat al-Taqrīb (The Story of the Rapprochement)*. Risalat al-Islam,
4th, Cario. 348–59.
Al-Sharq al-Awsat. (2006), *Dar Al-Taqrīb bayna al-Madhhib al-Islamiyya (The Society for
Rapprochement among Islamic Legal Schools)*. Available online: http://archive.aawsat.
com/details.asp?article=392788&issueno=10218 (accessed 13 April 2019).
Al-Sharqawi, M. (1959), *Al-Azhar wa al-Madhāhib al-Islamiya (Al-Azhar and the schools
of Islamic Jurisprudence)*. Majalit Al-Azhar, Cairo. 2nd edn, 142–6. Al-Azhar
Dar-aliftaa, A. (2011), *Encyclopedia of Islamic Fatwa*, 1st edn, 7–11, Vol. 38. Cairo: Dar
al-Iftaa.
Ibn Kathīr, I. (2018), *Al-Bedaya wa al-Nehaya*, 5th edn. Beirut: Dar Ibn Hazm.
Imara, M. (2011), *Sheik Shaltūt: Imam fi al-Ijtihad wa al-Tajdeed (Sheik Shaltūt: A pioneer
in Independent Legal Reasoning and Renewal)*, 1st edn. Cairo: Dar al-Salām.
IslamOnline. (2018), *Al-Qaradawy: No Fatwa for Shaltūt on Worship Based on the Jafari
Madhab*. Available online: https://archive.islamonline.net/?p=5449&fbclid=IwAR0do
_o_Nbef-bGDaRKwGZo2KhVk9SG2HWE-t4pOwhr_VAfKFe9MdIUNeD4 (accessed
6 April 2019).
IUMS International Union of Muslim Scholars. (2015), International Union of Muslim
Scholars Project. Available online: http://iumsonline.org/en/ContentDetails.
aspx?ID=8151 (accessed 13 April 2019).
Shaltūt, M. (1959), Fatwa Tarikhiyya (*Historic Fatwa*). Risalat al-Islam, 3rd edn, Vol. 11,
227–8. Cairo. August 1959.
Shaltūt, M. (2001), *Al-Islam: Aqeeda wa Sharia (Al-Islam: Creed and Legislation System)*,
18th edn. Cairo: Dar al-Shuruq.

English sources

Avery, P., Hambly, G. and Melville, C. P. (1991), *The Cambridge History of Iran. Volume 7, From Nadir Shah to the Islamic Republic*, Cambridge: Cambridge University Press.
Brown, N. J. (2011), *Post-revolutionary al-Azhar*, Vol. 3. Washington, DC: Carnegie Endowment for International Peace.
Brünner, R. (2004), *Islamic Ecumenism in the 20th Century: The Azhar and Shiism between Rapprochement and Restraint*, Vol. 91. Leiden: Brill.
Dodge, B. (1962), *Muslim Education in Medieval Times*, Washington, DC: Middle East Institute.
Goldziher, I., and Lewis, B. (1981), *Introduction to Islamic Theology and Law*, Princeton, NJ: Princeton University Press.
Hefner, R. W. (2010), *The New Cambridge History of Islam. Volume 6, Muslims and Modernity, Culture and Society since 1800*, Cambridge: Cambridge University Press.
'Ināyat, H. (1982), *Modern Islamic Political Thought: The Response of the Shiʿ I and Sunni Muslims to the Twentieth Century*, London: Macmillan.
Johnston Douglas, M. (2006), *Faith-Based Diplomacy: Bridging the Religious Divide*. Available online: https://2001-2009.state.gov/s/p/of/proc/79221.htm (accessed 1 January 2019).
Kramer, M. S., and American Council of Learned Societies (1986), *Islam assembled* [electronic resource]: the advent of the Muslim congresses, New York: Columbia University Press.
Lapidus, I. M. (2014), *A History of Islamic Societies*, 3rd edn, New York: Cambridge University Press.
Postel, D., and Hashemi, N. (2017), *Sectarianization: Mapping the New Politics of the Middle East*, New York: Oxford University Press.
Skovgaard-Petersen, J., and Bettina, G. (2009), *Global Mufti: The Phenomenon of Yusef Al-Qaradāwi*, London: C. Hurst.
Smith, W. C. (1977), *Islam in Modern History*, Princeton, NJ: Princeton University Press.
The Guardian. (2019), *Pope and Grand Imam Sign Historic Pledge of Fraternity in UAE*. Available online: https://www.theguardian.com/world/2019/feb/04/pope-and-grand-imam-sign-historic-pledge-of-fraternity-in-uae (accessed 15 April 2019).
UN (2019), Remarks at Al Azhar Mosque by *António Guterres*. Available online: https://www.un.org/sg/en/content/sg/speeches/2019-04-02/remarks-al-azhar-mosque (accessed 22 November 2020).
WOAG World Organization for Al-Azhar Graduates. (2019), 'The Human Fraternity Document for World Peace and Coexistence' Endorsed by the Grand Imam and the Pope. Available online: http://www.waag-azhar.org.uk/the-human-fraternity-document-for-world-peace-and-coexistence-endorsed-by-the-grand-imam-and-the-pope/ (accessed 15 April 2019).
Zebiri, K. (1993), *Maḥmūd Shaltūt and Islamic Modernism*, Oxford: Clarendon Press.

Appendix A

مكتب شيخ الجامع الأزهر

بسم الله الرحمن الرحيم

نص الفتوى

التي أصدرها السيد صاحب الفضيلة الأستاذ الأكبر
الشيخ محمود شلتوت شيخ الجامع الأزهر
في شأن جواز التعبد بمذهب الشيعة الإمامية

قيل لفضيلته :

ان بعض الناس يرى أنه يجب على المسلم لكي تقع عباداته
ومعاملاته على وجه صحيح أن يقلد أحد المذاهب الأربعة المعروفة وليس من بينها مذهب
الشيعة الإمامية ولا الشيعة الزيدية ، فهل توافقون فضيلتكم على هذا الرأي على إطلاقه
فتمنعون تقليد مذهب الشيعة الإمامية الإثنا عشرية مثلا ·

أجاب فضيلته :

١ – ان الإسلام لا يوجب على أحد من أتباعه اتباع مذهب معين بل نقول : ان لكل مسلم
الحق في أن يقلد بادىء ذي بدء · أي مذهب من المذاهب المنقولة نقلا صحيحا والمدونة
أحكامها في كتبها الخاصة ولمن قلد مذهبا من هذه المذاهب أن ينتقل الى غيره –
أي مذهب كان – ولا حرج عليه في شيء من ذلك ·

٢ – ان مذهب الجعفرية المعروف بمذهب الشيعة الإمامية الإثنا عشرية مذهب يجوز التعبد
به شرعا كسائر مذاهب أهل السنة ·

فينبغي للمسلمين أن يعرفوا ذلك ، وأن يتخلصوا من العصبية بغير الحق لمذاهب
معينة ، فما كان دين الله ولا شريعته بتابعة لمذهب ، أو مقصورة على مذهب ، فالكل
مجتهدون مقبولون عند الله تعالى يجوز لمن ليس أهلا للنظر والاجتهاد تقليدهم والعمل
بما يقررونه في فقههم ، ولا فرق في ذلك بين العبادات والمعاملات ·

السيد صاحب السماحة العلامة الجليل الأستاذ محمد تقي القمي
السكرتير العام
لجماعة التقريب بين المذاهب الإسلامية

سلام الله عليكم ورحمته أما بعد فيسرني أن أبعث إلى سماحتكم
بصورة موقع عليها بإمضائي من الفتوى التي أصدرتها في شأن جواز التعبد
بمذهب الشيعة الإمامية ، راجيا أن تحتفظوا في سجلات دار التقريب
بين المذاهب الإسلامية التي أسبغتم عليكم في تأسيسها ورعائها لطف التحقيق رسالتها ·
والسلام عليكم ورحمة الله ،،

شيخ الجامع الأزهر
محمود شلتوت

Shaltūt's Fatwa on Shia Madhāhib in 1959 AD

Shaltūt's Fatwa on Shi'i Madhāhib in 1959 AD

Head Office of Al-Azhar Mosque:

In the name of Allah, the Most Gracious, the Most Merciful

Text of the Fatwa issued by His Eminence the Grand Shaikh of Al-Azhar, Maḥmūd Shaltūt, *on the Validity of Following the Shi'i Imamiyyah* madhhab.

Appendix B

The Fatwa of Egypt's Dar Al-Iftaa on the Ruling on Takfir (Heretication) of Muslims (Ahl al-Qibla)

حكم تكفير أهل القبلة

المبادئ

١- أجمع المسلمون شرقًا وغربًا وخلفًا على أن المجتهد هو الذي يسمع كلامه في دين الله بعد أن يستوفي شروط الاجتهاد المبينة في علم أصول الفقه حتى يندرج تحت صفة أهل الذكر.

٢- من يتبع أي واحد من المذاهب الإسلامية أو يمارس في حياته شيئًا منها فهو مسلم صحيح الإسلام.

٣- المسلم الذي يشهد بلسانه الشهادتين يعصم نفسه وماله، إلا إذا أتى بشيء من المكفرات قاصدًا عالمًا مختارًا.

السؤال

سعادة/ سفير مصر بالمملكة المغربية

السلام عليكم ورحمة الله وبركاته... وبعد

فإشارة إلى الفاكس الوارد إلينا بتاريخ ١٣/ ٦/ ٢٠٠٥ والمتضمن طلب الإجابة عن حكم الشرع الحنيف في تكفير أهل القبلة: سنة وشيعة وزيدية وإباضية. فنحيط سعادتكم علمًا بما يلي:

الجواب

دين الإسلام في ذاته كدعوة ربانية أوسع من أفهام العلماء من لدن الصحابة وإلى يومنا هذا، قال تعالى: ﴿ذَٰلِكَ ٱلْكِتَٰبُ لَا رَيْبَ ۛ فِيهِ ۛ هُدًى لِّلْمُتَّقِينَ﴾ [البقرة: ٢]، وقال تعالى: ﴿وَمَآ أَرْسَلْنَٰكَ إِلَّا كَآفَّةً لِّلنَّاسِ بَشِيرًا وَنَذِيرًا وَلَٰكِنَّ أَكْثَرَ ٱلنَّاسِ لَا يَعْلَمُونَ﴾ [سبأ: ٢٨]، وقال تعالى: ﴿تَنزِيلُ ٱلْكِتَٰبِ لَا رَيْبَ فِيهِ مِن رَّبِّ ٱلْعَٰلَمِينَ﴾ [السجدة: ٢].

وإذا كان الإسلام أوسع دائرة من نتاج عقول المجتهدين، فإنه يصلح لكل زمان ومكان ولكل العالمين؛ فأمة الإسلام تخاطب كل الناس في جميع الأحوال، فمن صدق بالنبي المصطفى صلى الله عليه وسلم فهو من أمة الإجابة، ومن لم يصدق فهو من أمة الدعوة كما ذهب إلى ذلك غير واحد من العلماء، قال الحافظ ابن حجر في شرح البخاري (١١/ ٤١١): "أمته صلى الله عليه وسلم على ثلاثة أقسام أحدها أخص من الآخر:

أمة الاتباع، ثم أمة الإجابة، ثم أمة الدعوة.

فالأولى: أهل العمل الصالح، والثانية: مطلق المسلمين، والثالثة: من عداهم ممن بعث إليهم". اه.

وأجمع المسلمون شرقًا وغربًا وخلفًا أن المجتهد هو الذي يسمع كلامه في دين الله بعد أن يستوفي شروط الاجتهاد المبينة في علم أصول الفقه حتى يندرج تحت صفة أهل الذكر، والله سبحانه يقول: ﴿فَسْـَٔلُوٓاْ أَهْلَ ٱلذِّكْرِ إِن كُنتُمْ لَا تَعْلَمُونَ﴾ [النحل: ٤٣].

ولذلك حملوا أولي الأمر في مثل قوله تعالى: ﴿وَلَوْ رَدُّوهُ إِلَى ٱلرَّسُولِ وَإِلَىٰٓ أُوْلِى ٱلْأَمْرِ مِنْهُمْ لَعَلِمَهُ ٱلَّذِينَ يَسْتَنۢبِطُونَهُۥ مِنْهُمْ﴾ [النساء: ٨٣]، وقوله تعالى: ﴿أَطِيعُوا۟ ٱللَّهَ وَأَطِيعُوا۟ ٱلرَّسُولَ وَأُو۟لِى ٱلْأَمْرِ مِنكُمْ﴾ [النساء: ٥٩] على المجتهدين.

ولقد وصل بعض الصحابة إلى درجة الاجتهاد فنقلت مذاهبهم في كتب الفقه المعتمدة، كالمغني لابن قدامة المقدسي الحنبلي، والمجموع للإمام النووي الشافعي، والمحلى لابن حزم الظاهري، ونحو هذا، بل ونقلت مسندة في أمثال المصنف لعبد الرزاق، والمصنف لابن أبي شيبة، وغيرها من دواوين الأحاديث والآثار.

ثم جاءت طبقة التابعين وتابعيهم ومن بعدهم إلى القرن الرابع الهجري، فظهر فيهم المجتهدون حتى أحصينا نحو تسعين مجتهدًا قد اتبعت مذاهبهم واعتمدت آراؤهم ونظر في استدلالاتهم؛ لما عرف عنهم من العلم والذكاء والفطنة والتقوى.

ثم شاعت المذاهب الثمانية ووصلت إلينا بالتواتر مع قيام العلماء عبر العصور بخدمتها، كاستخراج أدلتها، والتثبت من منقولاتها، والقيام بتصحيح ما استدل به من كل مذهب من الحديث النبوي الشريف أو الآثار الواردة عن مصدرها، والبحث في دلالة الألفاظ الواردة في كتب تلك المذاهب من جهة اللغة ومن جهة الشرع، وتحليل المختصرات النافعة ونظمها وتلخيصها وشرحها والتفريع عليها والإلحاق بها، واستنباط القواعد والضوابط التي بنيت عليها وكتابة أصول ترد إليها، وغير ذلك من الخدمة التي جعلت هذه المذاهب هي الأكثر شيوعًا، والتي بقي لها أتباع قلوا أو كثروا في بلاد المسلمين، وهذه المذاهب الثمانية هي:

المالكية، والحنفية، والحنابلة، والشافعية -وهي التي يطلق عليها مذاهب أهل السنة- والجعفرية، والزيدية، والإباضية، والظاهرية، وهي التي يطلق عليها المذاهب غير السنية.

وإذا نظرنا إلى هذه المذاهب في فقهها وأصول فقهها رأينا أن الخلاف بينها إنما هو في نطاق المضمون، ولم يقع بينها خلاف في المقطوع به الذي يكفر منكره، والحمد لله رب العالمين.

وعلى ذلك فإنه من يتبع أي واحد من المذاهب الإسلامية، أو يمارس في حياته شيئًا منها فهو مسلم صحيح الإسلام، وهذا يتفق مع أمر الله والرسول صلى الله عليه وسلم لنا بأن نعتصم بحبل الله، وأن نكون أمة واحدة

The Ruling on Takfir (Heretication) of Ahl al-Qibla (Muslims)

The Principles

1- All Muslims scholars are unanimously in agreement that a Mujtahid (one who exercises independent legal reasoning) can be followed in religious matters as long as they meet the conditions stipulated in the books of *Usul al-Fiqh* (the principles of Islamic jurisprudence).
2- Whoever follows one of the Islamic Madhāhib shall be considered a Muslim.
3- A Muslim who proclaims the Islamic profession of faith becomes inviolable.

Question

Your Excellency the Ambassador of Egypt to the Kingdom of Morocco

May Allah's peace, mercy and blessings be with You.

In reference to the fax sent to us on 13/6/2005 including a request on clarifying the ruling of the noble Sharia on Takfir Ahl al-Qibla: Sunna, Shiʻa, Zaidiyya and Ibadiyya.

The Answer

Islam is a divinely revealed faith that encompasses all the attempts of evidence-based *ijtihad* conducted by the reliable scholars since the time of the companions till our present day. Allah Almighty says in the Noble Qur'an: (That is a book beyond any doubt) {Albaqara: 2} and Allah says: (We have not sent you (O Muhammad) except comprehensively to mankind as a bringer of good tidings and a warner) {Saba': 28}.

Consequently, Islam is suitable for all peoples at all times and spaces. All Muslims scholars are unanimously in agreement that a Mujtahid (one who exercises independent legal reasoning) can be followed in religious matters as long as they meet the conditions stipulated in the books of *Usul al-Fiqh* (the principles of Islamic jurisprudence). Allah Almighty says: (So ask the people of the knowledge if you do not know) {Al-Nahl: 43}.

Regarding the following two verses; (But if they had referred it back to the Messenger or to those of authority among them, then the ones who [can] draw correct conclusions from it would have known about it. And if not for the favor of Allah upon you and His mercy, you would have followed Satan, except for a few) {Al-nisaa': 83}; and (O you who have believed, obey Allah and obey the Messenger and those in authority among you. And if you disagree over anything, refer it to Allah and the Messenger, if you should believe in Allah and the Last Day. That is the best [way] and best in result) {Al-nisaa': 59}, the scholar of exegesis maintains that 'those of authority' refers to the Mujtahidoon (*plural of Mujtahid*). Some of the companions (may Allah be pleased of them) of the Prophet (Peace and blessings be upon Him) reached the level of Ijtihad and their schools of thought were verified and well documented, as the book of al-Mughni by Ibn Qudama al-Maqdisi, al-Majmou' by Imam al-Nawawi al-Shafi'i and al-Muḥalla by Ibn ḥazm al-Zahiri.

Afterwards, there came the generations of the successors till the fourth century AH with nearly ninety of Mujtahidoon whose legal opinions were authenticated and their schools of thought had wide following due to their attributes of knowledge, wisdom, intelligence and piety.

Then after that, the eight schools of thought (*Madhāhib*) became widespread and were passed down one generation after the other. Moreover, these *Madhāhib* have been, across the centuries, documented, verified, authenticated, abridged, elucidated and published. These eight Madhāhib are: al-Malikiia, al-Ḥanafiyya, al-Ḥanabila and al-Shafi'iyya – which are referred to as the Sunni Madhāhib – along with al-Ja'fariyya, al-Zaydiyya, al-Ibadiyya and al-Zahiriyya, which are referred to as the non-Sunni Madhāhib.

When we examine all the principles and jurisprudence of the aforementioned Madhāhib we conclude that the span of differences between them is within the speculative issues, and they agree on the core matters. Consequently, following any of these Islamic madhāhib is valid, and this goes in line with the command of Almighty Allah and His messenger PBUH to stand united on the straight path.

CONCLUSION

Samira Nasirzadeh, Elias Ghazal and Eyad Alrefai

Over the past two decades, the manifestation of sectarian tensions has had a dramatic impact on the political geography, institutional fabric and broader nature of political and social life across the Middle East. From the emergence of radical groups espousing messages of violent rejectionism to regimes manipulating communal differences in pursuit of survival, sectarian identity figured prominently across the political landscape of the region. The increased salience of sectarian differences has led to a growing presence of regional actors in the domestic affairs of other states as regional powers vie for influence in an increasingly precarious security environment, meaning that a nuanced analysis of local and regional politics requires consideration of the role played by the actors operating at different levels of analysis.

A direct consequence of this is the premise that to understand the geopolitics of the Middle East one must have a greater awareness of the impact of domestic politics, and to reflect on the nature of domestic politics one must be cognizant of regional politics. Since 1979, Saudi-Iranian tensions have escalated into a regional rivalry that resonates across the security environment of the Middle East. The geopolitical rivalry between the two states plays out in fragmented states and societies, capitalizing on shared ethno-sectarian identities in pursuit of their particular goals. Developments in regional and international politics exacerbate these tensions. For example, the US invasion of Iraq in 2003 altered the security dynamics in the region, creating an environment in which Shi'a groups gained prominence, causing a shift in the balance of power in favour of Iran in the process. Consequently, an anti-Shi'a rhetoric – best seen in the 'Shi'a Crescent' narrative articulated by the King of Jordan in 2004 – revealed fear among Sunni Arab states of rising Shi'a – Iranian – power in the Middle East. Later the Arab uprisings intensified regional tensions by creating political and social vacuums. The protests provided additional opportunities for Saudi Arabia and Iran to engage competitively across the region, leading to violence in Yemen, Bahrain and Syria (Mabon 2020).

Across the Middle East, constructing and mobilizing sectarian identities affect domestic and structural political dynamics. Processes of sectarianization from above – performed by political elites – (re)activated sectarian identities replete with political and socio-economic aspirations. This process produces complex relations between confessional communities and between sectarian elites and the masses across the region (Hinnebusch 2016–). The result is a continuous recalibration of power balancing, which involves various actors and diverse resources domestically and regionally. While sectarian elites conspire with external actors to achieve domestic and regional aims, that relationship does not yield political dividends without a popular support base. Mass adherence to a common sectarian narrative and allegiance to an imagined sectarian project underpin the pervasiveness of sectarianism.

In a crisis of politics and of the state, people have turned to sectarian groups for protection and other benefits, privileges and, invariably, material support. In states with fragmenting political systems, people put their trust in sectarian leaders and their agendas because that promises to bring them security and a future that is imagined to be free from threats emanating from other sectarian groups. Sect-based unity offers protection against perceived existential threats. There are undoubtedly religious and social elements that cause people to align themselves with sectarian leaders and their politics. However, the point to highlight is that just as people enable the permeation of sectarianism by accepting its presuppositions and rewards, they could neutralize sectarianism by questioning its pretences. In other words, people may have the agency to curb the spread of sectarianism and its damaging effects, a process known as de-sectarianization. Indeed, that is what a large number of people in Iraq, Lebanon and Syria have been doing (Dodge and Mansour 2020; Huber and Woertz 2021; Majed 2021).

A key observation emerging throughout this volume is that mobilizing sectarian identities is the result of disagreements over the proper place of religion in political life across the Middle East. In their bid to outdo each other, sectarian entrepreneurs manipulated communities and wider societies to advance their position and secure their power (see Belcastro: Chapters 8; Wyss: Chapter 6). Politically, the process of provoking sectarian cleavages involved interactions between units at all levels of political analysis: domestic, regional and international. Domestic and regional actors are involved in the process of sectarianization in the Middle East. Local actors, supported by external brokers, engaged in top-down sectarianization that influenced the public and elites to instigate sectarian othering in heterogeneous societies. Commonalities such as religion and language were reimagined to deepen sectarian cleavages.

In the Middle East, this comes as a result of the resilience of political interactions between states and societies in a historically interconnected environment. Writing on this issue in 2004, Bassel Salloukh and Rex Brynen argued that 'for more than two decades, scholars of domestic and international politics have pondered the changing "permeability" of Middle Eastern states to transnational political influences'. In reflecting about this after two decades, it can be seen that the dominance of transnational ideologies is not limited to the Middle East. Powerful global actors such as the United States and Russia, alongside aspiring regional powers such as Iran and Saudi Arabia, cannot be solely accountable for the sectarian violence that beset the region.

There are certainly multiple factors that cause tension and clashes between the diverse ethno-sectarian inhabitants of the Middle East. However, the role that foreign powers play in deepening and exploiting sectarian fissures remains important. Sectarian elites rely on external support to maintain their grip on power, and without that support they risk losing control over their spheres of influence. Support is solicited in the form of diplomatic, financial or coercive assistance. For their part, regional and international powers find it in their interest to back local leaders on the ground that can serve their ambitions and agenda for the region. Certainly, internal and external actors recognize the great potential that sectarian identities have for ordering public life and creating alliances.

Sectarianism is complicated but not unpredictable

In the first section of the book, several themes emerge from the case studies of Iraq, Lebanon and Syria as explored by Al-Habbal, Kalousian and Mace respectively. Among the main instigators of sectarianism are the ruling elites. Where democracy is deficient, regimes seek alternative means to legitimize and secure their rule. Elites evoke sectarian fears and affiliations in order to generate support and thwart off threats. They extort and selectively distribute state resources on patronage networks that earn them an unwavering popular base. In exchange for support and backing from their confessional communities, sectarian elites provide their loyalists basic services, overpriced government contracts and unmerited jobs in the public sector (Saouli 2019).

This exchange of material support for political rent administered on a sectarian basis fragments society and severely weakens the state. The state's failure to provide essential services and fair opportunities to all its citizens sets the stage for sectarian rulers to instrumentalize sectarian identities to entrench themselves in power. Rather paradoxically, sectarian elites compete with inter- and intra-confessional rivals for state power, but when they secure it, they hallow out the state by depleting its resources, weakening its institutions and corroding its infrastructure. As a result, instability and insecurity multiply, causing great dissatisfaction among the masses. In Lebanon, Syria and Iraq, the elites utilized the state for their narrow interests, but in the process, they sacrificed the future of the state and the unity of their citizenry.

By protesting in the streets against dismal living conditions and bleak futures, people were essentially objecting to the order that sectarian leaders imposed in collaboration with political elites (when the two were not the same). Mass inter-confessional protests in major Iraqi and Lebanese cities reflect widespread dissatisfaction with the ruling establishment and the sectarian modus operandi. Will popular mass movements be able to bring about a bottom-up change to the sectarian order? The answer will depend on the context, but any prospect of change will threaten the elites' grip on power. Therefore, it is expected that sectarian elites will utilize resources at their disposal, such as government institutions, power structures and foreign relations, to counter potential changes (Karam 2017).

In Lebanon, sectarian elites use their leverage over the legislature to provide themselves with legal immunity. At the same time, they exercise their influence over the judiciary to evade being questioned for offences and avoiding judicial processes. While sectarian leaders in Iraq have comparable sway over the legislature and the judiciary, it is the Popular Mobilization Forces that serve as the pre-eminent force in the hands of elites seeking to prolong the sectarian order and crush any opposition. In the Syrian context, by contrast, there are no power-sharing arrangements like those found in Iraq and Lebanon. Instead, the Assad regime has full control over state power. However, given the minority status of the Assad family, that creates unique circumstances for the deployment of sectarian narratives. The second section of the book studies how regional actors sought to manipulate those national fabrics, in Syria, Iraq, Yemen and Bahrain, by utilizing sectarian affiliations as a way to derive popular support for local and regional causes. In the third section concerning attempts of de-sectarianization, the three chapters engaged with analysing the instrumentalization of identities by institutions that belong to the state; therefore, authors have suggested a top-down understanding of the process.

Regional geopolitics of sectarianism and proxies

The second section of the book focuses on regional rivalries and proxy conflicts. Sectarian dynamics animated politics of the region and fuelled many civil wars. Many scholars approach the Middle East as a deeply interconnected region, or as Paul Noble calls it, an 'echo chamber' (Noble 2008) where local and external political, economic and cultural aspects interact to shape the regional system. Authors in this section focused on sect-based tensions that have an impact upon regional affairs. This part made an important contribution to the literature on sectarianism and regional politics by reflecting on the ways in which sectarian groups operate within and across state borders, with serious implications for the ordering of life across the Middle East. The regional geopolitical aspect of sectarianism questions the extent to which sectarian identities cut across state borders. The chapters in this section studied the relationship between sectarianism, symbolic politics and proxies' relations across the region. Writing on the complexity of the different forms of relationships between domestic and regional political players, Simon Mabon and Edward Wastnidge argue that

> While there is little doubting the existence of links between Iran and a range of groups across the Middle East, the nature of these links differs across time and space, shaped by a range of context specific factors. Networks are shaped by the interaction of their constituent parts and the organisation of power among their members and, as a consequence, networks are neither fixed nor universal. Here, context is key, resulting in different types of relationships across spaces. Moreover, while many refer to groups within these networks as Iranian proxies, emerging from power relations and the apparent dominance of Tehran,

this denies the agency of groups who have a degree of capacity to operate independently of Iranian dominance. (2019: 595)

Michel Wyss focused on non-state sponsorship and proxies in Syria. Building on the established scholarship on proxy warfare as well as agency–structure theory, this chapter offered a unique framework that accounts for the evolving role of non-state actors in proxy relationships, through which sponsors employ a cheaper option, plausible deniability and detach themselves form the actions of the proxies.

In the aftermath of the Arab uprisings, and especially the Syrian civil war, sectarianism appears to have become entrenched in the Middle East regional politics. Rivalries and alliances are increasingly framed in sectarian terms, and the main conflicts of the region from Yemen to Syria and Iraq can all be said to entail a sectarian dimension (Malmvig 2015). Such ideological and sectarian elements reside within MENA's political culture and discourse, although their ability to determine the region's politics and destiny is notably related to times of conflicts and regional polarization. From that perspective, the Middle East can be regarded as a 'regional security complex' (Beck 2014) in which identities, politics and geography interact to shape national and regional affairs.

In this context, Maria-Louise Clausen observed that Saudi Arabia discursively justified its military intervention in Yemen in March 2015. The Saudi justification comes through framing and constructing the Kingdom as a friend of Yemen and the Houthis as an Iranian proxy (enemy). The chapter specifically explored the normative aspect of Saudi Arabia's legitimization of the intervention. Subsequently, Francesco Belcastro focuses on the state in the rise of sectarianism, civil wars and broadly 'sectarianization' by recruiting foreign fighters. He emphasizes that the existence of sectarianized civil wars domestically leads to rise of sectarian tensions regionally.

In the Middle East, commonalities (religion, language, ideology and shared history) determine and define states' national interests and, consequently, regional realities. 'This situation has been exacerbated by the extensive permeability of Arab states and societies and their ensuing exposure to transnational political pressures' (Noble 2008). Symbolically, departing from the two countries' contrasting positions on the issue, Olivia Glombitza argued that the rivalry between Saudi Arabia and Iran has a symbolic dimension, where both parties aim at shaping the image of the Islamic Republic in connection to the nuclear deal and in accordance with their positions by exercising symbolic power and discursively mobilizing sectarian identities, feeding into the sectarian divide. Riyadh does so by employing frames and narratives that contribute to delegitimizing and negatively representing Iran and its actions.

Furthermore, Samira Nasirzadeh explored regional geopolitical dynamics focusing on securitization of Shi'a to 'violization' in Bahrain post-2011. The chapter goes beyond the 'primordial' and 'instrumental' understanding of the Sunni–Shi'a split, by applying a 'third-way' approach to understand unrest in Bahrain. Nasirzadeh argued that through the securitization of Shi'a, the regime did manipulate the ordering of political life in the country. This top-down approach of securitizing Shia identity in Bahrain rendered the country's majority framed by the regime as 'threat' and part of Iran's 'expansionist policy' leading to massive violization within the country.

It is obvious that the current struggle in the Middle East between Saudi Arabia and Iran was intensified post the Arab uprisings in 2011. However, this does not suggest that both were not locked in a struggle that started since the establishment of the Islamic order in Iran in 1979. As Kim Ghattas puts it while writing on the political effects of the year 1979 and precisely describing the Islamic Revolution and how it changed the region: 'The Saudi-Iran rivalry went beyond geopolitics, descending into an ever-changing competition for Islamic legitimacy through religious and cultural domination, changing societies from within, not only in Saudi Arabia and Iran, but throughout the region' (Black Wave 2020: 30).

Moving from sectarianization to de-sectarianization

The final section of the book reflects on ideas of de-sectarianization. Broadly speaking, de-sectarianization encapsulates the process of moving beyond sectarian politics. It adopts a critical approach to studying sectarianism, questioning its historicity, longevity and usefulness as an analytical framework. Emanating from a post-structuralist perspective, it focuses on how sectarian identity is conceptualized through discourse (Malmvig 2019). It builds on a growing body of literature that demonstrates how sectarian identity and sectarian relations are shaped and reshaped by a range of local, domestic, regional and international factors (Dodge 2019; Gause 2017; Lynch 2013; Mabon and Ardovini 2017; Malmvig 2014; Potter 2014; Salloukh 2017; Valbjørn and Hinnebusch 2019; Wehrey 2016). In a sense, de-sectarianization is forward-looking. It looks to a future or imagined state where sectarian identity is not a cause for division. It acknowledges that sectarian identities are not predetermined to clash.

De-sectarianization may be conceived as an organic reaction to sectarianization. Sectarianization exploits differences between people and fragments society. Sectarian elites provoke sectarian cleavages to advance their interests. Over time, however, the damage caused by sectarianization causes elites, as well as other constituents and stakeholders, to rethink about the utility of sectarian mobilization. From that perspective, de-sectarianization is akin to peacekeeping in the context of war. Warlords amass great fortune from provoking and prolonging wars. They profit from playing on people's fears and exploiting their insecurities. Yet, as war drags and its destruction increases, opposition to the war effort increases. Policies and people that sponsor the war are called out and resisted. Eventually, more actors push to end the war, including possibly former war profiteers.

At the same time, warring parties may get to a point where it's disadvantageous to prolong the war, even if they are not in losing. Following that logic, as sectarianization intensifies, the damage caused by sectarian competition incites people to rethink their sectarian identity. Alternatively, sectarian actors may find more effective means to mobilize people. At that point, de-sectarianization effort can be expected to increase, and former sectarianization actors can be seen to lead the de-sectarianization charge. This is one of the main themes that emerges from the articles by Umer Karim, Hossam Ed-Deen Allam and Nesibe Hicret Battaloglu in the final book section.

Top-down de-sectarianization, where states invest resources to build bridges between embittered sub-national groups, is considered in two of the largest sectarian brokers in the region. In the case of Saudi Arabia, Karim shows how the Kingdom under the leadership of King Salman and his son, Crown Prince Mohammed bin Salman, is making considerable efforts to rectify exclusionary policies that single out Shiites. This includes investing in nation-wide development projects, promoting nationalist discourse and disempowering the clergy, which acted as religious police. Having weighed the effectiveness of sectarianization in the current context, decision-makers in Riyadh were determined to find an alternative to Islamic–Sunni ideology to mobilize Saudi nationals as well as structure political alliances. By focusing on nationalist and Arab identity, and by promoting principles of liberal economy, the Kingdom made a sharp turn away from sectarianization and is embarking on a major de-sectarianization campaign.

On the other hand, Iran also has the capacity to engage in state-level de-sectarianization, though to a lesser extent and by different means. As an Islamic Republic, Iran is wedded to Islamic ideology as a founding principle. This poses major constraints to leaders in Tehran should they choose to reimagine their country's national identity. Nonetheless, Battaloglu explains how Iran can still leverage its Islamic identity as a form of soft power to facilitate inter-communal dialogue and promote multilateral relations. The extent to which Tehran engages in de-sectarianization depends on the context and regional circumstances. Iran's soft power is useful for building inter-sectarian bridges, but to deploy that power and to activate de-sectarianization Iran must feel unthreatened by regional actors. Here, the importance of context – historical, spatial, geopolitical, political and socio-economic – is seen, with Iran's engagement with other regional actors conditioned by its position in the Gulf and wider Middle East.

Top-down processes of de-sectarianization are subject to the political whims and desires of states, which may not necessarily result in a positive outcome. While top-down de-sectarianization may seem like the most viable form of de-sectarianization, given that it is sponsored by the state and would be sustained by financial and coercive means, bottom-up de-sectarianization efforts reveal a different form of political process, potentially leading to existential transformations of the *polis*. Top-down de-sectarianization can antagonize hardliners and ferment underground opposition.

In contrast, bottom-up de-sectarianization works at a slower pace as it seeks to navigate the complex structural environment, aiming at longer term change through the evolution of perspectives rather than enforced behavioural change. The case of Al-Azhar in Egypt provides a great example of promoting grassroots de-sectarianization. By issuing fatwas that affirm Shiite forms of worship, Allam makes a compelling case for how Al-Azhar contributed to Sunni–Shiite rapprochement. Al-Azhar clergymen can leverage the authority and popularity of their home institution to mend relations between Sunni and Shiite communities in ways that pave for peaceful coexistence in the future. Yet for Al-Azhar, as well as other grassroots de-sectarianization initiatives, to bear fruit, they must be allowed to operate without interference from the state or other external actors.

This collection has sought to demonstrate the complex interplay between actors found at different levels of analysis across Middle Eastern politics. Chapters across each section highlight the intersectionality of the nature of political life. To understand sectarianization and de-sectarianization it is important to contextualize such processes politically, socially, historically, economically, geopolitically and intellectually, across different disciplinary boundaries. Ultimately, this collection has sought to contribute to these intellectual efforts.

References

Beck, M. (2014), 'The Concept of Regional Power as Applied to the Middle East', in H. Furtig (ed.), *Regional Powers in the Middle East: New Constellations after the Arab Revolts*, New York: Palgrave Macmillan, 1–20.

Dodge, T. (2019), 'The Contradictions of Systemic Sectarianism in Iraq: Sectarianism in the Longue Duree', in Simon Mabon (ed.), *Sectarianism, Proxies, and De-Sectarianization*, Lancaster: Lancaster University, 20–4. Available online: https://www.sepad.org.uk/files/documents/Sectarianism%20in%20the%20Longue%20Duree%20copy.pdf

Dodge, T. and Mansour, R. (2020), 'Sectarianization and De-sectarianization in the Struggle for Iraq's Political Field'. *The Review of Faith & International Affairs*, 18(1): 58–69. DOI: 10.1080/15570274.2020.1729513

Gause, F. G. (2017), 'Ideologies, Alignments, and Underbalancing in the New Middle East Cold War', *PS: Political Science & Politics*. Cambridge: Cambridge University Press, 50(3): 672–5. doi: 10.1017/S1049096517000373.

Ghattas, K. (2020), *Black Wave: Saudi Arabia, Iran, and the Forty-Year Rivalry That Unravelled Culture, Religion, and Collective Memory in the Middle East*. New York: Henry Holt.

Hinnebusch, R. (2016), 'The Sectarianization of the Middle East: Transnational Identity Wars and Competitive Interference', *Project on Middle East Political Science (POMEPS)*, 21: 71–5.

Huber, D., and Woertz, E. (2021), 'Resilience, Conflict and Areas of Limited Statehood in Iraq', *Lebanon and Syria, Democratization*, 28 (7): 1261–79. DOI: 10.1080/13510347.2021.1940967.

Karam, J. G. (2017), Beyond sectarianism: understanding Lebanese politics through a cross-sectarian lens. Middle East Brief, 1(107). Brandies University, Waltham, MA. Available online: https://www.brandeis.edu/crown/publications/middle-east-briefs/pdfs/101-200/meb107.pdf (accessed July 2020).

Lynch, M. (2013), *The Entrepreneurs of Cynical Sectarianism*. 4 vols. POMEPS Studies 4: *The Politics of Sectarianism*. Mark Lynch (ed.). Project on Middle East Political Science. the George Washington University, Washington DC. 3–6. Available online: https://pomeps.org/wp-content/uploads/2014/06/POMEPS_Studies4_Sectarianism.pdf (accessed August 2019).

Mabon, S. (2020), *Houses Built on Sand: Violence, Sectarianism and Revolution in the Middle East*, Manchester: Manchester University Press.

Mabon, S., and Ardovini, L. (eds) (2017), *Sectarianism in the Contemporary Middle East*, London: Routledge.

Mabon, S., and Wastnidge, E. (2019), 'Transnational Religious Networks and Geopolitics in the Muslim World', *Global Discourse*, 9 (4): 593–603. https://oro.open.ac.uk/68403/8/68403ORO.pdf

Majed, R. (2021), 'In Defense of Intra-Sectarian Divide: Street Mobilization, Coalition Formation, and Rapid Realignments of Sectarian Boundaries in Lebanon', *Social Forces*, 99 (4): 1772–98.

Malmvig, H. (2015, August 19), Coming in from the Cold: How We May Take Sectarian Identity Politics Seriously in the Middle East without Playing to the Tunes of Regional Power Elites. Retrieved from Project on Middle East Political Science. Available online: http://pomeps.org/2015/08/19/coming-in-from-the-cold-how-we-may-take-sectarian-identity-politics-seriously-in-the-middle-east-without-playing-to-the-tunes-of-regional-power-elites/ (accessed May 2019).

Malmvig, H. (2014), 'Power, Identity and Securitization in Middle East: Regional Order after the Arab Uprisings', *Mediterranean Politics*, 19 (1): 145–8.

Malmvig, H. (2019), 'Allow Me This One Time to Speak as a Shi'i': The Sectarian Taboo, Music Videos and the Securitization of Sectarian Identity Politics in Hezbollah's Legitimation of Its Military Involvement in Syria', *Mediterranean Politics*, 26 (1): 1–24. DOI: 10.1080/13629395.2019.1666230.

Noble, P. (2008), 'From Arab System to Middle Eastern System? Regional Pressures and Constraints', in B. Korany and A. E. Hillal Dessouki (eds), *The Foreign Policies of Arab States: The Challenge of Globalization*, Cairo: The American University in Cairo Press, 67–165.

Potter, L. G. (2014), *Sectarian Politics in the Persian Gulf*, Oxford: Oxford University Press.

Salloukh, B. F., and Brynen, R. (2004), 'Pondering permeability: Some Introductory Explorations. Persistent Permeability', in B. F. Salloukh and R. Brynen (eds), *Persistent Permeability? Regionalism, Localism, and Globalization in the Middle East*, Burlington, VT: Ashgate, 1–14.

Salloukh, B. (2017), 'The Sectarianization of Geopolitics in the Middle East', in Nader Hashemi and Danny Postel (eds), *Sectarianization: Mapping the New Politics of the Middle East*, Oxford: Oxford University Press, 35–52.

Saouli, A. (2019), 'Sectarianism and Political Order in Iraq and Lebanon', *Studies in Ethnicity and Nationalism*, 19: 67–87. https://doi.org/10.1111/sena.12291.

Valbjørn, M., and Hinnebusch, R. (2019), 'Exploring the Nexus between Sectarianism and Regime Formation in a New Middle East: Theoretical Points of Departure', *Studies in Ethnicity and Nationalism*, 19 (1): 2–22. http://dx.doi.org/10.1111/sena.12293.

Wehrey, F. (2016), *Beyond Sunni and Shia: The Roots of Sectarianism in a Changing Middle East*, Oxford: Oxford University Press.

INDEX

Abu Dhabi 74, 127, 156, 158, 164, 194
Al Khalifa, Hamad bin Isa 90–3
Al Khalifa, Regime 85–98
Al Saud, Salman bin Abdulaziz 182, 187, 188–90, 193–5
Al-Assad, Bashar 49, 54–8, 108–10, 139, 145–9, 167, 193, 230
Al-Azhar 205–17
Al-Kadhimi, Mustafa 37–8
Amman 18, 89, 164, 171
Amnesty Law 36–9, 41–2
Arab Spring 13, 17–18, 49, 53, 85–7, 90–8, 137, 145, 149, 163, 166–72, 186, 188, 193
Armed non-state actor 25, 56, 104–7, 112, 120, 122–4, 130, 139, 173, 183, 231

Baghdad 13, 18, 20–5, 196–7, 207
Bahrain 18, 55, 71, 74, 85–98, 137, 156, 164–72, 193, 214, 227
Beirut 35–9, 42, 79
Biden, Joe 82

Cairo 205, 211
China 65
Civil wars 13–14, 32–6, 39, 41, 49, 54–8, 107, 112, 119–20, 135–50, 230–1
colonialism 35, 39, 53, 144, 164–6
consociationalism 15–16, 22

Damascus 43, 51–2, 109, 147
desectarianization 5–6, 13, 21, 26, 35, 57, 65, 149, 156, 159, 170–4, 179–83, 192, 196, 205, 215–6, 230–4
diplomacy 70, 161–2, 172, 205, 216
Doha 164, 168–70

external involvement 3, 5, 136–8, 149

Fatwa 80, 191, 205, 209–16

Gulf Co-operation Council 74, 92, 120, 125–6, 156–73, 193

Hariri, Rafik 37
Hariri, Saad 34, 41–2, 72
Houthi Movement 119–31, 193, 231

intervention 18, 21, 55, 85, 87, 91–3, 98, 103, 105, 108, 110, 119–20, 125–30, 137, 139, 142, 147, 193, 231
Iran, Islamic Republic of 65–73, 77–82, 85–8, 92–7, 103–4, 108, 119–31, 139–40, 144, 147, 156–74, 182–98, 205–7, 214, 227–33
Iraq 2–6, 13–26, 70–3, 77–80, 88–9, 105, 108–9, 138–9, 142, 147–8, 158, 164–8, 171–3, 179–83, 186, 192–8, 205, 227–30
Islamic Revolution 22, 66, 89, 108, 155, 158, 160–1, 168, 185, 192, 232
Islamic State in Iraq and Syria (ISIS) 104, 108, 138, 146, 161, 170, 173, 182–3, 196
Israel 107, 129, 156, 158, 162–4, 167–70

Jerusalem 163, 207
Joint Comprehensive Plan of Action (JCPOA) 8, 65, 67–9, 80–1

Khomeini, Ayatollah 78, 158, 160, 161, 163, 185, 192
Kuwait 74, 162, 164–6, 170–3, 191, 196

Lebanon 5–6, 15, 21, 31–2, 34–44, 53, 70, 72, 77, 103, 158, 163–4, 166–8, 205, 228–30

Manama 3, 92
media 143, 148
  coverage 18, 23, 67–8, 75, 164–5, 167, 215

outlet 20, 127, 162, 188–91
memory 36–9

Nasrallah, Hassan 41, 147, 163
non-state Armed Groups 5, 7, 16–17, 22, 25, 31, 56, 104–9, 111–12, 122–4, 139, 155, 173, 183, 231

October 2019 6, 13–15, 20–4, 26, 31–6, 39, 41
Oman 74, 158, 162, 164–6, 170, 172
Otherness 51, 123

People's Protection Units (YPG) 7, 104, 108–12
political violence 4, 14, 16, 18, 21–4, 32, 34, 39, 51, 55–6, 74, 86, 94–8, 104, 142, 144, 146, 225–6
power-sharing 13, 16, 25, 31, 32, 39, 40, 41, 43, 103, 230
protests 3, 5–7, 13–15, 17–30, 32–5, 37, 39, 41, 42, 43, 46, 58, 85, 91–6, 98, 107, 109, 110, 120, 121, 145, 146, 149, 158, 173–6, 186, 193, 197, 227, 229
proxy war (proxy warfare) 3, 7, 10, 61, 101, 103–8, 112, 119, 122–4, 130, 137, 151, 230–1
public opinion (perception) 75–7, 79, 142, 143, 150, 155, 157, 159, 163, 164, 171–73

regional security 2, 3, 19, 22, 66, 70, 71, 73, 74, 77, 80, 81, 82, 85, 87–9, 91–4, 97, 98, 119, 120, 127, 129, 168, 169, 172, 183–5, 194, 196, 229
revolution 2, 3, 13, 32, 33, 35, 41, 42, 44, 56, 66, 69, 73, 77, 78, 79, 80, 82, 85–7, 89–91, 94, 96, 97, 107, 108, 111, 127, 128, 147, 158, 169, 172, 185, 192, 213, 230
Riyadh 2, 3, 4, 70, 91, 92, 93, 122, 126, 132, 170, 191, 193–6, 203, 217, 229, 232

Salman
  Mohammed Bin 8, 71, 168, 179, 182–3, 188–90, 194–5, 197, 233
Sana'a 3, 121, 124, 129, 193
Saudi Arabia 1–9, 65–74, 76–82, 85, 88, 89, 91–3, 97, 103, 108, 119–120, 122–31, 140, 144, 147–9, 156, 158, 160–66, 168–74, 179–90, 192–7, 227–8, 231–3
Schmitt, Carl 4, 7, 49–55, 57
sectarianism 2–4, 6, 8, 11, 14, 15, 16, 18, 19, 31, 33, 36, 39, 49, 51–4, 57, 58, 67, 78, 87, 92, 94, 96, 97, 101, 103, 104, 109, 112, 119, 129, 131, 135, 137, 138, 140–6, 148–52, 170, 174, 180–1, 183, 186–7, 192, 205, 216, 228–32
securitization 4, 5, 7, 86–9, 91–4, 97, 98, 156, 189, 231
soft power 155–7
  Iran 8, 159–67, 170–3, 233
Solidere 37–9
sovereignty 7, 31, 49–53, 56–8, 78, 79, 81, 125, 128, 171, 197
state of exception 31, 49–51, 57–8
Sunni–Shi'i Rapprochement 2, 8, 66, 69, 129, 164, 167, 169, 172–3, 186, 192–4, 205–9, 211–6, 234
symbolic power 65–7, 74–6, 81, 160, 231
Syrian Arab Republic 3, 6–7, 33, 49–50, 53–7, 67, 71, 73, 103–4, 107–12, 136–7, 140–1, 143–9, 163, 166–8, 193, 227–9
Syrian Democratic Forces (SDF) 7, 109, 111–12

Taif Agreement 6, 31–2, 34–7, 39–40
Tehran 2–3, 70, 79, 128, 139, 147, 155–6, 158, 160–4, 166–74, 216, 230, 233
terrorism 20, 23, 39, 74, 77, 80–1
Thawrat Tishreen 13, 20, 23–5
Trump, Donald 68, 194
Turkey 2, 8, 108–9, 144, 147–8, 171, 179, 192–4, 197

United Kingdom 65
United Nations 120–1
United States 1, 14–15, 18, 23 65–6, 68–9, 82, 103, 108, 110–11, 120, 122, 129, 158, 170, 173, 193, 228

violization 85–6, 93–4, 96–8, 231–2

Yemen 2, 5, 7, 18, 67, 70–1, 73, 77, 80, 90, 103, 119–22, 124–31, 158, 166–9, 179, 188, 193, 230–31

www.ingramcontent.com/pod-product-compliance
Lightning Source LLC
Chambersburg PA
CBHW071825300426
44116CB00009B/1437